Organization Theory

Organization Theory

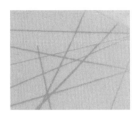  

Modern, Symbolic, and Postmodern Perspectives

Mary Jo Hatch
with Ann L. Cunliffe

OXFORD
UNIVERSITY PRESS

OXFORD

UNIVERSITY PRESS

Great Clarendon Street, Oxford OX2 6DP

Oxford University Press is a department of the University of Oxford.
It furthers the University's objective of excellence in research, scholarship,
and education by publishing worldwide in

Oxford New York

Auckland Cape Town Dar es Salaam Hong Kong Karachi
Kuala Lumpur Madrid Melbourne Mexico City Nairobi
New Delhi Shanghai Taipei Toronto

With offices in

Argentina Austria Brazil Chile Czech Republic France Greece
Guatemala Hungary Italy Japan Poland Portugal Singapore
South Korea Switzerland Thailand Turkey Ukraine Vietnam

Oxford is a registered trade mark of Oxford University Press
in the UK and in certain other countries

Published in the United States
by Oxford University Press Inc., New York

British Library Cataloguing in Publication Data
Data available

Library of Congress Cataloging in Publication Data
Data available

Typeset by Newgen Imaging Systems (P) Ltd, Chennai, India
Printed in Great Britain
on acid-free paper by
CPI Antony Rowe, Chippenham, Wiltshire

ISBN 978-0-19-926021-8   (Pbk)

10 9 8 7 6 5

With love, this book is dedicated to our daughters:
Jennifer Cron and Lauren Cunliffe

■ ABOUT THE AUTHORS

Mary Jo Hatch is the C. Coleman McGehee Eminent Scholars Research Professor of Banking and Commerce at the McIntire School of Commerce, University of Virginia. She is also an adjunct professor at the Copenhagen Business School in Denmark. She is an American organization theorist, who has taught management and organization theory, and published research on organizations and organizing in both the United States and Europe over the past twenty years. Her formal education took place at the University of Colorado, where she studied architecture as an undergraduate; Indiana University, where she studied English literature and creative writing and later earned an MBA in finance; and Stanford University, where she earned her Ph.D. in organizational behavior with an emphasis on organization theory. Before settling in at the University of Virginia, she held teaching posts at San Diego State University and UCLA in California, the Copenhagen School of Business in Denmark, and Cranfield School of Management in England. She is an active participant in the American Academy of Management, where she is a past officer of the Organization and Management Theory Division. You will find her published articles in *Administrative Science Quarterly, Harvard Business Review, Academy of Management Review, European Journal of Marketing, Human Relations, Organization, Organization Science* and *Organization Studies*. Her books include: *The Expressive Organization: Linking Identity, Reputation and the Corporate Brand* (with Majken Schultz and Mogens Holten Larsen, 2000, Oxford University Press) and *Organizational Identity: A Reader* (with Majken Schultz, 2004, Oxford University Press) and *The Three Faces of Leadership: Manager, Artist, Priest* (with Monika Kostera and Andrzej Koźmiński, 2005, Blackwell). She is the former European Editor of *Journal of Management Inquiry* and sits on the editorial boards of *Academy of Management Review, Human Relations, Organization Studies, Scandinavian Journal of Management, Journal of Management Inquiry, International Journal of Cross-Cultural Research, Corporate Reputation Review*, and *Management Learning*.

Ann L. Cunliffe is currently Associate Professor in the Department of Organizational Studies at the Anderson Schools of Management, University of New Mexico, having held teaching positions at California State University, the University of New Hampshire, and Blackburn College. She studied geography as an undergraduate at Aberystwyth University, and obtained her Master of Philosophy degree and Ph.D. from Lancaster University Management School. Recent publications in the field of management, management learning, reflexivity, and narrative research methods are found in the *Journal of Management Studies, Organization Studies, Administration and Society*, and *Management Learning*. She was awarded the 2002 'Breaking the Frame Award' from the *Journal of Management Inquiry* for the article that best exemplifies a challenge to existing thought. She also has a number of co-authored book chapters, including one with John Shotter in D. Holman and R. Thorpe's (eds.) *Management and Language: The Manager as Practical Author* (London: Sage). Ann is currently Associate Editor for *Management Learning* and the *International Journal of Qualitative Research in Work and Organizations*, and she is on the Editorial Boards of *Organization Studies* and the *Journal of Organizational Change Management*. She is involved in the International Conferences on Critical Management Studies and the Academy of Management.

■ PREFACE TO FIRST EDITION

Any narrative depends upon the perspective and location of its author. My perspective is as an American organization theorist, trained and employed in business schools, who has taught management and organization theory, and published research on organizations, in both the U.S. and Europe during the 1980s and 1990s. My formal education took place at the University of Colorado, where I studied architecture as an undergraduate; Indiana University, where I studied English literature and creative writing as an undergraduate, and later earned an MBA in finance; and Stanford University, where I earned my Ph.D. in organizational behavior with an emphasis on organization theory. My learning then continued in the context of my teaching posts—at San Diego State University and UCLA in the U.S., the Copenhagen Business School in Denmark, and now at the Cranfield School of Management in England— as well as through memberships in professional associations, including the American Academy of Management, the British Academy of Management, the Standing Conference on Organizational Symbolism (SCOS), and the European Group for Organization Studies (EGOS).

These days I live in a rural English village, in a thatched cottage built in the late 16th century, with beautiful countryside views. I spend my time doing research, reading, writing, traveling to conferences, giving lectures and seminars at a wide variety of universities, and doing a little oil painting. My research interests involve: organizational culture; identity and image; symbolic understanding in and of organizations; managerial humor as an indicator of organizational paradox, ambiguity and contradiction; and aesthetic (especially narrative and metaphoric) aspects of organizing. I consider myself to be a symbolic-interpretive researcher whose methodology shifts between interpretive ethnography and discourse analysis. It is upon all of these experiences that I draw in presenting organization theory. Unavoidable biases with regard to organization theory and its history are created by these particular experiences, and thus the book you are holding is influenced in ways that are difficult for me to specify. Other accounts of organization theory are available and will provide other versions of its story.

I came to write this book because, as a symbolic-interpretive researcher teaching organization theory, I was frustrated by the limited choices of textbooks for my classes. There seemed to be only two alternatives: either a modernist exposition on the content of organization theory with an expressly control-centered, rationalistic orientation; or a radical alternative that focused on criticising the modernist approach and displayed little or no sympathy for the substantial contributions modernist organization theory has made. I wanted a book that paid due respect to the modernist perspective, but that went beyond mere recitation of the findings of modernist research to explore the contributions of ethnographic studies that often challenge modernist notions, and that would give voice not only to the criticisms raised against organization theory as a tool of managerialism, but also to alternatives emerging from interdisciplinary research in the social sciences. I found that if I wanted such a book, I was either going to have to wait for someone else to get around to it, or I was going to have to write it myself. Being impatient, I chose the latter course.

Impatience, however, does not write books. It has taken me ten years to accomplish the task I first imagined in the mid-1980s. The process through which it materialized has been a labor of enthusiasm for the field of organization theory, and of determination to find a way to present material that is commonly believed to be difficult, dry, and boring in the extreme. To translate my vague image into this book required that I delve into my own subjective experience, to draw out the reasons for my enthusiasm and to develop the means of communicating them to others. These tasks I undertook in the classroom, and it is my students who deserve the lion's share of credit for this product—it is they who have been my teachers.

Each chapter of the book was developed through an iterative and interactive process of presenting ideas to my classes, followed by discussions in which I listened and responded to what the students chose to focus on, which generally involved application of the ideas to some aspect of their personal, professional, or anticipated managerial lives. In this way, I was able to observe how students handled the material I presented to them, what they found most interesting in it, and what they thought they might use it for. Along the way I discovered that the best way to present material in anticipation of discussion was to reflect upon what I found interesting in the topic, to press myself to learn something new about it just before going into class (which caused me to be in an active learning mode), and to share through open reflection what I found inspiring and what I was even now learning about it. The students responded well to this approach and appreciated the effort I took, because, as they told me, the enthusiasm I demonstrated for the material was contagious.

As I developed my learning-based style of teaching, I found that the students mimicked me in our discussions. A few would begin to focus on what was pertinent or attractive to them, would have insight based on their own experience in combination with the new material, and their unsuppressed enthusiasm diffused to other students who became engaged with the material until eventually (toward the end of our term of study together), most in the room had had the experience of finding organization theory interesting and useful—at least once in their lives. The effect overall was that, as we spent time together in these endeavors, the students became more and more active in their own education, taking an increasing share of the responsibility for their learning onto their own shoulders. This, of course, was not universally true, as in any classroom there were the perennial plodders, but by and large I was pleased that by focusing on the interesting, by following our collective intuition in the exploration of organization theory, we together carved out what I believe is a fair representation of the knowledge organization theory offers. While it is true that I polished the product through many rounds of review with both students and colleagues (who are experts in the subjects the book develops), on the whole the book was produced in dialogue with my students, and its contents reflect what they have been willing to take on board and use in their efforts to become educated future managers. The book is, in a way, a description of what we did together in the classroom.

A key element in my teaching/learning style is to allow students to explore in the directions their own curiosity takes them. The influence I exercise is then directed at developing their natural curiosity into genuine interest and mature engagement with the subject matter. Getting this process started is half the battle, and I see this book as a collection of stimulations for discussions of various aspects of organizing that have proven of lasting interest to the wide variety of students with whom I have shared the learning experience. This material has been developed over my years of teaching undergraduates, post-graduates (MBA and Ph.D.), and executives. Because I have not simplified the complex understandings that organization theory offers, but rather have clarified the language in which these ideas were originally (and often subsequently) presented, I find that the material in this book is useful, attractive, and accessible to a wide range of audiences.

There is another aspect to this book that bears mentioning here. At about the time that I concluded my Ph. D. training and took my first job as a faculty member, the push to internationalize business schools reached peak levels in the United States. At the time, I observed that attempts to internationalize the business school curriculum often consisted of simply using examples of companies headquartered or operating in foreign countries. As a culture researcher, I was suspicious of this approach to internationalization because I realized that examples will always be presented using concepts and perspectives that are rooted in the experiences of their author. Thus, if an author has only made brief (or no) visits to other cultures, then his or her analysis is unlikely to invoke anything like an international perspective. My opportunity to live and work in Denmark presented itself at just the moment these ideas were forming and provided me with an alternative. Moving to Denmark (I lived there three and one-half years all told) afforded me the chance to internationalize myself, along with the content of my course. My experiences taught me that internationalization goes way beyond the examples and knowledge that you offer, it is about profound changes in the ways you understand that affect your approach to description, analysis, and explanation—in other words, how you theorize.

My internationalization took root at about the same time that I was writing up the first version of this textbook. This coincidence had several important effects on what I was to produce. First, since I was teaching Danes who were fluent in English, but were not native speakers, I found that I had to restrict my vocabulary. While Danish students could easily follow complex and abstract arguments, and were, from my experience as an American, remarkably and delightfully fond of such arguments, they appreciated my keeping the language simple when I explained complex ideas. I obliged them and became intrigued by the puzzle of retaining the complexity of ideas, while reducing the complexity of how the ideas were presented. As I was teaching and writing at the same time, the language I used with my students slipped naturally onto the pages of my textbook. This turned out to be a real blessing, as it improved the means to write a demanding book about a complex subject that is accessible to anyone with a reasonable proficiency in the English language, a proficiency that has become practically essential in the international world of business. When I returned to the U.S. two years later and began using my manuscript as a text in my American MBA classes, I was startled at the strength of the positive response it received. In retrospect, I suppose it is not surprising that accessibility to complex ideas was appreciated by native as well as by non-native English speakers.

A second effect of my time in Denmark was the profound appreciation for multiple perspectives that it provided. I had already been introduced to the idea of multiple perspectives through my research training which involved struggling with debates over whether qualitative or quantitative methods provided a better means of addressing the problems of organizing—a debate that was raging at the time of my Ph.D. training. After moving to Denmark, the idea of accepting multiple perspectives began to take on new meaning. First of all, I became aware of the differences between European academic traditions of social science that focused on ontology and epistemology, and American academic traditions that were far more concerned with the issues of theory and method. At first I simply substituted my preferred set of terms (theory and method) for theirs (ontology and epistemology), but slowly I began to discern the differences. Eventually I came to an understanding of just how much slips between the cracks of translations of any sort, and on this foundation built my concern to preserve differences even while acknowledging the importance of crossing between different views which highlights their similarities. Out of these experiences, my views about organization theory as offering a fundamentally multiplicitous approach to understanding began to take shape. It is this theme that, as my Scandinavian friends would say, provides 'the red thread' that holds this book together.

The particular perspectives that I identify as crucial to grasping what organization theory has to offer I label modernist, symbolic (or, to be more accurate, symbolic-interpretive), and postmodern, after current fashion in the field today. At other times and in other places, these perspectives have been labeled differently. The **modernist perspective** has also been known as the rational perspective, the open systems view, the positivist school, and the quantitative approach. The **symbolic-interpretive perspective** has been known as the qualitative approach and is sometimes equated with the organizational culture school. The **postmodern perspective** has links to critical organization theory, the labor process school and radical feminism as well as to poststructuralist philosophy and literary theory. While these three perspectives will be distinguished throughout the book, in the end it must be admitted that the contours of these and other perspectives constantly shift and change so that there can be no final categorizing of ideas.

Still, there is value in making, for the moment at least, distinctions between several perspectives. For one thing, this practice broadens intellectual horizons and stimulates the imagination, both of which help to build knowledge and feed creativity. For another, learning to appreciate and rely upon multiple perspectives increases tolerance for the views of others and the capacity to make positive uses of the diversity multiple perspectives bring to organization and to life in general. It is my belief that, if we are ever to realize the value of theory for practice, then we must master the use of multiple perspectives, for it is in bringing a variety of issues and ideas to the intellectual table that we will learn how to be both effective and innovative in our organizational practices.

Please be aware that I am not attempting integration of the multiple perspectives of organization theory. Each perspective has contributed something of value to my understanding of organizations and I want to relate that understanding to new students of the subject of organization theory, whether they be undergraduates, postgraduates, or practicing managers. I have attempted to communicate my enthusiasm for these ideas and to bring them to life for the reader. The structure I offer, such as it is, is provided by the chronology of the ideas, which typically progresses from modernist, through symbolic-interpretive to post-modernist. I am not trying to privilege any particular viewpoint, I just want to let students vicariously experience the ideas in the rough order of their influence on the field (which was not always their order of appearance in the larger world).

Above all, I want students to feel free to play with ideas, but also to accept the discipline of focused study. To learn through their own experience that the hard work of studying other peoples' ideas can liberate their own thinking. The book is demanding—students who have used the book say they feel they have to underline *everything* because it all seems important. They report that they must (and do!) read the chapters multiple times.

What is most important, they start talking about these ideas in class, and by their reports, outside of it as well. The book seems to stimulate interest in organization theory, and that, I think, is its greatest strength.

I do not, however, suffer under the illusion that the book has no faults. I am sure it has plenty. Most of all, it is incomplete—a work in progress as any book on a dynamic field of study must be. I know also that it inspires contradictory opinions—postmodernists complain that it isn't postmodern enough, modernists have said that it goes too far. My view is that organization theory is an open field, filled with controversy and contradiction. I want this book to reflect the many aspects of the discipline and to grow along with the field. In this I rely upon your support and feedback; together we can make this a book that gets better rather than worse with each successive edition. But I get ahead of myself here. First let me thank those who have already provided volumes of feedback and who have shaped the book you have in your hand.

The most important group to thank for inspiring this project, and for providing feedback in its progress, are the many students whose company I have enjoyed in the classroom as well as in private discussions outside of class. The learning experiences we have shared are what made writing this book possible and enjoyable. I have had enormous help from colleagues and friends who, along the way to finishing this version, have offered their expertise as advisors on various chapters. They checked and corrected the content, offered suggestions about the flow and structure of the arguments, and without their sound criticism, guidance, and encouragement, I would not have the confidence necessary to publish this material. I offer my deep gratitude to Ria Andersen, David Boje, Finn Borum, Frank Dobbin, Eigil Fivelsdahl, Joe Harder, Gerry Johnson, Kristian Kreiner, Livia Markoczy, Bert Overlaet, Susan Schneider, Ellen O'Connor, Jesper Strandgaard Pedersen, Mary Teagarden, Carol Venable, Dvora Yanow, and several anonymous reviewers. I am also indebted to Majken Schultz and Michael Owen Jones with whom I have worked closely in developing related classroom material and on numerous research projects.

In addition to those already mentioned I would like to single out two people whose extraordinary contributions have improved the quality of this book enormously: my husband Doug Conner and OUP editor David Musson. Both of these individuals read every chapter start to finish on multiple occasions and made many helpful suggestions as to both style and substance. Thanks also to Ann Davies of Cranfield University, and to Donald Strachan and Brendan Lambon of OUP for their efforts in bringing this project from manuscript to published work. San Diego State University, the Copenhagen Business School and Cranfield University each supported my work in this project during its various critical stages. The friendship, support, and inspiration of my close friends Kirsten and Jacob Branner helped to sustain me during the long hours that this project has filled. Last, but certainly not least, I would like to thank my daughter, Jennifer Cron, whose consternation at my confusion about her ways of viewing the world initially inspired me to open my mind to the myriad possibilities of exploring multiple interpretations.

M.J.H.

Cranfield
September 1996

■ PREFACE TO SECOND EDITION

Much has changed since I wrote the first edition of *Organization Theory: Modern, Symbolic, and Postmodern Perspectives*. The field has expanded considerably, for one, and to tackle its wider reach I happily relate that Ann Cunliffe proved indispensable in producing the second edition. Ann is originally from Manchester, England. She completed an M.Phil. and Ph.D. at Lancaster University in the United Kingdom, and since 1987 has lived and worked in the United States. She now enjoys life in the high desert, where she teaches and does research at the University of New Mexico.

You can find me in the United States again as well. The University of Virginia became my home institution in 2000 when I was hired by the McIntire School of Commerce. The move meant that I gave up the thatched cottage in England for a cabin in the woods just outside Charlottesville, where I continue to enjoy my life of writing and painting. Apart, that is, from the regular visits of a peliated woodpecker, who seems determined to eat the entire outer layer of my house. Except for him, things are pretty peaceful and extraordinarily beautiful.

As for the second edition of *Organization Theory*, you will find several major changes, though there is also much you will recognize from the first edition. The most important continuity is the presentation of organization theory as a multidisciplinary field woven from multiple perspectives. The perspectives, naturally, have been elaborated, extended and challenged by an enormous and ever-growing body of research, and giving these developments their due has been the primary task undertaken by Ann and I in preparing this edition.

One example of a major change to the second edition is the incorporation of more critical theory, which has so deeply infiltrated the field over the last ten years that Ann and I added it in many places in the new edition. Although critical theory was hugely influential in the United Kingdom and some circles elsewhere in Europe even when the first edition was written, it only came into prominence for the rest of the field along with postmodernism sometime in the 1990s, and for a time the differences between these two perspectives were not well articulated. They have, however, become clearer with time so in this edition you will see distinctions being made that were previously ignored. What is perhaps the biggest change in regard to critical theory is the addition of a chapter on organizational power, politics and conflict to Part II: The Core Concepts of Organization Theory. The placement of this chapter reflects the now established importance of critical theory to the field.

Of course adding power, politics and conflict to the core concepts covered in Part II meant gutting Part III of the first edition. This made room for other important contributions that Ann and I have grouped into two chapters focused on applications of organization theorizing—one to practice and the other to recent developments. In the new Part III you will find Chapter 9 devoted to a question my students often ask: 'What has all this got to do with the real world?', while Chapter 10 addresses the question most often raised by those who are, or who are studying to become, organization theorists: 'Where do we go from here?'

Other important changes to the first edition have been made. Both symbolic-interpretive and postmodern perspectives receive much more attention in this edition of the book to reflect their growing influence on the field. More examples have been included throughout, along with additional suggestions for ways readers can develop concepts and their capacity to theorize. I have retained as much of the style of the first edition as was possible—no mean feat given the vocabulary of postmodernism!—and I hope that you will find the writing to be as accessible as it was in the first edition.

The new topics covered in the second edition are too numerous to list exhaustively, but include among others: extended discussions of symbolic and postmodern aspects of social structure and technology; the inclusion of narrative, storytelling, discursive and poststructuralist approaches to organizational analysis; and issues relating to gender, hegemony, disciplinary power and reflexivity. Of course you will encounter many old friends as well. The biggest concession I made was to leave out the chapter on strategy. The field of strategy has enjoyed almost as much growth over the last ten years as has organization theory and I found it impossible to keep up with both. I have, however, retained the bits of strategic thinking that touch most directly on organization theory, so you will find most of what was covered in the first edition absorbed into various discussions throughout the book.

Beyond her many contributions during revision, Ann has built a website to accompany the second edition. On the website you will find a host of goodies including cases and suggestions for ways to adapt them to the subject matter of the book, downloadable slides, web links to additional material, teaching ideas and resources, and exam questions (for instructors only!!!).

As always the list of people to thank is long. Our students have been our most important partners in the process of revising the book, and we have benefited from the insights of all the people whose works we will tell you about in the pages to follow. In addition, the support and insight provided by Phil Mirvis and my colleagues at the McIntire School is much appreciated. Ann wanted me to thank Mary Ellen Pratt and Michael Clifford for their generous help, which I gladly do. Several anonymous reviewers contributed greatly to refining various chapters, and thanks also to everyone at OUP who helped to get this edition out of our heads and into print!

Finally, to the many friends of the first edition, let me say that I hope you will be pleased by the second. Ann and I have worked hard to make it a useful and enjoyable study tool and we look forward to hearing your comments and suggestions for improving the third edition!

M.J.H.

Charlottesville, Virginia
July 2005

■ BRIEF TABLE OF CONTENTS

◼ DETAILED CONTENTS

■ LIST OF FIGURES

■ LIST OF TABLES

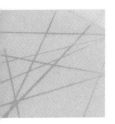

What is Organization Theory?

theorist /ˈθɪərɪst/ n. a holder or inventor of a theory or theories.

theorize /ˈθɪəraɪz/ v. intr. (also **-ise**) evolve or indulge in theories. **theorizer** n.

theory /ˈθɪərɪ/ n. (pl. **-ies**) **1** a supposition or system of ideas explaining something, esp. one based on general principles independent of the particular things to be explained (opp. HYPOTHESIS) (*atomic theory; theory of evolution*). **2** a speculative (esp. fanciful) view (*one of my pet theories*). **3** the sphere of abstract knowledge or speculative thought (*this is all very well in theory, but how will it work in practice?*). **4** the exposition of the principles of a science etc. (*the theory of music*). **5** *Math.* a collection of propositions to illustrate the principles of a subject (*probability theory; theory of equations*). [LL *theoria* f. Gk *theōria* f. *theōros* spectator f. *theōreō* look at]

Oxford Encyclopedic English Dictionary

Why Study Organization Theory?

Organization theory is not an easy sell. Unless you are naturally drawn to the abstract, you probably expect this subject to be dry, unconnected to practical matters and perhaps a little boring. Even if you are enthusiastic about abstractions, it can be daunting to confront as many of them at one time as organization theory asks you to do. So why would anyone sign up to study this complex and difficult subject matter?

There are many different answers to this question. For some, studying organization theory is motivated by curiosity. They wonder what it would be like to think like an organization, to get inside organizing processes far enough to reveal the intricate organizational patterns that make organizations understandable. Others are motivated by the attraction of stretching their minds in new ways. For example, organization theory draws on the sciences, the humanities and the arts, and so presents the intellectual challenge of thinking in interdisciplinary ways. Some turn to organization theory in the hope that it will improve their chances of becoming successful executives in business, government or non-profit organizations. Table 1.1 lists some of their specific reasons. For me, it was something else entirely. I came to organization theory reluctantly when it was foisted upon me as a requirement of my doctoral program. To say that I did not appreciate organization theory when I first encountered it would be putting it mildly.

In a way, my initial disaffection with organization theory inspired this book. Once I began using organization theory, my experiences convinced me that this field of study is not only valuable—it is interesting! Organization theory has helped me time and again to analyze complicated situations in the organizations with which I have worked, and to discover or invent effective and creative means for dealing with them. It has opened my mind to many aspects of life both inside and outside organizations that I previously took for granted, and it has given me both mental discipline and a wide-ranging knowledge of many different subjects. My amazement at how relevant and valuable organization theory can be caused me to reverse my initially low opinion of the field and find great enthusiasm for it. It is this change in my perception that led me to write this book. Through it I hope to share my insights and enthusiasm with you as you discover the benefits and attractions of organization theory for yourself.

Whether you come to organization theory out of curiosity, a desire to improve your chances of success in life, or simply because somebody made you do it, there are three interrelated things I can tell you that will ease your way into this complex subject. The first involves theories and theorizing, the second concerns abstraction and its place in theory development, and the third explains why you need to study organizations from multiple perspectives. I will introduce you to each of these topics in the following sections of this chapter.

Table 1.1 Some applications of organization theory

Strategy/Finance	Those who want to improve the value of a company need to know how to organize to achieve organizational goals; those who want to monitor and control performance will need to understand how to achieve results by structuring activities and designing organizational processes.
Marketing	Marketers know that to create a successful corporate brand they need to get the organization behind the delivery of its promise; a thorough understanding of what an organization is and how it operates will make their endeavors to align the organization and its brand strategy more feasible and productive.
Information technology	The way information flows through the organization affects work processes and outcomes, so knowing organization theory can help IT specialists identify, understand and serve the organization's informational needs as they design and promote the use of their information systems.
Operations	Value chain management has created a need for operations managers to interconnect their organizing processes with those of suppliers, distributors and customers; organization theory not only supports the technical aspects of operations and systems integration, but explains their socio-cultural aspects as well.
Human resources	Nearly everything HR specialists do from recruiting to compensation has organizational ramifications and hence benefits from knowledge provided by organization theory; organizational development and change are particularly important elements of HR that demand deep knowledge of organizations and organizing, and organization theory can provide content for executive training programs.
Communication	Corporate communication specialists must understand the interpretive processes of organizational stakeholders and need to address the many ways in which different parts of the organization interact with each other and the environment, in order to design communication systems that are effective or to diagnose ways existing systems are misaligned with the organization's needs.

Theories and Theorizing Organizations

You might be surprised to learn that you use theory everyday, and so does everyone else. Take for example any old adage that seems true or wise to you. One of my favorites is 'You can lead a horse to water, but you can't make it drink.' Old sayings like this one are filled with common sense (e.g., about what you can and cannot do for others) and common sense is a theory about how to understand and negotiate life. More generally, whenever you create your own meaning or grasp someone else's, you make things, feelings, ideas, experiences, values and expectations into ideas or concepts. In doing this you explain yourself and your world and this constitutes theorizing. Organization theorists specialize in developing this human capacity to make and use theory. They hone their theorizing skills by refining conceptual distinctions and using them to create sophisticated explanations (theories) that far outstrip common sense. As they do so they participate in the invention of new ways of looking at experience and its phenomena. The basic difference between common sense theorizing and the theorizing academics do is the added care academics take to specify their practice, correct its errors and share their theories with others, thereby contributing to systematic knowledge-building efforts.

Theories are built from abstractions known as concepts. One concept—called the **phenomenon of interest**—is selected from all the others as a focus for theorizing and then related concepts are defined and used to explain that one. Consider Albert Einstein's theory that $E = mc^2$. Energy (E) was Einstein's phenomenon of interest and he explained it using the concepts of mass (m) and a constant representing the speed of light (c). The squaring of c, and its multiplication by m, specify how these explanatory concepts are related to the phenomenon of interest and form Einstein's theory about the relationship between energy and matter. In a nutshell, $E = mc^2$ shows what **theory** is—a set of concepts and the relationships between them proposed to explain the phenomenon of interest.

Sometimes the explanation of a phenomenon is too complex for precise specification using a mathematical formula. This is the usual case for phenomena involving human behavior because human behavior is notoriously unpredictable, except under tightly constrained conditions like those psychologists create in laboratories where the ordinary influences of everyday life can be controlled. For this reason explaining organizations where humans are at work often demands the use of statistical probabilities rather than precise formulae. Alternatively, researchers turn to metaphor or analogy to explain their phenomena. Sometimes theorists do not even attempt to explain phenomena; instead they develop understanding and appreciation or give practical guidance. You will meet all of these kinds of theorizing in the pages that follow as we wend our way from theories of organization that take physical science as their model, to those that find their foundations in the humanities and the arts.

Given the volume and variety of organization theories, you may find it somewhat ironic to call this field of study organization theory. While the name suggests that there is only one—a single, integrated, overarching explanation for organizations and organizing— in fact there are many organization theories and they do not always fit neatly together. Some people see this diversity as a stumbling block for an academic discipline because, in their view, if there is no agreement on what a field has to offer then it probably has little to offer at all. Others try to excuse the situation arguing that organization theory is a young field that will eventually work out its differences and come around to the singular perspective that they believe defines a mature academic discipline.

I take an altogether different view. Along with a number of other organization theorists, I believe that organization theory always has and always will embrace multiple perspectives because it draws inspiration from a wide variety of other fields of study, and because organizations will remain too complex and malleable to ever be summed up by any single theory. In my view the diverse theoretical base of organization theory is something to celebrate, not only because it offers a broad perspective on organizational life that encompasses scientific explanation, human understanding and artful appreciation, but because it creates more possibilities for effectively designing and managing organizations.

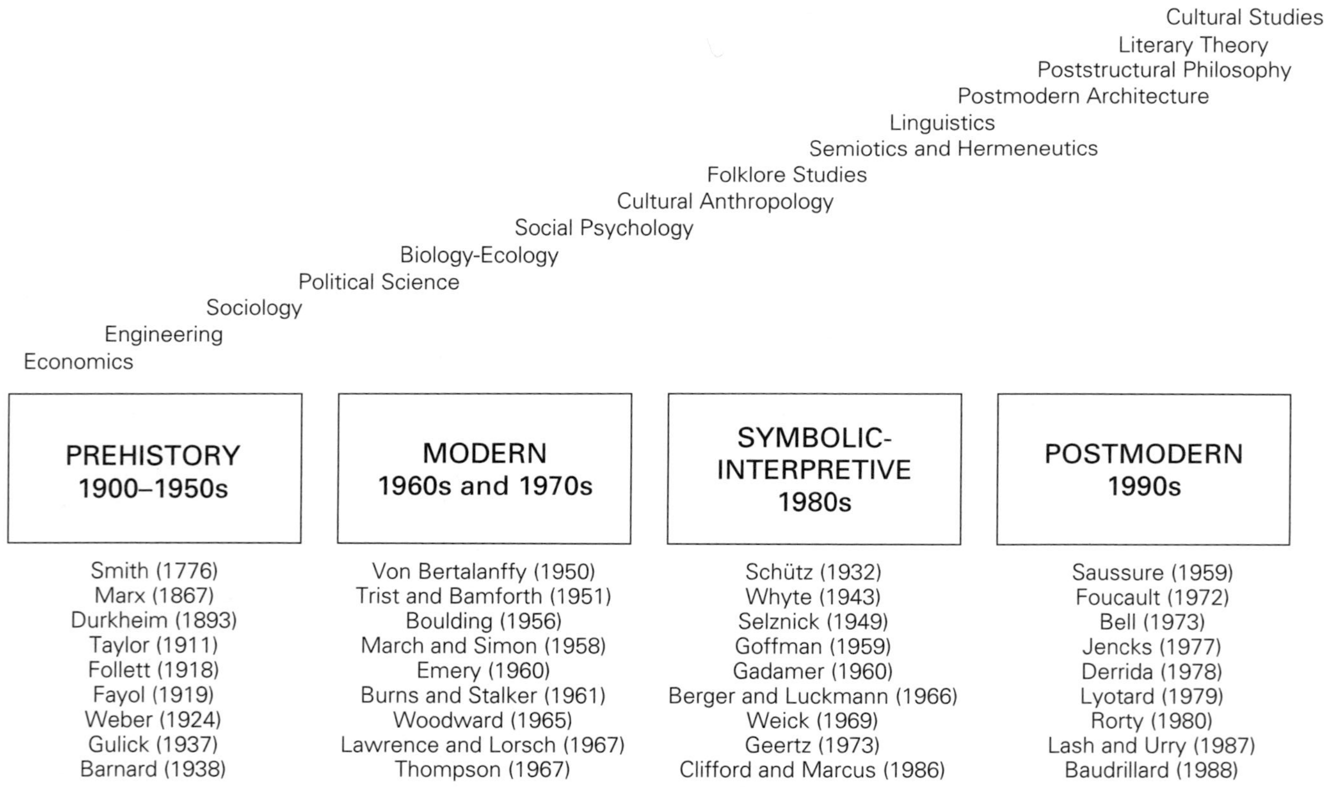

Economics
Engineering
Sociology
Political Science
Biology-Ecology
Social Psychology
Cultural Anthropology
Folklore Studies
Semiotics and Hermeneutics
Linguistics
Postmodern Architecture
Poststructural Philosophy
Literary Theory
Cultural Studies

PREHISTORY
1900–1950s

Smith (1776)
Marx (1867)
Durkheim (1893)
Taylor (1911)
Follett (1918)
Fayol (1919)
Weber (1924)
Gulick (1937)
Barnard (1938)

MODERN
1960s and 1970s

Von Bertalanffy (1950)
Trist and Bamforth (1951)
Boulding (1956)
March and Simon (1958)
Emery (1960)
Burns and Stalker (1961)
Woodward (1965)
Lawrence and Lorsch (1967)
Thompson (1967)

SYMBOLIC-
INTERPRETIVE
1980s

Schütz (1932)
Whyte (1943)
Selznick (1949)
Goffman (1959)
Gadamer (1960)
Berger and Luckmann (1966)
Weick (1969)
Geertz (1973)
Clifford and Marcus (1986)

POSTMODERN
1990s

Saussure (1959)
Foucault (1972)
Bell (1973)
Jencks (1977)
Derrida (1978)
Lyotard (1979)
Rorty (1980)
Lash and Urry (1987)
Baudrillard (1988)

Figure 1.1 Sources of inspiration for organization theory

The boxes show the four major perspectives on organizations used as a framework for this book. The dates inside the boxes indicate the decade when the perspective became recognizable within the field. Contributing disciplines are indicated above the boxes and some of their influential thinkers are listed below. Notice that some contributions pre-date their influences on organization theory considerably, indicating the lag in communication between disciplines.

Figure 1.1 will give you appreciation for the ambitious reach of organization theory. The figure displays the many academic disciplines from which organization theorists have drawn inspiration. The top part of the figure shows the academic disciplines that have contributed to organization theory while the bottom part names some major thinkers from these disciplines whose ideas have shaped the field. Be sure to notice that the contributing disciplines range from the natural and social sciences to the humanities and arts.

Now look at the middle part of Figure 1.1. The first box, labeled prehistory, represents sources of ideas about organizations that occurred before anyone considered organization theory to be a discipline in its own right. Thus the authors listed below the prehistory box did not theorize organization from a single perspective nor did they intend to create the field of organization theory; they had their own disciplinary communities, shown at the top of the figure, to which they were oriented when they wrote. Nonetheless the authors grouped in the prehistory category provided organization theory with its formative concepts and their ideas served as reference points around which the perspectives of organization theory later developed. When you become familiar with these authors, you will hear echoes of their words in the many concepts and theories that make organization theory what it is today, and you will recognize how their work contributed to one or more of the three perspectives that form the remaining boxes in the middle of Figure 1.1.

The order of the boxes from left to right in the middle of this figure gives a sense of how the field has changed over time (don't panic, you will get more information about the multiple perspectives of organization theory in a minute). But it would be a mistake to think that newer perspectives have replaced older ones; perspectives accumulate in organization theory and over time they influence one another as organization theorists take in more and more of the ideas this field of study offers.

To get a grip on what I mean by perspectives, you may find it helpful to compare them to literary or film genres (e.g., drama, romantic comedy, horror), styles of painting (e.g., classical, impressionist, post-impressionist, cubist) or types of jazz (Big Band, Bebop, Cool Jazz, Fusion). Just as these genres encourage certain forms of artistic expression, theoretical perspectives encourage certain ways of thinking and speaking. And not unlike genre in the arts, it is only after the appearance of a critical mass of theories using similar underlying logics and vocabularies that anyone identifies them as having come from the same perspective and articulates what the assumptions underpinning that perspective are. Thelonious Monk, among others, was playing Bebop before anyone acknowledged this as a new type of jazz or gave it a name. Similarly Max Weber, Émile Durkheim and Karl Marx were writing about bureaucracy and authority before organization theory was known by this name. Thus, the different perspectives on organization theory developed at different times and continue to develop in reaction to one another. Today their proponents form communities within organization theory whose members think and do research in similar ways that you will soon learn to distinguish from one another.

Interplay among the perspectives of organization theory produces continuous change in each of them, which is one reason why it can be difficult to make a case for one particular way of sorting through the ideas of organization theory, including the one diagramed in Figure 1.1. However, if you are a newcomer to the field, you will probably appreciate a little order; most people find it useful to hear about how others have come to terms with the diversity of organization theory. But please feel free to rearrange, change or even abandon any of the schemes presented throughout this book when you are ready to create your own. In Part III I will introduce you to the organization theorists who are currently challenging the dominant perspectives by inventing new concepts and theories. Eventually some of them will combine their work into new perspectives that will stand alongside those that provide the framework for this book. But before you are ready to tackle all these current issues in organization theory, you need to know something about what organization theory is and where it came from. Let me start you off with some basics concerning theory and theorizing.

Concepts and Abstraction in Theory Development

Concepts provide mental categories for sorting, organizing and storing experience in memory. They are ideas formed by the process of abstraction. Webster's *New World Dictionary* defines **abstraction** as the 'formation of an idea by mental separation from particular instances.' This means that you build concepts in your memory on the basis of your acquaintance with instances that are familiar to you, either as the result of personal experience, or based on what others tell you. For example, your concept of dog is built upon your personal encounters with representatives of this class of animal such as dogs you have owned or that have bitten you; upon stories you have heard others tell about their experiences with dogs; and upon encounters with non-dogs that, when you were a young child, helped you to build this concept by teaching you what a dog is not ('No, that's a cat').

Think of your concepts as empty baskets to be filled with experience. If you first encounter concepts through academic study, you will likely experience it as empty. This is one reason why organization theory appears to many as dry and boring when they first encounter it. To enrich your concepts you must fill them with meaning by relating personal experiences to them in much the same way you did when you learned the concept of dog as a young child. That is, you must gather specific examples that fit each concept until it is more or less fully formed. Of course you can continue enriching your concepts for the remainder of your life, like experts do. For example, a person who trains dogs learns more about them all the time, just as an organization theorist continually seeks different ways of understanding and explaining organizations. This means that, at least for experts, some concepts will be continually expanding. There is no end to the subtlety you can develop by enriching your concepts and, of course, by adding new concepts to your knowledge base. The trick is to get the process of abstraction going.

It is important to remember that, in this book, you will mostly encounter other peoples' concepts. Your task will be to relate these concepts to your own experience and other knowledge that you have stored in your memory. I will present the concepts of organization theory in ways designed to trigger associations with experiences you have had so that you can fill your concepts with your own meanings. With each new concept you encounter, try imagining what it is that you have personally experienced that might relate to it. Keep a journal of these ideas with different sections dedicated to describing the examples you relate to each concept. Be playful. Do not feel constrained to obvious associations; also challenge yourself to consider experiences you only intuitively sense are applicable. As you do this you will begin to embed concepts in your own experience as well as placing your experience in the context of your conceptual knowledge. Comparing your examples to those of your classmates, colleagues, or others you know who are interested in organizations will also expand your understanding and hone your conceptual abilities.

As your pool of concepts and theories expands, you will find yourself analyzing your experiences in new ways, for instance, by relating experiences that you never before thought of as related, or by seeing hidden or disregarded aspects of a situation in which you were involved. In other words, use your personal experience to develop concepts with which you can understand or build theories, and then use your concepts and theories to better understand your experiences. This sort of give and take between theoretical understanding and personal experience is essential to the development of your theorizing skills of abstraction, reasoning and application as well as to your knowledge of organizations and organizing.

Although concepts are associated with specific examples, a concept is not a simple aggregation of all the information you remember about specific examples. A concept is much more compact than this. To form a concept, ignore the unique elements or features you associate with specific examples and focus on only those aspects that are common to all the instances to which the concept applies. Thus, the concept dog is associated with four legs, a tail, a cold wet nose when it is healthy, and two ears, but not black spots, big paws, or a habit of jumping on strangers, which are features of particular dogs, but not all dogs. Seen in these terms, abstraction is the process of removing the unique details of particular examples so that only their common aspects remain. Of course abstraction does not happen in one move; learning is involved in the movement from multiple concrete examples to an abstraction.

You may wonder why you would want to drop all the interesting details out of your daily experiences in order to build concepts. One reason is that abstraction gives you an increased ability to process more information and/or to process information more quickly. When you encounter a new example of a well-developed concept, you have numerous bits of information about that object or idea at your fingertips. If you recognize an object as a dog, you may instantly be aware of the possibility that it will growl if it feels threatened. This information has immediate practical value. Concepts also make it possible to communicate knowledge to others. For instance, once your children know what a dog is, you can tell them that some dogs bite and so they should not reach out their hands to a strange dog until they are confident it is friendly.

In addition to giving you the ability to communicate with others, abstraction gives you enormous powers of thought. It allows you to associate volumes of information with a single concept and thereby to process this information rapidly whenever you think of, or with, the concept. You can see the importance of this aspect of abstraction in terms of the psychological process known as **chunking**. Cognitive psychologists tell us that humans have the capacity to think about, roughly, seven pieces of information (plus or minus two) at one time.[1] This means that you can think about seven different dogs and nothing else, or, through chunking larger portions of your knowledge, you can think about all the dogs in the universe and six other kinds of animal as well. You can even think about the entire animal kingdom and have room to think about six more things besides. Chunking illustrates the power of abstraction—using concepts allows you to consider large blocks of knowledge at once, a handy capacity to have when your daily activity demands that you understand and stay abreast of developments within a complex entity such as an organization.

Chunking makes an important contribution to theorizing—it permits us to relate large bodies of knowledge to each other. Remember, a theory is an explanation rooted in the specification of the relationships between a set of concepts (e.g., $E = mc^2$). When the concepts upon which a theory is built are defined at very high levels of abstraction, the theory becomes very general which means that it applies across many situations with few or no limiting conditions. Of course this is part of the danger with theory; by leaving out so many of the details of specific circumstances and meanings as we ascend the heights of abstraction, we can be lulled into thinking that we understand everything. If we assume our knowledge is more general than it is, we may apply it to the wrong situations or be willing to impose our beliefs on others when it is inappropriate or misleading to do so. Therefore, be sure to notice that there is both something gained and something lost when you use abstraction. You gain the ability to think about numerous instances, but you lose the rich detail that the individual cases contain and the depth of knowledge these details describe.

As a theorist, you will want to learn to use abstraction because it permits you to communicate and understand general ideas about complex subjects, such as organizations. This will enable you to see day-to-day issues in a larger perspective that expands your thinking and gives you ready access to accumulated knowledge. But you should also remember that abstract reasoning alone will not provide the important details that you will confront in your role within a specific organization. Applying theory, which is wedded to abstract reasoning, demands that you be able to add critical details back into your formulations after you have analyzed and understood the more abstract aspects of the situation at hand. You will want to develop both concepts and theorizing skills with a broad base of personal experience and then translate your abstractions back into specific understanding.

I believe a great deal of the frustration with organization theory that many students and practitioners report feeling is the result of not recognizing that the application of theory is a creative act. A belief that abstract theory can generate instant solutions to specific problems is naïve. It is equally naïve to reject theory as having little value simply because you have not yet learned how to use it. Theory is better suited to raising important questions at critical moments and reminding you what relevant knowledge is available, than it is to providing ready-made answers to your problems. Use theory as a tool to help you reason through complex situations; do not expect it to guarantee your success.

Multiple Perspectives

Different ways of looking at the world produce different knowledge and thus different perspectives come to be associated with their own concepts and theories. This is the case with the **multiple perspectives** you will study in this book—modern, symbolic-interpretive and postmodern. The concepts and theories of a particular perspective offer you distinctive thinking tools with which to craft ideas about organizations and organizing. Depending upon your intentions, you may find that particular perspectives have greater appeal than others for your purpose. The more knowledge you have of multiple perspectives, concepts and theories, the greater will be your capacity to choose a useful approach to dealing with the situations you face in your organization.

British sociologist Gibson Burrell and British organization theorist Gareth Morgan were among the first to draw attention to the multiple perspectives of organization theory in their highly acclaimed book *Sociological Paradigms and Organizational Analysis*, published in 1979.[2] They argued that knowledge is based on different paradigms, each with its own assumptions about the world. Paradigms encourage researchers to study phenomena in different ways.[3] However, be sure to notice that paradigm differences are not just academic; they become practical when knowledge is used to create a more desirable reality or better ways of organizing. Beliefs, assumptions and knowledge of the world influence how researchers carry out their research, how leaders design and manage their organizations and how each of us relates to the world and to other people. For example, whether you assume that your organization is best run as a well-oiled machine, a web of meaning, or a broken mirror will influence what you perceive to be the best way of designing your organization and managing its people. As you will see, the three perspectives used in this book draw upon significantly different assumptions about the organizational world and consequently will lead you to think about organizations in different ways (e.g., as machines, cultures or fragmented images) and thus to seek different kinds of knowledge about them.

I am committed to maintaining multiple perspectives in organization theory for a number of reasons. First, today few would disagree that organizations operate in complex, uncertain, and often contradictory situations. Managers and employees are expected to do more with less, to maximize both short-term gain and long-term investment, and be more efficient as well as more humane and ethical. Confronting such a variety of contradictory forces demands the broadest set of concepts and theories that your mind can grasp. Learning to think about organizations using the multiple perspectives presented in this book will help you embrace complexity and uncertainty and their contradictory demands. Second, recent corporate scandals, such as those that occurred at Enron, the FBI, and Parmalat, raise questions about the nature of ethical action and the pressures managers face when trying to act in socially and organizationally responsible ways. Learning to use multiple perspectives can help make you aware of the assumptions and values underlying your theory and practice, which in turn should make you more conscious of your reasons for doing things and better able to understand the reasons behind the actions taken by others. As you begin to grasp the differences between perspectives, you will become aware that what you consider reasonable is defined by the perspective you take. Being able to reflect on your own reasoning processes and compare them to those used by the people around you will develop your ethical awareness. Third, by learning organization theory, by knowing how to theorize, and by understanding how different perspectives influence the way you and others experience, interpret and shape organizational realities, you will become a more effective member of any organization you join.

In order to compare modernism, symbolic-interpretivism and postmodernism, you will need to examine the assumptions underlying each of these perspectives. A good place to begin is with the important philosophical choices of ontology and epistemology. Ontology is concerned with how you choose to define what is real, whereas epistemology is concerned with how you form knowledge and establish criteria for evaluating it. Thinking about ontology and epistemology is a useful place to begin because these philosophical choices explain basic differences between the perspectives of organization theory. Although they are difficult philosophical issues, by giving ontology and epistemology some attention now, you will begin to learn why different perspectives lead to different ways of theorizing organizations and how modern, symbolic-interpretive and postmodern perspectives make distinctive contributions to organization theory.

Ontology

Ontology concerns our assumptions about reality. Is there an objective reality out there or is it subjective, existing only in our minds? In ordinary, everyday life, you probably take your assumptions about what exists for granted because you believe you know what the real world is. You get up, drive to work, do your job as a student, manager or administrator, go to meetings, write reports, establish policy etc. You don't question whether these things are real or have an existence independent of you; you know your car exists because you drive it. But does your job exist if you are not there to perform it? Does your report describe what is *really* going on or does it describe only what you *think* is happening? Philosophers sometimes refer to these as existential questions because they attribute existence to one set of things (reality), but not to another (the unreal, metaphysical or fantastical). Depending upon your perspective, you will give some things the status of being real, while you disregard others. These ontological assumptions about whether a particular phenomenon exists or is merely an illusion (e.g., culture, power, control) lead to arguments between those who maintain different perspectives and cause them to set up separate and sometimes conflicting research communities.

Ontology is also concerned with the question of agency—do people have free will and are they wholly responsible for their own actions, or is life predetermined, whether by situations or by God? **Subjectivists** stand at one end of the reality continuum in their belief that something exists only when you experience and give it meaning. At the other end, **objectivists** believe reality exists independently of those who live in it. Seen from the subjectivist point of view, people create and experience realities in different ways because individuals and groups have their own assumptions, beliefs, and perceptions that lead them to do so. Seen from the objectivist point of view, people react to what is happening around them in predictable ways because their behavior is part of the material world in which they live and is determined by causes, just as is the behavior of matter. In between these points of view you can find many combinations of subjectivism and objectivism.

Epistemology

Epistemology is concerned with knowing how you can know. Typical questions asked by those investigating epistemology include: how do humans generate knowledge, what are the criteria by which they discriminate good knowledge from bad (e.g., true from false, valid from invalid, rational from irrational, scientific from pseudoscientific), and how should reality be represented or described? Epistemology is closely related to ontology because the answers to these questions depend on, and in turn help to forge, ontological assumptions about the nature of reality.

Table 1.2 summarizes the key ontological and epistemological differences of the modern, symbolic-interpretive and postmodern perspectives and their implications for organization theory.

Positivist epistemology assumes you can discover what truly happens in organizations through the categorization and scientific measurement of the behavior of people and systems. Positivists also assume that language mirrors reality, that is, reality and its objects can be described using language without any loss of meaning or inherent bias.[4] For positivists, good knowledge is generated by developing hypotheses and propositions, gathering and analyzing data, and then testing the hypotheses and propositions against the external reality represented by their data to see if they are correct. In this way, modernists can develop general theories explaining many different aspects of one overarching reality, and make predictions about the future.

Positivist epistemology is based on foundational principals that celebrate the values of reason, truth and validity. Positivist organization theorists study organizations as objective entities and are attracted to methods adapted from the physical or hard sciences. They gather data using surveys and laboratory or field experiments relying upon measures of behavior that their assumptions lead them to regard as objective. Based on statistical analysis of the data collected using these methods, they derive theoretical models that they believe provide factual explanations of how organizations operate.

Antipositivist or **interpretive** epistemology assumes that knowledge can only be created and understood from the point of view of the individuals who live and work in a particular culture or organization. Interpretivists assume that each of us acts in situations and makes sense of what is happening based on our experience of that situation and the memories and expectations we bring to it. This means that there may be many different understandings and interpretations of reality and interpretive epistemology leads us to use methods designed to access the meanings made by others and describe how they come to make those meanings. However, we know that our understanding of others is filtered through our own experiences, and therefore we can never be objective about the interpretations made by others.

What interpretivists believe they can do is work alongside others as they create their realities and, by studying their interpretations and interactions in particular situations, develop intersubjective awareness of and appreciation for the meanings produced. This stance is what turns a researcher into an interpreter, bridging meaning between the researcher's academic experiences and the experiences of organizational members. Both of these experiences are subjective, and bias is controlled (but never eliminated) through

Table 1.2 Summary of the three perspectives of organization theory

Modernism	Symbolic interpretivism	Postmodernism
Ontology Objectivism—belief in an objective, external reality whose existence is independent of our knowledge of it	**Ontology** Subjectivism—the belief that we cannot know an external or objective existence apart from our subjective awareness of it; that which exists is that which we agree exists	**Ontology** Postmodernism—the belief that the world appears through language and is situated in discourse; what is spoken of exists, therefore everything that exists is a text to be read or performed
Epistemology Positivism—we discover Truth through valid conceptualization and reliable measurement that allows us to test knowledge against an objective world; knowledge accumulates, allowing humans to progress and evolve	**Epistemology** Interpretivism—all knowledge is relative to the knower and can only be understood from the point of view of the individuals who are directly involved; truth is socially constructed via multiple interpretations of the objects of knowledge thereby constructed and therefore shifts and changes through time	**Epistemology** Postmodernism—knowledge cannot be an accurate account of Truth because meanings cannot be fixed; there is no independent reality; there are no facts, only interpretations; knowledge is a power play
Organizations are Objectively real entities operating in a real world. When well-designed and managed they are systems of decision and action driven by norms of rationality, efficiency and effectiveness for stated purposes	**Organizations are** Continually constructed and reconstructed by their members through symbolically mediated interaction. Organizations are socially constructed realities where meanings promote and are promoted by understanding of the self and others that occurs within the organizational context	**Organizations are** Sites for enacting power relations, oppression, irrationality, communicative distortion—or arenas of fun and playful irony. Organizations are texts produced by and in language; we can rewrite them so as to emancipate ourselves from human folly and degradation
Focus of Organization Theory Finding universal laws, methods and techniques of organization and control; favors rational structures, rules, standardized procedures and routine practices	**Focus of Organization Theory** Describing how people give meaning and order to their experience within specific contexts, through interpretive and symbolic acts, forms and processes	**Focus of Organization Theory** Deconstructing organizational texts; destabilizing managerial ideologies and modernist modes of organizing and theorizing; revealing marginalized and oppressed viewpoints; encouraging reflexive and inclusive forms of theorizing and organizing

rigorous training in self-reflection. Such training is designed to teach you to separate your interpretations from those of the people you study. This method allows you to describe how meaning was made in particular situations and among particular people and to offer your understanding for others who were not there to witness what you experienced.

Taking an interpretive epistemological stance helps you to become sensitive to how people make meaning to the point where, while you will never be able to fully understand or predict the meanings others will make, you can develop your intuitive capacity to anticipate the range of meanings that are likely to emerge in given circumstances by specific people with whom you share adequate intersubjective understanding. Perhaps most importantly, your growing appreciation for the limits of understanding will prevent you from ever claiming to fully know another's meaning and will open you to deep listening.

Comparing Modern, Symbolic and Postmodern Perspectives

You might think of ontology and epistemology as commitments you make to your preferred genre of organization theory. To take a modernist perspective, you must commit to limiting what you count as knowledge to what you can know through your five senses. Of course modernists augment their five senses with sense-enhancing devices (e.g., microscope, telescope), but what counts as data is what is collected by the eyes, ears, nose, tongue or skin. Modernists claim that 'I saw (heard, smelled, tasted or touched) my data, and you can confirm them for yourself by replicating my procedures'.

Symbolic-interpretivists are willing to extend the definition of empirical reality to include forms of experience that lie outside the reach of the five senses, as do emotion and intuition. As a result of this subjectivity, their findings cannot be easily replicated by others. The commitment these researchers make is to be true to their personal experience and to honor the accounts and explanations made by others. What is more, symbolic-interpretivists focus on meaning and understanding as it occurs in particular contexts; consequently their findings should not be generalized beyond the context in which they were produced. Modernists find this problematic—can we really call what we create knowledge if we are unable to replicate studies or apply their findings to other organizations? As opposed to generalizability, symbolic-interpretivists sometimes use verisimilitude (the resonance of one's own experience with the experiences of others) as the basis for claiming they have made a contribution to understanding.

Because of the differences in their assumptions, modernist and symbolic-interpretive researchers endlessly debate methodology. For instance, modernists say subjectivity undermines scientific rigor, while symbolic-interpretivists say it cannot be avoided and, indeed, is required if we are to study meaning. Modernists typically believe that subjective understandings introduce bias, and bias is precisely what science seeks to eradicate in pursuit of the rational ideals of modernism. Lurking behind these epistemological positions is an irresolvable debate between their differing ontologies that permit symbolic-interpretivists to investigate meaning as a subjective phenomenon, while modernists are precluded by their ontological assumption of objectivity from allowing the subjective to enter their science. As you will see in the following chapters, these differences in assumptions mean that modernist and symbolic-interpretive organization theorists define organizational concepts differently and use different research methods that often cause them to disagree rather violently with one another.

Turning to postmodern perspectives, there is even more trouble to be found. Postmodernism diverges from the other two perspectives in its unwillingness to seek Truth (spelled with a capital T to indicate the idea of truth in any final or irrefutable sense), or to make permanent ontological or epistemological commitments such as those that give rise to modernist forms of scientific endeavor or to symbolic-interpretive descriptions of meaning and human meaning making activity. Seen from these other perspectives, post-modernists seem to flit between philosophical positions. They often refuse to take even a temporary philosophical stand because they believe that doing so privileges some forms of knowledge over others and this violates postmodern ethics.

Many postmodernists trace the ethical foundations of postmodernism to the French poststructural philosophers, especially to Michel Foucault and Jacques Derrida. For example, Foucault argued that, since knowledge is power, when anyone privileges particular forms of knowledge, they push other forms to the margins where they are likely to be ignored.[5] Derrida observed that this is because modern thought is binary and binary thinking leads us to center our attention on one element of a pair while ignoring or denigrating its opposite or other (e.g., true/false, nature/culture, reality/representation). Therefore the development and use of knowledge are always power plays that must be resisted for the sake of the power-less. Many postmodernists commit themselves to uncovering and challenging all forms of power (including knowledge) in order to expose the sources of domination that are so easily taken for granted. They do so by decrying the privileged and bringing those people and ideas relegated to the margins out of the shadow of their repression. (If this and other statements about postmodernism confuse you, don't worry, you will find a more elaborate introduction to postmodernism in Chapter 2 and a more thorough treatment of power in Chapter 8.)

The other two perspectives have not ignored the challenge laid down by postmod-ernists. First, symbolic-interpretivists, and more recently modernists, have tried to respond to this challenge within their own systems of belief and commitment. The result has been some movement toward greater self-consciousness about the assumptions each perspect-ive makes, and how these commitments apply to the practice of social science and the theories that result from their application. For example, postmodernists have critiqued cultural anthropologists (both modernist and symbolic-interpretive) for their co-optation by Western governments to aid in the subordination of indigenous and aboriginal cultures. Postmodernists argued that cultural anthropologists, seduced by the allure of government grants and a romantic vision of helping less advanced cultures progress toward the ideals of Western civilization, conspired in the colonization of non-Western peoples to the detriment if not the destruction of many native cultures. The response by Western anthropo-logists was to give voice to the members of the cultures they studied by inviting them to help interpret the data collected about them, and in some cases to write cultural reports themselves. Aboriginal reports are, of course, no freer of self-interest than any other, but by juxtaposing reports from many perspectives you can begin to learn about the range of biases that appear in all data. Watch the film *Rabbit-Proof Fence* to get a taste of aboriginal self-reporting on the injustices experienced by native Australians when European colonizers attempted to Westernize their culture.

As you can see, the issues of ontology and epistemology are complex and are understood differently when viewed from within each perspective. To get a feel for how different these perspectives can be, take the well-known question: if a tree falls in a forest and no one is there to hear it, does it make a sound? To the modernist the answer is yes because the tree and sound are real and can be measured; therefore it doesn't matter whether anyone is there to experience the tree falling or not—knowledge of what happens when a tree falls generalizes to all falling trees. To the symbolic-interpretivist there is no way of knowing the answer to this question because there is no one to experience the tree falling. Although a symbolic-interpretivist could study how different people make sense of the question, if no one is present when the tree falls then there is no meaning to address apart from that of the rhetorical move of asking a hypothetical question. To a postmodernist the answer is likely to be a set of entirely different questions: Who has the right to ask or answer this question? Whose interests have been marginalized and violated in the process?

Returning to our prior discussion of concepts, you should now be ready to refine your understanding of a concept by applying the three perspectives. Notice that modernists emphasize the representative aspect of concepts—concepts align with objects in the real world (e.g., the concept of dog represents real dogs). Symbolic-interpretivists emphasize the agreement among the people of one culture to call things by the same names (e.g., the English word *dog* versus the French *chien*), pointing out that you construct concepts in the context of intersubjective meanings and vocabularies shared with other members of your culture. Postmodernists emphasize the ever-changing relationship between concepts. For the postmodernist all words, including concepts, are defined in relation to other words (dog versus cat, mouse, house, life) rather than in relation to objects in the real world; no word's meaning can be fully or finally determined because each use brings a word into relationship with a different set of other words and this continually changing juxtapositioning causes its meaning to endlessly shift.

It is important to understand the differences in the applications of the perspectives because these differences are not only crucial to how theory is created but also to the way organizing is practiced. If you take the objectivist stance that an organization is a formal structure with an internal order, a set of natural laws governing its operation, and roles that must be carried out in a deterministic manner by organizational members, you will manage your organization and act differently toward it and others within it than if you adopt either the subjectivist stance or the postmodern perspective. Similarly, if you take the subjectivist stance, that organizations have no objective structure but are continually constructed and maintained by people as they try to make sense of what is going on, you will manage your organization differently than if you assume the postmodern perspective and thereby maintain skepticism toward the idea that knowledge is anything more than a ploy to gain power over others. It is important to know what your underlying assumptions are when you apply your theories because each set of ontological and epistemological assumptions will exercise a different influence on the way you design and manage your organization.

Plan of the Book

Part I of the book describes the approach I will use to help you learn organization theory and develop your capacity to theorize. Chapter 1 has introduced you to several core ideas—theory, theorizing, concepts and abstraction—and to the three perspectives that form the framework of this book—modern, symbolic-interpretive, and postmodern. Chapter 2 presents a historical account of the economists, sociologists and classical management scholars whose work inspired the first organization theorists and to some of the theories that subsequently shaped the three perspectives of organization theory.

Part II of the book will present you with the core concepts that contemporary organization theorists use to explain, understand and theorize organizations. In these chapters you will learn to look at organizations as constituents of a larger environment (Chapter 3); as social structures ordering the activities of their members (Chapter 4); as technologies for producing goods and services for society (Chapter 5); as cultures that produce and are produced by meanings that form the symbolic world of the organization (Chapter 6); as physical structures that support and constrain both activity and meaning (Chapter 7); and as arenas within which power relations express themselves through organizational politics, conflict and control (Chapter 8). These core concepts are related in numerous ways, yet each will contribute something unique to your understanding of organizations and organizing. As you read and reread these chapters, strive to develop your appreciation for both the similarities and differences between the concepts because this will develop your imagination for theorizing.

In addition to providing exposure to the core concepts of organization theory, Part II will present several different theories of organization that were built using the core concepts. Within each chapter these theories will be presented in historical order; in most cases this means beginning with modern and proceeding to symbolic-interpretive and postmodern perspectives, although organizational culture is an exception in that symbolic-interpretivists were complicit with modernists in introducing this concept into organization theory. This format should help you to experience organization theory as an unfolding series of challenges and disagreements among theorists and their ideas about and different perspectives on organizations and organizing.

The theories I am going to present will not only give you exposure to the various types of explanation, understanding and appreciation offered by organization theory, they will also provide a means to describe some of the skills and practices organization theorists use. In discussing how theorists produce theory, I mean to encourage you to become more actively theoretical in your approach to organizations and in your management practices. In this regard, Part III will show you how organization theorists sometimes combine concepts, theories and perspectives to analyze and recommend action on practical issues and problems such as organizational design, organizational change, knowledge management and organizational learning (Chapter 9). The final chapter will introduce you to ideas that lie on the horizon for organization theory: critical realism, network theory, organizational aesthetics, complexity theory and organizational identity (Chapter 10). Thus Part III will show you some of the tricks of the trade practiced by organization theorists.

A Conceptual Model of Organization

Throughout this book I will provide many conceptual models such as you see in Figure 1.2. These models visually represent theories as sets of concepts and their relationships. Organization theorists use them to make abstractions seem more tangible. Figure 1.2, for example, is a visual way of communicating my definition of organizations as technologies, social structures, cultures and physical structures that exist within and respond to an environment. The grey tint over the entire model indicates that all of these elements of organizing are colored by relations of power.

Diagrams such as Figure 1.2 can help you to remember a great deal about the theories you will be studying. Giving these diagrams close attention will often reveal aspects of organization theory that are subtle but important. For example, let the interconnections of the four small circles in Figure 1.2 remind you that none of these concepts or the theories and perspectives associated with them is complete in itself; each shares some aspects with the others and it is the combination of these different ways of knowing that will allow you to produce rich and complex explanations and descriptions of organization, or to

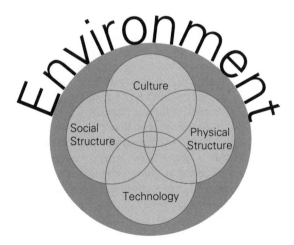

Figure 1.2 A model for the concept of organization

The five intersecting circles of this model represent the organization as five inter-related phenomena conceptualized as shown. Power, a sixth core concept, is symbolized by the grey tint that infuses the other circles. These six concepts will be examined in depth in Part II of the book.

challenge theories offered by others. Now imagine that each of the circles is a sphere spinning on its axis and rotating around the others. Let this image remind you that these core concepts are dynamic, mutually reactive parts of an organization interacting with and within an environment. Then focus on the intersections of the circles and the gray tint infusing them all. Let these features of the model remind you that any conceptual distinction can be regarded as insupportable, that from some other perspective your distinctions will break down and blend into each other.

I should warn you that, as you move toward understanding each core concept, there will be times when you get caught in the intersections and become confused as to which concept, theory or perspective you are using. Expect this. Try not to feel discouraged when it happens because this is part of the process of becoming knowledgeable about organization theory. Trust that out of your confusion new possibilities for theorizing, designing and managing organizations will emerge in ways that you would never have imagined before you studied organization theory.

SUMMARY

A theory attempts to explain (modernist), describe so as to produce understanding and appreciation of (symbolic-interpretive), criticize or create (postmodernist) a segment of reality. Which of these purposes you believe theory serves depends on your ontological and epistemological assumptions. The particular focus of a theory is called its phenomenon of interest. In organization theory the primary phenomenon of interest is the organization. A theory consists of a set of concepts and the relationships that tie them together into an explanation (or an understanding, critique or creation) of the phenomenon of interest.

Because of the complexity and pluralism of organizations, managers who make sense of and use multiple perspectives are better able to bring their knowledge of organization theory to bear on the wide range of analyses, decisions and plans their organizations make each and every day. This book is built upon the framework of multiple perspectives, and in particular, modern, symbolic-interpretive, and postmodern perspectives will structure our discussion. Studying organization theory from multiple perspectives will help you to enlarge your knowledge base, master a wide range of skills and see situations in different ways—all of which are crucial for understanding, analyzing and managing the complexities of organizational life.

The modernist perspective focuses on the organization as an independent objective entity and takes a positivist approach to generating knowledge. Modernist organization theorists focus on how to increase efficiency, effectiveness and other objective indicators of performance through the application of theories relating to structure and control. The symbolic-interpretive perspective focuses on the organization as a community sustained by human relationships and uses a predominantly subjectivist ontology and an interpretive epistemology. Instead of treating organizations as objects to be measured and analyzed (modernist perspective), symbolic-interpretivists treat them as webs of meanings that are jointly created, appreciated and communicated. Symbolic-interpretive organization theory explores how meanings are created and realities (note the plural) made sensible to those who participate in sustaining them.

Meanwhile postmodernism will generate healthy skepticism toward any dominant theory and will license you and others to try something completely different. The postmodern perspective does all this by expanding the focus of theorizing from the organization per se, to how we speak and write about organizations. Thus one phenomenon postmodern organization theory addresses is theorizing itself: how what you may perceive as stable or objective elements of organizations and organization theory (structure, technology, culture, control, etc.) are but the outcomes of linguistic convention and discursive practice. As such, postmodernism always makes you aware that theories are open to revision and invites you to ask who supports them and why. You should recognize, however, that most postmodernists would object to being categorized as they are in Figure 1.1 and Table 1.2. Remember, postmodernism challenges categories, seeking to undermine them by blurring their boundaries and exposing the motivations that produced or maintain them. In the case of Figure 1.1, for instance, a postmodernist would probably argue that this typology objectifies organization theory and theorizing in ways that reproduce and legitimize seeing the field as constructed of modern, symbolic-interpretive and postmodern perspectives, when other perspectives might be promoted at the same time or instead of these (some others will be discussed in Chapter 10).

I believe that the best theories are those that you have found or invented to match your own experience of organization. In this book you will learn about the theories of organizations and organizing that others have developed and the skills they used to formulate them. This will give you a foundation for your own theorizing. You can use the already formulated theories as they stand, if this proves useful to your purposes, or as inspiration for your own theory-building efforts, but in either case, using organization theory will require both the mastery of existing theories and personal development of the skills of theorizing, analysis, interpretation and critique. Just remember: when you want to apply your abstract reasoning to concrete situations you will need to reverse the process of abstraction and that will require you to perform a creative act.

Finally, you have your own reasons for studying organization theory. Mine are that organization theory broadens my appreciation of organizations and the world in general and opens my mind to new ideas and possibilities for change and transformation. I am constantly renewed by my work in this field and find that the ideas it has given me promote an increased ability to develop new concepts and theories and enhance my ability to learn. Although it may hold other meanings and possibilities for you, I hope that my enthusiasm, which is built on my own particular needs, values and experiences, will inspire you to explore and learn to use organization theory in ways that enhance your life and career.

KEY TERMS

phenomenon of interest	*postmodern*
theory	ontology
concepts	*objectivist*
abstraction	*subjectivist*
chunking	epistemology
multiple perspectives	*positivist*
modern	*interpretive*
symbolic-interpretive	

ENDNOTES

1. See Miller (1956).

2. The multiple perspectives approach to organization theory has been employed by a variety of researchers. One of the earliest and most influential of these was American political scientist Graham Allison (1971), who analyzed the Cuban Missile Crisis using several different theoretical perspectives. John Hassard (1988, 1991; Hassard and Pym 1990) has been particularly active in promoting Burrell and Morgan's (1979) framework. W. Richard Scott (1992) presented rational, natural, and open system views of organizations, while Joanne Martin (1992) built her analysis of organizational culture theory around a multiple perspective

approach including integration, differentiation, and fragmentation perspectives.

3. This assumption is important because theorists use language to create and communicate their theories and if language did not align with reality then it would be impossible to lay claim to positive knowledge.

4. See Schneider (1993) for further discussion and analysis of this ongoing debate.

5. Foucault (1977).

REFERENCES

Allison, Graham (1971). *The essence of decision: Explaining the Cuban missile crisis*. Boston: Little, Brown.

Burrell, Gibson, and Morgan, Gareth (1979). *Sociological paradigms and organizational analysis*. London: Heinemann.

Foucault, Michel (1977). *Power/knowledge* (ed. Colin Gordon). New York: Pantheon.

Hassard, John (1988). Overcoming hermeticism in organization theory: An alternative to paradigm incommensurability. *Human Relations*, 41/3: 247–59.

—— (1991). Multiple paradigms and organizational analysis: A case study. *Organization Studies*, 12/2: 275–99.

—— and Pym, Denis (1990) (eds.). *The theory and philosophy of organizations: Critical issues and new perspectives*. London: Routledge.

Martin, Joanne (1992). *Cultures in organizations: Three perspectives*. Oxford: Oxford University Press.

Miller, George A. (1956). The magical number seven, plus or minus two: Some limits on our capacity for processing information. *Psychological Review*, 63/2: 81–97.

Schneider, Mark A. (1993). *Culture and enchantment*. Chicago: University of Chicago Press.

Scott, W. Richard (1992). *Organizations: Rational, natural, and open systems* (3rd edn.). Englewood Cliffs, NJ: Prentice-Hall.

WORK CITED IN FIGURE 1.1 IN CHRONOLOGICAL ORDER BY PERSPECTIVE

Prehistory

Smith, Adam (1957). *Selections from "The Wealth of Nations"* (ed. George J. Stigler). New York: Appleton Century Crofts (originally published in 1776).

Marx, Karl (1954). *Capital*. Moscow: Foreign Languages Publishing House (first published in 1867).

Durkheim, Émile (1949). *The division of labor in society*. Glencoe, Ill.: Free Press (first published in 1893).

Taylor, Frederick W. (1911). *The principles of scientific management*. New York: Harper.

Follett, Mary Parker (1923). *The new state: Group organization and the solution of popular government*. New York: Longmans, Green and Co. (originally published 1918).

Fayol, Henri (1919/1949). *General and industrial management*. London: Pitman (first published in 1919).

Weber, Max (1947). *The theory of social and economic organization* (ed. A. H. Henderson and Talcott Parsons). Glencoe, Ill.: Free Press (first published in 1924).

Gulick, Luther, and Urwick, Lyndall (1937) (eds.). *Papers on the science of administration*. New York: Institute of Public Administration, Columbia University.

Barnard, Chester (1938). *The functions of the executive*. Cambridge, Mass.: Harvard University Press.

Modernist perspective

Bertalanffy, Ludwig von (1950). The theory of open systems in physics and biology. *Science*, 111: 23–8.

—— (1968). *General systems theory: Foundations, development, applications* (revised edn.). New York: George Braziller.

Trist, Eric, and Bamforth, Kenneth W. (1951). Some social and psychological consequences of the long-wall method of coal-getting. *Human Relations*, 4: 3–38.

Boulding, Kenneth E. (1956). General systems theory—The skeleton of science. *Management Science*, 2: 197–208.

Simon, Herbert (1957). *Administrative behavior* (2nd edn.). New York: Macmillan (first published in 1945).

March, James G., and Simon, Herbert (1958). *Organizations*. New York: John Wiley.

Emery, Fredrick (1960) (ed.). *Systems thinking*. Harmondsworth, Middlesex, England: Penguin.

—— and Trist, Eric L. (1960). Socio-technical systems. In *Management science models and techniques*, Vol. 2. London: Pergamon.

Burns, Tom, and Stalker, G. M. (1961/1995). *The management of innovation*. Oxford: Oxford University Press.

Woodward, Joan (1958). *Management and technology*. London: Her Majesty's Stationery Office.

—— (1965). *Industrial organization: Theory and practice*. London: Oxford University Press.

Lawrence, P. R., and Lorsch, J. W. (1967). Differentiation and integration in complex organizations. *Administrative Science Quarterly*, 12: 1–47.

Thompson, James (1967). *Organizations in action*. New York: McGraw-Hill.

Symbolic-interpretive perspective

Schütz, Alfred (1967). *The phenomenology of the social world* (trans. G. Walsh and F. Lehnert). Evanston, Ill.: Northwestern University Press (first published in 1932).

Whyte, William F. (1943). *Street corner society*. Chicago: University of Chicago Press.

Selznick, Philip (1949). *TVA and the grass roots*. Berkeley: University of California Press.

Goffman, Erving (1959). *The presentation of self in everyday life*. Garden City, NY: Doubleday Anchor.

Gadamer, Han-Georg (1994). *Truth and method* (second revised edn., translation revised by J. Weinsheimer and D. Marshall). New York: Continuum (originally published as *Wahrheit and Methode*.by J. C. B. Mohr/Paul Siebeck, Tubingen, 1960).

Berger, Peter, and Luckmann, Thomas (1966). *The social construction of reality: A treatise in the sociology of knowledge*. Garden City, NY: Doubleday.

Weick, Karl E. (1979 [1969]). *The social psychology of organizing*. Reading, Mass.: Addison-Wesley.

Geertz, C. (1973). *Interpretation of cultures*. New York: Basic Books.

Clifford, James, and Marcus, George E. (1986) (eds.). *Writing culture: The poetics and politics of ethnography*. Berkeley: University of California Press.

Postmodern perspective

Saussure, Ferdinand de (1959). *Course in general linguistics* (trans. Wade Baskin). New York: McGraw-Hill.

Foucault, Michel (1972). *The archeology of knowledge and the discourse on language* (trans. A. M. Sheridan Smith). London: Tavistock Publications.

—— (1973). *The order of things*. New York: Vintage Books.

Bell, Daniel (1973). *The coming of post-industrial society*. New York: Basic Books.

—— (1976). *The cultural contradictions of capitalism*. New York: Basic Books.

Jencks, Charles (1977). *The language of post-modern architecture*. London: Academy.

Derrida, Jacques (1978). *Writing and difference* (trans. Alan Bass). London: Routledge & Kegan Paul.

—— (1980). *Of grammatology* (trans. Gayatri Chakravorty Spivak). Baltimore: Johns Hopkins University Press.

Lyotard, Jean-François (1979). *The postmodern condition: A report on knowledge* (trans. G. Bennington and B. Massumi). Minneapolis: University of Minnesota Press.

Rorty, Richard (1980). *Philosophy and the mirror of nature*. Princeton: Princeton University Press.

Bakhtin, Mikhail (1981). *The dialogic imagination: Four essays* (trans. Chorale Emerson and Michael Holquist). Austin: University of Texas Press.

Lash, Scott, and Urry, John (1987). *The end of organized capitalism*. Cambridge: Polity Press.

Baudrillard, Jean (1988). *Selected writings* (ed. M. Poster). Palo Alto, Calif.: Stanford University Press.

2

A Brief History of Organization Theory

There are many ways to talk about the history and development of a field of study. I presented one of them in Chapter 1. Figure 1.1 shows an academic genealogy that identifies theorists from a wide range of academic disciplines who contributed ideas to the modern, symbolic-interpretive and postmodern perspectives of organization theory. In this chapter we will explore some of the ideas of these influential thinkers. This ideological history will help you understand how each perspective emerged in organization theory, its defining vocabulary and themes, and the logic supporting the various theories you will encounter in later chapters. As in the rest of the book, I will present these ideas more or less in the chronological order of their influence on organization theory so that you can experience for yourself the continuities and discontinuities in thought from which the three perspect-ives and the field emerged. But remember that the order of appearance of ideas is related to their influence on organization theory; quite often these ideas influenced other disciplines before organization theorists caught wind of them. For example, the dates in parentheses after the names of theorists listed at the bottom of Figure 1.1 are publication dates, whereas those inside the boxes of the figure indicate the time frames during which these ideas were incorporated into the field of organization theory.

A word of warning—the ideas in this chapter come from vastly different disciplines and there are quite a few of them. If you start to feel overwhelmed, try reading through the most difficult material quickly and then rereading it after you have finished Part II of the book. Once you are more familiar with the concepts and theories to which this history relates, Chapter 2 should make more sense to you. But be sure to familiarize yourself now with the key terms highlighted in the text because they will give you the vocabulary you will need to tackle the rest of the book.

I have chosen the ideas presented in this chapter on the basis of their common use by theorists representing each perspective. In most cases, other terms might have been chosen and you will encounter some of the others as you work through the remainder of the book. Remember, these terms are more than jargon; they are the concepts from which organization theories are formed. You will need to master a sufficient number of them before you can begin to theorize, so don't fall behind! Oh, and if you get hooked on any of the concepts or theories presented here or elsewhere in the book, look for additional readings at the end of each chapter that will help you on your way to learning more about them.

The first section of the chapter presents scholars whose work forms the prehistory of organization theory. These individuals provided the field—particularly the modernist perspective—with its foundational ideas. In this section I will introduce you to several important sociologists and classical management scholars and trace the ways their ideas live on in organization theory today. In the second section I will present three of the most important modernist contributions to organization theory: general systems theory, socio-technical systems theory and contingency theory. The third section will direct your attention to important ideas drawn from the symbolic-interpretive perspective: social construction theory, enactment theory, and reflexivity. Following this I will present a handful of the most widely debated postmodern concepts to have infiltrated organization theory including language games, grand narratives, power/knowledge, discourse, decentering, deconstruction, différance, simulacra and hyper-reality. As you read about the variety of ideas that shaped organization theory and its perspectives, do not forget that the three perspectives are not just of academic interest; they have many applications to organizing and managing, some of which I will point out as we go along to help you learn to connect theory and practice. Later on, in Chapter 9, I will treat the subject of theory in practice directly.

Organization Theory at Its Inception: Principles, Typologies and the One Best Way

I would now like to introduce you to some of the pioneers of social science and tell you how their ideas provided inspiration to the three perspectives of organization theory. As you read through this material remember that, since organization theory did not emerge as a recognizable field of study until sometime in the 1960s, those whose scholarship contributed to its prehistory were only connected to the field in retrospect. At the time these scholars did their research and writing there was no organization theory for them to contribute to. Furthermore, you should be aware that organization theory is just one of several disciplines inspired by the theorists discussed here. Other disciplines that trace their origins to these scholars include industrial relations, industrial and organizational psychology, organizational sociology, management, administrative theory, and organizational behavior. Some people refer to all of these fields collectively as organization studies.

Using key terms you learned in Chapter 1, the scholarship of organization theory's prehistory is situated mainly in objectivist ontology but combines both positivist and interpretive epistemologies. Theorists who today are considered to have founded organization theory were a mix of academic scholars and management practitioners, some of whom used **inductive** modes of reasoning (developing theory from practice using an interpretive epistemology), while others used **deductive** modes (testing theory against practice using a positivist epistemology). The logic of grouping these theorists into one box in Figure 1.1 lies in their mutual fondness for developing principles, rules and typologies and in their search for the best, most rational, and therefore most efficient way of structuring and managing organizations. Although they may seem obvious to you, remember that most organizations of the day were managed so unsystematically that these ideas seemed revolutionary when they were first proposed.

There are two major sources of thought that formed the prehistory of organization theory, one sociological and the other managerial. The sociological source, represented here by Émile Durkheim, Max Weber, and Karl Marx, focused on the changing shapes and roles of formal organizations within society and the influences of industrialization on the nature of work and its consequences for workers. Classical management theory was shaped by Frederick Taylor, Mary Parker Follett, Henri Fayol, Luther Gulick, Chester Barnard, and others who worked as executives or management consultants and focused on the practical problems faced by managers of public and private sector organizations. The often remarked tension in organization theory between theory and practice traces to the different interests represented by these two sources of thought.[1] The ideas of both go back even further to those of the famous political-economist Adam Smith, which is where I will begin this brief historical survey of the influences that shaped organization theory at its inception.

Adam Smith, Political-Economist (1723–1790, Scottish)

Because he was the first to articulate a theory to explain efficient production in systematically organized work practices, many organization theorists give the Scottish political-economist Adam Smith the place of honor in their intellectual histories. In 1776, Smith published *An Inquiry into the Nature and Causes of the Wealth of Nations*, in which he described the techniques of pin manufacturing as an illustration of how the **division of labor** can produce economic efficiency at work.[2] The theory Smith presented in his book foreshadowed important industrial management practices like work and production simplification, and time and motion studies. Smith wrote:

> The effects of the division of labour, in the general business of society, will be more easily understood, by considering in what manner it operates in some particular manufactures. It is commonly supposed to be carried furthest in some very trifling ones; not perhaps that it really is carried further in them than in others of more importance: but in those trifling manufactures which are destined to supply the small wants of but a small number of people, the whole number of workmen must necessarily be small; and those employed in every different branch of the work can often be collected into the same workhouse, and placed at once under the view of the spectator. In those great manufactures, on the contrary, which are destined to supply the great wants of the great body of the people, every different branch of the work employs so great a number of workmen, that it is impossible to collect them all into the same workhouse. We can seldom see more, at one time, than those employed in one single branch. Though in such manufactures, therefore, the work may really be divided into a much greater number of parts, than in those of a more trifling nature, the division is not near so obvious, and has accordingly been much less observed.
>
> To take an example, therefore, but one in which the division of labour has been very often taken notice of, the trade of the pin-maker; a workman not educated to this business (which the division of labour has rendered a distinct trade), nor acquainted with the use of the machinery employed in it (to the invention of which the same division of labour has probably given occasion),

could scarce, perhaps, with his utmost industry, make one pin in a day, and certainly could not make twenty. But in the way in which this business is now carried on, not only the whole work is a peculiar trade, but it is divided into a number of branches, of which the greater part are likewise peculiar trades. One man draws out the wire, another straights it, a third cuts it, a fourth points it, a fifth grinds it at the top for receiving the head; to make the head requires two or three distinct operations; to put it on, is a peculiar business, to whiten the pins is another; it is even a trade by itself to put them into the paper; and the important business of making a pin is, in this manner, divided into about eighteen distinct operations, which, in some manufactories, are all performed by distinct hands, though in others the same man will sometimes perform two or three of them . . . I have seen a small manufactory of this kind where ten men only were employed, and where some of them consequently performed two or three distinct operations. But though they were very poor, and therefore but indifferently accommodated with the necessary machinery, they could, when they exerted themselves, make among them about twelve pounds of pins in a day. There are in a pound upwards of four thousand pins of a middling size. Those ten persons, therefore, could make among them upwards of forty-eight thousand pins in a day. Each person, therefore, making a tenth part of forty-eight thousand pins, might be considered as making four thousand eight hundred pins in a day. But if they had all wrought separately and independently, and without any of them having been educated to this peculiar business, they certainly could not each of them have made twenty, perhaps not one pin in a day; that is, certainly, not the two hundred and fortieth, perhaps not the four thousand eight hundredth part of what they are at present capable of performing, in consequence of a proper division and combination of their different operations.

In every other art and manufacture, the effects of the division of labour are similar to what they are in this very trifling one; though, in many of them, the labour can neither be so much subdivided, nor reduced to so great a simplicity of operation. The division of labour, however, so far as it can be introduced, occasions, in every art, a proportionable increase of the productive powers of labour.[3]

As you will learn in Chapter 4, the division of labor, including the differentiation of work tasks and the specialization of laborers, is central to the concept of social structure in organization theory. However, as you will see in the section on postmodernism below, Smith and the modernists who followed him assumed that the economic development provided by industrialization led to social progress, an assumption postmodernists later called into question.

Karl Marx, Philosopher-Economist and Revolutionary (1818–1883, German)

Karl Marx is perhaps best known for his **theory of capital** and related ideas about the exploitation and alienation of the working classes. Along with Max Weber and Émile Durkheim (see below), Marx is regarded to be one of the founders of the field of sociology. His theory of social conflict provided the basis for critical theory by offering an early critique of capitalism.

Marx's theory of capital begins by considering the human need to survive the dangers presented by the physical world. Survival needs create an economic order when humans, in trying to cope with danger and sustenance issues, discover the efficiencies of collective labor. The need to work together occasions the development of social roles and structures and subsequently leads to resource surpluses of raw material and time that can then be invested in cultural development. In Marx's theory, societies and cultures build upon this economic foundation and the particular forms taken by society and culture are therefore subject to the relations of power worked out between those who comprise the economy.

Having narrowed the explanation of society and culture to economic order, Marx then argued that capitalism rests upon a fundamental antagonism between the interests of capital (i.e., capitalists who own the factories and other means of production) and those of labor (i.e., workers whose activities produce the output of the production process). The antagonism, in part, arises over how to divide the excess profits generated when products or services are exchanged on a market at a price that is higher than their costs. According to Marx, since profit is generated by a combination of labor and capital, each side, naturally, can reasonably claim that the surplus should belong to them. The laborers think that a large share should be theirs because they did the work, while capitalists argue that, without the investment their capital makes possible, there would be no work to do and therefore the larger share should be theirs. Thus is the capitalist system forever conflicted by the never-ending struggle between the interests of capital and those of labor.

Antagonism between labor and capital also arises from the necessity to ensure profitability. Without profitability, the survival of the individual firm and the entire capitalist economy would be in jeopardy. Profitability depends upon the organization and control of work activity. This is because competition from other firms puts downward pressure on the prices for a firm's products and services. This pressure translates into a need to reduce the costs of production. Since labor is a large component of the costs of production, capitalists pressure laborers to work more efficiently (or at least more cheaply), which is achieved by continuously imposing new forms of **managerial control** on work processes.

Alienation refers to the disenfranchising of workers from the product of their work efforts. Because, in the drive for efficiency, labor is defined as a cost of production, rather than as a means to achieve a collective purpose for the good of society, labor comes to be defined as a commodity to be bought and sold on an exchange market. This concept of labor gives humans a purely instrumental relationship with one another based on the economic value of their potential to do work. When managers accept this alienating assumption they are encouraged to treat labor like any other raw material, that is, to exploit it for its economic value. Unless workers organize their resistance (e.g., via unions) to such managerial exploitation, the disempowerment and alienation of workers will grow unabated. Thus, according to Marx, the result of antagonism between capital and labor is a continual build up of institutionalized forms of mutual control and resistance (e.g., management versus unions) held in place by the dynamics of a capitalist economy.

Building on Marx's theories, critical organization theorists are particularly concerned to challenge the rights claimed by owners and managers to suppress conflicting interests and control the lives of others for the purpose of generating profit. In addition, they offer theories to explain the dehumanizing effects of managerial control based on Marx's theory of alienation. Their work, known as **critical organization theory**, focuses on the structural, economic and social system determinants of the distribution of power in organizations, and is concerned with the emancipation of workers and with establishing more democratic structures and forms of corporate governance. Postmodernists tend to disagree with emancipation, arguing it merely replaces one form of privilege with another;

however, they build on critical organization theory when they study ideology and the various forms of domination that it produces in the workplace. You will read more about Marxist critiques of power and control in Chapter 8 and to appreciate what critical theory has contributed to the postmodern perspective.

Émile Durkheim, Sociologist (1858–1917, French)

Over one hundred years after Adam Smith described the economic benefits of the division of labor, the French sociologist Émile Durkheim wrote his book on the subject. Published in 1893, *The Division of Labor in Society* extended Smith's ideas about the structural shift from agricultural to industrial societies brought about by the industrial revolution. Following Smith, Durkheim described this shift in terms of increases in specialization, but also emphasized hierarchy and the interdependence of work tasks. Early modernist organization theorists regarded these concepts as key dimensions for defining and describing complex organizations, as you will see in Chapter 4.

Durkheim also proposed the distinction between **informal** and **formal organization** that placed attention on workers' social needs in addition to the demands of formally organizing work. The theme of social needs within work groups is of major interest to the fields of organizational behavior, and industrial and organizational psychology. And the concept of informal organization grounds the notion of organizational culture, which is the subject of Chapter 6. The distinction between the informal and formal organization exposed a tension between humanistic and economic aspects of organizing that challenges managers to this day.[4]

In addition to his work on the division of labor, Durkheim made a major contribution to establishing sociology as a scientific discipline through his development of objectivist (i.e., quantitative) research methods. With his books *The Rules of Sociological Method* and *Suicide*, which emphasized objective measurement and statistical description and analysis, Durkheim helped lay positivistic methodological foundations, not only for sociology but also for modernist organization theory.

Karl Emil Maximillian (Max) Weber, Sociologist (1864–1920, German)

Like Durkheim, the German economic-sociologist Max Weber wanted to understand the ways in which industrialization affected society, especially through its effects on authority structures. According to Weber, before industrialization societies organized themselves either around traditional or charismatic forms of authority. **Traditional authority** is an inherited status defined and maintained by the ways of the past. For example the inheritance of property from father to son defines the aristocracy of many different societies both past and present. In **charismatic authority** the rights of leadership fall to individuals whose magical powers of attraction for others justify their authority with little need for any other legitimization. Historical examples of charisma include religious leaders such as Christ or Mohammed, while modern examples often come from politics, such as Gandhi,

Winston Churchill, John F. Kennedy and Martin Luther King, Jr. Kings and queens are an interesting mixture of both charismatic and traditional authority—the divine rights of monarchs are believed by their subjects to flow through bloodlines but also draw upon metaphysical connections to God that deliver unquestionable power.

Weber believed that industrialization created a third form of authority and he considered the emergence of bureaucratic authority structures as superior to both charismatic and traditional authority because, in bureaucracies the choice of who should be given authority is rationally determined by rules and legally binding procedures. In these authority structures, laws and norms are the basis and justification for rules. Using **rational-legal authority** allows a society to avoid both the succession problems of finding another charismatic person when a leader is lost (think of the turmoil created in the Civil Rights Movement when Martin Luther King, Jr. was assassinated), and the problem of ceding authority through inheritance to those who are ill-fit or unwilling to lead. Under rational-legal authority, a society has an endless supply of people to whom it can give authority because it can make rational choices on the basis of superior leadership or technical abilities. At least this was the ideal Weber saw as arising from the industrial system and its norms for technical efficiency. In his imagination rational social systems would replace cults of personality and nepotism with merit-based selection of those who would have authority over others.

Weber's **theory of bureaucracy** with its central themes of authority and rationality was presented in his book *The Theory of Social and Economic Organization*, published in German in 1924 and in English translation in 1947. In this book Weber proposed that bureaucracy could rationalize the social order in a manner similar to technology's rationalizing influence on the economic order. This association led modernist organization theorists of the 1950s and 1960s to believe that bureaucratic rationalization would promote technical efficiency. This belief persists in the minds of many modernist organization theorists, some of whom have devoted their research to studying the relationship between organizational structure and technology, which you will learn more about in Chapter 5.

Weber himself, however, recognized that the uses of rationalization rest upon value-based criteria. Evidence for this is found in his distinction between formal and substantive rationality. **Formal rationality** involves techniques of calculation (such as those developed by engineers to measure technical efficiency or by accountants to track costs), while **substantive rationality** refers to the desired ends of action that direct the uses of calculative techniques. Different desired ends will lead to different uses of formal rationality. Weber warned that formal rationality without conscious consideration of substantive rationality would lead, in his colorful phrase, to an 'iron cage' capable of imprisoning humanity and making every human being a 'cog in an ever-moving mechanism'.[5] Such sentiments position Weber close to those who criticize modernist organization theory and attempt to free humankind from the often restrictive practices of management. His interest in how cultural rules, beliefs, customs and morality influence social behavior is carried on by symbolic-interpretive researchers who study organizational culture and sensemaking, concepts you will read more about later in this chapter and in Chapter 6.

Frederick Winslow Taylor, Founder of Scientific Management (1856–1915, American)

At the turn of the twentieth century, big business was accompanied by the professionalization of industrial management. As part of this professionalization process, management journals were created to enable the exchange of information among practitioners. Within this milieu, Frederick Taylor proposed his philosophy of scientific management.

At the age of 28, Taylor had been named chief engineer at the Midvale Steel Company. Based on his experience there and on experiments he later conducted at the Bethlehem Steel Company, among other places, he developed procedures for enhancing the efficiency and productivity of factories. His early efforts to manage Midvale followed common management practices combining persuasion and force to encourage workers to perform, and the disgruntlement of workers and his own disaffection with the result of this management style led him to realize that he needed to know at least as much about the technical aspects of work as his workers knew. So Taylor conducted experiments in such matters as the handling of raw material, the use of machines and other tools and worker motivation. These studies prompted Taylor to develop work standards (a target rate of performance generally set higher than the average at which workers had produced prior to being exposed to scientific management), uniform work methods to guarantee workers could achieve the standards set for them (including instruction cards, order-of-work sequences, materials specifications, inventory control systems, etc.), skill-based job placement methods, methods of supervision and incentive schemes.

Taylor integrated these elements into the **scientific management** system whose philosophy was that applying scientific methods to labor would both maximize the benefits of the factory to society and achieve high levels of cooperation between management and labor. His system was scientific in that it called for managers to employ research and experimentation to find the correct standards, principles and processes that would allow them to pay high wages while simultaneously lowering production costs. That is, science would be used to ensure profit maximization without the conflict generally associated with worker–management relations in factories.

In addition to the scientific investigation of work methods, Taylor applied science to the study of management. Research and analysis were at the time uncommon in business, and Taylor and his followers promoted their use so effectively that today the reverse is more often observed—managers whose reliance on research and analysis prevent them taking full advantage of intuition and creativity. The dominance of the technical aspects of management today (e.g., cost savings, control systems) is a tribute to the influence Taylor exercised.

For example, Taylor's work inspired an international efficiency movement. The husband and wife team of Frank and Lillian Gilbreth, well-known representatives of this movement, devoted their lives to studying work methods in order to reduce the motions and thus the time required to perform work. For example, while working as a bricklayer Frank Gilbreth invented a method that reduced the number of movements required to lay one interior brick from 18 to 2, thus increasing the bricklaying rate from 120 to 350 bricks per man-hour. Taylor also inspired heads of state and business leaders to adopt the principles of scientific management. Lenin, Stalin and Henry Ford all implemented Taylor's ideas, each in their own way. Even today, the practice of quantifying workers' inputs and outputs for the purpose of evaluation and control can be observed in businesses in the United States, Japan and Germany, as well as the former Soviet Union. Yet in spite of this, scientific management was considered by many workers and business owners to be dangerous and subversive. In the United Kingdom, France, Sweden and Denmark, where worker rights have been historically better defended, scientific management was resisted.

Those who resist scientific management do so on the grounds that strict work methods alienate most workers who lose control over their labor practices through the application of Taylor's methods, and that worker solidarity is eroded by offering differential pay for performance. The displacement of master craftsmen and foreman with managers causes resentment as well. The furor over the control of work methods earned scientific management considerable and lasting ill-repute as being ruinously ignorant of the trust and cooperation between management and workers upon which organizations depend. Scientific management was the subject of an American Congressional investigation after attempts to introduce Taylor's principles into a government organization led to union opposition and a strike. The controversy recently re-emerged in critical organization theory, and in the postmodern critique of Taylorism associated with assembly line technology (also known as Fordism because Henry Ford adopted Taylor's principles to the assembly of automobiles), total quality management (TQM) and business process re-engineering (BPR).[6]

Perhaps the most enduring image of Taylor is as a promoter of rationalization in organizations. His belief in the powers of objective measurement and the discovery of laws governing work efficiency carry over into the modernist perspective where scientific management techniques lay the groundwork for management control systems. Critics see Taylor's system, not so much as a means to make organizations more efficient, but rather as a rationale justifying the power managers enjoy. The topics of managerial control and resistance to it will be presented in Chapter 8.

Mary Parker Follett, Scholar, Social Reformer, Government and Management Consultant (1868–1933, American)

Based on her consulting work with community centers, government and business organizations, Mary Parker Follett developed the idea that the same principles that contribute to strong social communities could be applied to creating successful organizations. Long before such ideas became popular, Follett promoted democratic forms of organization and employee involvement, as she did in her 1911 book *The New State: Group Organization and the Solution of Popular Government*.

In 1924 Parker published *Creative Experience*, in which she proposed a management theory based on the principle of self-government which she claimed would facilitate 'the growth of individuals and of the groups to which they belonged'. She argued that 'by directly interacting with one another to achieve their common goals, the members of a group fulfilled themselves through the process of the group's development.' Thus, her ideas anticipated by many decades recent interest in **workplace democracy** and nonhierarchical networks of self-governing groups. She envisioned self-governing organizations, pointedly suggesting that organizations within a democratic society should embrace democratic ideals, and that power should be power *with* not power *over* people. For example, Follett stated:

> You cannot coordinate purpose without developing purpose, it is part of the same process. Some people want to give the workmen a share in carrying out the purpose of the plant and do not see that that involves a share in creating the purpose of the plant.[7]

Although her work is currently experiencing a revival, it is surprising how often it has been overlooked in historical surveys of organization theory. For instance, her work on organizations as communities can be seen as a precursor to organizational culture studies as well as to much recent scholarship focusing on organizations as communities of knowledge, practice and learning. The value of her work has been more widely recognized in Japan where, in the 1950s, her influence spawned the Mary Parker Follett Association dedicated to the dissemination of her ideas. This association continues its work to this day.

Henri Fayol, Engineer, CEO, and Administrative Theorist (1841–1925, French)

French administrative theorist Henri Fayol had been an engineer and manager in the mining industry, and eventually became CEO of an ailing French mining company. His successful turnaround of that company earned him great admiration, and upon his retirement he established a center for the study of administration in an effort to codify and pass on the wisdom he had gained. In his book *General and Industrial Management*, first published in 1919 but not available in English translation until 1949, he presented what he believed to be universal principles for the rational administration of organizational activities.

Fayol's theory inspired much discussion among management scholars about the precise specification of his **administrative principles**. The principles themselves involved issues such as the span-of-control (the maximum number of subordinates that can be overseen by one manager); exceptions to routine (subordinates should handle routine matters, leaving managers free to handle exceptions to rules and standard operating procedures); departmentalization (departments formed around the grouping of similar activities); unity-of-command (each subordinate should report to only one boss); and hierarchy (the scalar principle links all organizational members into a control structure resembling a pyramid). Fayol's belief that the best way to administer organizational activities could be achieved by applying his principles proved to be too ambitious. Nonetheless, his approach to organization theory identified many of the measurable dimensions of organizational social structure that underlie this modernist concept, as you will see in Chapter 4.

In addition to his administrative principles, Fayol emphasized the importance of esprit de corps among organizational members. He argued that unity of sentiment and harmony contribute to the smooth functioning of an organization. A similar idea arose in the modernist concept of organizational culture, to be discussed further in Chapter 6. Fayol also specified the responsibilities of the manager as: planning, organizing, commanding, coordination, and control. These came to be known as the functions of management and were elaborated by the American administrative theorist Luther Gulick.

Luther H. Gulick, Administrative Theorist (1892–1992, American)

In 1936 Gulick, who was Professor of Municipal Science and Administration at Columbia University, became a member of the Brownlow Committee on Administrative Management established by President Franklin Delano Roosevelt. The committee was concerned with restructuring the Executive Branch of government and resulted in 1937 in a collection of papers entitled *Papers on the Science of Administration* that Gulick edited with Lyndall Urwick. Gulick's contribution to the book entitled 'Notes on the Theory of Organization' built on Fayol's theory that organizational efficiency could be increased by dividing work into small, specialized segments, allotting the work to those skilled in that specific segment, and coordinating the work through supervision, clear task definition, instruction, and direction. He saw technical expertise as crucial to the efficient running of government, and efficiency as 'one of the things that is good for [the common man] because it makes life richer and safer'. But Gulick is probably best known for the mnemonic he devised to define the work of the chief executive:

P lanning
O rganizing
S taffing
D irecting
Co ordinating
R eporting
B udgeting

Many generations of students have used the acronym POSDCoRB to remember the functions of the executive. Gulick thought that a science of administration built on knowledge of these functions could be a means of rationalizing and professionalizing business management and public administration. His work highlights one of the central tenets of modernism—that universal rules and principles can be found and applied to any organization, in this case any administrative institution whether it be a business, hospital, government, prison or school.

Chester Barnard, Executive and Management Theorist (1886–1961, American)

In his 1938 book *The Functions of the Executive*, Chester Barnard, former president of the New Jersey Bell Telephone Company, extended one of Durkheim's ideas to management theory by suggesting that managing the informal organization was a key function of successful executives. Barnard emphasized the ways in which executives might develop their organizations into **cooperative social systems** by focusing on the integration of work efforts through communication of goals and attention to worker motivation, ideas that echo those of Mary Parker Follett. However, postmodernists sometimes blame the significance Barnard and his followers attached to the cooperative aspects of organizations for having blinded early organization theorists to the importance of conflict as a fundamental aspect of all organizations (see Chapter 8). Nonetheless, the consideration Barnard gave to issues of value and sentiment in the workplace identified themes that reappear in contemporary research on organizational culture, meaning, and symbolism, concepts you will meet again in Chapter 6. In this regard Barnard's focus on the informal—what really goes on in organizations—foreshadowed participant-observation studies that were later used to establish the symbolic-interpretive perspective (see Chapter 6).

Modernist Influences on Organization Theory

Modernism is rooted in the Enlightenment of seventeenth- and eighteenth-century European philosophy associated with Descartes, Locke and Kant. Often described as the Age of Reason, the Enlightenment sought to replace feudalism and superstition with rational knowledge. The belief of the times was that rationality would free humankind from slavery and the fear that superstition brings and would allow humans to control their environment through scientific knowledge and its application via technological means. Much of the hope the Enlightenment gave to those emerging from the Dark Ages was built upon the modern idea of human progress.

The idea that humankind progresses by building new knowledge on the back of old goes back much further than the Enlightenment. According to American comparative literature scholar Matei Calinescue, the idea of progress first appeared in medieval times when the word 'modern' (*modernus*) was coined in a bid to distinguish what was then the current period from the times of the ancients. Although the word 'modern' appeared in the late fifth century, it took until the twelfth century for the debate between the moderns and those representing the ancients to reach its zenith. The debate was centered on the modernists' claim that the idea of progress meant modern humans knew more than the ancients did because they possessed all the ancients' knowledge plus some of their own. Even so, those modernists living in the twelfth century were not irreverent of ancient knowledge. For example, in 1159 John of Salisbury wrote down a popular analogy that survives today:

> We frequently know more, not because we have moved ahead by our own natural ability, but because we are supported by the mental strength of others, and possess riches that we have inherited from our forefathers. Bernard of Chartres used to compare us to puny dwarfs perched on the shoulders of giants. He pointed out that we see more and farther than our predecessors, not because we have keener vision or greater height, but because we are lifted up and borne aloft on their gigantic stature.[8]

Although modernists of the twelfth century thus called for humility in the face of ancient wisdom, modernists of the twentieth century were more likely to accentuate the superior value of the farther view. Such thinking underpins modernistic love for the newest ideas and latest techniques, and supports the notion of scientific progress as a series of linear, cumulative steps toward the ideals of complete knowledge and human perfection. Thus, Calinesque argued, the encyclopedia is the perfect symbol of modern sensibilities because it offers a compendium of all human knowledge. Today modernist Westerners are still inspired by German philosopher Immanuel Kant who believed in a human race unified by the ideals of justice and individual freedom, an ideology subsequently used to justify colonialism on the grounds that it led to universal improvement of the human condition. Meanwhile, elsewhere in the world, this ideal has been reinterpreted as modernization—belief in the value of copying the scientific progress of the West in order to gain its material advantages without necessarily adopting Western ideology.

Modernist organization theorists believe that complete knowledge means understanding how and why organizations function the way they do and how their functioning is influenced by different environmental conditions. They develop ways of diagnosing organizational problems so as to manage in more effective and efficient ways that create competitive advantage and profitability. Specifically, from a modernist perspective, effective organizations are able to balance internal and external pressures, develop core competencies, increase efficiency and adapt to change. Three theories provided much of the logic underpinning modernist organization theory today: general systems theory, socio-technical systems theory and contingency theory.

General Systems Theory

In the 1950s, the biologist Ludwig von Bertalanffy presented the outline of a theory intended to explain all scientific phenomena across both natural and social sciences from the atom and molecule, through the single cell, organ, and organism, all the way up to the levels of individual, group, and society. He recognized that these phenomena formed a hierarchy: societies contain groups, groups contain individuals, individuals are comprised of organs, organs of cells, cells of molecules, and molecules of atoms. To generalize across all these phenomena, he referred to each as a system. Bertalanffy then sought the essential laws and principles that he believed govern all systems regardless of their level in the hierarchy. Thus, he envisioned a theory that would draw generalizations at such a high level of abstraction that the essence of all scientific knowledge would be distilled. He called his vision **general systems theory**.

Bertalanffy based general systems theory on the assumption that the scientific method shared by all the sciences implies, or at least permits, theoretical unity. He did not expect the theory to do away with the varied branches of science, he predicted that the branches would continue to investigate the unique features of their phenomena of interest. Instead, systems theorists would focus on the lawlike regularities underlying and uniting all phenomena across the various branches of natural and social science, an early attempt at interdisciplinary research.

To understand the importance of systems thinking for organization theory, it is necessary to grasp the concept of a system and its characteristics. A **system** is a thing with mutually interrelated parts called **subsystems**. Each subsystem affects the others, and each in turn depends upon the whole. The use of the term 'thing' shows you just how general, general systems theory is. This theory can be applied to any *thing* that science takes as its phenomenon of interest. However, any whole is greater than the sum of its parts and the essence of a whole can only be discovered when the system is confronted on its own terms. This is because subsystem interdependence produces features and characteristics that are unique to the system.

Consider the example of an automobile. No matter how much you know about each automotive subsystem (e.g., the electrical or fuel systems), unless you understand how all the parts relate to each other to affect overall performance, it will be difficult to assemble a car in a workable way. In other words, a system must be apprehended holistically; it can never be fully understood merely by analyzing its parts.

The car example illustrates another important feature of systems: that systems are highly differentiated, that is, each subsystem performs (specializes in) a particular function or activity. **Differentiation** provides the system with the benefits of **specialization**, for example, having an efficient and optimal fuel system. Of course, specialization at the subsystem level eventually creates a need for **integration** and coordination at the system level (building the fuel system into the car and making sure it works smoothly with other subsystems like the engine), or in other words, a need for organization. The systems approach does not imply that analyzing subsystems is a bad idea, only that it is partial because it misses something essential about the system. The implication is that to comprehend a system you must not merely analyze (or synthesize or integrate), you must also be willing to transcend the view of the individual parts to encounter the entire system at its own level of complexity. It is this assumption of a transcendent position from which to understand organization that postmodernists later attacked as untenable. I will return to this matter in the section on postmodern influences below.

You may have noticed that what we have called subsystems could also be discussed as systems in their own right. Kenneth Boulding, an American economist, outlined a **hierarchy of systems** ordered from the simplest to the most complex described in Table 2.1.[9] Notice that each level of Boulding's hierarchy has its own unique characteristics but also incorporates the characteristics of lower levels. This means that if you look only at a lower level system, you will be blind to the uniqueness that the higher level system manifests. For example, you may study the structure of an organization, but this does not tell you about the characteristics and complexity of the industry or society in which the organization operates (both higher level systems).

When you analyze a subsystem it is important for you to carefully define your **level of analysis**. Allow the particular system you wish to focus on (your phenomenon of interest) to define your level of analysis. For example, if you are studying how an organization functions as a whole, your level of analysis is the organization, which means that units or departments will be regarded as subsystems and the environment will be the supersystem. If you define a department within the organization as your system of interest, then groups within the department form its subsystems and the organization embedded in its environment comprises its supersystem. Learning to use levels of analysis will give you the flexibility to apply general systems theory to any phenomenon you choose to study, but you need to be wary of the confusion you will create by forgetting what level you have defined as your focus.

Table 2.1 Boulding's hierarchy of systems

Level	Characteristics	Examples
1. Framework	• labels and terminology • classification systems	anatomies, geographies lists, indexes, catalogs

2. Clockwork	• cyclical events
	• simple with regular
	  (or regulated) motions
	• equilibria or states of
	  balance
		solar system
		simple machines
		  (clock or pulley)
		equilibrium system
		  of economics

3. Control	• self-control • feedback • transmission of information	thermostat homeostasis auto pilot
4. Open (living)	• self-maintenance • throughput of material • energy input • reproduction	cell river flame
5. Genetic	• division of labor (cells) • differentiated and mutually dependent parts • growth follows 'blue-print'	plant
6. Animal	• mobility • self-awareness • specialized sensory receptors • highly developed nervous system • knowledge structures (image)	dog cat elephant whale or dolphin
7. Human	• self-consciousness • capacity to produce, absorb, and interpret symbols • sense of passing time	you me
8. Social organization	• value system • meaning	businesses governments
9. Transcendental	• 'inescapable unknowables'	metaphysics, aesthetics

Based on: Boulding (1956).

Organizational theorists who apply general systems theory try to model how the organization functions as a system. Their focus can be how subsystems relate to each other or how gaps or misalignments between subsystems affect organizational performance; what feedback mechanisms are or should be in place; how the organization interacts with its environment; and how to structure the organization to maximize efficiency. This is one way you might read Figure 1.2: the organization is a system comprised of four subsystems (technology, social structure, culture and physical structure) situated within a supersystem (the environment) of which it is a part. In the chapters that follow you will find that general systems theory provides the logic for many modernist organization theories.

Socio-Technical Systems Theory

You may have noticed that people do not play a big role in general systems theory, except that they occupy the individual level in the hierarchy of systems. In the 1960s, renewed concern for the human dimensions of work led to the development of socio-technical systems theory. The Tavistock Institute of Human Relations in the United Kingdom proposed the idea that human behavior and technology are interrelated and that any changes in technology will affect social relationships, attitudes and feelings about work which in turn affect the output of the technology. According to Tavistock researchers, managers therefore need to identify the best fit between technical and social systems and maintain a balance between them that may mean compromising the optimality of one or both subsystems.

Socio-technical systems theory evolved from the work of two Tavistock researchers, Eric Trist and Ken Bamforth, who examined the impact of technology on worker productivity, motivation, morale and stress in a British coalmine in the early 1950s.[10] In the traditional long-wall method of coal mining, all miners worked independently at stations situated along a conveyor belt that ran the length of the coal face. Miners working in the dangerous and monotonous environment of long-wall mines had little influence over their work or the work of others because each person and work shift had little contact. Trist and Bamforth noted a number of shortcomings with this method including constantly shifting blame to other workers, high stress, absenteeism, labor turnover and low productivity.

One Durham mine had adopted a short-wall method in which multi-skilled work groups were responsible for the whole cycle of coal mining on their shift. These **autonomous work groups** allowed the miners to control their task assignment. Trist and Bamforth found that although the methods developed by the autonomous work groups were technically not as efficient as those designed by the engineers, more work was accomplished and workers were much more satisfied with their jobs. They predicted that new forms of work organization using short-wall principles would enjoy both improved productivity and morale. In other words, the version of technical suboptimization they observed paradoxically optimized the performance of the social and technical systems taken together, and they believed that this result would generalize to other work settings.

Fred Emery, another Tavistock researcher, conceptualized socio-technical systems theory in a number of papers and books.[11] He mapped the impact of the technical and social systems on the psychological needs of individuals, and suggested that production systems be redesigned to allow for teamwork, multi-skilling and self-management. He stated that the success of the organization depends upon each subsystem (or group) being able to adapt to problems and integrate with each other subsystem and the whole. Be sure to notice the spirit and terminology of general systems theory in use here. Many of Emery's ideas are contained in contemporary theories of self-organizing systems and complexity theory, to be discussed further in Chapters 9 and 10, respectively.

The work of all the Tavistock researchers focused attention on a number of humanistic issues: organizations as social systems, the social and psychological consequences of work design, the importance of the work group compared to the individual, and the need for a division of labor that considers increasing rather than decreasing the variety of work skills and tasks. They also suggested that self-managed teams should be the building blocks of organizational design, and that this could lessen the need for hierarchical forms of organizing. As you can see, this proposal was contrary to many of the principles of scientific management and offers a way to overcome the disempowering tendencies of capitalism. Tavistock researchers took their work into many organizations around the world including calico mills in India, ship building and fertilizer plants in Norway, an American mining company, and Shell oil refining plants in the United Kingdom and Canada. Socio-technical systems ideas underpin new forms of organization such as matrix structures and networks (see Chapters 4 and 9) and workplace democracy (see Chapter 8).

Contingency Theory

Contingency theory arose in the 1960s when empirical studies challenged the classical management belief in finding the one best way to organize. Those who promote it believe that the most appropriate way of designing and managing an organization depends upon the characteristics of the situation in which the organization finds itself.[12] In other words, organizational design is contingent upon many factors, including the environment, goals, technology, and people, and effective organizations are those in which these various elements are aligned. The analogy of a jigsaw puzzle may be helpful to you—each piece has to be shaped to fit others as well as displaying the appropriate part of the overall picture. Unless this happens, the puzzle will be impossible to solve. Contingency theorists try to identify the key contingencies in each situation (the pieces of the puzzle) and try to determine the best fit between them. You can usually identify a contingency approach by the general phrase '*If* this situation exists . . . *then* this should be done.' For example, *if* a manufacturing organization exists in a highly competitive environment and has to produce a dependable number of widgets each day to precise quality standards—*then* the production process should be highly standardized, there should be clear output goals, written standards and operating procedures, and close supervisory control.

One reason contingency theories have remained so popular over the years is because they take the seductive form of recipes for success. Note that contingency theory takes an objectivist stance and is typically assessed on criteria of technical rationality and efficiency. You will learn more about contingency theory in the remaining chapters of the book, as this is still the dominant approach to modernist organization theorizing.

Symbolic-Interpretive Influences

Symbolic-interpretivists played a crucial role in the history of organization theory by being the first to successfully challenge the objective science of modernism and offer an acceptable alternative. In many respects, symbolic-interpretive organization theory was inspired by the crisis of confidence faced by anthropologists in the early 1980s. Spearheaded by the collapse of colonialism, Western anthropologists raised self-critique to international prominence by admitting to having conspired (if unwittingly) with powerful Western governments to impose their values on other cultures of the world. Originally legitimated by the claim to bring progress to primitive cultures, colonization crumbled amid demands from the colonized for self-determination and native rights.

The specific academic claim that came under fire was whether anthropologists were capable of representing native cultures accurately.[13] In their ethnographic descriptions of native peoples, anthropologists had represented indigenous cultures in ways framed by the anthropologists' own cultural understandings and for their own purposes, some of which supported colonial governments. Some members of the colonized cultures felt that their views had been ignored and their concerns silenced by the anthropologists' accounts. They typically saw the anthropologists' representations of them as contributing to their subjugation and exploitation by the colonizers. Since the anthropologists' main claim to scientific validity rested on having understood the native point of view, they were completely upended by this critique. How could they deny the counterclaims of colonized people and their demands for self-representation, particularly when they were made on the pages of the anthropologists' own scholarly journals, which the natives (who relabeled themselves aboriginals or first peoples) by this time had invaded by educating themselves in the ways of Western anthropology?

The debate surrounding anthropology's methods came to be known as the **crisis of representation**.[14] There is a famous photograph that nicely captures this concept. The image shows a group of natives lined up outside an anthropologist's tent. They watch intently as Bronislaw Malinowski (one of the founders of cultural anthropology) types his field notes. Malinowski is so absorbed by the task of recording his observations about the natives that he fails to observe them observing him! The photograph subverts the modernist view of anthropology by reversing the relationship between observer and observed, thereby demonstrating through irony that cultural natives are the real cultural experts.

Amid the hullabaloo surrounding the crisis of representation, culture became a topic of nearly universal interest along with the question of who has the right to represent whom. In organization theory this debate opened the way to studying organizational cultures as webs of significance socially constructed by their members—a view of culture most forcefully articulated by the American cultural anthropologist Clifford Geertz in his influential book *The Interpretation of Cultures*, published in 1973. Geertz's ideas about context and thick description encouraged organization theorists to apply interpretive ethnographic methods to organizations and ultimately invited critiques of managers and researchers on the grounds that they acted like colonizers within their own organizations (i.e., by imposing their views on, and ignoring the understandings of, their employees). Most importantly, Geertz's book became a template for the study of how employees make sense of their organizations and life within them, and helped to make ethnography the method of choice among symbolic-interpretive organizational researchers. More will be said about thick description and Geertz's contributions to organization theory in Chapter 6.

The logic of symbolic-interpretivism is based on the belief that organizational realities are socially produced as members interact, negotiate and make sense of their experience, and symbolic-interpretivists study how people make and communicate meaning in particular situations. Because meaning is embedded in human interactions and in symbols and artifacts that may be interpreted differently by different people, we need to address **multiple interpretations** and the role **context** plays in shaping how situations and events are interpreted by those who experience them. In doing so, we need to be particularly sensitive to language because it is through language (both verbal and written forms) that we construct, modify, make sense of and communicate reality. Symbolic-interpretive organization theorists therefore focus on common sense and experiential understandings, often reflecting on their own understandings and interpretations as they study those of their subjects. In particular, they study:

- How people (including researchers) create meanings in organizations through their interpretations of utterances, stories, rituals, symbols, actions, interactions and so on.
- How different individuals and groups (subcultures) produce multiple meanings and interpret them from within their own cultural contexts.
- How the multiple interpretations of individuals and subcultures blend to socially construct organizational reality.

Below I will introduce you to four important influences on the development of the symbolic-interpretive perspective in organization theory: social construction theory, enactment theory, institutionalization and reflexivity. The idea of the **social construction of reality** forms a common thread connecting these ideas because all symbolic-interpretive researchers assume that we construct the social realities within which we live out our lives.

Social Construction Theory

In their influential book of 1966, *The Social Construction of Reality*, German sociologists Peter Berger and Thomas Luckmann proposed that our social world is negotiated, organized, and constructed by our interpretations of what is happening around us. Berger and Luckmann argued that interpretations are based on implicit understandings found in our **intersubjectivity** (i.e., built between our subjective understandings) via shared experience that is influenced by shared history. They also emphasized that symbolism (language and conversation)—not structure—creates and maintains social reality because it forms the domain within which intersubjective meaning is constructed.

Social construction theory may seem objective in the sense that, from this viewpoint, the social world appears as an objective reality (e.g., social facts). However, social constructionists believe that reality is not so much objective as it is **objectified** (socially constructed in a way that makes it *seem* objective). This introduces both stability and instability into our understanding of organizations and emphasizes the potential for organizational change. If organizations are social constructions whose stability is created by continuous reconstruction, we can change them through our interactions with others. The human tendency to repeat past behavior, along with the collective nature of intersubjectivity, however, limits this potential for change by giving socially constructed realities the stability we often think they have and by encouraging us to regard them as objectively real.

Social construction works like this: humans and their social worlds interact with each other in ways that produce both individual identity and experienced reality. There are three components to the process of social construction: externalization, objectification and internalization. Few humans can maintain a life of quiet interiority; most need to express themselves through activity that often occurs in interaction with others. Human social activity then constructs the world and in the process humans externalize their meanings as both personal and shared realities. Intersubjectively produced realities are then taken as objective (i.e., objectivized) in the perceptions of those who externalize it. Following objectivization, it becomes possible for a group's participants to socialize new members (e.g., children, foreigners), causing them, in turn, to internalize the group's social constructions by taking on some of its roles and accepting most of its meanings. Once internalization occurs, new members will externalize and objectivize right along with other group members, thus sustaining shared social constructions of reality. In these ways, humans act and interpret action within socio-cultural contexts of their own collective making. This is the idea behind Geertz's famous phrase: 'man is an animal trapped in webs of significance he himself has spun.'[15] Change occurs when members externalize something new by borrowing it from another group or acting idiosyncratically, and the new element is taken up by others within their social construction processes.

Socially constructed reality is more complicated than this description suggests because it consists of subworlds (subcultures, e.g., social institutions and organizations), each with their own socio-cultural context that is internalized by its members. This makes sense if you think about entering a new subworld. When you first begin college or a new job, you learn (internalize) established ways of doing things and of getting along with others (their objectivized reality). These objectivized realities are maintained or changed through your actions and those of other members (externalized). But because subworlds are interconnected by encounters with one another, and by mutual members, the processes contributing to stability and change are extremely complex and therefore difficult to track, often requiring methods like Geertz's thick description (see Chapter 6) to expose them.

Sensemaking Theory and Enactment

American social psychologist Karl Weick brought social construction into organization theory with his theory of sensemaking in organizations.[16] According to **sensemaking theory** organizations exist largely in the minds of organization members in the form of cognitive maps, or images of particular aspects of experience.[17] Humans form these maps and images as they look for order in their experiences; however, this order does not preexist their search. Weick claimed that sensemaking is not based on discovering the truth about organizations, but on ordering our experiences so that our lives make sense.

Weick compared sensemaking to cartography, arguing metaphorically that humans create mental maps of particular aspects of their experience to help them find their way around the social world. Of course we do not usually create these maps individually, rather there is a certain amount of social agreement and cooperation involved that derives from the human propensity for social interaction. Furthermore, in mapping and talking about organizations and their environments, we make them real, a process Weick labeled **reification**. Be sure to notice the parallel with Berger and Luckmann's concept of objectification; as humans enact an environment, a culture, a strategy or an organization, they make sense of their actions using constructions of reality produced by objectivization and reification.

In Weick's theory of organizing, organizational realities are socially constructed by organizational members as they try to make sense of what is happening both as it occurs and in retrospect, and then act on that understanding. Weick called this process **enactment**, a concept he introduced in his influential 1979 book *The Social Psychology of Organizing*, where he stated that he purposely used the term 'en*act*ment to emphasize that managers construct, rearrange, single out, and demolish many "objective" features of their surroundings'. He claimed: 'When people act they unrandomize variables, insert vestiges of orderliness, and literally create their own constraints.'[18] Autonomous structures, inter-organizational networks and populations of organizations are 'convenient fictions' talked into existence by organizational members.

In enactment theory, the environment of an organization does not exist independently of the organization, rather it is socially constructed and reconstructed as people gather and analyze information, make decisions and take action based on their analysis. Extending enactment to legislators, Weick observed that: 'When people enact laws, they take undefined space, time, and action and draw lines, establish categories, and coin labels that create new features of the environment that did not exist before.'[19] While legislators and other organizational members generally assume the environment is objective and provide the data for analysis, it is actually their analysis that creates (objectifies) the environmental features to which they then respond. Organizational members therefore enact the environment by responding to their social constructions of it.

An example of enactment provided by Weick comes from stock trading. Consider the case in which a rumor that a trader has a good record for finding hot stocks leads others to mimic the trader's buying pattern. This in turn increases the exchange activity around certain stocks, in all likelihood raising their value (i.e., making them hot) and thereby confirming that the trader is worth watching. Further mimicry of the trader's buys attracts more buyers and purchases and temporary enhancements of stock prices. As Weick stated: 'The fact that a bandwagon effect drove up share prices, and not the quality of the stock, suggests a powerful pathway for enactment in the investment community.'[20]

Institutionalization

In 1949 Philip Selznick wrote about the Tennessee Valley Authority (TVA) in his book *TVA and the Grass Roots*. The TVA was a U.S. government funded project created as a grassroots organization to develop the Tennessee Valley by building dams to produce electricity and control flooding in this important agricultural region. In addition, TVA was supposed to protect forest lands, develop recreational areas and aid local farmers. In this book, Selznick famously decried the TVA for allowing itself to be co-opted by various interests including land grant colleges, county extension agents and political and business leaders. Co-optation transformed the organization from an efficient distributor and coordinator of tasks into a unique and distinctive American institution. Selznick used the concept of **institutionaliza-tion** to criticize the ways in which the idealization of the TVA's role and character made it a desirable object of identification to its members but also caused it to lose focus on the purposes for which it had been created.

The process of institutionalization, described by Selznick as degenerative and pathological, was subsequently recast in a positive light by symbolic-interpretivists who used it as an explanation for the importance of symbolism in the study of organizations.[21] This so-called new institutionalism was developed by a variety of organizational socio-logists in the United States including W. Richard Scott, John Meyer, Paul Hirsch, Woody Powell and Paul Di Maggio (see Chapters 3 and 4). Selznick's theory was also a resource for organizational theorists like Lou Pondy (United States), Barry Turner (United Kingdom), Pasquale Gagliardi (Italy), Per Olaf Berg (Sweden/Denmark) and Peter Frost (Canada) who helped found the organizational symbolism movement, which itself became institutional-ized as the Standing Conference on Organizational Symbolism (SCOS). The institutional-ization of SCOS was instrumental in legitimating the symbolic-interpretive perspective in organization theory and helped establish organizational culture as a mainstream concept (see Chapter 6 for more on symbolic-interpretive organizational culture theory).

Reflexivity

Reflexivity is part of both social constructionist and postmodernist ways of thinking. Reflexive approaches to organization theory have been influenced by work in cultural anthropology and sociology (constructionist approaches), and more recently by postmod-ernism and poststructuralism (deconstructionist approaches). The implication proposed by both constructionists and deconstructionists is that our explanations of the world should not be accepted at face value; instead we should explore how social and organiza-tional realities are constructed through our meaning-producing interactions including, especially, our use of language.

In a controversial book entitled *Writing Culture: The Poetics and Politics of Ethnography*, American anthropologists James Clifford and George Marcus claimed that research accounts are partial fictions because they are products of the situated perspective of their authors. By situated perspective, Clifford meant that the interpretive community of which the researcher is a member has its own interests and ways of talking about the world that influence what and how researchers describe and interpret their phenomena. For example, you may study an organization as a system, identifying its subsystems and feedback mechan-isms, but organizational members may not share your theory or use this vocabulary. This becomes problematic when you value your perspective above that of organizational mem-bers and thereby impose your theory on them.

Clifford suggested that to avoid this problem, researchers need to study how they conduct themselves and make sense of their research, for example, by applying ethnographic research methods and organizational culture theories to themselves. In doing so they become self-reflexive—able to observe themselves as they would observe others and thereby able to appreciate the degree to which, whatever they study, they are in some senses always studying themselves as well. Being reflexive in a research context means asking questions such as: what are the assumptions underlying my research design; how do they influence the way I see the world and carry out my research; what impact does this have on knowledge in general and on those studied? A reflexive researcher or manager recognizes that social realities and our explanations of those realities are accomplishments, that is, they are incomplete and continually negotiated accounts open to multiple interpretations and meanings, our own being but one among many.

Some Postmodern Influences

Postmodernists embrace so many different ideas that it is difficult to find points of agreement among them. Nonetheless, they do seem to share the desire to challenge modernist notions of reality, knowledge and identity. With its purpose to undermine modernism, postmodernism often appears to be critical in its orientation, though it can also be playful. Postmodernists believe that there is no objectively definable social reality; that everything you or I know is relative to the moment of our experience; and that since language has no fixed meaning, there can be no accurate accounts of our world nor can we make definitive statements about it or ourselves. As French poststructuralist philosopher Michel Foucault put it: 'Do not ask who I am and do not ask me to remain the same.'[22]

Postmodern organization theory can be traced to two main sources. The first is critical theory as developed by the Frankfurt School scholars of post-World War II Germany, especially Adorno, Horkheimer, Marcuse. The second is the poststructuralist movement in French philosophy that was later extended into literary theory, most notably in the United States and the United Kingdom.

Early critiques of modern thought were aimed at the Enlightenment and its devotion to rationality, hence early postmodernists labeled modern ambitions to free humans from superstition and produce universal knowledge **The Enlightenment Project**. This terminology was their way of pointing out how Enlightenment values and ideals legitimated efforts to impose Western ideology on the rest of world (its project). For example, postmodernists accused Charles Darwin of placing Western values for progress above all other human motives. Darwin's theory of evolution was all the rage following publication of his book *On The Origin of Species* in 1859. The book recounted Darwin's voyage around the world during which he recorded scientific observations about the vast array of species that populate the planet. His conclusions, much contested by those adhering to the view that God created the universe, proved to the progressive modern mind that humans belonged to the most advanced species in a chain of being that reached back to the beginning of life on this planet. Darwin's theory fed belief in the right of humans to dominate nature by making continued human evolution seem like an uncontestable scientific fact, part of nature itself.[23]

Progress was an equally attractive target of early postmodern criticism. Early postmodernists used the term **Progress Myth** to refer to the unreflexive belief that scientific and technological advance is universally desirable and that progress is therefore a sufficient motive for all sorts of things (including colonialism and management power). According to these postmodernists, belief in progress is so widespread and taken for granted in the West that it has attained the status of modern myth (non-Westerners often call it dogma). Much postmodernist organization theory is directed at exposing this myth in its many forms as an outmoded and often dangerous belief that destroys human freedom and threatens life on this planet. For instance, postmodernists have pointed to the irony that the pursuit of enlightened human freedom has produced domination, oppression and alienation as people have become subordinated to rational systems and technology—in other words modernism makes us slaves rather than masters of our worlds.

At the same time that postmodernists were attacking modernists for their devotion to rationality, poststructuralist literary theorists took on structuralism—the modernist belief that identifiable patterns underlie all systems and determine their behavior. Poststructuralism was built upon the theory of signs proposed in the late 1800s by Swiss linguist Ferdinand de Saussure.[24] Saussure's theory contradicted the prevalent modernist view of language as a mirror that accurately reflects reality. This modernist view of language, still dominant today, assumes that particular names are attached to particular things because of some essential link between word and thing that can only be recovered by studying the history of language. Saussure assumed instead that there is no essential bond between word and thing, their connection is arbitrary, and therefore language exists independent of reality. For Saussure, the meaning of a word is not determined by the thing or concept it represents, but by its position within language, that is, by its relationship to other words. For example, when you look a word up in the dictionary you find only more words. Saussure himself was a structuralist, and on the basis of his theory of meaning proposed semiology—the science of sign systems. However, poststructuralists used his insights about the arbitrariness of language to make the argument that meaning shifts constantly as words change their referents and therefore we need to absorb ambiguity and uncertainty into our theorizing. Many postmodern ideas are challenging because they draw on this radical philosophical stance.

In the rest of this section you will see that the Saussurian theory of language played a central role in developing postmodernism. As difficult as they may at first seem, it is important that you persevere in your study of postmodern organizational ideas because they have profound implications for understanding how organizations are studied and managed. As you work through the applications of postmodernism presented in the chapters that follow this one, these ideas will become more familiar, if not more comfortable.

Language and Language Games

According to Saussure, language is a system of signs (e.g., letters, words), and all signs have two parts: the **signifier** (a sound pattern) and the **signified** (the concept to which the signifier refers). In Saussure's theory, the relationship between the signifier and the signified is arbitrary because there is no natural or necessary relationship between a word and a concept. For example, consider the vast diversity of signifiers for feathered flying creatures across different languages—English: bird, Danish: fugl, French: oiseau, to name only a few.

A number of poststructuralists and postmodernists take Saussure's idea of the arbitrary nature of signs to the logical extreme of believing that language allows for the construction of any reality that words can produce, including absurdity and fantasy. Saussure claimed that as there is no thought without language, the way we put together a sequence of words in phrases, sentences, and so on, shapes meaning and thereby our ideas about reality. He also suggested that the use of language and other signs to make meaning is community specific, and that particular communities have their own sign systems. For example, the word 'merit' has different meanings depending on whether you are address-ing a business, government organization or law firm. In business, this term usually refers to a bonus given for good performance (e.g., merit-based pay), but throughout the U.S. government it refers to the formal rules governing the treatment of employees (e.g., hiring, promotion and firing decisions made on a formalized assessment process), whereas in law firms it refers to the acceptable qualities (the merits) of a case.

The idea of communities of meaning is related to the German philosopher Ludwig Wittgenstein's notion of **language games**.[25] Just as games such as soccer and chess have their own rules of play, so too does language by which words take on meaning in relation to the rules used in specific communities. For example, the implicit rules of what can be said, how and by whom differ in a classroom discussion, a conversation with a customer, or a lively debate in the pub—you probably wouldn't tell a customer or your professor, even in jest, that they have no clue what they are talking about, whereas you might say this to a friend. So the type of language you use and how you respond to statements differs depend-ing on the language game in which you are engaged. Sometimes those who subscribe to one language game find it difficult to communicate with those who play a different language game, and switching between language games during the course of conversation can create considerable confusion.

To put this idea in a familiar organizational context, consider how difficult it can be to align what you have learned from your study of one university subject with another, for example, astronomy and business. Because professors often subscribe to different language games embedded in separate communities of meaning, they may present knowledge in a way that you find difficult or impossible to integrate, even when you sense that there is a powerful connection between them. A relevant example occurs within organization theory—adopting a modern, symbolic-interpretive or postmodern perspective places organization theorists in different language games that promote different ideas about what is true, how organizations can be described and explained and therefore which journals will publish their work. In important respects, one opportunity you face in studying orga-nization theory is to learn several different language games at once. Learning how language games work and how to move comfortably between them will serve you well when working in cross-functional teams, or across other boundaries created by the communities to which you belong.

Grand Narratives and Giving Voice

The artist Francesco de Goya made a famous etching showing a philosopher asleep over his books.[26] The air over the philosopher's head swarms with frightening bats and owls swooping down on him as if from out of his nightmare. The caption reads: *The sleep of reason produces monsters*. The philosopher's nightmare depicts the fear modernists associate with letting go of reason. They see rationality as having saved humankind from the nightmares of unreason, such as being vulnerable to those who would prey on their fears and lead them around by their superstitions.

In *The Postmodern Condition* (1979), Lyotard painted the opposite picture. For him, reason was the nightmare because of what it brings to the world. He criticized the **grand narratives** of the Enlightenment Project (the Progress Myth, emancipation of labor, wealth creation through scientific advance, and the search for universal truth and justice) as intellectually and politically totalitarian. Lyotard called them narratives because they form the story that modernists tell themselves in order to justify their devotion to reason (it brings progress, creates wealth, makes us free, leads us to truth). In Lyotard's view, knowledge and society are closely linked because institutions such as education, business, and government are created on the basis of expert knowledge, which in turn legitimates particular ways of thinking and acting. For example, universities expound particular forms of knowledge (notably scientific), and businesses embrace prevailing norms of management (most often to do with maximizing profit) to which students and employees are expected to conform. Grand narratives therefore mask the ambition of modernists to create knowledge and institutions that promote their own interests over those of unsuspecting others.

Following Wittgenstein's notion of language games, Lyotard believed that scientific facts are simply agreements within communities of scientists to regard certain claims as true and that those who decide what truth is will dominate a community of discourse. However, Lyotard suggested that truth claims collapse when other, more widely-accepted claims come along, or when a different community of scientists is consulted. In this view, no truth can last because another community will sooner or later take over and establish their version of truth as the correct one. Furthermore, the present distribution of power in a community determines how that group defines its body of knowledge, therefore, when the distribution of power changes, truth shifts.[27] Seen in this light, resistance to changes in power structures by the currently powerful is easily understood as a desire to maintain the truth value of one's own claims.

Once you accept the proposition that power is involved in knowledge creation, you can easily understand Lyotard's concern about the uses of power to silence or eliminate a member from the knowledge community. He regarded the silencing of opposition to be an act of totalitarianism, pointing out that this also occurs whenever a community has no procedures for presenting what is different. He claimed that if different views and ideas are silenced, there can be no new ways for a community to think or act; therefore, **giving voice** to silence is the antidote to totalitarianism. The belief that free speech repels totalitarianism is one reason why so many critical theorists and some postmodernists support democracy and advocate for pluralism.[28] Yet many postmodernists argue that, in forming a shared ambition to overturn totalitarian tendencies, you are in danger of creating alternative grand narratives that only privilege different groups rather than overthrowing privilege. Their call for the creation of multiple texts and for tolerating different interpretations of them is what they mean by giving voice.

Discourse and Discursive Practices

French poststructuralist philosopher Michel Foucault argued that approved knowledge is a primary tool for the exercise of power over those branded as deviant within the discourse that knowledge creates and reproduces.[29] This is because deciding who can speak and what can be said determines what is regarded as normal behavior. Those who do not conform are considered abnormal—deviant troublemakers who must be excluded, disciplined or institutionalized. Foucault studied the history of psychiatric hospitals and prisons to investigate how psychiatry and social work established categories of insanity and delinquency into which people were sorted for institutional treatment. He claimed that by making insanity and delinquency into problems that society needed to address, psychiatrists and social workers established their own powerful social positions from which they could incarcerate or otherwise control certain people in order to protect society.

Foucault went on to study the histories of literary criticism, psychology, psychoanalysis, sociology, anthropology, criminology, political science and economics and concluded that modern Western societies have delegated to the human sciences the authority to determine social norms.[30] In the process of raising and answering questions about what is normal, Foucault believed the human sciences forged and maintain a link between power and knowledge. Furthermore, because the knowledge these academic disciplines produce is used to categorize, control and in some cases incarcerate the least powerful members of society, knowledge and power are really the same thing and we should not think of them as power and knowledge, but as **power/knowledge**. Power/knowledge is exercised through discursive practices that arise in the discourses that regulate normativity (the normalization of behavior). According to Foucault, **discursive practices** include phenomena such as the jargon of academic fields, or the technical terminology used in industry or in the many branches of government.

The normalizing effects of discursive practices take place within a context that Foucault and others defined as a **discourse**. The concept of discourse emerged in poststructuralist linguistics as a means of discussing the collective process that constructs and shapes language in use. As it was promoted by Foucault among others, discourse came to refer to a mode of thinking or mindset, a set of cultural practices and/or an institutional framework that provides the always partial perspective of a particular group.[31] For Foucault, discourse was constructed historically within a society according to existing relationships of power. Those who exercise power allow some things to be said, written and thought, but not others.

There are many implications of Foucault's ideas about discourse and the effects of discursive practices. One is that, when people become part of a particular discourse, their identity is a discursive formation that is part of that discourse. In other words, what you take to be your identity—the self—is merely an effect of the way your community uses language. To illustrate, it is customary to make self-references when we speak ('I did this or that'), and these self-references, coupled with what others say about us ('you are lazy') and about others ('she is brilliant'), give us the idea that we exist even though this impression is only the effect of the way we use language. By this reasoning Foucault came to his contentious claim that man only appeared in modern times and will disappear again 'like a face drawn in the sand' if ever we stop talking about ourselves.[32] Thus he presented a logical corollary to the German philosopher Martin Heidegger's proposition that: 'It is in the saying it comes to pass that the world is made to appear.' According to Foucault, by not saying man, man disappears from the discourse in which reality appears.

To give you an organizational sense of what the disappearance of man might mean, consider the recent importance attached to the customer by the management community.[33] Where once employees were encouraged to attend to the wishes of their managers, the new management discourse encourages employees to attend to their customers, thereby disappearing man(agers), or at least **decentering** them within the reality the discourse creates. A similar example comes from discussions of the democratic process in the field of public administration where citizens have recently taken center stage away from administrators who traditionally staved off responding to citizen needs by using administrative systems and processes as reasons why something could not be done. In theory at least, by moving citizens to the center of the discourse, concerns over administrative procedures are less potent and this allows the discussion to shift from why something cannot be done to how to do it. In this way the once dominant identity of the administrator can be disappeared in conversations about governance, and administrative power can be decentered.[34]

Another implication of Foucault's notion of discursive practices is that focusing on the repressed or hidden elements of a discourse will change existing discursive practices and thereby alter the construction and maintenance of current mindsets. For example, modern discursive practices within the field of history repressed the use of novels, myths and diaries. New historicists believe that because they are embedded in the times in which they were written, fiction, myth and autobiography give important historical evidence that should be incorporated into our histories.[35] Their work attempts to alter the discursive practices of historians by forging links between discourses in the fields of history and literature.

Deconstruction, Différance

According to Algerian born, French poststructuralist philosopher Jacques Derrida, language has no fixed meaning; the meaning of anything spoken or written is unstable, constantly inviting multiple and opposite interpretations.[36] You can find a simple illustration of Derrida's argument in the well-known phenomenon of taking someone's words out of context. As Saussure demonstrated, the meaning of a particular set of words depends upon the context of other words to give them their meaning. On this basis Derrida claimed that since contexts are interchangeable, no context can claim to be more appropriate than another; therefore one meaning cannot possibly be more correct than another, and you need only wait for a new context to form in order for another meaning to appear. An important implication of Derrida's theory is that, by changing the context surrounding a text (a set of symbols), you can change its meaning. This idea underlies Derrida's practice of deconstruction.

Deconstruction is a way of reading and rereading texts using different contexts in order to expose their fundamental instabilities and multiple interpretations. Through deconstructive readings of several novels, Derrida showed that meaning always eludes us due to the contradictory nature of language (différance) and because texts are always situated within historical, cultural, political and institutional contexts. Every reading brings a new context even as it refers to the contexts of previous readings and so meaning is unstable. Most particularly for postmodernism, Derrida convincingly argued that truth and knowledge are as unstable as any other element of language. The purpose of deconstructing a text is not to find an ultimate or alternative meaning, but to reveal a text's assumptions, contradictions and exclusions—to show that it does not mean what it says but rather that its multiple audiences continually produce its meaning.

Another use of deconstruction is to make the central features of constructed reality visible and to contest their dominance over our ways of thinking and acting. Saussure suggested that language operates through differences in the meanings of words. Derrida took this idea a step further by claiming that binary or dichotomous thinking is a structural underpinning of the way modernists use language. This allowed him to deconstruct the central concepts of modernist discourse (e.g., monarch/subject, master/slave, boss/subordinate) to show how modernists construct centers and peripheries within our societies and organizations by privileging one set of terms (monarch, master, boss) over others (subject, slave, subordinate). Thus it is through the use of language that we create categories, name centers, draw boundaries, express social power and reproduce or change it.

Take the example of race. Racism (white center, non-white periphery) has been shown to lead to disparities in income, housing, healthcare and education, with whites systematically enjoying more of these benefits than non-whites do. Deconstructive analysis provides an explanation of these and other effects of racism by pointing out that whiteness has been made a focal center within discourse but that its centrality depends upon maintaining the difference between white and non-white. Thus the meaning of whiteness provided by contrasts with non-whiteness determines the value of all other races by their proximity to the white center that, in turn, justifies racial inequality within any discourse community that uses this terminology.[37]

While developing deconstruction, Derrida invoked the term **différance**—a play on the French verb *differer* that means both to differ and to defer.[38] Derrida argued that a word derives its meaning from differences with its opposite (e.g., truth/falsehood, good/bad, male/female) thus even when you use only one term in a binary, you implicitly draw on its opposite. So, for example, when modernist organization theorists talk about organization they implicitly draw meaning from the difference between the concepts of organization and disorganization. This analysis reveals that at least part of the value modernists place on organizations and organizing derives from the ability to keep disorganization at bay. You can see how such thinking would justify modernist organization theory. Try deconstructing some of the core concepts you have studied in other academic fields and see if you can reveal evidence of social power lying behind them.

In regard to différance Derrida argued further that meaning is deferred or postponed because, as you try to explain the meaning of one word, you replace it with other words that must be explained by still other words and so on. As you speak or write, you move further and further away from the original word or object you are attempting to describe because the processes of differing and deferring are unending. Thus the concept of différance shows how meaning becomes ever more diffuse and distant from its starting point as it travels across time and space. It also explains why postmodernists regard meaning as fluid.

Simulacra and Hyperreality

In the Wachowski brothers' film *The Matrix*, we see a world taken over by artificial intelligence, in which machines breed and keep humans in pods as a power source for the computer that controls human thought and thereby produces images of human lives and realities that do not exist. The humans think they are living normal lives, but instead a computer program, the matrix, simulates the world of the late twentieth century, a world that is now a nuclear wasteland. The film's central character, symbolically named Neo, takes a pill that allows him to awaken from the computer-simulated reality to find that what he thought was real is not. In order to survive and rescue others from the treachery of the machines, he has to move between the post-nuclear reality, where he and a small band of other awakened humans battle the machines, and the pre-nuclear simulation. In the simulation, Neo fights computer-enhanced images of superhuman bureaucrats with his own superhuman powers. Neo's powers come from his knowledge that the world is only a simulated reality; denying its power to persuade him of its existence gives him the freedom and strength to resist and overthrow the machines.

As in *The Matrix*, the confusion of real and simulation is a central theme in the work of possibly the most controversial of the postmodern scholars, French social philosopher Jean Baudrillard. In *Simulacra and Simulation*, Baudrillard argued that the image has passed through a progression of successive phases that make it impossible to talk about what is real. The stages the image passed through are, according to Baudrillard:

- reflecting a profound reality.
- masking and denaturing a profound reality.
- masking the absence of a profound reality.
- no relation to any reality whatsoever: the image is its own pure simulacrum.[39]

According to Baudrillard, in premodern times a simulation was assumed to represent reality, just as a map was assumed to represent the physical geography it described. However, the distinction between reality and the image began breaking down in modern times when mass production led to the proliferation of copies of originals (e.g., reproductions of artwork, imitations of designer fashions). In modern times people began to discover that it was possible for images to mask reality or even to hide the absence of reality; for example, British artist David Hockney made images on a photocopy machine that looked like copies of original artworks but for which there were no originals (apart from the copies!). When governments disseminate propaganda or disinformation they participate in a similar masking of the absence of reality. The postmodern age is marked by a further development in which simulations create reality from images. So-called reality TV produces fabrications that have no relation to any reality but the show's own pretensions. Disneyland provides another example in which real actors portray cartoon characters and guests take real riverboat rides down a fake Mississippi. In **simulacra** there is no deep meaning or underlying structure hidden beneath the surface on which images play. Simulacra show that ideals like meaning and structure can be overthrown by postmodern thinking of the sort suggested by the aphorism: what you see is what (all!) you get.

Baudrillard claimed that in postmodernism the opposite poles of reality/image, fact/fantasy, subjective/objective, public/private, active/passive implode to create **hyperreality** where 'illusion is no longer possible, because the real is no longer possible'.[40] In the hyperreal, we are immersed in simulations, nostalgically trying to produce what we thought was real, but which has always been nothing but images. Although you may like reality TV whereas your friend hates it, both of you are responding to hyperreality. According to Baudrillard, simulacra like reality TV programs form the contexts of our lived experiences. For example, Baudrillard described Disneyland as the ideal simulacrum because it creates, the architecture, community and traditional family values of a Main Street America that never existed.[41] He suggested that although we may think Disneyland is imaginary (just a performance) and the rest of the world is real, it is the rest of the world that is an ongoing performance through which we strive to live up to the images fed to us by Disneyland along with those provided by the media, government, businesses and other modern institutions. Just as the film *The Matrix* portrayed a simulation within which humans live, we create our lives in terms of the images we use to define ourselves to ourselves.

While Baudrillard's ideas might at first seem unrelated to organization theory, you get a sense of hyperreality when you consider how images floating around us everyday are produced by the organizations they serve. For example, most consumer-oriented businesses count on our willingness to buy products because the images they project through advertising seduce us. For a time Enron managed to hide billions of dollars in debt and operating losses by creating fake partnerships (with names inspired by the film *Star Wars*), misleadingly complex accounting schemes, and nonexistent departments. For example, when Wall Street analysts visited Enron in 1998 to assess its credit rating, 75 people relocated to an empty floor and a fake trading room where they pretended to buy and sell energy contracts. The simulacrum was staged with ringing phones and family photos on desks—a performance used unethically to support Enron's falsely inflated stock price.[42] Although such sting operations have occurred throughout history, the difference now is that they are becoming the rule rather than the exception and this has the potential to radically alter our norms concerning ethical behavior.

SUMMARY

This chapter provided background on the three perspectives of organization theory that frame this book and offers some help identifying the focus, types of theories and vocabulary associated with each. Hopefully you are beginning to understand why theorists from each perspective view the others' ideas as suspect—because they are judging them with their own, very different assumptions and from within their own distinctive discourses. Whereas the links between the modernist perspective and organization theory may be clear to you already, those between symbolic-interpretive and postmodern perspectives may be less so. One reason for this is that these two perspectives are openly concerned with how we think about reality and generate knowledge (i.e., ontology and epistemology), whereas modernists tend to take these issues for granted. By emphasizing the constructed, contradictory and indeterminate nature of reality and knowledge, symbolic-interpretivists and postmodernists ask us to think more reflexively about our work as managers and researchers than do modernists who are generally unreflexive about their values for order, rationality, structure, progress and efficiency and the practices these values encourage including domination and control. Modernist work is important because it provides a number of analytical frameworks, predictive models and principles for organizing that managers use to diagnose problems and design organizations. However, a multiple perspectives approach cautions you not to take modernist frameworks and tools for granted—they have important limitations and there are useful alternatives to explore.

Symbolic-interpretivists study how we construct organizational realities as we make meaning and coordinate our activities. They emphasize the role humans play in creating organizational life. For example, if you recognize that realities are constructed, and think about how you and others construct those realities, then you can explore possibilities for change inherent in the reinterpretation of the assumptions and values that underlie those realities. For their part, postmodernists argue that organizations are not characterized by order and unity, as modernists claim, but by uncertainty, image, complexity and contradiction. In taking a postmodern view you should give up relying on structures and other stable patterns, and focus instead on flux and différance, being particularly aware of language and its many uses.

Some contrasts between the focal concerns and modes of thinking preferred by each perspective are offered in Table 2.2. Some of the distinctions contained in this table are subtle (e.g., cohesion versus coherence; diversity versus plurality). As you make your way through the book, see if you can bring these differences between perspectives into high relief. Try to locate your own examples of concepts discussed in the chapters and see if you can relate them to any or all of the distinctions between perspectives described in Table 2.2. As you do this you may find you want to add your own distinctions or replace those in the table. In doing so remember différance—like Derrida, you may discover that the process of seeking meaning in these comparisons is unending!

Table 2.2 Some comparisons among the three perspectives

	Modern	Symbolic-interpretive	Postmodern
Reality is a	Pre-existing unity	Socially constructed diversity	Constantly shifting and fluid plurality
Knowledge is believed to be	Universal	Particular	Provisional
Knowledge is developed through	Facts and information	Meaning and interpretation	Exposure and experience
Knowledge is recognized via	Convergence	Coherence	Incoherence, fragmentation, deconstruction
Model for human relationships	Hierarchy	Community	Self-determination
Overarching goal	Prediction and control	Understanding	Freedom

KEY TERMS

inductive and deductive reasoning
division of labor
theory of capital
managerial control
alienation
critical organization theory
formal and informal organization
authority
   traditional
   charismatic
   rational-legal
theory of bureaucracy
formal vs. substantive rationality
scientific management
workplace democracy
administrative principles
POSDCoRB
cooperative social systems
general systems theory
   system
   subsystem
differentiation
specialization
integration
hierarchy of systems
level of analysis
autonomous work groups

contingency theory
crisis of representation
multiple interpretations
context
social construction of reality
intersubjectivity
objectification
sensemaking theory
reification
enactment
institutionalization
reflexivity
The Enlightenment Project
Progress Myth
signifier and signified
language games
grand narratives
giving voice
power/knowledge
discursive practices
discourse
decentering
deconstruction
différance
simulacra
hyperreality

ENDNOTES

1. For discussions of organization theory as the product of this tension, see Perrow (1973) and Barley and Kunda (1992).

2. C. S. George, Jr. (1968) compiled a short history of management in ancient times in which he observed that the division of labor, along with other managerial practices, has been used from the time of the Egyptians and was probably a feature of prehistorical life as well.

3. From A. Smith, *An inquiry into the nature and causes of the wealth of nations*, Vol. 1, ed. R. H. Campbell and A. S. Skinner, W. B. Todd (textual ed.) (Oxford: Clarendon Press, 1976), 14–16.

4. This tension has been discussed by Wren (1987); Bernard (1988); Boje and Winsor (1993); Steingard (1993); O'Connor (forthcoming).

5. Weber (1946: 228).

6. It is uncertain where the term originated, but Aglietta used Fordism in his 1979 book *A theory of capitalist regulation* (London: Verso).

7. Cited in Graham (1995: 56).

8. Cited in Calinescu (1987: 15).

9. Boulding (1956).

10. Trist and Bamforth (1951).

11. For example see Emery (1969).

12. See Donaldson (1985) for a review and defense of contingency theory.

13. See Clifford and Marcus (1986).

14. Stocking (1983).

15. Geertz (1973: 5).

16. Weick (1995).

17. Weick and Bougon (1986).

18. Weick (1979 [1969]: 243).

19. Weick (1995: 30–31).

20. Weick (2003); see also Mitch Abolafia and Martin Kilduff (1988), who described attempts to corner the silver market in the 1980s using enactment theory.

21. Gagliardi (forthcoming).

22. From the introduction to Foucault's Archeology of Knowledge (1969) cited in *The Penguin Dictionary of Critical Theory*, 134.

23. See Rorty (1999: 262–71) for further discussion of Darwin's role in the development of the modernist system of belief.

24. Saussure (1959).

25. Wittgenstein (1965).

26. From the series by Francesco de Goya, *Los Caprichos*, etching number 48.

27. Lyotard (1983).

28. For example, see Calas and Smircich (1991).

29. Foucault (1977).

30. Foucault (1973).

31. Moran (2002: 14).

32. Foucault (1970: xxiii), cited in Moran (2002: 135–36).

33. See articles about relationship marketing in business periodicals such as the *Harvard Business Review*.

34. King, Feltey, and Susel (1998).

35. Moran (2002: 136–37).

36. Derrida (1976).

37. See Dwyer and Jones (2002), Linstead (1993) and Kilduff (1993) on deconstructing organizations.

38. Derrida (1978).

39. Baudrillard (1994: 6).

40. Baudrillard (1994: 19).

41. Baudrillard (1994: 7).

42. *Wall Street Journal*, February 20, 2002.

REFERENCES

Abolafia, Mitchell Y., and Kilduff, Martin (1988). Enacting market crisis: The social construction of a speculative bubble. *Administrative Science Quarterly*, 33: 177–93.

Barley, Stephen, and Kunda, Gideon (1992). Design and devotion: Surges of rational and normative ideologies of control in managerial discourse. *Administrative Science Quarterly*, 37: 363–99.

Barnard, Chester (1938). *The functions of the executive*. Cambridge, Mass.: Harvard University Press.

Baudrillard, Jean (1994). *Simulacra and simulations* (trans. S. F. Glaser). Ann Arbor: University of Michigan Press.

Berger, Peter L., and Luckmann, Thomas (1966). *The social construction of reality: A treatise in the sociology of knowledge*. Garden City, NY: Doubleday.

Bernard, Doray (1988). *From Taylorism to Fordism: A rational madness*. London: Free Association Books.

Bertalanffy, Ludwig von (1968). *General systems theory: Foundations, development, applications* (revised edn.). New York: George Braziller.

Boje, David M., and Winsor, R. D. (1993). The resurrection of Taylorism: Total quality management's hidden agenda. *Journal of Organizational Change Management*, 6/4: 58–71.

Boulding, Kenneth E. (1956). General systems theory—The skeleton of science. *Management Science*, 2: 197–208.

Calas, Marta, and Smircich, Linda (1991). Voicing seduction to silence leadership. *Organization Studies*, 12: 567–602.

Calinescu, Matei (1987). *The five faces of modernity*. Durham, NC: Duke University Press. First published in 1977 by Indiana University Press.

Clifford, James, and Marcus, George E. (1986) (eds.). *Writing culture: The poetics and politics of ethnography*. Berkeley: University of California Press.

Darwin, Charles R. (1936). *On the origin of species*. New York: Modern Library.

Derrida, Jacques (1976). *Of grammatology*. Baltimore: Johns Hopkins University Press.

—— (1978). *Writing and difference* (trans. Alan Bass). London: Routledge & Kegan Paul.

Donaldson, Lex (1985). *In defence of organisation theory*. Cambridge: Cambridge University Press.

Durkheim, Émile (1966). *Suicide: A study in sociology* (trans. John Spaulding and George Simpson). New York: Free Press (first published in 1897).

—— (1982). *The rules of sociological method* (trans. W. D. Halls). New York: Free Press (first published in 1895).

—— (1984). *The division of labour in society* (trans. W. D. Halls). New York: Free Press (first published in 1893).

Dwyer, O., and Jones III, J. P. (2002). White socio-spatial epistemology. *Social and Cultural Geography*, 1: 209–22.

Emery, Fred E. (1969). *Systems thinking*. Harmondsworth, England: Penguin.

Fayol, Henri (1949). *General and industrial management*. London: Pitman (first published in 1919).

Follett, Mary Parker (1923). *The new state: Group organization and the solution of popular government*. New York: Longmans, Green and Co.

—— (1924). *Creative experience*. New York: Longmans, Green and Co.

Foucault, Michel (1973). *The order of things: An archaeology of the human sciences* (trans. Alan Sheridan-Smith). New York: Vintage Books.

—— (1977). *Power/knowledge* (ed. Colin Gordon). New York: Pantheon.

Gagliardi, Pasquale (forthcoming). The revenge of gratuitousness on utilitarianism. *Journal of Management Inquiry*.

Geertz, Clifford (1973). *The interpretation of cultures*. New York: Basic Books.

George, Claude S., Jr. (1968). *The history of management thought*. Englewood Cliffs, NJ: Prentice-Hall.

Graham, P. (1995) (ed.). *Mary Parker Follett: Prophet of management*. Boston: Harvard Business School Press.

Gulick, Luther, and Urwick, Lyndall (1937) (eds.). *Papers on the science of administration*. New York: Institute of Public Administration, Columbia University.

Kilduff, Martin (1993). Deconstructing organizations. *Academy of Management Review*, 18: 13–31.

King, C. S., Feltey, K. M., and O'Neill, Susel B. (1998). The question of participation: Toward authentic public participation in public administration. *Public Administration Review*, 58/4: 317–26.

Linstead, Steve (1993). Deconstruction in the study of organizations. In John Hassard and Martin Parker (eds.), *Postmodernism and organizations*. London: Sage, 49–70.

Lyotard, Jean-François (1979). *The postmodern condition: A report on knowledge* (trans. G. Bennington and B. Massumi). Minneapolis: University of Minnesota Press.

—— (1983). *The differend: Phrases in dispute* (trans. G. Van den Abeele). Minneapolis: Minnesota University Press.

Marx, Karl (1973). *Grundrisse: Foundations of the critique of political economy*. Harmondsworth, UK: Penguin (first published in 1839–41).

—— (1974). *Capital*, Vol. 1. London: Lawrence and Wishart (first published in 1867).

—— (1975). *Early writings* (trans. R. Livingstone and G. Benton). Harmondsworth, UK: Penguin (first published as *Economic and philosophical manuscripts*, 1844).

Merton, Robert (1965/1993). *On the shoulders of giants*. Chicago: Chicago University Press.

Moran, Joe (2002). *Interdisciplinarity*. London: Blackwell.

O'Connor, Ellen S. (forthcoming). Lines of authority: Readings of foundational texts on the profession of management. *Journal of Management History*.

Perrow, Charles (1973). The short and glorious history of organizational theory. *Organizational Dynamics*, Summer: 2–15.

Rorty, Richard (1989). *Contingency, irony, and solidarity*. Cambridge: Cambridge University Press.

—— (1999). *Philosophy and social hope*. London: Penguin Books.

Saussure, Ferdinand de (1959). *Course in general linguistics* (trans. Wade Baskin). New York: McGraw-Hill.

Selznick, Philip (1949). *TVA and the grass roots*. Berkeley: University of California Press.

Smith, Adam (1776/1937). *An inquiry into the nature and causes of the wealth of nations*. New York: Modern Library.

Steingard, D. S. (1993). A postmodern deconstruction of total quality management (TQM). *Journal of Organizational Change Management*, 6/4: 72–87.

Stocking, G. W., Jr. (1983) (ed.). *Observer observed: Essays on ethnographic fieldwork, a history of anthropology*, Vol. 1. Madison: University of Wisconsin Press.

Taylor, Frederick W. (1911). *The principles of scientific management*. New York: Harper.

Trist, Eric L., and Bamforth, K. W. (1951). Some social and psychological consequences of the long wall method of coal getting. *Human Relations*, 4: 3–38.

Weber, Max (1906–24/1946 trans.). From *Max Weber: Essays in Sociology*, Gerth, Hans H. and Mills, C. Wright (eds) New York: Oxford University Press.

Weber, Max (1947). *The theory of social and economic organization* (ed. A. H. Henderson and Talcott Parsons). Glencoe, Ill.: Free Press (first published in 1924).

Weick, Karl E. (1979 [1969]). *The social psychology of organizing*. Reading, Mass.: Addison-Wesley.

—— (1995). *Sensemaking in organizations*. Thousand Oaks, Calif.: Sage.

—— (2003). Enacting an environment: The infrastructure of organizing. In R. I. Westwook and S. Clegg (eds.), *Debating organization: Point-counterpoint in organization studies*. London: Blackwell, 184–94.

—— and Bougon, Michel (1986). Organizations as cognitive maps: Charting ways to success and failure. In Sims, Jr. H.P. and Gioia, D.A. (eds.) *The thinking organization*, 102–35. San Francisco: Jossey-Bass.

Wittgenstein, Ludwig (1965). *Philosophical investigations*. New York: Macmillan.

Wren, D. (1987). *The evolution of management thought* (3rd edn.). New York: Wiley.

FURTHER READING

Clegg, Stewart (1990). *Modern organizations: Organization studies in the postmodern world*. London: Sage.

Harvey, David (1990). *The condition of postmodernity*. Cambridge, Mass.: Blackwell.

Hassard, John, and Parker, Martin (1993) (eds.). *Postmodernism and organizations*. London: Sage, 49–70.

Jencks, Charles (1992) (ed.). *The post-modern reader*. London: St. Martin's Press.

—— (1996). *What is post-modernism?* (4th edn.). New York: Wiley.

Knudsen, C., and Tsoukas, H. (2003) (eds.). *The Oxford Handbook of Organization Theory: Meta-theoretical Perspectives*. Oxford: Oxford University Press.

Kumar, Krishan (1995). *From post-industrial to post-modern society: New theories of the contemporary world*. Oxford: Blackwell.

Lash, Scott, and Urry, John (1987). *The end of organized capitalism*. Cambridge: Polity Press.

Piore, Michael, and Sabel, Charles (1984). *The second industrial divide*. New York: Basic Books.

Reed, Michael I., and Hughes, M. D. (1992) (eds.). *Rethinking organization: New directions in organizational research and analysis*. London: Sage.

Rosenau, Pauline Marie (1992). *Post-modernism and the social sciences: Insights, inroads, and intrusions*. Princeton: Princeton University Press.

Rousseau, Denise (1985). Issues of level in organizational research: Multi-level and cross-level perspectives. In L. Cummings and B. M. Staw (eds.), *Research in organizational behavior*, Vol. VII: 1–37. Greenwich, Conn.: JAI Press.

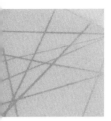

Core Concepts and Theories

You now begin your immersion into the depths of organization theory and theorizing. In the chapters that make up Part II, you will build your understanding of six core concepts that organization theorists rely upon to construct their theories—environment, social structure, technology, culture, physical structure and power/control. As you move through the chapters of Part II, I will help you first to build these concepts and then use them to create theories, gradually increasing the complexity of the theorizing as we go. In keeping with our theme of multiple perspectives, all of the core concepts will be discussed from modernist, symbolic-interpretive and postmodern perspectives.

Organization and Environment

In modernist organization theories, the organizational environment is conceptualized as an entity that lies outside the boundary of the organization, providing the organization with raw materials and other resources (inputs) and absorbing its products and services (outputs, see Figure 3.1). It influences organizational outcomes by imposing constraints and demanding adaptation as the price of survival. The organization, for its part, faces uncertainty about what the environment demands and experiences dependence on the multiple resources that its environment provides. Modernist organization theorists use combinations of dependence and uncertainty to explain the forms organizations take in response to their environments.

In some ways, the trickiest part of analyzing an organization's environment is the first step—defining the organization. This is because the definition implies that you know where the **organizational boundary** lies and that you have defined it in the best possible way considering your reasons for doing the analysis. Boundary definition is easier said than done. Take the university as an example and consider the case of students. Are you a

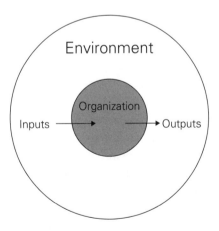

Figure 3.1 The organization in its environment

A simple distinction showing the organization as an entity (subsystem) embedded within a larger system that supplies its resource inputs and absorbs its outputs (goods and services). Notice the presumption of a boundary separating the organization from its environment.

member of the university? Are you a customer? A raw material? A product? Each answer is accurate in some ways and, what is more, each suggests a different definition of what lies inside and what lies outside the organization. Similar analytical choices await you when considering the membership status of faculty (especially visiting and non-tenured faculty), continuing education students, guest lecturers, alumni and benefactors. Drawing a boundary around an organization is a difficult exercise and the implications of various definitions for different decision-making situations must be taken into account when you make an analysis.

It is not that one proposal for locating an organizational boundary is the correct one; rather boundary definition is determined by your reasons for conducting an analysis. Consider the case of a university. If you are analyzing the environment because the university is considering a tuition increase, then it will be useful to consider students to be customers and, thus, members of the environment rather than of the organization. If you want to analyze the environment because the university wants to apply for outside research funds, then it may be helpful to think of students as members of the organization who will aid in, and learn from, the performance of proposed research activities. If, however, you are interested in discovering how the environment is responding to the university's new general education programs, then viewing students as products of the organization is likely to provide a useful analysis; from this point of view firms recruiting on campus are customers consuming graduating students. If you want to focus on how students can influence the decisions of university administrators, think of students, not just as low status members of the organization, but also as special interest groups, or as regulatory agents (e.g., allow students to sit as voting members on faculty committees) or unions (e.g., give students negotiating rights).

Symbolic-interpretivists, in contrast to modernists, view environments as social constructions. In their perspective, environments are constructed from intersubjectively shared beliefs about their existence and by expectations that are set in motion by these beliefs. Weick's enactment theory (see Chapter 2) is an example of this way of conceptualizing organizational environments. From the symbolic-interpretive perspective, while environments have material consequences, organizational members enact their environment by constructing the features they think are significant and need to be addressed. Different organizations may therefore construct their environment in different ways depending on the interpretations of their managers.

Postmodern organization theory offers many approaches to the subject of organizations and environments. One is to problematize the distinction between them, as suggested by the notions of boundaryless and virtual organizations. Another is to critique modernist theories of organization–environment relations for being anti-environmental in the sense that they justify exploitation of limited natural resources (including human beings) for competitive advantage while silencing demands for environmentally and socially responsible action.

Until recently, most organization theorizing about environments was conducted from a modernist perspective. However, the symbolic-interpretive perspective has now firmly established itself within this debate by building on Selznick's institutional theory. What is more, postmodern critiques of modernist theories of the environment have helped to support stakeholder theory as a means of introducing ethical concerns and democratic ideals into mainstream organization theory. Thus all three perspectives have made their mark on the theory of organizational environments.

This chapter begins with several modernist definitions of environment. Next you will read about four theories of organization–environment relations—contingency theory, resource dependence theory, population ecology, and institutional theory—the last of which introduces symbolic-interpretive thinking into theorizing about organizational environments. The postmodern perspective on organization–environment relations will be explored via applications of post-industrial history, stakeholder theory and deconstruction. The chapter concludes with some practical advice about analyzing organizational environments.

Defining the Organizational Environment

General systems theory introduced the notion of levels of analysis (see Chapter 2) and this idea spread to modernist theories of organization, not just in terms of different hierarchical levels within the organization, but of the higher level system of which the organization is a part: its supersystem, the environment. You can think about levels of analysis as a set of nested Russian dolls. Take the largest doll apart (the environment) and you find a smaller one (the organization) inside, take that one apart and you find still smaller ones (divisions or departments) within, and so on. In systems theory, higher order systems contain lower order systems.

One implication modernists draw from the distinction between organizations and their environments is the existence of organizational boundaries from which arises the question of how to manage them. American sociologist W. Richard Scott, a staunch modernist, suggested buffering and boundary spanning as two boundary management practices that organizations can use.[1] **Buffering** involves protecting the internal operations of the organization from interruption by environmental shocks such as material, labor, or capital shortages. This is generally accomplished by assigning some members of the organization responsibility for seeing that the organization's production of goods and services continues uninterrupted. Those who protect the productive capacity of the firm act out the buffering role. For instance, in traditional manufacturing organizations, purchasing agents and sales people buffer production workers from interruptions due to the lack of raw materials from suppliers or orders from customers. Buffering frees those working in production centers from concerns that might distract them from efficiently performing their work. **Boundary spanning** is the label given to environmental monitoring activities including passing needed information to decision makers such as the adoption of new production techniques by suppliers or customers. It also describes the activity of representing the organization or its interests to the environment, not only via public relations or advertising, but also through sales, recruiting efforts and myriad other activities through which stakeholders learn about the organization.

The difference between boundary spanning and buffering roles is primarily what is transferred between the organization and its environment. In the case of buffering, transfers of material, services and money between the organization and the environment are of primary concern. Boundary spanners work mainly with the transfer of information across the organization's boundary. It is not uncommon to find that some organizational members engage in activities that can be described as both buffering and boundary spanning. Sales people, for instance, are responsible for transferring the organization's output to its customers (the buffering role), but they also bring important information about changing customer demands into the organization and represent the organization's capabilities and reputation to the customer (their contribution to boundary spanning).

Just as an organization can be differentiated from its environment by using the idea of levels of analysis, so too can the environment be conceptually divided into levels. For example, modernist organization theorists often use three different levels of environment in their analyses: the interorganizational network, the general environment, and the international environment. Each of these levels can, in turn, be broken into several constitutive elements, as described below. Just remember: no level in any system is completely independent of the others, so rarely will you only consider one level in your theorizing about organizations and their environments. On the other hand, be aware that it is easy to get lost and confused by switching between levels of analysis when you are theorizing. Always state the level you are focused on to help avoid losing your way.

Stakeholders and the Interorganizational Network

Every organization interacts with other members of its environment. Through these interactions organizations do things such as acquire raw materials, hire employees, secure capital, obtain knowledge, and build, lease or buy facilities and equipment. Since organizations produce one or more products or services for the environment to consume, they also interact with their customers. Other environmental actors participate in, regulate or oversee these exchanges, including investors, competitors, suppliers, distributors, partners, advertising agencies, trade associations, government regulators and the media. Taken as a whole, all of these interacting individuals, groups and organizations are described as the **stakeholders** of the organization. In its narrow sense, stakeholder refers to any actor (individual, group, organization) that is vital to the survival or success of the organization. A wider definition includes any actor that affects or is affected by the organization.[2] A typical stakeholder analysis would identify the actors shown in Figure 3.2.[3]

An **interorganizational network** analysis involves more than stakeholder analysis. It focuses attention on the complex web of relationships in which a group of organizations is embedded (see Figure 3.3). A network analysis would typically show the relative positions of all organizations involved in the network. In Figure 3.3, for example, centrality is shown by the number of linkages an organization has with other elements of its network. The links in the network represent channels through which resources, information, opportunities and influence flow. Network analysis promotes sensitivity to the variety and complexity of interactions that sustain organized activity within the environment.

Figure 3.2 The organization operates within a network of stakeholders and competitors

Although one's own organization is not always central within its network, defining the actors relevant to your organization using this model will help you to assess and monitor key stakeholders.

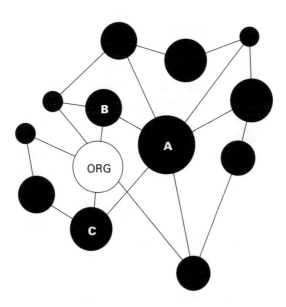

Figure 3.3 The interorganizational network

This model depicts an interorganizational network in which Organization A, a competitor of your organization (ORG), is most central, B is a supplier of both ORG and A, and C is a customer to both firms.

An application of the interorganizational network concept with which you may be familiar is value chain management.[4] It has become increasingly common for businesses to consider the flow of raw material and value-added activities as a chain of connections that originate with suppliers of the most basic raw materials (e.g., petroleum) and then flow through intermediary organizations (e.g., oil refineries, petroleum distributors and gasoline stations) to end users (e.g., drivers of gasoline-powered vehicles). A value chain links organizations on the basis of the economic value they add to a product or service as it moves through them on its way to the end user. Visually, a value chain cuts a slice through an interorganizational network like the one shown in Figure 3.3 and would include all suppliers, distributors and end users. You should be aware that it is this way of thinking about interorganizational networks that sparked the customer relationship movement in business and inspired the client relationship model used by some nonbusiness organizations and service firms.

The General Environment

In addition to specific actors in the interorganizational network, there are a host of general forces at work in an environment. These forces will have an effect throughout the network, yet, analysis of the network alone is unlikely to pick them up. Thus you will need to analyze conditions and trends in the **general environment** in addition to the interorganizational network in order to fully appreciate the links between an organization and its environment. To conduct an analysis of these conditions and trends, organization theorists typically divide the general environment into different sectors including some or all of the following: social, cultural, legal, political, economic, technological and physical (see Figure 3.4).

Social Sector

The social sector of the environment is associated with class structure, demographics, mobility patterns, life styles, social movements and traditional social institutions including educational systems, religious practices, trades and professions. In the United States and Western Europe, aging populations, increasing workforce diversity and professionalization of many types of work, including management, are all examples of recent trends in the social sector surrounding organizations that do business in those parts of the world. Recent migrations of people from Eastern Europe and North Africa into the wealthier nations of Western Europe are examples of social mobility patterns of importance in the general environment of organizations that operate in these areas. Recycling has become a social movement in many countries around the world.

Cultural Sector

Concern with the cultural sector revolves around issues such as history, traditions, normative expectations for behavior, beliefs and values. Examples of conditions in the cultural sector for US firms include emphasis on leadership, technical rationality and material wealth, while cultural sector trends show a decreasing value for hierarchical authority (especially among the growing ranks of professionals) and increasing value for ethical

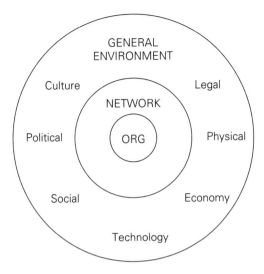

Figure 3.4 Sectors of the general environment

You may find it useful to make finer grained distinctions than these to track all the general conditions and trends in the environment of your organization, or you may discover that you can collapse one or more of these categories. The point is to be sure that you are tracking the conditions and trends that can influence the success or survival of your organization.

business practices, human rights and protection of the physical environment. Be sure to notice how social and cultural trends intersect. For instance, the increasing diversity of the US workforce is showing up as a change in values for the contributions that differences of gender, race and cultural background bring to many organizations. These value shifts have, in turn, influenced the legal and political sectors of the general environment of organizations operating in the United States.

Legal Sector

The legal sector is defined by the constitutions and laws of the nations in which the organization conducts its business, as well as legal practices in each of these domains. This sector involves such areas of law and legal practice as corporate, antitrust (anti-monopoly), tax and foreign investment law. Examples of trends in the legal sector are often difficult to separate from trends in the political and economic sectors. For instance, trends involving both regulation and deregulation of certain industries are of major concern to affected organizations operating in the European Community, the Asia/Pacific region and Latin America. The legal sector has close links to social and cultural trends because cultural values and social institutions create pressures to legalize various behaviors, or to declare them illegal. For example, a heightened concern over unethical behavior in US businesses led to the passage of the Sarbanes-Oxley Act in 2002. This piece of legislation created mechanisms to expose and punish acts of corporate corruption, promote greater accountability by financial auditors and protect small investors and pension holders. You can easily see how Sarbanes-Oxley arose from activities within both the political and economic sectors.

Political Sector

The political sector is usually described in terms of the distribution and concentration of power and the nature of political systems (e.g., democratic vs. autocratic) in those areas of the world in which the organization operates. The renunciation of communist rule across Eastern Europe in 1989 is an example of significant change in the political (and economic) sector of organizations doing or seeking to do business in this region. The political sector has close ties with the legal sector and both are influenced by trends in other sectors. For example, in the United States women and minorities have become more politically active since their entry into the workforce (social sector), and their increased political participation (political sector) has resulted in affirmative action, anti-discrimination and anti-harassment legislation (legal sector).

Sometimes the political and economic sectors are so intertwined that it does not make sense to try to analyze their influences separately. For example, many governments (political sector), under pressure from businesses (economic sector), have relaxed trade barriers via trade agreements with other countries that reduce national autonomy, as has happened in relation to free trade zones. Economically driven political alliances such as the EU, ASEAN, MEROCUR and NAFTA further erode national autonomy in favor of supporting the free flow of trade in various regions of the world. Similarly, privatization has made businesses out of organizations that were formerly run by governments including prisons, hospitals, airlines, schools and universities. These and other transfers of power from political leaders to business leaders bring the political and economic sectors ever closer together in many parts of the world.

Economic Sector

The economic sector is comprised of labor markets, financial markets and markets for goods and services. The extent to which private versus public ownership is typical in the place where an organization conducts its affairs, whether or not centralized economic planning is attempted, fiscal policies, consumption patterns, patterns of capital investment and the banking system all contribute to the economic sector. Examples of economic conditions commonly found in economic sector analyses include: the balance of payments, hard currency issues, economic alliances with other countries, trade agreements, price controls, access to raw materials markets, interest and inflation rates, price indexes, unemployment rates, excess production capacity and investment risk. Economic sector trends have implications for the other sectors of the general environment. For instance, the shift from a communist planned economy to democratic capitalism in Poland (political-economic sector change) had implications for nearly every other sector in the general environment of Polish organizations.

Technology Sector

The technological sector provides knowledge and information in the form of scientific developments and their applications that the organization can acquire and use to produce output (goods and services). In a sense, the environment possesses the knowledge to produce its desired outputs and contributes this knowledge to various organizations that then carry out production processes for the benefit of others in the environment. Organizations receive knowledge from the environment in such forms as pre-trained and culturally socialized employees, equipment and software purchases, and the services provided by consultants and other professionals. A significant recent trend in the technological sector of many organizations has been the availability of computer-based technologies such as personal computers, robots, video-recording equipment and computer-aided design and manufacturing (CAD-CAM). Applications of these technologies to multimedia and wireless communication are creating enormous changes in organizations around the world that are rapidly adapting to doing ever larger portions of their business over the Internet. Promises of further technological advances are coming from the fields of genetics, quantum physics and fiber optics.

There are endless examples of ways in which the technological sector intertwines with other sectors of the general environment. Software pirating, reverse engineering and theft of copyrighted material become easier with digitization, a trend that began in the technological sector and has spread to the legal and economic sectors in the form of threats to intellectual property rights. Satellite communication replaces some travel and connects previously remote places in Africa, Latin America, Asia and elsewhere to the global economy. Computer technology inspires shifts in organizational forms and practices such as network organization and outsourcing. Businesses now operate 24/7, partly as a result of advances in global communication technology that have affected cultural expectations for access and responsiveness. Changes in the technological sector affect the social and economic sectors as technology creates further socio-economic divisions between those who have electricity and can read, and those who do not read or have no electricity.

Physical Sector

The physical sector includes natural resources and the effects of nature. Some organizations have direct and immediate concerns with physical sector elements ranging from coal and oil reserves (e.g., firms operating in the oil industry), accessible harbors (e.g., firms in import/export trades or those operating shipping companies), viable transportation routes (e.g., trucking companies), and pollution levels (e.g., manufacturing concerns), to severe weather conditions (e.g., firms in the air transportation, shipping, construction and tourism industries). Examples of general conditions and trends worth watching in the physical sector include changing weather patterns (e.g., global warming), the disappearance of the rain forests, and disasters such as drought, earthquake, flood, famine and volcanic activity.

Except for the case of dwindling natural resources, changes in the physical sector are extremely difficult to predict. Nonetheless, firms that depend on this sector for resources or favorable working conditions will obviously be economically affected by events and changes that occur here. Disasters such as the earthquakes in San Francisco and Los Angeles in the United States and in Kobe, Japan in the 1990s, however, had more than economic impact. For example, changes in attitudes and values about safety issues (cultural sector) initiated changes in building codes (legal sector) that stimulated the development of new building techniques (technical sector). The tsunami of 2004 not only killed many who lived in or were visiting the East Asian countries that were hit by the waves but devastated economies throughout the region. Of course other sectors influence the physical sector as well, such as when population growth or migration (social sector) taxes the physical resources of those regions of the world where settlement occurs.

A Comment

Many more examples of the sectors of the general environment could be given, of course, and I invite you to think of others to help you develop these concepts. However, remember that, although organization theorists separate the general environment into sectors in order to identify and analyze their distinctive influences, the sectors are not really separable as was illustrated by the examples of cross-sectoral influences given above. The seven sectors shown in Figure 3.4 are conceptual distinctions that organization theorists use to help them address environmental complexity. After you become familiar with these categories you may find that you prefer to use only five or six sectors. For instance, collapsing the social and cultural or political and legal categories makes good sense to many people. Or, you may find you need more than these seven sectors to accommodate all the variety you see in the environment of your organization. The model of the general environment presented in the figure is offered merely as a starting point for understanding how modern organization theorists think about general conditions in an organization's environment. It is meant as a stimulus, not a rigid solution. Don't forget that the usefulness of this, or any other organization theory model, will depend upon your elaborating it with specific information based upon your knowledge and experience. Please do not be reluctant to change a theoretical model if the change enables you to better understand or more effectively influence your world, but be prepared to explain to others how your model differs from theirs.

International Environment and Globalization

In many respects the same distinctions we made under the headings of the interorganizational network and general environment apply to the **international environment**. This is because as soon as an organization begins to expand its activities beyond the boundaries of its home nation, it will interact regularly with representatives of organizations from other nations—joint venture partners, consumer groups, tariff collecting agencies, tax authorities and licensing agents, to name only a few—and all of these stakeholders will become part of the organization's network. Even before entering into international operations or exchanges, the organization will be affected by competitors that operate in international markets, and by firms that enter the organization's domestic markets from abroad.

However, the international/global environment is not simply 'another layer of things to worry about', as one student put it. It represents a fundamental shift in perspective such as the one shown in Figure 3.5. From this perspective the environment of the organization is composed of many interrelated environments. The complexity of this level of

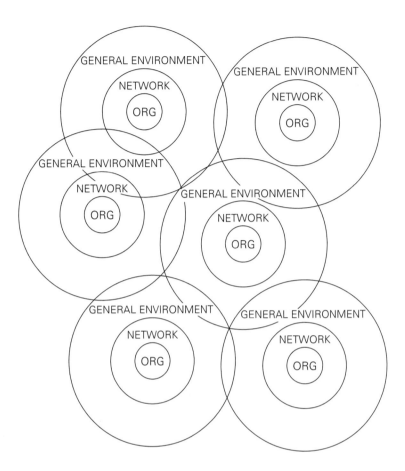

Figure 3.5 The international environment

This model shows how organizations can be embedded within multiple overlapping networks that are influenced by the general conditions and trends in their own environments, as well as in the environments of those with whom they interact.

environmental analysis is immensely greater than the conceptualizations we considered earlier in the chapter. Thus, once you have learned to take the international environment into account, you will have broadened yourself in a way that changes your orientation toward even the most local aspects of the interorganizational network. This bigger picture is the value of an international perspective and many people now believe that this picture will soon be replaced by a perspective better equipped to engage the contradictions and paradoxes of global life such as those evoked by slogans like 'think global, act local' and its obverse 'think local, act global'![5]

The international environment includes organizational actors that cross national boundaries or operate on a global scale. Actors operating within and constituting an important part of the international environment include institutions such as the United Nations (UN), the World Trade Organization (WTO), the North Atlantic Treaty Organization

(NATO), the International Monetary Fund (IMF), the Red Cross and the World Bank, not to mention a growing number of NGOs (nongovernmental organizations created to voice public concerns and exert pressures for change throughout the world). International businesses and consulting firms are international actors that form and influence international markets and push them toward global inclusion. For example, the markets of the Pacific Rim and the European Community have recently been formed and the global reach of brands such as Coca-Cola, Toyota, Heineken, McDonald's and L'Oréal symbolizes the growing interdependence of a world economy. However, the existence of widely accepted products and growing international markets does not constitute the level of interdependence that is evoked by the image of a global environment. There is still some distance to go before Coca-Cola or any other global brand is accessible to everyone everywhere in the world. Nonetheless, the anticipation of a global future is clearly creating the very activities from which that future will be constructed. American strategy professor C. K. Prahalad's book *The Fortune at the Bottom of the Pyramid: Eradicating Poverty through Profits* gives many examples of the ways that capitalism and consumerism are being encouraged among even the most impoverished of people.[6]

Trends can appear in different sectors of the international environment, just as they do in the general environment. In this regard it can be difficult to separate out general sector and international sector trends and conditions in the overall environment. The growth of markets in China is one example of an economic trend that is global in its scope and implications because the size of China's markets has the potential to attract resources from around the globe and to create new dependencies that will reorganize the world economy. Terrorism represents a political trend of global significance that has affected all other sectors of the global environment as well as many nations, organizational networks and organizations throughout the world.

Concern for the natural environment is an example of an international trend that began in the physical sector, mobilized parts of the social and cultural sectors, and is having effects on political, legal and economic sectors in many parts of the world. The shift in values that promotes protecting natural resources and reclaiming polluted regions encourages people to organize themselves politically through the Green movement. Since the sentiment underlying the Green movement crosses national boundaries, this movement can be interpreted as an example of an international trend with national implications that reach into networks and organizations. For instance, the shifting of cultural values affects national political institutions through establishment of Green parties in various democratic societies and produces pressures that influence international law and cross-national trade relations that are part of the legal and economic sectors of many organizations. These forces may one day become fully organized at the global level. Consider, for example, the Earth Summit first held in Rio de Janeiro, Brazil, in 1992. Managers need to maintain awareness of the specific ways in which changes like those introduced by the Green movement affect their interorganizational network and, through it, their organization.

Globalization refers to economic, political, socio-cultural, legal, technological and physical interconnections and exchanges that render existing borders and boundaries (such as those dividing nation-states or economic partnerships) permeable or irrelevant.[7] Cultural homogenization is one widely feared affect of the globalizing economy as English, the language of business, becomes increasingly commonplace along with blue jeans, training shoes and American fast food. But cultural homogenization is not all that is taking place; the threat of homogenization triggers desires to maintain local cultural values and customs. Thus global cultural trends toward emphasizing religion and community are translated differently in different parts of the world and this leads paradoxically to growing cultural diversity and to the appeal of democratically inspired concepts of self-determination and individual freedom.

Some people interpret globalization as primarily a socio-cultural development, while others see it as largely economic and political. As it involves all sectors of the general and international environment it is probably useless to try to restrict the definition to trends in any one sector. Instead globalization merges the sectors into one extremely complex and highly dynamic whole. It is this holistic picture of the global environment of organizations that has persuaded some modernist organization theorists to pin their hopes on complexity theory (see Chapter 10), a recent development in the natural sciences that suggests that even the smallest change in one part of an interconnected system can create repercussions in seemingly unrelated parts of the system, just as in the global ecosystem the batting of a butterfly's wings can change weather patterns on the other side of the globe. For example, where once banks dominated capital markets, today they are increasingly influenced by mutual and hedge-fund investors whose search for returns create rapid transfers of capital to areas of the world able to show economic growth and political stability. Some of the elements from particular sectors of the general environment that many believe are converging globally to transform the world are shown in Table 3.1.

The crosscutting influences of the different sectors of the general and international environments make an important point about theoretical models: they are always based in conceptual distinctions that are open to deconstruction and/or alternative constructions. In the case of the phenomenon of the organizational environment, I am not presenting a bunch of different environments, as my language seems to suggest. Rather, I am talking about different aspects of one, highly complex environment. In fact, the organization itself cannot really be separated from its environment because it makes up the environment along with other organizations with which it is involved. You will perhaps more easily see this with reference to another figure (see Figure 3.6).

Figure 3.6 shows the organization operating within its network that, in turn, operates within the general environment and thus is subject to its myriad influences, including international factors. The conditions and trends in the general environment are separated for purposes of analysis into the seven sectors: cultural, social, political, legal, economic, physical and technological. The figure traces these conditions and trends as they move through the network and into the organization itself to show that the organization is not simply an outcome of environmental influence, it is a contributing member of the environment—it is both embedded in, and an active part of, its environment. Therefore, the conceptual distinction between organization and environment, like those

Table 3.1 Contributions of environmental sectors to global complexity and change

Sector	Contribution to global change
Technology	Personal computers The Internet and WIFI Digital cameras and HDTV Cell phones Communication satellites Rapid transit trains, space shuttles, supertankers
Economic	Global capital markets Technology exchanges Worldwide trade Transnational corporations International economic institutions (e.g., IMF, World Bank, WTO) Regional trading systems and global retailing
Political/Legal	Breakdown of the authority of the nation-state Erosion of territorial borders Institutions of global governance (e.g., UN, WHO, World Court)
Social/Cultural	Global media coverage Popular culture (e.g., slang, fashion, brands, music) English as global language of science, politics, business and the Internet Materialism and consumerism Tourism Multi-racialism, multi-culturalism and multi-lingualism
Physical	Population growth Loss of biodiversity Hazardous waste and industrial accidents Global warming and climate change Pollution Disease and food insecurity Genetically modified (GM) foods

Based on: Steger (2003).

between different environmental sectors, are somewhat arbitrary. In general, you will want to make analytical distinctions because without them you might fail to examine aspects of the environment that are critical to your understanding and thus important for effective action. These particular distinctions are recommended because they are in common use among modernist organization theorists and managers. Later in this chapter we will consider what postmodernists have to say about these and other modernist ideas about the environment of organizations and about the arbitrariness of conceptual distinctions.

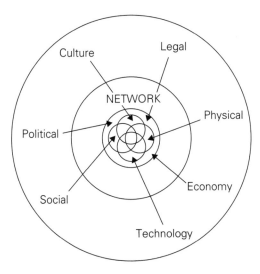

Figure 3.6 How the general environment penetrates the interorganizational network and the organization

The conditions and trends of the sectors of the general environment penetrate the interorganizational network and the organization even as networks and organizations constitute the environment and contribute to its conditions and trends.

Modernist Theories Relating Organizations to Their Environments

During the late 1950s the concept of environment was introduced to organizational analysis by an extension of systems theory. Prior to this, a closed systems view predominated, especially in classical management theory whose proponents treated organizations as if their internal operations were the sole source of concern for managers. Using systems theory, modernists established the idea that organizations are open to their environments and devoted themselves to conceptualizing and demonstrating the importance of the new concept. By the late 1970s most organization theorists and managers had taken the influence of the environment for granted, and interest shifted to explaining how environmental influence operates, thus creating the first theories of organization–environment relations. Three of the most influential of these theories are presented to you here: environmental contingency theory, resource dependence theory and population ecology. A fourth—institutional theory—will be presented in the next section of the chapter because its theoretical assumptions position it within the symbolic-interpretive perspective.

Environmental Contingency Theory

British sociologists Tom Burns and George Stalker and American organization theorists Paul Lawrence and Jay Lorsch were among the first to argue that an organization's structure should be based on the conditions it faces in its environment. Burns and Stalker, for example, presented one of the first empirical tests of contingency theory showing that, in stable environments, successful organizations specialize in routine activities with strict lines of authority and distinct areas of assigned responsibility, while in rapidly changing environments, organizations require flexibility and employees are encouraged to apply their skills as needed, fitting into the changing work patterns in whatever way they find to be useful.[8]

Notice that there is no theoretical reason to consider either organic or mechanistic organizational forms to be universally superior; each is appropriate to different environmental conditions. In stable environments, the mechanistic form is advantageous because of the efficiencies it can generate by using standard procedures to perform routine activities. Under these conditions organizations can learn to optimize their activities with respect to minimizing costs and maximizing profit. Under rapidly changing conditions, however, many of the advantages of mechanistic organization are lost. The logic and profitability of routinization breaks down when the organization must constantly alter its activities in order to adapt to rapid changes in the environment. The flexibility that comes with organic forms of organization is preferred in a changing environment because this supports needed innovation and adaptation. The explanation of when to use mechanistic versus organic forms of organization is an example of environmental contingency theory, that is, which form you should use is contingent on a set of environmental factors specified by the theory.

In early environmental contingency theories, uncertainty was presented as a property of the environment resulting from complexity and rate of change. **Complexity** refers to the number and diversity of the elements in an environment. **Rate of change** refers to how rapidly these elements change. **Environmental uncertainty**, as this perspective came to be known, was defined as an interaction between varying amounts of complexity and change in the environment (Figure 3.7).

The problem with environmental uncertainty theory was that it assumed that conditions in the environment were experienced in the same way by everyone. Empirical studies of uncertainty, however, found that this was not a valid assumption. The same environment might be perceived as certain by one set of managers and uncertain by another. The term 'environmental uncertainty' turned out to be quite misleading—environments do not feel uncertain, people do. Furthermore, it became apparent that what affects organizations is not conditions in the environment so much as the perceptions of organizational decision makers about how uncertain their environment is.[9] Today organization theorists recognize that uncertainty lies not in the environment, but in the individuals who consider the environment when they make organizational decisions. In modernist organization theory this viewpoint is associated with the **information perspective on uncertainty**.[10]

The information perspective argues that managers experience uncertainty when they perceive the environment to be unpredictable, and this occurs when they lack the information that they feel they need to make sound decisions. Figure 3.8 helps to visualize the links between perceived environmental conditions, uncertainty, and information.

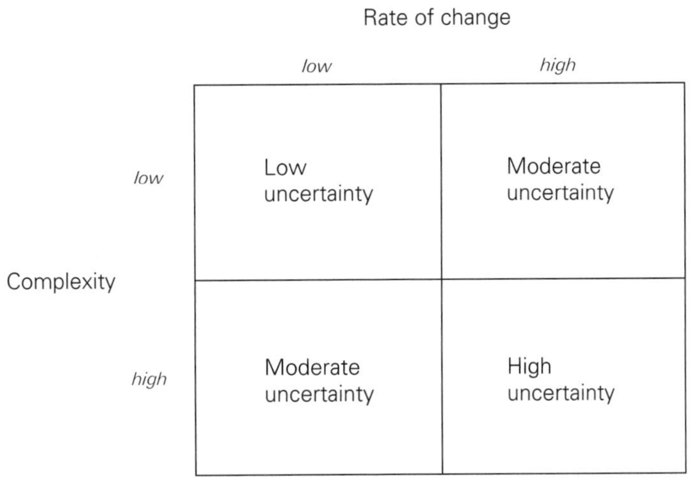

Rate of change

	low	high
low	Low uncertainty	Moderate uncertainty
high	Moderate uncertainty	High uncertainty

Complexity

Figure 3.7 Environmental uncertainty is defined by the amount of complexity and the rate of change in the organization's environment

Based on: Duncan (1972).

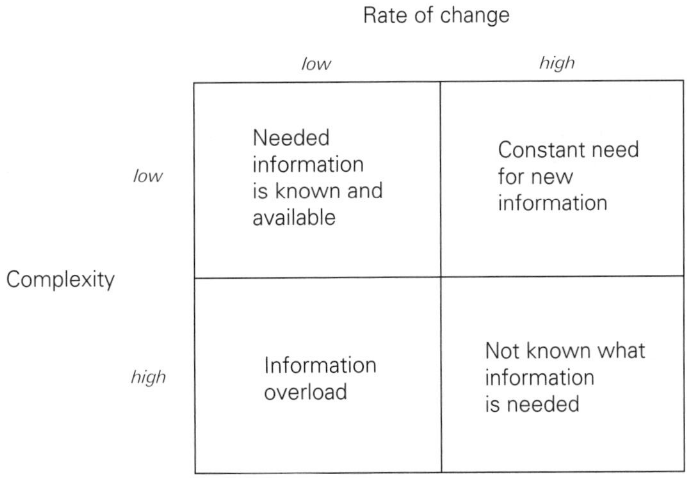

Rate of change

	low	high
low	Needed information is known and available	Constant need for new information
high	Information overload	Not known what information is needed

Complexity

Figure 3.8 Links between conditions in the perceived environment, uncertainty, and information

Figure 3.8 shows that managers perceive environments as stable and as having minimum complexity when the information they need is both known and available; when this occurs they experience low levels of uncertainty in their environment. Managers perceive environments to have either high complexity or to be rapidly changing when they confront either too much information or constantly changing information, in which case moderate levels of uncertainty are experienced. Managers experience high uncertainty and perceive a highly complex and changing environment when they face an overwhelming amount of information that is constantly changing. For instance, advances in computer technology and the internationalization of markets create conditions of increasing diversity that make it difficult for managers to locate and process all the information they need to make sound decisions. But what is most uncertainly provoking is not knowing what information is needed amidst an overabundance of information.

Early efforts to explain how organizations respond to uncertainty relied on the concepts of requisite variety and isomorphism. The **law of requisite variety**, borrowed from general systems theory, states that for one system to deal effectively with another it must be of the same or greater complexity. In organizational terms this means that successful organizations map perceived environmental complexity with their internal structures and management systems, thus creating isomorphism. *Iso* means same and *morph* means form; therefore **isomorphism** means that the organization takes on the same form as its environment. For instance, if the environment is simple, the organization should take a simple form. In a complex environment, the isomorphic organization will be complex too. Under changing conditions, of course, the concepts of isomorphism and requisite variety suggest that successful organizations will change in response to changes in their environments in order to maintain fit.

American organization theorists Paul Lawrence and Jay Lorsch discussed the implications of isomorphism in their 1967 book *Organization and Environment*. They suggested that organizations confront many different conditions and elements in their environments. The different environmental demands create pressure for internal differentiation. Put another way, differentiation allows different parts of the organization to specialize in handling responses to different demands from the environment. It is this differentiation of the organization into specialized units for confronting different aspects of the environment that produces the internal complexity of organizational structures and systems that allows them to isomorphically map complex environments.

Resource Dependence Theory

Resource dependence theory was most fully developed by American organization theorists Jeffrey Pfeffer and Gerald Salancik who published their ideas in 1978. Their book was provocatively titled *The External Control of Organizations*, to emphasize their point that the environment is a powerful influence on strategic action. Although resource dependence theory is based on the assumption that organizations are controlled by their environments, these theorists also suggested how managers could learn to navigate the harsh seas of environmental determination.

The basic argument of **resource dependence theory** is that an analysis of the interorganizational network can help an organization's managers understand the **power/dependence** relationships that exist between their organization and other network actors. Such knowledge allows managers to anticipate likely sources of influence from the environment and suggests ways in which the organization can offset some of this influence by creating countervailing dependence.

An organization's vulnerability to its environment is the result of its need for resources such as raw materials, labor, capital, equipment, knowledge and outlets for its products and services—resources that are controlled by the environment. The environment derives its power over the organization from this dependence. The environment uses this power to make demands on the organization for such things as competitive prices, desirable products and services, and efficient organizational structures and processes. However, the dependency the organization has on its environment is not one single undifferentiated dependency, it is a complex set of dependencies that exist between an organization and the specific elements of its interorganizational network.

A resource dependence analysis begins by identifying an organization's needed resources and then tracing them to their sources. This procedure can be visualized using the interorganizational network model shown in Figure 3.9. Applying open systems thinking, you first identify the resource inputs and outputs of the organization. You then define where the resource flows begin and where the outputs end up. For example, firms that provide raw materials and equipment will be found among the organization's suppliers. Tracing the organization's outputs will identify specific customers in the network. Labor, capital, and knowledge are also brought into the organization and these are supplied by other actors in the network (e.g., labor from employment agencies, capital from financial institutions, knowledge from universities and think tanks).

After specifying resources and their sources and destinations in the interorganizational network, the resource dependence perspective moves your attention to those environmental actors who can affect these organization–environment relationships and thereby support or interfere with the organization's resource exchanges. Competition over raw materials, customers and employees is one source of potential influence, and this is where you should bring the organization's competitors into your analysis. Another source is regulatory agencies, and the special interests that compete with the organization for

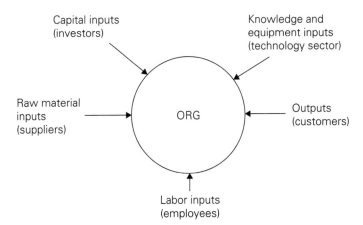

Figure 3.9 Applying resource dependence theory

Use this model to remind you to trace your organization's resources to their sources in the interorganizational network.

influence over the regulators. Regulatory agencies have legal control over organizational activities, for example, tax authorities, licensing agencies and customs inspectors. Special interests are people or groups that attempt to influence the activities of the organization via political, economic and/or social pressure. Examples of special interests include nongovernmental organizations (NGOs) and other groups concerned with world health, human rights, fair trade, shareholder rights, labor relations, women's issues, environmental protection and consumer interests. To the extent that regulatory agencies, special interest groups or competitors affect the organization's dependencies, these will also be drawn into focus.

Of course the procedure given above is too ambitious. In practice it will be impossible to consider every source of dependence that an organization has on its environment or every potential competitive, special interest or regulatory move. The practical solution offered by Pfeffer and Salancik is to prioritize elements in your analysis according to the criticality and scarcity of the resources involved. **Criticality** is an estimate of the importance of a particular resource. Without critical resources, the organization cannot function. For instance, beef is a critical resource for McDonalds, whereas drinking straws are not. **Scarcity** is an estimate of resource availability. Gold and platinum are scarce, air and water are not (yet). Resources that are both scarce and critical are given the highest priority in organizational efforts to track and manage dependencies because these create the strongest power base for other network actors.

Managing dependencies requires the establishment of countervailing power with respect to the particular environmental elements upon which the organization's dependence rests. This means that the first step toward applying the resource dependence perspective is to thoroughly understand the interorganizational network with respect to criticality and scarcity of resources. The second step is to seek ways to avoid dependency or to make other environmental actors dependent upon your organization.

Organizations have found many different ways to manage their resource dependencies and Pfeffer and Salancik documented quite a few. In the area of managing suppliers of raw materials, one common technique is to establish multiple sources of supply. This reduces the power of any one supplier. Where there are benefits to using a limited number of suppliers, such as with supply chain management systems where the cost of changing suppliers is high, contracting is a common strategy for managing dependencies. Dependency on suppliers (or customers, from the suppliers point of view) is sometimes counteracted by creating joint ventures or acquiring or merging with suppliers (called **vertical integration strategies**) or by forming alliances or merging with competitors in order to have more negotiating power with suppliers; similar strategies also are useful for managing competitor relations (called **horizontal integration strategies**). Strategies useful for managing all kinds of dependencies include: developing personal relationships with members of firms on which yours is dependent, and establishing formal ties such as taking up membership on their board of directors or inviting one of their officers to sit on your board. In the area of managing regulatory dependencies, a common strategy is to send lobbyists to influence legislators, for example, to work for competitive trade agreements or to vote for favorable corporate tax laws or government funding of research and development. All aspects of marketing—sales, advertising, distribution, branding—can be seen as attempts to manage output dependencies via influence on consumer purchases of company products. For example, counteracting negative public opinion or the negative influence of special interest group pressures or reports in the media is sometimes achieved with advertising, for example, using corporate image campaigns or corporate citizenship programs.

Labor and knowledge dependencies can be managed with recruitment strategies for attracting executives and other personnel away from competitors. A strategy that can aid in the management of dependency with respect to competitor organizations and regulators is the formation of trade associations. These associations enable their members to share the costs of monitoring conditions and trends in the environment and to pool their influence by jointly hiring lobbyists to represent their common interests to the government or through category marketing. Of course trade associations are open to criticism and even legal action if they are not careful to guard themselves against price fixing and other unfair or illegal business practices. In societies in which price fixing is not outlawed, price agreements and cartels are common means of managing environmental dependence between competitors. OPEC is a prime example. Finally, if all else fails, the organization can release itself from unwanted dependencies by changing its environment, as when an organization enters or exits a line of business or alters its product/service mix through diversification or retrenchment (e.g., joint ventures, spin-offs, mergers, acquisitions). Notice, however, that these strategies merely alter the organization's dependencies; they do not eliminate the need to manage them.

Managing resource dependence requires careful definition and monitoring of the environment. It also calls for imagination with respect to balancing the power of others by developing countervailing power within your own organization. The topic of organizational power and politics will be examined further in Chapter 8.

Population Ecology

In modernist organization theory, ideas about variation, selection and retention processes form the basis for population ecology theory that was developed by American organization theorists Michael Hannan, John Freeman, Howard Aldrich and Glen Carroll, among others.[11] Like resource dependence theory, **population ecology** starts from the assumption that organizations depend on their environments for the resources they need to operate. Both theories assume that this dependency gives the environment considerable power over the organization. However, whereas the viewpoint of resource dependence theory was rooted in the organizational level of analysis, population ecology operates at the level of the environment. What interests the population ecologist is not one particular organization seeking its own survival via competition for scarce and critical resources (the resource dependence view), but rather the patterns of success and failure among all the organizations that compete within a given resource pool.[12]

The environment is not studied as a whole in population ecology; instead, a specific area within an environment, called an **ecological niche**, is studied. A niche consists of the resource pool upon which a group of competitors depends. While similar to an interorganizational network, a niche differs in that its focus is the group of organizations that compete within the resource pool the niche offers, rather than the links between a competitor and the organizations that support and regulate it. Population ecologists assume that organizations sharing a resource pool are competitively interdependent and that the patterns of interdependence that they adopt within the group, called the **population**, affect the survival and prosperity of individual members. Thus population ecology is based on the assumption that organizations compete for their survival and this competition is the phenomenon of interest. Population ecology studies have focused, for example, on competition in populations of restaurants, newspapers, small electronics firms, day care centers, and labor unions.[13] Population ecologists try to predict such things as organizational birth and death rates, and the forms and strategies that successful organizations adopt (e.g., being generalists with many lines of business in multiple markets, or specialists that devote their attention to one line of business or a single market). Their main interest is to explain how competitive ecological processes result in all the various types of organization we see around us today.

In population ecology the environment of an organization is given the power to select from a group of competitors those organizations that best serve its needs. You might say that population ecology is an organizational version of Darwin's survival of the fittest principle. As in Darwin's theory of evolution, three processes—variation, selection, and retention—explain the dynamics of a population of organizations. **Variation** occurs primarily through entrepreneurial innovation that gives birth to new organizations. But it also occurs through the adaptation of established organizations as they respond to new threats or opportunities in their environments. Organizations that are formed or transformed through birth or adaptation provide diversity to the selection process. **Selection** occurs as organizations that best fit the needs and demands of their ecological niche are supported with resources, while those that do not meet the criterion of fitness starve. Non-selection does not always necessitate organizational decline and death however, instead it can lead to flight from an existing environment to inhabit a different resource niche (e.g., exiting a business that does not have long-term profit growth potential, entry into new businesses). Such flight feeds back into variation by producing organizational adaptations such as downsizing, spin-offs, mergers, acquisitions and new business development. **Retention** means that resources are continuously fed to the organization; thus maintaining fitness equals organizational survival. However, survival in one period is no guarantee of success over the long run. Constant change in environments demands continual adaptation so that retained organizations need to take part in further variation. And on it goes.

Because population ecology takes the point of view of the environment rather than the organization, using it means giving up a certain amount of identification with the organization. Such detachment is useful for considering alternatives and making decisions such as which organizations to finance or own, to whom to extend credit, or with whom to start a joint venture. Thus population ecology offsets the organization-centered perspective resource dependence theory sometimes encourages. The population ecology viewpoint is also useful for communicating with members of government or regulatory agents whose perspective is normally defined by the environmental level of analysis due to the large numbers of organizations that their policies affect.

In spite of its benefits, there are several constraints on the usefulness of the population ecology view. First, as with Darwin's theory, the definition of fitness is a problem—survival is explained by fitness, but fitness is defined as survival—there is a tautology at the heart of population ecology theory that means you cannot predict survival on the basis of an independent assessment of fit. You can only recognize survival after it occurs. Second, the theory applies most readily to populations that are highly competitive. Not all populations fit this description. Populations with significant barriers to entry or exit such as high start-up costs (e.g., automobile manufacturing) or complex legal regulation (e.g., pharmaceuticals) do not make ideal candidates for population ecology studies. Also, environments that are dominated by a few large organizations (e.g., airplane manufacturing) make unsuitable populations for ecologists to study. When competitiveness is compromised by the existence of enormously powerful organizations or barriers to entry or exit, the population ecology model loses much of its explanatory power. In these circumstances the institutional view often proves useful.

Symbolic-Interpretive Environmental Analysis

The symbolic-interpretive perspective has fostered one of the great debates in organization theory: whether organizational structure or human agency has the greater significance for understanding organizations. Institutional theory anchors the structuralist side of this debate, while enactment theory provides an illustration of the agency position. Institutional theorists typically take the position that institutions are relatively durable social structures that shape and constrain the behavior of actors operating within a given social system (actors can be individuals, groups or organizations). Those propounding enactment theory take the view that regularities in individual actions and interactions produce the patterns of relationship that, when viewed at the organizational level of analysis, appear as structures. For institutionalists, actors are often unwitting agents of systems (or institutional fields) that organize their actions and activities, whereas for enactment theorists systems are constructed through the social interactions and relationships arising between individual actors. A third position—structuration theory—lies midway between these two. I will leave structuration theory until Chapter 4 as it represents an important compromise between modernist and interpretive theories of organizational social structure.

Institutional Theory

Many organization theorists regard American sociologist Philip Selznick to be the grandfather of institutional theory. Selznick based institutional theory on his observation that organizations adapt, not only to the strivings of their internal groups, but to the values of external society. Elaborating on this idea, American sociologists Paul DiMaggio and Woody Powell argued that 'organizations compete not just for resources and customers, but for political power and institutional legitimacy, for social as well as economic fitness.'[14] In other words, environments can put demands on organizations in two different ways. First, they may make technical, economic and physical demands that require organizations to produce and exchange their goods and services in a market or a quasi-market. Second, they may make social, cultural, legal or political demands that require organizations to play particular roles in society and to establish and maintain certain outward appearances. Environments dominated by technical, economic or physical demands reward organizations for efficiently and effectively supplying the environment with goods and services. Environments dominated by social, cultural, legal and/or political demands reward organizations for conforming to the values, norms, rules and beliefs upheld by social institutions such as government, religion and education.

Recognizing the social and cultural basis of external influence on organizations, however, is only one contribution of institutional theory. Neo-institutionalists attempt to move beyond mere recognition of the social and cultural foundations of institutions to describe the processes by which practices and organizations become institutions. For instance, W. Richard Scott defined **institutionalization** as 'the process by which actions are repeated and given similar meaning by self and others.'[15] Thus, not only government, religion and education can be conceptualized as institutions, but so can actions, such as voting, bowing or shaking hands. This grounds the definition of institutions in repeated actions and shared conceptions of reality.

Sometimes actions are repeated because explicit rules or laws exist to ensure their repetition (legal and political influences). Sometimes activity patterns are supported by norms, values and expectations (cultural influences); sometimes by a desire to be or look like another institution (social influences). Powell and DiMaggio distinguished between these three different institutional pressures and gave them distinctive labels.[16] These institutional theorists argued that when the pressure to conform comes from governmental regulations or laws, then **coercive** institutional pressures are at work. When the pressure comes from cultural expectations, for instance via the education of organizational members, then **normative** institutional pressures are at work. DiMaggio and Powell called desires to look like other organizations **mimetic** institutional pressures and explained them as responses to uncertainty that involve copying other organizational structures, practices or outputs in order to conform to expectations. When an environment becomes organized around social, cultural, political and legal expectations via these institutional pressures, it is said to be institutionalized.[17] According to Scott, the aspects of the environment through which institutional influences operate include: regulatory structures, government agencies, laws and courts, professions, interest groups and mobilized public opinion.[18]

The difference between institutionalized and noninstitutionalized environments often appears to be simply a matter of rationality. In this view, the technical/economic success factor is viewed as the product of rational decision making, while social conformity is a victory for symbolic management. Conforming to institutional demands wins social support and ensures survival to an organization, not because it makes more money or better products, but because it goes along with accepted conventions.[19] However, rationality alone will not distinguish institutionalized from noninstitutionalized environments because rational talk can become institutionalized. That is, the making of decisions that only superficially conform to the norms of rationality can be an effective way to legitimize organizational choices.[20]

You have probably made many rational arguments in favor of decisions that were emotionally based—to buy a particular car, for example, or to drop a course that was unappealing. This sort of framing of nonrational logic as rational argument occurs in organizations just as it does in your private life. John Meyer and Brian Rowan suggested that, in organizations, these rationalized arguments take the form of myths that are never objectively tested because everyone knows them to be true. In their view, rationalized myths (e.g., that organizations are efficient mechanisms for maximizing the use of scarce resources) and their ceremonial expressions (e.g., annual budget reviews) are part of the institutional context in which organizations operate and to which they must adapt if they are to maintain their social legitimacy.[21]

In the institutional perspective, the environment is a culture that provides a more or less shared view of what organizations should look like and how they should behave. Often certain structural characteristics, such as bureaucracy in the public domain or matrix structures in the defense industry, become institutionalized standards by which organizations are judged as appropriate and thus granted the social legitimacy required to continue using resources (particularly capital and/or public support). Meyer and Rowan's rather cynical assessment of this perspective is that, once an organization has learned how to look good (e.g., to look like a rational organization), it need do only face work to survive. Meanwhile, the actual activities of the firm may be at odds with outward appearances and the lack of any objective criteria by which to judge the organization's performance means that institutionalized organizations are not accountable to society except in a very superficial sense.

One important theoretical contribution of the institutional perspective is the addition of **social legitimacy** to the list of inputs depicted by the open systems model of organization (see Figure 3.10). Not only do organizations require raw materials, capital, labor, knowledge, and equipment, they also depend upon the acceptance of the society in which they operate. Organizations whose environments question their right to survive can be driven out of business. For instance, public outcry at unethical business practices either killed outright or severely threatened the survival of a wide range of organizations in the late 1990s (e.g., Enron and Arthur Anderson in the United States, Parmalat in Italy). Human and animal rights activists as well as environmental protection groups are just some examples of numerous forces that have attempted to de-legitimize various organizations and even entire industries (e.g., the fur trade) through the mobilization of public opinion and action (e.g., boycotts, demonstrations, letter writing or e-mail campaigns).[22] These examples reveal the importance of social legitimacy by showing what can happen if it is threatened or taken away.

In applying institutional theory to an analysis of a particular organization you should consider how the organization adapts to its institutional context. For instance, analyze the sources (e.g., regulatory agencies, laws, social and cultural expectations) and types of institutional pressure (e.g., coercive, normative, mimetic) exerted by the environment on the organization. Also consider how decision-making processes are shaped by institutional

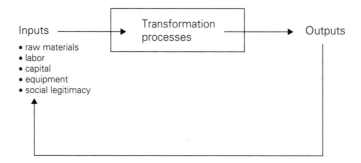

Figure 3.10 Social legitimacy as an organizational resource

Institutional theory suggests that social legitimacy be considered an input to the organizational transformation process along with raw materials and other resources upon which this process depends.

myths versus rational choice. Finally, try to imagine how the organization might gain greater legitimacy within its institutional context.

The Enacted Environment

Cognitive organization theorists like Karl Weick start from the assumption that conditions in the environment cannot be separated from perceptions of those conditions. Weick suggested that if organizational decision makers assume the environment is real, they will gather and analyze information in order to create accurate forecasts and make rational decisions. If decision makers perceive the environment as complex and unanalyzable, then more qualitative data and improvised approaches to managing the environment will be used. This is similar to the modernist information perspective that I presented earlier in this chapter except that, instead of arguing that complexity and change challenge organizational decision makers with an increased need for information, the **enacted environment** view maintains that when decision makers respond to their perceptions, they enact the environment they anticipated by constructing an interpretation that seems sensible.[23] An interesting paradox arises—as decision makers experience uncertainty, they search for and find more information, and as the database grows, the environment appears more complex and uncertain. In this formulation, people interpret their uncertainty as a lack of information and then attribute their experience to environmental complexity and change.

It is also important to understand that the way organizations respond to their environment will depend on how they construct and interpret that environment. Weick suggested that, if an organization constructs the environment as a given that is highly complex and unmanageable, it may not try to influence events but will react only to crises. An alternative is for an organization to create its environment. For example, Apple Computer enacted a world in which personal computers and iPods are a necessary part of everyday life.

While enactment theory is not enough to explain everything we observe in organizations (from where, for instance, does the initial sense of uncertainty come?), it does offer an interesting way to explain the sudden radical shift to greater complexity and more rapid change experienced by organizations caught up in the computer revolution and the information age. The computer allows us to process rapidly changing and steadily increasing amounts of information that, in turn, permits us to construct ever more complicated and changing realities. In the cult film classic *The Gods Must be Crazy*, someone on an airplane passing overhead inadvertently dropped a Coke bottle into a village inhabited by a primitive tribe. Tribe members, not knowing what it was, proceeded to find many uses for it (e.g., a rolling pin, hammer, ant collector) and eventually found it so indispensable to their lives that they began to fight over it. Their wise chief, realizing the danger, threw it away and soon thereafter the tribe resumed its former peaceful existence. A major point of the film was that we create enormous complexities when we introduce alluring technologies into a society. In the case of organizations, the alluring technology is the computer.

Ambiguity Theory

A corollary to Weick's enactment theory is his concept of **equivocality**. According to Weick, when humans equivocate they multiply perceived possibilities and then enact them as contradictory realities that they use to justify their further equivocation. Introducing a closely related concept, American organization theorist James March argued that **ambiguity** is 'a strategy for suspending rational imperatives toward consistency [that helps organizations] explore alternative ideas of possible purposes and alternative concepts of behavioral consistency'.[24] Eric Eisenberg, an American communication theorist, expanded upon March's insight claiming that people in organizations do not always promote correspondence between their intentions and the interpretations given to their messages; at times they purposely omit contextual cues to allow for multiple interpretations by others.[25] Eisenberg claimed that strategically encouraging multiple interpretations of goals and vision can produce unified diversity (as opposed to Gulick's notion of the unity of command described in Chapter 2).

American organization theorist Deborah Meyerson provided an example of unified diversity in her study of the ambiguities confronted by hospital social workers.[26] She found that social workers in the hospitals she studied shared a common orientation and purpose as well as facing similar problems, but that they used different techniques to arrive at different solutions to those similar problems. Furthermore, she found that, when a hospital's culture accommodated different beliefs and supported multiple and sometimes conflicting meanings, social workers experienced less burnout from their work. In addition to illustrating unified diversity, cultures like those Meyerson described exemplify the organizational benefits of equivocality and ambiguity, while her descriptions of how hospital social workers do their work revealed enactment processes.

In summary, the implications of symbolic-interpretive perspectives are that to a certain degree the environment is what we make it, and therefore the interpretations of organizational decision makers may have more influence on the environment than the environment has on organizational decision makers.[27] This has implications for strategy, which can be crafted around the interpretation of the environment. Scenario analysis, an approach associated with initiatives at Royal Dutch/Shell, reflects ideas from the symbolic-interpretive perspective. Instead of carrying out a rational analysis of environmental characteristics, scenario analysis requires organizational decision makers to create narratives about what the future of the organization will look like. These scenarios are then used to identify environmental and business forces that may be currently in play and to assess their likelihoods and risks. For example, each scenario can be acted out with decision makers playing the roles of key actors to help them imagine how their decisions are likely to affect the future of the organization.[28]

Postmodernism and Organization–Environment Relations

One implication of the enactment view not normally taken up by symbolic-interpretivists is that, once we recognize our role as social constructors of organizational realities, we can free ourselves from situations we do not like. This is the sort of thinking advocated by postmodernists pushing for radical change via deconstruction. For example, it has been said that this type of thinking brought down the Berlin Wall. However, one might also do well to consider the consequences of a choice to alter an existing reality—the consequences for Central and Eastern Europeans that have emerged from razing the wall are both exciting and terrifying (new economic and political relationships with the West, war, genocide). It is one thing to decide you want to deconstruct an undesirable reality, replacing it with something else is another story. The postmodern perspective often has a strong ethical tinge, reminding us that responsibility for constructing organizations and the other realities we inhabit ultimately rests on our own shoulders. Stakeholder theory examines the ethics of constructing our organizations in ways that acknowledge the rights of those whose lives are influenced by the organization. It is an ethical interpretation of the interorganizational network model that builds on the concept of legitimacy from institutional theory.

Another symbolic-interpretive idea that filtered into postmodern organization theory is the importance of considering context. Some postmodern organization theorists are particularly interested in the historical contexts of organizing and so take as their departure point the history of industrialization. For example, leading postmodern thinkers such as Jean-François Lyotard, Daniel Bell, and David Harvey, whom you met in Chapter 2, believed that recent changes in the technological sector had such a profound influence on the world that it is forever changed in all of its aspects.[29] Below you will read a historical account of the three phases of industrialization adapted from the industrial sociology of British sociologist Tom Burns. This particular version, though modernist in its origin, illustrates how postmodern organization theory aligns with post-industrial organizing practices, just as modernist organization theory aligned with industrialization in an earlier period of history. Following our discussion of Tom Burns's history, I will present some postmodern challenges to the notion of organizational boundaries using organizational ethics as a countervailing force to strictly economic theory.

Three Phases of Industrialization

Tom Burns defined the trajectory of Western industrial development in terms of three distinguishable phases.[30] The first phase, which ushered in the factory system, grew out of the use of machines to extend and enlarge the productivity of work. The factory system offered an alternative to subcontracting, which was the way industrial labor was organized before factories appeared. In subcontracting, groups of individuals, typically working under a master craftsman, contracted out for specific jobs. In factories, the subcontractor's role was replaced by that of the foreman who worked under the direction of a general manager or the factory owner. A foreman's responsibilities and freedoms were considerably less than those of a subcontractor even though the social status of both remained roughly the same. For example, while subcontractors were responsible for hiring and firing, assigning work tasks, and defining the pace of work, these responsibilities belonged to owners or their executives in the factory system.

Factories first appeared in the British textile industry. They consisted of collections of machines located in one building and were tended by feeders and by maintenance and repair workers. In phase one of industrialization, the machines in a factory were typically all of a single type involving only one task or simple, repetitive process. More complex tasks were still carried out using the older system of subcontracting. While the maintenance workers and supervisors in the early factories were nearly always men, most of the machine operators were women who were, in turn, assisted by children. Thus in phase one of industrialization in Britain, gender relations in factories generally reflected gender relations in society (men had higher status and greater opportunity than women and both had greater status and opportunity than children).

During the second phase of industrial development, which began roughly in the 1850s and 1860s, the factory system diffused into clothing and food manufacturing, engineering, and chemical, iron, and steel processing, all of which depended upon more complex production processes than those of the textile industry. According to Burns, the increased technical complexity of manufacturing operations demanded parallel growth in systems of social organization and bureaucracy with emphasis on control, routine and specialization. These changes were reflected in large increases in the ranks of managers and administrative staff personnel (e.g., professional and clerical workers) and were accompanied by improvements in transportation and communication, freer trade, growing public interest in the consumable products of industrialism, and the armaments revolution that followed improvements in steel and chemical technology and the development of machine tools. Developments similar to those in industry were seen in the growth of national armies and governmental administrations. It was changes introduced in the second phase of industrialization that attracted the attention of sociologists who would later found organization theory. For instance, Weber and Marx both predicted that the changes mentioned above would lead to the creation of a new middle class of managers, clerical workers, and professionals employed in large, hierarchical organizations. According to Burns, many parts of Western industrial society still operate in phase two, while much of the rest of the world is preparing to skip from phase one (or even from no industrial development whatsoever) directly to phase three.

Burns claimed that the third phase of industrial development has only recently appeared in the West. In this phase, production catches up with and overtakes spontaneous domestic demand. In these circumstances, the capitalist organization's dependence on growth leads to enhanced sensitivity to the consumer, to new techniques to stimulate consumption (e.g., product development, design, consumer research, market research, advertising, marketing, branding), to the internationalization of firms in search of new markets, and to new technical developments that increasingly occur within industrial firms (e.g., via research and development). This relationship with their markets demands greater flexibility of organizations, that are required to be customer-oriented, internationally active and technically innovative. What is more, higher levels of commitment to the economic performance of the firm demanded of all organizational members leads to more participative styles of organizing, greater complexity and more rapid change. These ideas, which Burns equated with the third phase of industrialization, have been interpreted by others as indicating a more fundamental change, at least in the West, from industrialism to post-industrialism.

According to futurist Alvin Toffler in his 1970 book *Future Shock*, a good way to envision the extent of the social transformation initiated by computer and telecommunications technology is to compare it to the transformation from agricultural to industrial societies that occurred during the industrial revolution. The American sociologist Daniel Bell gave these new developments the name **post-industrialism** in his 1973 book *The Coming of Post-Industrial Society*. There he argued that, whereas industrial societies are organized around controlling labor for the production of goods, post-industrial society is organized around the creation of knowledge and the uses of information. According to Bell, post-industrial society is shaped and defined by its methods of acquiring, processing, and distributing information, all of which have been revolutionized by the computer. This emphasis on information led Bell, among others, to label the current era the information age and to predict the rise of the service sector and the decline of manufacturing, with knowledge workers (technicians and professionals) replacing capitalists as the most powerful members of society.

Bell and others attribute the emergence of the global economy to the ability to instantaneously share knowledge and information, which they defined as a product of the computer revolution. A further implication of the computer revolution, initially remarked by futurist John Naisbitt in his popular book *Megatrends*, is the abandonment of hierarchies in favor of communication networks with a consequent shift from vertically to horizontally structured organizations. This aspect of the information age provides the departure point for most discussions of the post-industrial or post-bureaucratic organization.

Discussions of post-industrial or post-bureaucratic organization typically involve comparisons of the forms of work and organization that became familiar during phase two of industrialism with those anticipated as a consequence of the shifts equated with the information age. Much energy has been devoted to describing what, in particular, is changing. Table 3.2 groups some typical ideas in relation to the environment, technology, social structure, culture, physical structure (space-time) and the consequences of these changing conditions for the nature of work in organizations. Be sure to compare

Table 3.2 Comparison of characteristics associated with industrialism and post-industrialism

	Industrial period	**Post-industrial period**
Environment	Nation-states regulate national economies Mass marketing Standardization The Welfare State	Global competition De-concentration of capital with respect to nation-state Fragmentation of markets and international decentralization of production Rise of consumer choice, demand for customized goods Rise of social movements, single-issue politics, service class Pluralism, diversity, location
Technology	Mass production along Taylorist/Fordist lines Routine Manufacturing output	Flexible manufacturing, automation Use of computer for design, production, and stock control Just-in-time systems (JIT) Emphasis on speed and innovation Service-information output
Social structure	Bureaucratic Hierarchical with vertical communication emphasized Specialization Vertical and horizontal integration Focused on control	New organizational forms (e.g., networks, strategic alliances, virtual organization) Flatter hierarchies with horizontal communication and devolved managerial responsibility Outsourcing Informal mechanisms of influence (participation, culture, communication) Vertical and horizontal disintegration Loose boundaries between functions, units, organizations
Culture	Celebrates stability, tradition, custom Organizational values: growth, efficiency, standardization, control	Celebrates uncertainty, paradox, fashion Organizational values: quality, customer service, diversity, innovation
Physical structure	Concentration of people in industrial towns and cities Local, nationalistic orientation Time is linear	Deconcentration of people in urban areas Reduction in transportation time links distant spaces and encourages international orientation and globalization Compression of temporal dimension (e.g., shortening of product lifecycles)
Nature of work	Routine Deskilled labor Functional specialization of tasks and jobs	Frenetic, complex Knowledge-based skills Cross-functional teamwork Greater emphasis on learning More outsourcing, subcontracting, self-employment, teleworking

Based on: Clegg (1990); Harvey (1990); Heydebrand (1977); Kumar (1995); Lash and Urry (1987, 1994); Piore and Sabel (1984).

the post-industrial column of Table 3.2 to the sector changes listed in Table 3.1—is everything you know to have changed in the last 100 years accounted for by these two tables?

While most observers agree that something has changed drastically, there is little agreement about whether this change is out there in the real world, or whether it is in here, in our understanding of ourselves and our relationships with the world we construct around us. The industrialization thesis was originally developed using the assumption that these changes are objectively real. Modernist critics of the post-industrial argument propose that the so-called changes associated with post-industrialism, although real, have been with us throughout the modern period and so, since they are nothing new, they are not nearly as transformative as proponents of the post-industrial thesis claim. Meanwhile, many symbolic-interpretivists and postmodernists think that the changes associated with the computer are not located in the objective world but rather in our experiences and reactions, which have been fundamentally altered by our use of the computer, multi-media and various forms of rapid transportation and instant communication. Where do you stand on this issue?

Stakeholder Theory

The prototypical post-industrial organizational form is the network, but other forms associated with post-industrialism include joint ventures, strategic alliances, and virtual organizations as well as the democratically inspired labor-managed firm and the post-bureaucratic organization (you will learn more about these organizational forms in Chapters 4 and 9). One important distinguishing feature shared by post-industrial organizations is boundarylessness—for them boundaries are either transparent or permeable. Boundaries between internal groups also disappear in post-industrial organizations as distinctions cease to be made between departments, hierarchical positions and even jobs. Instead employees collaborate with an ever-changing mix of others in temporary cross-functional and cross-organizational teams that emphasize learning in order to keep up with the rapid and never ending change to which these organizations are well suited. Post-industrial organizational life is thus characterized by uncertainty, contradiction and paradox; states that contrast sharply with the industrial organization's stability, routine and rationality. Such views take the organic form of organizing well beyond its initial conceptualization.

This organicism and boundarylessness extends to the organization's stakeholders whose interests become one with those of the organization. Although different interests are represented by the environment, it becomes impossible to set these off against one another or to privilege one set of interests, an argument that has been examined in depth by American ethics professor R. Edward Freeman.[31] According to Freeman, corporations operate via a social contract with society that guarantees certain rights to those who have an interest (a stake) in the organization's activities and/or outcomes. The theory is that organizations that attend to the demands of all stakeholders will out-perform organizations that ignore some of their stakeholders. Notice that stakeholder theory expands the concept of a contract from its narrow political-legal meaning to include social legitimacy. For example, consider the issue of corporate governance to which Freeman applied stakeholder theory. Legal interpretations of corporate responsibility are often restricted to the protection and enhancement of shareholder wealth. Freeman argued that although this is part of corporate responsibility, it is not to be achieved at the expense of respecting ethical considerations such as the potential of organizational activities to do harm (e.g., pollute local air or water supplies, damage a local economy with a plant closing). In its adoption of social legitimacy as a criterion for governance, stakeholder theory appears to be an application of institutional theory. Furthermore, insofar as stakeholder theory offers a justification for reining in the self-interested actions of a privileged stakeholder group (i.e., owners and executives), it resonates with key aspects of critical theory and postmodernism.

One important implication of stakeholder theory is that ethics obligates organizations to consider their impact on the wider social and physical environments from which they take their resources. Environmental sustainability and corporate social responsibility are two movements in which some companies participate in acknowledgement of these obligations. For example Interface, the US-based floor cover manufacturing company, a self-professed former 'plunderer of the Earth', underwent enormous change when it opened itself to the influence of environmental activists and became the standard bearer for environmental protection through environmentally sustainable manufacturing.[32] Danish pharmaceutical company Novo Nordisk provides another example. This company was one of the first to use triple bottom line accounting practices and to publicly report the company's annual performance in terms of environmental and social responsibility as well as using traditional measures of economic performance.

Avoiding Hegemony in Organization Theory

Some postmodernists oppose replacing modernist theories of organization with yet more theories. They have a natural distaste for theoretical abstraction based on their conviction that abstractions are used to disguise hegemonic intentions (e.g., using an efficiency rationale to disguise Western exploitation of resources around the world). As you learned in Chapter 2, postmodernists redefine modernist organization theories as grand narratives and deconstruct their rhetoric to reveal the complicity of modernist organization theorists with the capitalist hegemonic order. In Marxist theory, **hegemony** refers to the practice of interpreting the interests of the ruling class as universal.

Other postmodernists move beyond deconstruction. For them, deconstruction is merely an emancipatory move to free oneself from modernist habits of thought, such as assuming that economic rationality is universally desirable. These postmodernists imagine organizational reconstructions based on alternative, non-modernist conceptions. Sometimes alternative assumptions and values are sought among the indigenous peoples of the world whose voices have been silenced by modernist hegemonic practices. For example, the belief of native American Indians that their role in life is to protect the environment (Mother Earth) is contrasted with modern exploitative practices such as strip mining, traditional logging, hunting species to extinction, overgrazing prairies and destroying the rainforests.

A key to understanding and using the postmodern perspective lies in attending to the ways in which language is used to construct reality, and within that reality, to define identity. For instance, the distinction between the First and Third Worlds implies a hierarchy of dominance and submission that seems natural once you accept these identifying labels. Postmodernists often support the efforts of marginalized people to define their own identities with empowering labels by insisting that those in positions of dominance use the preferred language of those being labeled (e.g., developing world versus Third World). The use of such language symbolically equalizes the parties within a new discourse opened by this change in speaking habits. While such linguistic strategies do not perform miracles, there is reason to believe they unleash transformative powers. Take the U.S. cases of women and African-Americans whose powers of self-determination greatly increased along with choosing their own identity labels—woman instead of girl or lady; Black or African instead of Negro or colored.

According to some postmodernists, similar work needs to be done to reconceptualize the environment. Organization theorist Paul Shrivastava, for example, argued that modernist views of the organizational environment are denatured. He claimed that by historically giving so much voice to capitalistic concerns about markets, competitors, industry and regulation, the natural environment has been discursively reduced to 'a bundle of resources to be used by organizations'.[33] Views such as Shrivastava's suggest that the modernist rhetoric of economic necessity has silenced concern for environmental sustainability and justified possibly irreversible abuses to our environment. Conceptions of the environment that marginalize these concerns are provided by the categories and language of modernist theories of organization–environment relations. Postmodernism offers a method for deconstructing these arguments and truth claims and suggesting alternative futures such as Shrivastava's call to place the protection of nature at the center of organizational discourse and to replace the value for wealth with a value for health.

SUMMARY

In conducting environmental analysis from a modernist perspective you must first define the organization whose environment you are interested in analyzing. Then identify the links between this organization and others with which the organization interacts, or that can influence these relationships through competition, regulation, or social pressure. Use the stakeholder model given in Figure 3.2 to make sure you have not left out any important elements of the interorganizational network. Following this, consider conditions and trends in the general and international sectors of the environment. Next, assess how the relationships between the organization and its network are likely to be affected by the specific conditions and trends you have identified. In this effort you are likely to find resource dependence theory, population ecology, institutional theory and enactment theory quite helpful. Although one or two of these theories will seem most obviously useful for a particular analysis, be sure to try them all to see what insights they offer. Finally, try to imagine what biases you bring to your analysis and seek ways to counteract them.

Remind yourself that distinct points of view are represented in the theories of resource dependence and population ecology relative to institutional, enactment and ambiguity theory. These viewpoints derive from differing levels of analysis as well as different assumptions such as whether the organization is simply at the mercy of its environment (population ecology and institutional theory) or whether it has some degree of influence over the environment (resource dependence theory and enactment theory).

Ambiguity theory focuses on the conflicting and contradictory ways individuals construct their organizational contexts while resource dependence theory and enactment theory are both formulated at the organizational level of analysis and provide the perspective of individuals looking outward from the organization to its surrounding environment. Resource dependence and enactment theory can be distinguished from population ecology and institutional theory in that the latter two are formulated at the level of the environment. However, whereas population ecologists attempt to explain why there are so many different kinds of organizations, institutional theorists try to explain why so many organizations look alike. Nonetheless, both population ecology and institutional theory answer their fundamental questions by referring strictly to the influence of the environment on the organization, not the other way around.

In terms of Figure 3.4, population ecology explains the influences generated by the technical, physical, and economic sectors of the general environment, while institutional theory focuses on the influences associated with social, cultural, political and legal sectors. Enactment theory is unique in regard to its assumption that all aspects of the environment are socially constructed and thus focuses our attention on explaining how and why certain types of environmental analysis hold sway at a particular point in time. In spite of their differences, population ecology and institutional theory are similar in that organizations are depicted as relatively passive elements of an environment that shapes them and determines their outcomes. Resource dependence and enactment theory, on the other hand, represent organizations as having an active role through counteraction or outright creation of the environment.

According to Scott, environments vary in the degrees to which they are institutionalized.[34] When environments have many rules and expectations to which organizations must conform if they are to receive needed social legitimacy, institutional theory is a useful point of departure for explaining the organization's structure and outcomes. When environments are not highly institutionalized, and are influenced more by economic and technical competition, the population ecology perspective is a better starting point.

It is important to consider both population ecology and institutional views in your environmental analyses. The same goes for the inclusion of resource dependence and enactment theory. Even though one theory may seem to fit an organization better than the others, it is good practice to look at the situation through the different lenses provided by these different theories of organization–environment relations. Only after trying the different theories will you be in a position to evaluate their usefulness to your analysis. Try to be open to any surprises the juxtaposition of different perspectives offers you. The qualitative methods preferred by symbolic-interpretivists emphasize that valuable insight often emerges when your data surprise you.

Theoretical categories are not cast in stone, they are ways to think—different categories stimulate different thoughts. Postmodernists encourage you not to be rigid in your use of categories. When new categories are first encountered nearly everyone feels some anxiety about putting examples in the wrong box, and there is often a sense of satisfaction that comes when a box is filled. However, in organization theory it is generally the case that a given example will fit more than one category, and it is usually also true that shifting examples from one category to another brings new insight. This shifting around of examples and categories makes some students uncomfortable. What frustrates them is not organization theory, as they generally claim, but their desire to pin everything down. Everything cannot be pinned down where organizations are concerned and this is reflected in the ambiguity of the concepts of organization theory and perhaps in your discomfort in using them. To make effective use of organization theory, you need to learn to accept some ambiguity in your concepts and to cultivate a certain amount of equivocality. This is where postmodern organization theory comes in handy. Postmodernism introduces healthy skepticism about categories and encourages their continual deconstruction. Always ask: what assumptions lie behind these categories and whose voices are silenced by a particular construction of reality? My message is not to stop categorizing or making distinctions—these are necessary for thought and action. The message I encourage you to take from postmodernism is to think, talk and act in full consciousness or, in other words, be self-reflexive.

KEY TERMS

organizational boundary
buffering
boundary spanning
stakeholders
interorganizational network
general environment
  social, cultural, legal, political, economic,
    technology and physical sectors
international environment
globalization
machine metaphor and mechanistic
  organizations
organic metaphor and organic organizations
uncertainty
  complexity
  rate of change
  the information perspective on uncertainty
  law of requisite variety
  isomorphism
resource dependence theory
  power/dependence

criticality
scarcity
population ecology theory
  ecological niche
  population
  variation
  selection
  retention
institutional theory
  institutionalization
  coercive
  normative
  mimetic
  social legitimacy
the enacted environment
  equivocality
  ambiguity
post-industrialism
stakeholder theory
hegemony

ENDNOTES

1. Scott (1992: 180–225).

2. Freeman and Reed (1983).

3. This formulation can be traced to Dill (1958), Evan (1966), and Thompson (1967).

4. Porter (1985).

5. See Dru (1996) on the power of local advertising to inspire global sales efforts.

6. Prahalad (2005).

7. Steger (2003).

8. Burns and Stalker (1961).

9. Duncan (1972).

10. Galbraith (1973), Aldrich and Mindlin (1978).

11. Hawley (1950) is often cited by population ecologists as a source of inspiration. See Aldrich (1979) for an early review and Weick (1979 [1969]) for a symbolic-interpretive application of these ideas in organizational theory.

12. Aldrich and Pfeffer (1976).

13. Hannan and Freeman (1977), Caroll (1984), Singh (1990).

14. DiMaggio and Powell (1983: 150).

15. Scott (1992: 117).

16. DiMaggio and Powell (1983), Powell and DiMaggio (1991).

17. Selznick (1957).

18. Scott (1987).

19. Zucker (1983, 1987, 1988), Powell and DiMaggio (1991).

20. Feldman and March (1981).

21. Meyer and Rowan (1977).

22. Baron (2003).

23. Duncan (1972).

24. March and Olsen (1976: 77).

25. Eisenberg (1984: 230).

26. Meyerson (1991).

27. Daft and Weick (1984).

28. Schwartz (1991).

29. Lyotard (1979), Bell (1973), Harvey (1990).

30. Burns (1962).

31. Freeman (1984), Freeman and Reed (1983).

32. Amodeo (2005).

33. Shrivastava (1995: 125); see also Boje and Dennehy (1993).

34. Scott (1992).

REFERENCES

Aldrich, Howard E. (1979). *Organizations and environments*. Englewood Cliffs, NJ: Prentice-Hall.

—— and Mindlin, Sergio (1978). Uncertainty and dependence: Two perspectives on environment. In Lucien Karpik (ed.), *Organization and environment: Theory, issues and reality*. London: Sage, 149–70.

—— and Pfeffer, Jeffrey (1976). Environments of organizations. In A. Inkeles, J. Coleman, and N. Smelser (eds.), *Annual review of sociology*, Vol. 2. Palo Alto, Calif.: Annual Reviews, 79–105.

Amodeo, Romona Ann (2005). 'Becoming sustainable': Identity dynamics within transformational culture change at Interface. Doctoral Dissertation, Benedictine.

Baron, David (2003). Face-off. *Stanford Business*, August.

Bell, Daniel (1973). *The coming of post-industrial society*. New York: Basic Books.

Boje, David, and Dennehy, Robert (1993). *Managing in the postmodern world: America's revolution against exploitation*. Dubugue, Ia.: Kendall Hunt.

Burns, Tom (1962). The sociology of industry. In A. T. Walford, M. Argyle, D. V. Glass, and J. J. Morris (eds.), *Society: Problems and methods of study*. London: Routledge, Kegan and Paul.

—— and Stalker, George M. (1961). *The management of innovation*. London: Tavistock.

Caroll, Glenn R. (1984). Organizational ecology. *Annual Review of Sociology*, 10: 71–93.

Clegg, Stewart (1990). *Modern organizations: Organization studies in the postmodern world*. London: Sage.

Daft, Richard, and Weick, Karl (1984). Toward a model of organizations as interpretation systems. *Academy of Management Review*, 9: 284–95.

Dill, William R. (1958). Environments as an influence on managerial autonomy. *Administrative Science Quarterly*, 2: 409–43.

DiMaggio, Paul J., and Powell, W. W. (1983). The iron cage revisited: Institutional isomorphism and collective rationality in organizational fields. *American Sociological Review*, 48: 147–60.

Dru, Jean-Marie (1996). *Disruption: Overturning conventions and shaking up the marketplace*. New York: John Wiley.

Duncan, Robert B. (1972). Characteristics of organizational environments and perceived environmental uncertainty. *Administrative Science Quarterly*, 17: 313–27.

Eisenberg, Eric (1984). Ambiguity as strategy in organizational communication. *Communication Monograph*, 51: 237–42.

Evan, William (1966). The organization set: Toward a theory of interorganizational relations. In D. Thompson (ed.), *Approaches to organizational design*. Pittsburgh: University of Pittsburgh Press, 175–90.

Feldman, Martha S., and March, James G. (1981). Information in organizations as signal and symbol. *Administrative Science Quarterly*, 26: 171–86.

Freeman, R. Edward (1984). *Strategic management: A stakeholder approach*. Boston: Pittman.

—— and Reed, D. (1983). Stockholders and stakeholders: A new perspective on corporate governance. *California Management Review*, 25/3: 88–106.

Galbraith, Jay (1973). *Designing complex organizations*. Reading, Mass.: Addison-Wesley.

Hannan, Michael T., and Freeman, John H. (1977). The population ecology of organizations. *American Journal of Sociology*, 82: 929–64.

Harvey, David (1990). *The condition of postmodernity*. Cambridge, Mass.: Blackwell.

Hawley, Amos (1950). *Human ecology*. New York: Ronald Press.

Heydebrand, Wolf (1977). Organizational contradictions in public bureaucracies: Toward a Marxian theory of organizations. *Sociological Quarterly*, 18 (Winter): 83–107.

Kumar, Krishan (1995). *From post-industrial to post-modern society: New theories of the contemporary world*. Oxford: Blackwell.

Lash, Scott, and Urry, John (1987). *The end of organized capitalism*. Cambridge: Polity Press.

—— —— (1994). *Economies of signs and space*. London: Sage.

Lyotard, Jean-François (1979). *The postmodern condition: A report on knowledge*. Minneapolis: University of Minnesota Press.

March, James G. (1978). Bounded rationality, ambiguity, and the engineering of choice. *Bell Journal of Economics*, 9: 587–608.

—— and Olsen, Johan P. (1976). *Ambiguity and choice in organizations*. Bergen: Universitetsforlaget.

Meyer, John W., and Rowan, Brian (1977). Institutionalized organizations: Formal structure as myth and ceremony. *American Journal of Sociology*, 83: 340–63.

Meyerson, Debra (1991). 'Normal' ambiguity? In P. Frost et al. (eds.), *Reframing organizational culture*, 131–44. Newbury Park, Calif.: Sage.

Pfeffer, Jeffrey, and Salancik, Gerald R. (1978). *The external control of organizations: A resource dependence perspective*. New York: Harper & Row.

Piore, Michael, and Sabel, Charles (1984). *The second industrial divide*. New York: Basic Books.

Porter, Michael (1985). *Competitive advantage: Creating and sustaining superior performance*. New York: Free Press.

Powell, Walter W., and DiMaggio, Paul J. (1991) (eds.). *The new institutionalism in organizational analysis*. Chicago: University of Chicago Press.

Prahalad, C. K. (2005). *The fortune at the bottom of the pyramid: Eradicating poverty through profits*. Upper Saddle River, NJ: Wharton School Publishing (Pearson Education).

Schwartz, Peter (1991). *The art of the long view*. New York: Currency Doubleday.

Scott, W. Richard (1987). The adolescence of institutional theory. *Administrative Science Quarterly*, 32: 493–511.

—— (1992). *Organizations: Rational, natural, and open systems* (3rd ed.). Englewood Cliffs, NJ: Prentice-Hall.

Selznick, Philip (1957). *Leadership in administration*. New York: Harper & Row.

Shrivastava, Paul (1995). Ecocentric management for a risk society. *Academy of Management Review*, 20: 118–37.

Singh, Jitendra V. (1990) (ed.). *Organizational evolution: New directions*. Beverly Hills, Calif.: Sage.

Steger, Manfred B. (2003). *Globalization: A very short introduction*. Oxford: Oxford University Press.

Thompson, James D. (1967). *Organizations in action*. New York: McGraw-Hill.

Weick, Karl E. (1979 [1969]). *The social psychology of organizing*. Reading, Mass.: Addison-Wesley.

Zucker, Lynn G. (1983). Organizations as institutions. In S. B. Bacharach (ed.), *Research in the sociology of organizations*. Greenwich, Conn.: JAI Press, ii. 1–47.

—— (1987). Institutional theories of organization. In W. R. Scott (ed.), *Annual review of sociology*, 13: 443–64.

—— (1988) (ed.). *Institutional patterns and organizations: Culture and environment*. Cambridge, Mass.: Ballinger.

FURTHER READING

Donaldson, T., and Preston, L. E. (1995). The stakeholder theory of the corporation: Concepts, evidence, and implications. *Academy of Management Review*, 20/1: 65–91.

Hannan, Michael T., and Freeman, John H. (1989). *Organizational ecology*. Cambridge, Mass.: Harvard University.

Karpik, Lucien (1978) (ed.). *Organization and environment: Theory, issues and reality*. London: Sage.

Lawrence, Paul R., and Lorsch, Jay W. (1967). *Organization and environment: Managing differentiation and integration*. Cambridge, Mass.: Harvard University Press.

Meyer, John W., and Scott, W. Richard (1992). *Organizational environments: Ritual and rationality*. Beverly Hills, Calif.: Sage.

Oliver, Christine (1991). Strategic responses to institutional processes. *Academy of Management Review*, 16: 145–79.

4

Organizational Social Structure

Organization theorists often claim that organizations arise from activities that individuals cannot perform by themselves or that cannot be performed as efficiently and effectively alone as they can be with the organized effort of a group. Adam Smith's pin manufacturing example from Chapter 2 illustrates the latter point, while NASA illustrates the former in that a single individual acting alone would never have been capable of human space flight or putting a man on the moon. NASA's extraordinary achievements in space exploration were accomplished through the organized efforts, not only of scientists, engineers and astronauts, but also technicians, production workers, maintenance workers, clerical employees and managers, not to mention equally important organized efforts within the scientific community, the defense industry and the United States government. NASA also illustrates how failures of organizing can destroy lives and careers and threaten an organization's survival. All these things happened when NASA lost two space shuttles and their crews in horrific explosions.

In this chapter you will learn about the theoretical concept with the longest association to organizing—organizational social structure. The term structure refers to the relationships among the parts of an organized whole. As such, this concept can be applied to almost anything. For example, a building relies upon a structure of relationships between its foundation, frame, roof and walls. Relationships between bones, organs, blood and tissue form the structure of a human body. Organization theorists are particularly interested in two types of structure—physical and social. Physical structure refers to the spatial (and temporal) relationships between physical elements of an organization such as its buildings and their geographical locations. In organization theory, social structure refers to relationships among people who assume the roles of the organization and to the organizational groups or units to which they belong (e.g., departments, divisions). Of course spatial and social aspects of organizations are not completely separate; they overlap in the same sense that people have both physical bodies and social identities. In this chapter we discuss organizational social structures; the physical structure of organizations will be the subject of Chapter 7.

This chapter begins with the elements and dimensions of organizational social structure (sometimes simply called organizational structure) that were defined during the prehistory of organization theory by the scholars you met in Chapter 2. The assumptions these scholars used influenced the way organizational structures were first studied by modernists. One of these assumptions was that social structure is an objective entity with identifiable and measurable characteristics. Another was that an organization's social structure is stable unless management decrees a change. Thus, at the inception of modernist organization theory, most theorists unquestioningly accepted social structure as a fact of organizational life and assumed it to be a significant determinate of both human behavior and organizational performance. Because of this influence, modernists believed social structure could be used as a tool to control organizational outcomes. As organization theory developed, first one and then the other of the assumptions underpinning this view was upended resulting in our having a more sophisticated understanding of organizational social structure today.

The first challenge to the initial assumptions about organizing came when modernists introduced ideas about how organizational structures change over the lifecycle of an organ-ization. Drawing on open systems and contingency approaches, these theorists acknow-ledged change and presented models of the best way to adapt organizational structures to environmental demands as well as to available technology and preferred strategy. Once freed from the assumption of stability, organization theorists began to look at social structure as a process rather than an entity. Then, along with the symbolic-interpretive perspective came subjective interpretations of social structure that produced structuration theory and models of organizations as communities of meaning. Ethnographic studies of emergent organizing practices such as routines and improvisation have recently contributed further sophistica-tion to understanding the dynamics of social structuring. Meanwhile, critical theorists and postmodernists, believing social structure equates to the domination and marginalization of some groups by others, either attempt to replace structures of domination with democratic structural forms, or seek ways to expose and resist their inherent inequalities.

Origins of the Social Structure Concept

As was explained in Chapter 2, ideas developed by a group of sociologists and classical management scholars combined to form the field of organization theory. These early organ-ization theorists shared a preference for structural definitions of organizing and, being for the most part prescriptive, they emphasized finding the best, most practical, ways of achieving an organization's stated purpose or goal through the structural arrange-ment of people, positions and work units. The trouble was, there was no agreement on how to best define organizational structure. This section of the chapter begins with Weber's definition, part of his theory of **bureaucracy**. Some of the characteristics of orga-nizational social structure defined by classical management scholars will be presented next, followed by a list of commonly used dimensions of social structure that trace to this prehistory of organization theory.

Weber's Ideal Bureaucracy

Max Weber published his theory of organizational structure in the early 1900s, though his work was not translated into English until the mid-1940s. In numerous essays, Weber

Table 4.1 Characteristics of Weber's ideal bureaucracy

- A fixed division of labor
- A clearly defined hierarchy of offices, each with its own sphere of competence
- Candidates for offices are selected on the basis of technical qualifications and are appointed rather than elected
- Officials are remunerated by fixed salaries paid in money
- The office is the primary occupation of the office holder and constitutes a career
- Promotion is granted according to seniority or achievement and is dependent upon the judgment of superiors
- Official work is to be separated from ownership of the means of administration
- A set of general rules governing the performance of offices; strict discipline and control in the conduct of the office is expected

Source: Parsons (1947), Scott (1992).

offered an ideal model of organizations as bureaucracies, whose main characteristics are summarized in Table 4.1.[1]

Weber's use of the term ideal might not be what you expect; he used it in the sense of a pure idea—something that can only be known through the imagination—rather than a perfect or desirable state. In his original discussion of ideal types, he made reference to similar notions in other academic disciplines, such as ideal gases in physics, or ideal competition in economics. Note that ideal does not equate with goodness or virtue. With Weber's usage there can also be ideal crimes or ideal diseases. Ideals only provide a basis for theorizing because they are abstract; they cannot be expected to exist in the world around us. The ideal bureaucracy that Weber imagined was a means for turning employees of average ability into rational decision makers serving their clients and constituencies with impartiality and efficiency. Conceptualized in this way, the bureaucratic form promised reliable decision making, merit-based selection and promotion and the impersonal and, therefore, fair application of rules. Organization theorists have defined three components of organizational social structure on the basis of Weber's theory: the division of labor, the hierarchy of authority and formalized rules and procedures.

Division of Labor

Division of labor defines the distribution of responsibilities and assignment of work tasks within an organization. When labor is properly divided the combination of work tasks produces the desired output of the organization. Smith's description of the division of labor in a pin manufacturing firm (see Chapter 2) provided a simple example of how the division of labor organizes work. You can think of other examples ranging from the manufacture of automobiles, computers or airplanes, to the provision of services such as banking, education and insurance. In all of these examples the work of the organization is divided among employees, each of whom performs only a piece of the whole.

The ways that jobs are grouped into organizational units such as departments (e.g., purchasing, production, marketing) or divisions (e.g., consumer products, international sales) is also part of the division of labor. **Departmentation** has to do with grouping similar or closely related activities together into organizational subunits. Because administrators or managers typically oversee the subunits created by departmentation, this concept links the division of labor to the hierarchy of authority, the second Weberian component of organizational social structure.

Hierarchy of Authority

Hierarchy refers to the distribution of authority in an organization. Some people believe that hierarchy is a fundamental aspect of life; their evidence is that feeding order and activities like sexual reproduction are organized hierarchically throughout much of the animal kingdom. They regard organizational hierarchies as extensions of these natural tendencies. Regardless of whether or not you think organizational hierarchies are natural, you will probably recognize hierarchy as a common feature of most organizations. According to Weber, a high position in the hierarchy confers legal authority, consisting of the right to make decisions, give direction, and reward and punish others. Authority is strictly a matter of position, so when individuals leave their positions (e.g., through promotion, retirement or replacement), their authority remains behind to be taken up by the next job incumbent.

Hierarchy also defines formal reporting relationships that map the vertical communication channels in an organization—downward (directing subordinates) and upward (reporting to management). When each position in an organization is made subordinate to some other position, authority and vertical communication combine to permit the most highly placed individuals to gather information from, and to direct and control the performance of, all individuals throughout the organization. This is what Fayol referred to as the scalar principle (see Chapter 2).

In the past, many managers believed that every member of the organization should report to only one person so that each member has one clear path through the hierarchy stretching from themselves to their boss, to their boss's boss, and all the way to the top person in the organization. Fayol called this the unity-of-command principle. Today, dual reporting relationships are more acceptable. Likewise, lateral (i.e., nonhierarchical or network) connections are recognized for the increasingly important part they play in integrating an organization's diverse activities and promoting flexibility of responses to environmental pressures.

Formalized Rules and Procedures

Formalization involves the extent to which explicit rules, regulations, policies and procedures govern organizational activities. Indicators of formalization in an organization include: written policies, handbooks, job descriptions, operations manuals, organization charts, management systems such as Management by Objectives (MBO), and technical systems such as PERT (program evaluation review techniques). Formal rules, procedures, position descriptions and job classifications specify how decisions should be made and work performed.

Government organizations are often associated with both bureaucracy and high levels of formalization. For example, in 2003 the State of California had 4,500 formal written job classifications (groupings of jobs defined by similar responsibilities and training) for a total number of 230,228 active employees.[2] These job classifications defined the division of labor, specified the type of position appropriate to each level in the hierarchy and provided the basis for making hiring decisions, determining pay levels and coordinating work throughout the state.

Formalization tends to reduce the amount of discretion employees have in performing their work tasks while increasing the sense of control managers maintain over their employees. Along with strict observance of positional authority, formalization contributes to the feeling of impersonality often associated with bureaucratic organizations. Studies have shown that formalization tends to discourage innovation and leads to reduced communication levels.[3] This can be contrasted with a lack of formalization, sometimes referred to as informality, that denotes the flexibility and spontaneity of non-bureaucratic or post-bureaucratic organizations. However, to really appreciate the concept of bureaucracy it is important to recognize the difference between Weber's ideal bureaucracy and the organizational reality with which you are likely to be familiar.

For Weber, bureaucracy was not the ponderous frustrating bastion of mediocre service that many people associate with this concept today, but in its ideal form is a rationalized moral alternative to the common practice of nepotism and other abuses of power that were rampant in the feudal preindustrial world from which the modern industrial organization emerged. Since Weber's time we have learned much about the negative face of bureaucracy, particularly its tendency to over-rationalize decision making to the point of turning people into unfeeling and unthinking automatons, a tendency satirized in Joseph Heller's novel *Catch 22* and Terry Gilliam's film *Brazil*, both of which depicted the nonsensical outcomes of overreliance on bureaucratic formalities. Weber himself recognized the potential for trouble, warning that bureaucracy could easily become an iron cage. Nonetheless, when organizations are large and operate routine technologies in fairly stable environments, bureaucracy apparently offers benefits enough for many societies to continue to create and maintain numerous bureaucracies in spite of distaste for the working conditions they foster and disappointment in the level of service they provide. Today bureaucratic features are characteristic of most governments, nearly every university, the Catholic Church, and large business organizations such as McDonalds, Telefónica, and Royal Dutch Shell.

Dimensions of Organizational Social Structures

Inspired by the same idealism that infused Weber's theory of bureaucracy, the scholars of classical management theory sought laws of organizing from which they could derive practical advice regarding how to best organize employees to perform the work of the organization. The classical management scholars had considerable practical experience as executives and consultants to industry, and they drew on their experiences to offer advice to others who were in similar positions. See Table 4.2 for a sample of the numerous dimensions of organizational social structure that competed for the attention of early modernist

Table 4.2 Commonly used dimensions of organizational social structure

Dimension	Measure
Size	Number of employees in the organization

Administrative component
  Line function
  Staff function
	Percentage of total number of employees that have administrative responsibilities
	Departments involved directly in the production of organizational outputs (e.g., production departments, medical and nursing staff)
	Departments that advise and support line functions such as strategic planning, finance, accounting, human resources

Differentiation
  Vertical
  Horizontal
	The number of levels in the hierarchy
	The division of labor, which involves:
	    number of departments in the organization
	    span of control or number of employees reporting to a manager

Integration	The coordination of activities through accountability, rules and procedures, liaison roles, cross-functional teams or direct contact
Centralization	Extent to which authority to make decisions concentrates at the top levels of the organization; in a decentralized organization, decision making devolves to all levels in the hierarchy
Standardization	The extent to which standard procedures govern the operations and activities of the organization as opposed to the use of individual judgment and initiative in dealing with events as they arise
Formalization	Extent to which an organization uses written (i.e., formal) job descriptions, rules, procedures and communications, as opposed to communication and relationships based on informal, face-to-face interaction
Specialization	Extent to which the work of the organization is divided into narrowly defined tasks assigned to specific employees and work units

organization theorists who used them to develop empirical measures for their statistical studies.

The measures of organizational social structure developed by early modernist organization theorists added specificity to Weber's bureaucratically defined characteristics of division of labor, hierarchy of authority and formal rules and procedures and rendered them amenable to statistical analysis and empirical study. For example, consider the relationship between the division of labor and the dimensions associated with one of its aspects: differentiation. The division of labor between different departments is known as **horizontal differentiation**, the division of authority into different hierarchical levels is known as **vertical differentiation**. You can measure horizontal differentiation by counting the number of units or departments within the organization, and vertical

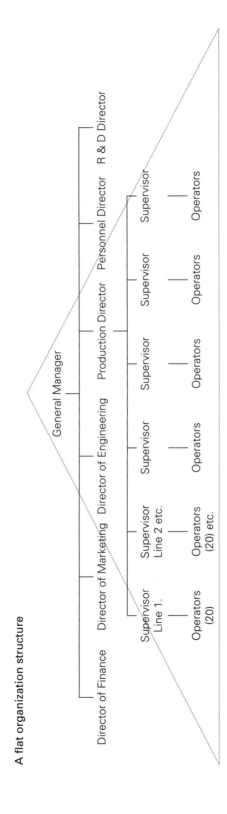

A flat organization structure

Figure 4.1 A comparison of flat and tall organization structures

These organization charts give you a quick impression of what is meant by steep or tall hierarchies as opposed to flat or less hierarchical organizations.

A tall organization structure

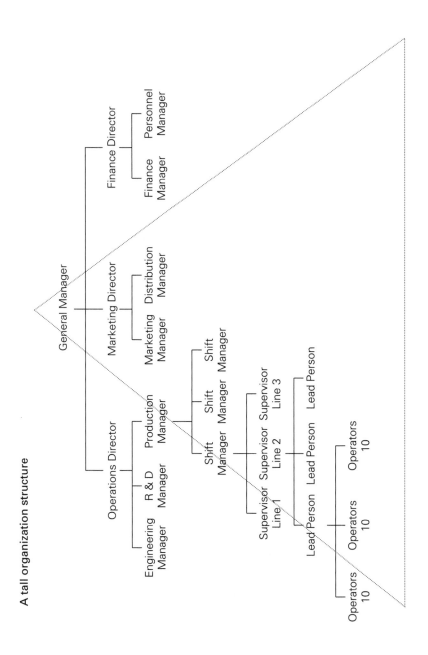

Figure 4.1 *(Continued)*

differentiation by counting the number of hierarchical levels. You can also look at the shape of an organization chart. An organization with a **flat organizational structure** has many departments (a high degree of horizontal differentiation) and few hierarchical levels (low vertical differentiation). A **tall** organizational structure has fewer departments (low horizontal differentiation) and many hierarchical levels (high vertical differentiation). Figure 4.1 gives a visual illustration of the contrast between flat and tall organization structures and shows two simple organization charts (more will be said about organization charts in Chapter 9).

Modernist Theories of Organizational Social Structure

In the late 1950s and throughout the 1960s, early modernist organization theorists were eager to measure organizational social structure using the dimensions defined by Weber and the classical management scholars in the hope of finding the best way of organizing. They were looking for a means to predict high levels of organizational performance and thought that by examining statistical relationships between dimensions of structure and performance they could arrive at a formula for success. They focused on identifying the organizational principles and structural elements that lead to optimal organizational performance in the belief that, once basic laws governing these relationships were discovered, the perfect organization could be designed.

Empirical research revealed, however, that what works for one organization may or may not work for others. This result led to the development of contingency theory and the organizational design school (see Chapter 9). Contingency theorists claim that the dimensions of organizational structure relate to each other differently depending upon the environment the organization faces and on other aspects of the organization such as its technology, size and strategy. By analyzing relationships between structural dimensions and these other aspects, contingency theorists believe they can offer recipes for the best organizational structure.

This section of the chapter will first present some of the main contributors to structural contingency theory followed by material relating to more recent contributions. These include structural typologies and taxonomies and dynamic models of structural growth and change. The section concludes with a theory that plays organizational structure against the micro notion of agency and thereby examines the boundary between organizations and the people whose actions give rise to them. This theory, called structuration, also crosses the boundary between modernist and symbolic-interpretive foundational assumptions by considering not only the objective properties that shape organizations, but their interpretive characteristics as well.

Structural Contingency Theory

Contingency theorists have long been focused on discovering what constellations of organizational factors contribute to organizational survival and success. Many organizational contingencies have been proposed and validated by empirical study such that, in his 1996 review of contingency theory, Australian organization theorist Lex Donaldson could claim that:

> There are several contingency factors: strategy, size, task uncertainty and technology. These are characteristics of the organization. However, these organizational characteristics in turn reflect the influence of the environment in which the organization is located. Thus, in order to be effective, the organization needs to fit its structure to the contingency factors of the organization and thus to the environment. Hence the organization is seen as adapting to its environment.[4]

In their 1961 book *The Management of Innovation*, British organization theorists Tom Burns and George M. Stalker first suggested that effective organizational design is based on fitting the internal organizational structure to the demands of the environment. In 1967 Paul Lawrence and Jay Lorsch followed with their book *Organization and Environment: Managing Differentiation and Integration*, in which they examined how contingencies created by the environment influenced an organization's patterns of differentiation and integration. At roughly the same time, a group of researchers from Aston University in the United Kingdom conducted research showing that an organization's social structure is contingent on its size.[5] Taken together these empirical studies shaped the approach that became contingency theory and so will be described in some detail below to give you the flavor of this influential organization theory.

Mechanistic and Organic Management Systems

Burns and Stalker studied a number of organizations in the electronics and R & D industries, and identified two management systems—mechanistic and organic—that appear to be at opposite ends of a continuum defined by the stability–instability of the environment in which they operate (see Table 4.3). According to Burns and Stalker, **mechanistic organizations** operate like machines in that they consist of specialized parts (the different tasks and jobs that employees do) that can be engineered into a high-performance system. Like other living things, **organic organizations** need to adapt to their ever-changing circumstances, therefore they have less specialization and formalization and are less hierarchical than mechanistic organizations; they also engage in considerably more lateral communication and coordination.

You can discover the difference between mechanistic and organic forms of organizing for yourself by comparing some common organizations; most college libraries, post offices and other government organizations, and telephone companies have the characteristics of mechanistic organizations while hospital emergency rooms, research laboratories and outings with your friends tend to be organic. Of course, organizations always combine mechanistic and organic characteristics. For example, most administrative work in universities is done in a mechanistic way, while research activities are organic. Actually, both of these types of work activity (along with most others) combine elements of mechanistic and organic forms of organizing, as does university teaching. Teaching activities are partly

Table 4.3 Comparing mechanistic and organic organizations

Mechanistic Structures *(predictability, accountability)*	Organic Structures *(flexibility, adaptability, innovation)*
High horizontal and vertical *differentiation*—a hierarchical structure of authority and control.	High/complex horizontal and vertical *integration*—a network of authority and control based on knowledge of the task.
High formalization—the definition of roles, responsibilities, instructions and job methods is stable.	Low formalization—tasks and responsibilities are redefined depending on the situation.
Centralization—decisions made at the top of the hierarchy.	Decentralization—decisions made by those with knowledge.
Standardization through written rules, procedures, SOPs.	Mutual adjustment and redefinition of tasks and methods through joint problem-solving and interaction.
Close supervision with authority and prestige based on position.	Personal expertise and creativity without supervision. Prestige attached to expertise.
Vertical (superior–subordinate) communication in the form of instructions.	Frequent lateral communication, often in the form of consultation between people from different departments.

mechanistic (e.g., testing knowledge, reporting grades) and partly organic (e.g., designing curricula, facilitating group learning experiences) and within each of these tasks you will discover both mechanistic and organic components as well. Nonetheless, the overall distinction remains useful as a way to characterize the central tendencies of different forms of organizing that appear in two extreme types of environments that lie on opposite ends of the dimension of environmental stability–change.

Burns and Stalker noticed that in stable environments, mechanistic organizations outperformed organic organizations, while in unstable environments organic organizations tended to be more successful. Innovation was the key contingency they used to explain their finding—in rapidly changing environments, organizations need to innovate to survive, and to do so they need teams of knowledgeable employees who can work together to anticipate and respond quickly to environmental change.

The explanation Burns and Stalker offered for their finding is as follows: innovation tends to be limited in mechanistic forms of organization where high levels of hierarchical control, clearly defined roles and tasks, and centralized decision making impede flexibility and creativity. Formalization interferes with responsiveness because change requires rewriting policies and rules and disseminating the revisions to supervisors who must then implement the new rules and ensure that others comply with them. Whenever innovation is a primary consideration in work, mechanistic structures hinder performance. Organic forms, characterized as informal, decentralized and requiring a high degree of coordination across departments, are more likely to be innovative and to grant greater discretion to employees performing tasks since they are not bound by strict rules and procedures, and decision making is pushed to lower levels of the hierarchy. This means that employees hired for their knowledge and expertise have the discretion to use their skills and training, and the flexibility to experiment and solve problems as they arise. In organic forms, so the theory goes, systems and people are more proactive and adaptable to changing circumstances.

Differentiation and Integration

Like Burns and Stalker, Lawrence and Lorsch believed that effective organizational performance is determined by the fit between an organization's social structure and its environment. In particular, the most successful organizations are those where the degree of differentiation and the means of integration match the demands of the environment. In their initial study of six organizations in the plastics industry (a complex and unstable environment), they focused on internal structure and found that organizational subunits were confronted with different degrees of uncertainty that caused each department (sales, production, applied research and fundamental research) to vary in terms of its degree of differentiation. Using four dimensions of **differentiation**—the degree of formality, emphasis given to task vs. relationships, orientation to time and goal orientation—they found that:

- departments operating in more stable environments (production) were more formalized, hierarchical, and carried out more frequent performance reviews than those facing environmental uncertainty (R & D); sales and applied research departments fell in between these two extremes.

- departments with greater task uncertainty (sales) were more relationship-oriented, while departments facing less task uncertainty (production) were more task-oriented.

- the time orientation of departments (short or long term) varied: sales and production had a short-term orientation and required rapid feedback on results, while R & D had a long-term orientation (several years depending on the length of projects).

- finally, departments differed in terms of goal orientation, with sales being concerned with customer issues and production with cost and process efficiency.

You may be able to relate Lawrence and Lorsch's findings to departments in your own organization. Differentiation occurs as sales departments focus on customer satisfaction and building long-term relationships with customers. They are often concerned with meeting individual customer requests for a modified product and driving down average response times. Production departments are more task-oriented, with daily and weekly output goals. They focus on a more efficient use of people and equipment by producing large amounts of a standardized product and minimizing the downtime required to retool equipment for individual customer orders. In this way, production departments increase output quantity and reduce defect rates and production process conversion times. You can see how these different orientations might lead to conflict between departments, especially when performance measures are tied to substantial rewards.

The more complex the organization, both in terms of horizontal and vertical differentiation, the greater the strain on communication and the greater the need for coordination or integration.[6] Lawrence and Lorsch defined **integration** as the collaboration required to achieve unity of effort (i.e., getting everyone to pull in the same direction). The most common integration mechanism is hierarchy—creating formal reporting relationships to managers whose task it is to coordinate activities and resolve problems. However, adding levels to the hierarchy creates vertical differentiation that requires even more integration. Although the hierarchy of authority makes a substantial contribution to overall coordination, hierarchy alone cannot keep up with a growing organization's endless demands for coordinated activity.

Numerous additional integrating mechanisms have been devised to complement the hierarchy of authority: rules, procedures and schedules being the most common examples, especially in bureaucracies. Schedules specify the period of time in which activities are to be accomplished. They can also be used to communicate task assignments. When activities conducted by different persons must occur in a particular order, such as in the construction of a building or the work done on an assembly line, schedules are a key element in coordination. Other means of integration include: liaison roles, committees, task forces, cross-functional teams, and direct communication between departments. For example, an organization might have a technical sales engineer in a liaison role to talk with the customer, coordinate with purchasing, production planning, production, quality control, finance, and the legal department to ensure a contract is satisfactorily completed on time. A hospital might have a cross-functional team of medical, nursing, therapy, finance and social services staff to manage an individual patient's health care program.

In the second phase of their study, Lawrence and Lorsch examined the relationship between environmental stability and internal structure. They selected two organizations from the packaged food industry (a relatively diverse and unstable environment) and two from the container industry (a stable environment) as comparisons to the firms from the plastics industry (unstable). They concluded that high performing organizations had the appropriate degree of differentiation for their environments and used forms of integration consistent with the coordination demands of their differentiated activities. In particular they found that:

- unstable environments required a higher degree of differentiation than stable environments in order to meet varying and complex demands;

- both stable and unstable environments required a high degree of integration, but the means of integration differed: in stable environments, hierarchy and centralized coordination was more appropriate, in unstable environments there is a need to push decision making to lower levels in the hierarchy so that problems can be dealt with through direct communication with those possessing relevant knowledge.

Lawrence and Lorsch concluded that appropriate levels of differentiation and methods of integration vary depending on the particular organization and its environment. Their data showed that goodness of fit correlated with higher levels of organizational performance in the sample of businesses they studied.

Size, Specialization and Centralization

Researchers from Aston University in the United Kingdom developed quantitative measures of six dimensions of organizational social structure: the degree of specialization, standardization, formalization, centralization, configuration and flexibility.[7] They gathered comparative data from 52 organizations on each of these dimensions. On the measure of the degree of **centralization**, the researchers assessed the level at which 37 common decisions were made in the organizations being measured. The measurement instrument asked which management or administrative level had the authority to make each decision, and the data for all 37 decisions were averaged for an overall centralization score. Analysis of this data suggested that **size** can be a factor affecting structure: the larger the organization, the greater the degree of specialization and centralization. In a centralized organization, final choices are made almost exclusively at high levels and unquestioning acceptance of top-level decisions is expected. As a result, there tends to be a minimum of participation from lower level members. In decentralized organizations, decisions are made by the individuals who are closest to the situation. Decentralized organizations rely on the participation of many members of the organization in decision-making processes.

Subsequent studies revealed a difficulty with measuring centralization that results from the different kinds of decisions organizations make. For example, an organization may be highly decentralized with respect to work-related decisions, but highly centralized with respect to strategic decisions.[8] In universities, for instance, decisions about course offerings, new faculty hires and the distribution of travel funds are made in the academic departments, and so you would consider them to be decentralized decisions. Decisions about university fundraising campaigns or charting new directions for university growth and development are centralized, since these decisions are made by the university president and the board of trustees.

Studies of centralization show that the amount of communication, involvement and satisfaction tends to be higher in decentralized firms, but coordination and control are more difficult to accomplish. Centralized organizations are quicker to respond to the dictates of higher authority because of the relative efficiency of communication compared with decentralized structures. However, when centralized organizations are large, decision bottlenecks can undermine organizational performance by slowing organizational response to environmental pressures. Most studies of large organizations indicate a negative relationship between formalization and centralization, that is, you can trade off centralization for formalization because rules and procedures direct subordinates to make the same decisions their managers would make. Thus large decentralized organizations are more likely to be formalized than are large centralized organizations.[9] Such is the case with many bureaucracies.

You may think that mechanistic and bureaucratic are two words for the same thing. Experience with bureaucracies tends to confirm this belief because the image of an unfeeling machine fits with the red tape and runaround that are associated with bureaucracy. Notice, however, that there is one feature of bureaucracies that distinguishes them from mechanistic organizations—the bureaucracy is *de*centralized whereas the mechanistic organization is centralized. The trick to resolving the decentralization puzzle is to understand what it means to say that a bureaucracy is simultaneously highly formalized and decentralized. In a bureaucracy, many routine decisions are pushed to low levels of the organization, but there are strict rules and procedures that govern how those decisions are made. Thus street-level bureaucrats (police, social workers, teachers, clerks, etc.) often use their discretion, but only within set limits. Like mechanistic organizations, the bureaucracy remains highly controlled, but it does so by being decentralized in such a way that lower level bureaucrats make all the programmed decisions, which frees higher level bureaucrats to form policy and make unprogrammed decisions.

Contingency Theory Today

In his survey of the history of contingency theory, Donaldson insisted that the contingency approach is the essence of organization theory, and although others have argued that its measurement problems and seemingly endless discovery of new contingencies have rendered it too complex for practical purposes, I would argue instead that it lives on in the logic of modernist organization theory in the sense that nearly all modernists try to find predictive relationships between variables representing aspects of the organization, its environment and its performance, and all acknowledge that their theories have boundary conditions, that is, they only apply to a subset of all organizations that can be defined by their similar contingencies. Thus the primary contribution of contingency theory has been to make us aware that there are many different ways to organize successfully and to begin to enumerate the possibilities and their consequences.

Some extremely useful general statements have been made on the basis of contingency theory. For example, there are several situations in which mechanistic forms are decidedly inappropriate. Small organizations do not need formalization, since direct supervision through daily contact with the boss is cheaper and more satisfying for members of the organization than are formal rules and procedures. Nonroutine technologies and unstable environments also undermine the effectiveness of mechanistic organizations, but for different reasons. In these situations, formal rules and procedures cannot cover all the possibilities and problems that arise in the course of doing business.

Large organizations that exist in stable environments and provide standardized services or products operate most efficiently when they use mechanistic forms, but as environments change, organizations need to change also. Most people are familiar with McDonalds—the hamburger organization that operates under the sign of the Golden Arches. McDonalds has 30,000 restaurants in 119 countries, 1.6 million employees, and serves 50 million people per day. Their goal is to be the world's best quick service restaurant experience.[10] Ten years ago, McDonald's was known for its mechanistic structure and high degree of formalization—including an operations manual with over 400 pages. The result was that you could recognize McDonalds anywhere in the world and know exactly what you would be buying. Given its size and standardized products a mechanistic structure allowed McDonalds to be a highly successful organization. However, since then, increasing competition and changes in nutritional habits have led McDonalds to take a more flexible, organic approach. A recent statement on their website reads, 'Decentralization is fundamental to our business model—and to our corporate responsibility efforts. At the corporate level, we provide a global framework of common goals, policies, and guidelines rooted in our core values. Within this framework, individual geographic business units have the freedom to develop programs and performance measures appropriate to local conditions.'[11]

Types and Taxonomies

Following Weber's lead in differentiating ideal types of organizations (e.g., bureaucracies), many modernist organization theorists devoted themselves to creating typologies of organizational forms. The best known of these is probably Henry Mintzberg's structure in fives, a typology in which this Canadian organization theorist distinguished between the organizational forms shown in Table 4.4.[12] Typologies have contributed many prescriptive theories of organizational structure sometimes collectively referred to as the organizational design school (see Chapter 9 for more on organizational design).

A different approach to addressing the variety of organizational forms was offered by modernist organization theorist William McKelvey.[13] He proposed that, just as biological organisms are categorized and compared by taxonomists on the basis of their genetic makeup, so an organizational taxonomy might be created to account for different species of organizations. McKelvey's work suggests an extension of systems theory in the sense of using emerging knowledge of the human systems level (genetic theory from the field of biology) to better understand the higher level system of organization. The idea of applying genetic theory to organizations is reflected in popular calls to find organizational DNA, a metaphoric reference to the code or essence that explains the form an organization takes or predicts its behavior.

Models of Structural Change

In spite of its inclusion of organic organizational forms as responses to changing environmental conditions, contingency theory itself presents a fairly static approach to organizational structure in that the contingencies determining organizational success are assessed at specific moments in time. Other modernist models focused on how organizational social structure changes and thus complement and extend the contingency approach.

Models describing how organizational social structures change typically take one of two forms. Evolutionary models explain how an organization develops over time through a progression of static states or stages. The other type of structural change model focuses on the dynamics of change as these occur in the course of everyday organizational life. In these dynamic theories the seeming stability of social structure is undermined by discovering that numerous interactions shape and transform social structure on a more or less continuous basis. Evolutionary stage models tend to stay within the boundaries of the modernist approach, while models of the dynamics of everyday interaction move into symbolic-interpretive territory.

Two theories, one proposed by Larry Greiner and the other by Daniel Katz and Robert L. Kahn, portray different ways to think about the stages of development that organization

Table 4.4 Mintzberg's structure in fives

	Description	Appropriate for
Simple structure	Most basic structure. Power centralized in top management, with few middle managers employed. Usually small companies use this form and control is exercised personally by managers who are able to know all their workers and talk to them directly on a daily basis.	Entrepreneurial companies, companies with simple or single products. Examples: most start-ups.
Machine bureaucracy	Emphasizes standardization of production processes. Most employees are low-skilled and perform highly specialized tasks. The organization needs detailed planning and so requires administrative management. These organizations are highly efficient but not flexible.	Companies involved in mass production, or that produce simple products in stable environments. Examples: McDonalds, UPS.
Professional bureaucracy	Relies on standardized skills, rather than standardized processes. Use of professionals permits organization to give its employees discretion in performing tasks for which they have been professionally trained. Have less hierarchy than machine bureaucracies although professionals are supported by more mechanistically organized staff.	Best suited to companies operating in complex, stable environments. Examples: universities, hospitals, large consulting houses such as McKinsey and KPMG.
Divisionalized form	Relatively autonomous divisions each run their own businesses in the sense that each produces specialized products for particular markets. The divisions are overseen by executives and their corporate staff who set divisional goals, control their behavior by regulating their resources, and monitor and compare their performance using standardized financial measures (e.g., sales targets, rates of return, brand equity).	Best in complex, somewhat unstable environments because divisions can shut down or be spun off and new businesses started up more easily than with bureaucratic forms. Examples: General Electric, General Motors.
Adhocracy	A structure of interacting project teams whose task is to innovate solutions to constantly changing problems. Employs many experts who produce non-standardized products to their customers'/clients' specifications. Decision making is highly decentralized and strategy emerges from actions taken throughout the company.	Best in turbulent environments when company needs constant innovation. Examples: small consulting houses such as advertising agencies, biotechnology firms, think tanks.

Based on: Mintzberg (1981, 1983).

structures typically go through. Greiner's popular lifecycle theory depicts organizational growth as a sequence of evolutionary periods punctuated by revolutionary events, while Katz and Kahn's open systems model illustrates how social structure emerges from organizational responses to both technical and environmental pressures. Anthony Giddens's structuration theory and his conception of the duality of structure and agency will describe the dynamic play of elements that constitute organizational structure. Because Giddens' theory combines modernist and symbolic-interpretive reasoning it will make a good transition point to the next section of this chapter where you will read about how those using the symbolic-interpretive perspective think about organizational social structures.

The Organizational Lifecycle

American organization theorist Larry Greiner described organizations as if they, like humans, have a lifecycle that moves through stages of development.[14] Just as a child passes through infancy and childhood to adolescence and maturity, so, according to Greiner, an organization passes through entrepreneurial, collectivity, delegation, formalization and collaboration stages (see Figure 4.2). Greiner theorized that, in each stage of its lifecycle an organization is dominated by a different focus. Each stage ends with a crisis that threatens organizational survival and brings about a revolutionary change through which the organization passes into its next developmental stage.

In the **entrepreneurial stage**, the organization is embroiled in creating and selling its product. This phase usually takes place in a small setting in which every member of the organization is familiar with what the other members are doing. The entrepreneur can easily control most activities personally and this personal contact makes it easy for other

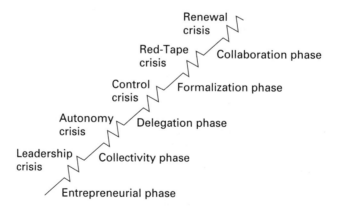

Figure 4.2 Greiner's model of organizational lifecycles

employees to sense what is expected of them and to receive direct feedback and close supervision. If successful (and remember, the majority of organizations fail at this early stage), the entrepreneurial organization will find itself in need of professional management. Entrepreneurs are usually idea people or technical experts rather than organizers, and further organizational development often necessitates bringing management skills in from outside the organization, although sometimes professional management develops from within. In rare cases the entrepreneur evolves along with the needs of the organization (e.g., Bill Gates at Microsoft, Michael Dell from Dell Computers).

It often takes a crisis to convince the entrepreneur that professional management is required, since the early successes that allowed the organization to survive and prosper will also give the entrepreneur the impression that things are fine the way they are. However, growth brings differentiation and sooner or later the organization becomes too complex for a single individual to monitor everything that is going on. This condition can be compounded by an entrepreneur's distaste for management activities. According to Greiner, the result of this early differentiation, coupled with inadequate attention to integration due to lack of managerial oversight, throws the organization into a **leadership crisis**. Successful resolution of the leadership crisis moves the organization into a new stage of development—the collectivity stage.

The introduction of the organization's first professional management usually brings the organization through the leadership crisis and provides it with centralized decision making and a renewed focus on its purpose. The primary concern of the new management is to give the organization a sense of direction and to provide integration among the differentiated groups operating within the organization. In this **collectivity stage**, concern for establishing clear goals and routines takes over the manufacturing and marketing focus of the entrepreneurial stage. In this stage the organization's complexity grows through differentiation until, once again, the organization becomes too much for the existing social structure and its management to handle. This time the crisis occurs because the decision-making process becomes overloaded—the result of too much centralization.

During the collectivity stage centralization gives the organization its sense of a clear direction because decisions are coordinated by a set of well-integrated decision makers (i.e., the new professional management). However, at some point even the most effective managers of a centralized social structure cannot keep pace with the decisions required by an ever more differentiated organization. Thus, sooner or later, centralized decision making becomes a bottleneck for action, and decisions must be pushed down the hierarchy if the organization is to continue functioning. Greiner called this the crisis of autonomy. The reason this situation produces a crisis is that most managers find it difficult to relinquish control over formerly centralized decisions. It is typical, therefore, for management to wait overlong in initiating decentralization and their hesitation is what provokes the **autonomy crisis**.

The solution to the autonomy crisis is delegation, and the next stage of the organizational lifecycle is described as the **delegation stage**. However, once delegation is initiated, usually via decentralization of decision making, the need for further integration arises. This need grows steadily until a **crisis of control** occurs. The response to loss of control is usually to create formal rules and procedures to ensure that decisions are made in the way that management would make them if they could do so themselves. This is the point at which bureaucracy appears; Greiner labeled it the formalization stage.

During the **formalization stage**, the organization continues to grow and differentiate, adding more and more formal control mechanisms in an attempt to integrate an increasingly diverse set of activities through planning, accounting and information systems, and formal review procedures. The tendency to control through bureaucratic means eventually leads to the **crisis of red tape**. The red-tape crisis is what has given bureaucracy a bad name. It is not, however, that bureaucracy is the villain, but rather that, in this situation, management overindulges and ends up with too much of a good thing. Attempts to apply formal rules and procedures in a universal and impersonal manner create an organizational environment that becomes not only ineffective, but increasingly distasteful to workers. Things will generally worsen when management's first response to the breakdown of bureaucratic controls is to implement even more bureaucracy. The problem reaches crisis proportions when employees either cannot figure out how to make the system of rules and procedures work, or when they rebel against or sabotage it.

If the organization is to emerge from the red-tape crisis, it will generally proceed to the **collaboration stage**. During this stage the organization uses teamwork as a means of re-personalizing the organization by distributing the now overdifferentiated tasks into more recognizable chunks and assigning shared responsibility for them to groups of individuals in ways that make work once again comprehensible. What was too complex for rule-making to regulate can be reorganized into smaller units managed from within by teams that are granted decentralized decision-making authority. A greater focus on trust and collaboration is often required in these circumstances.

The collaboration stage of organizational development requires a qualitative change in organizational form as well as in the integration skills and leadership styles demanded of managers. Instead of the former emphasis on controlling the organization, top management must shift its concern to constantly regenerating motivations to work and to stay organized. However, if at some point the management fails to provide regeneration, the organization will undergo a **crisis of renewal** marked by what in humans would be described as lethargy. The primary symptom of this crisis is employees and managers who suffer from burnout and other forms of psychological fatigue due to the strains associated with temporary assignments, dual authority, and continuous experimentation. According to Greiner, the crisis of renewal will either lead to a new form of organization or to organizational **decline** and eventual death.

Greiner used his theory to emphasize the point that every stage of an organization's development contains the seeds of its next crisis. This is because the organizational arrangements and management strategies that are adaptive for one stage in the lifecycle will be seen as maladaptive when the organization grows more complex. Therefore, old structural arrangements and leadership styles must be constantly replaced by new patterns and leaders throughout the life of the organization.

Greiner's model has been extremely popular, but his emphasis on leadership obscured some important information about how the social structure of the organization develops. Katz and Kahn's theory made up for this deficiency.

An Open Systems Model of the Development of Organizational Structures

According to Katz and Kahn's **open systems model**, structure first develops out of technical needs and later from internal integration pressures in combination with shifting demands from the environment.[15] At first, a primitive organization emerges from cooperation between individuals who wish to pool their efforts to achieve a common goal, such as bringing a new product to market. This primitive organization is not actually structured in the usual sense of the term because the cooperative effort is more the result of individual motivation than it is an organizational achievement. However, if the primitive organization is going to survive beyond its initial project, it will begin to develop a social structure. The development from primitive to fully elaborated organizational structure will occur in several stages, each of which involves differentiation and integration. Katz and Kahn's model describes these stages.

In the first stage, activities such as purchasing and marketing are structurally differentiated from core production tasks. This initial differentiation is a natural extension of the primitive production process that also required procurement and disposal processes, but on such a restricted scale as to be easily accomplished by members of the production core who take time away from production to purchase raw materials or distribute output to customers. This stage of differentiation provides the organization with buffering capacity in the sense that it permits employees working to produce organizational output to focus all their attention and energy on transforming raw materials into products. Meanwhile, other individuals specialize in the tasks of purchasing raw materials to feed the transformation process and transferring the organization's products to its environment so that new inputs can be acquired and production can proceed uninterrupted (see Figure 4.3). Katz and Kahn called these **support activities**.

Once the initial differentiation of activities is underway, pressures to integrate begin to appear. In elaborating itself to ensure continuous input of raw material, and production and sale of output, the organization produces three different pockets of activity that can lose track of one another. The three functions of purchasing, production, and sales must be aligned, so that the correct levels of raw materials are brought into the organization and so that production output balances with sales. This requires integration that is usually provided by a general manager who oversees purchasing orders and production schedules while taking sales projections into account.

At this point in the development of its social structure, the organization has usually survived long enough to require maintenance—employees quit and others must be recruited and trained, bookkeeping tasks expand to include corporate tax considerations and financial planning, physical facilities require regular upkeep and modification, and the community may begin making inquiries about the organization and demands regarding its community involvement. It now becomes necessary to supplement core production and support activities with accounting, personnel, facilities management and public relations. Katz and Kahn grouped all of these into the category of maintenance activities.

Maintenance activities help to preserve the organization in a steady state of readiness to perform, while the production core does the performing. Because the activities of the

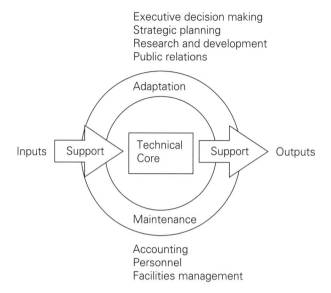

Executive decision making
Strategic planning
Research and development
Public relations

Accounting
Personnel
Facilities management

Figure 4.3 Katz and Kahn describe the development of social structure in relation to the needs of the technical core and demands of the environment

According to their historical view, a primitive technical core is first elaborated with support structures, then maintenance structures appear, and finally adaptive structures are added. *Based on*: Katz and Kahn (1966).

maintenance group are not highly interdependent with those of purchasing, production and sales, the maintenance function can be carried out with considerable independence of the production core. This represents further differentiation of the organizational social structure, which, in turn, demands more integration. The addition of managers to achieve this integration is typical, but now, with multiple managers, a new level of management emerges in the form of an executive to oversee the other managers. Thus integration designed to overcome the problems introduced by differentiation breeds further differentiation by creating hierarchy.

If the organization survives the early stages of development described above, it will probably exist long enough to encounter some change in the environment that affects demand for the organization's product. Such changes create problems for the organization, such as predicting what amount of output will be sold and, thus, what level of raw material needs to be ordered and how much product should be produced. Mistakes in scheduling production runs will be acutely felt as both over- or undersupply of customers' demand can threaten the firm's cash flow position as well as its reputation. If demand for the company's product is waning, new products may need to be developed to keep the organization in business. In order to face these problems, another elaboration of social structure occurs. This one introduces adaptive activities into the social structure.

Adaptive activities are responsible for attending to changes in the environment and for interpreting the meaning of the changes for the rest of the organization. The earliest manifestation of the adaptive function is executive decision making, which in one form or another exists from the beginning. However, other, more specialized, adaptive activities emerge over a longer period of time, including strategic planning, economic forecasting, market research, research and development, tax planning, legal advising and lobbying.

Structuration Theory

A long-standing debate in sociology pits agency (free will) against structure (determination). Those favoring structure claim that the societies into which we are born, and the institutions, organizations and groups to which we belong, structure our lives by imposing rules and controlling our access to resources to the point of (pre)determining our roles and outcomes in life. Those who favor agency ask about where structures come from, what sustains them and how structural change can be explained. Sociologists who favor agency see humans constructing the very social structures that structuralists claim determine behavior. A few social theorists have tried to reconcile these views by studying structur*ing* as opposed to structure. They emphasize the ways in which social structures are patterns produced by interacting agents whose actions are influenced by the structures they construct. In studying structure and agency simultaneously, structuration theorists crossed between individual and organizational levels of analysis, thus setting the stage for thinking about organizational structure as a human social process with both material and symbolic aspects.

British social theorist Anthony Giddens described how structuring occurs through the mutual influences of action (agency) and the residue of past action (structure).[16] This idea reminds me of M. C. Echer's famous etching showing two hands drawing each other. According to **structuration theory**, structure both enables and constrains the activities of interacting individuals even as those same activities create the structure that enables and constrains them. Giddens called this idea the **duality of structure and agency** according to which agents of the organization are both enabled and constrained by structures of resources, routines and expectations. Agents are enabled to the extent that structures of signification, domination and legitimation support their activity, and constrained whenever they do not. But of course the activities shaped by these structures fuel the next round of structuration, and so on (see Figure 4.4).

Everyone experiences the duality of structure and agency on a daily basis. For example, we construct systems to manage information and then tell ourselves we cannot do something because the system and its routines will not allow it. Our failure to recognize that the system does not exist as a fixed entity prevents us from realizing that it can be changed using the same creative forces that produced it in the first place. What prevents us from doing so are our own habits, routines and expectations, and these are typically sustained by those in power who use their influence to sanction behavior in support of the status quo. This line of reasoning frames the structure side of structuration theory. On the agency side, structuration theory emphasizes the minute changes and the ever-present dynamics that occur within, produce and reproduce our social structures. Accordingly, social structures are defined by fragile cooperative movements sustained by the complicity of the individuals involved at particular places in specific moments of time.

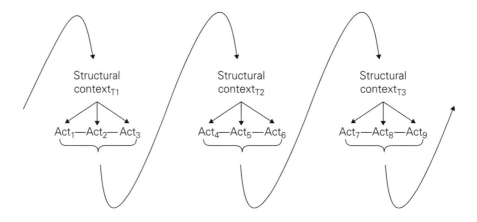

Figure 4.4 The duality of structure and agency

The mutual construction of structure and agency as portrayed in Giddens's structuration theory. *Based on:* Barley and Tolbert (1997).

Table 4.5 How rules and resources mediate agency and structure

Structures of:	Signification	Domination	Legitimation
Rules and resources mediating structure and agency:	Interpretive schemes	Relationships within which power is exercised	Normative influence
Forms of Agency:	**Communication**	**Power**	**Sanction**

Giddens explained social system dynamics in terms of three mutually supportive dualities of structure and agency: signification–communication, domination–power, and legitimation–sanction. According to Giddens, these dualities are mediated by three different types of rules and resources that actors use to construct their structural contexts: interpretive schemes for defining what symbols mean (e.g., language games, discourses and speech genres), relationships within which the exercise of power occurs (e.g., hierarchy, division of labor), and norms (e.g., found in the exercise of conformity pressure, socialization). Table 4.5 shows structures, forms of agency, and rules and resources that mediate between them as a matrix of material and symbolic social practices that, through mutual influence, produce the social context and outcomes (both structures and actions) of social systems.

While Giddens has been criticized for emphasizing the agency side of the structure-agency reconciliation, French social theorist Pierre Bourdieu presented two concepts that emphasize the structure side: field and habitus.[17] According to Bourdieu, a **field** is a structure with an internal logic that establishes hierarchical relationships on the basis of the distribution of capital. Bourdieu defined capital as resources used by the powerful and influential to distinguish themselves from those without power or influence. He then claimed that capital takes various forms, one for each field. For example, the cultural field is structured by cultural capital (celebrity status, prestige), the academic field by academic capital (academic reputation and honors) and the field of economics by economic capital (wealth).

According to Bourdieu's version of structuration theory, a field is constituted through the signifying practices of its agents whose actions, therefore, are capable of transforming it. Bourdieu used the field of literature as an example. In literature, a subsystem of the cultural field, including authors, critics, publishers and readers, produces and consumes literary works wherein their responses, interpretations and texts legitimize social differences. The structure of these social differences, in turn, determines which individuals get to have enough power and influence to change the field, which of course they are then unlikely to do unless they are certain it will not affect their standing.

Permeating any given field, the **habitus** gives individuals a feel for the game that allows them to know how they and others should behave depending upon their hierarchical position which, in turn, is determined by the amount of field-relevant capital they control. Because the internal logic of a field can be kept hidden, the habitus can be well protected from outsiders and may operate as tacit knowledge among insiders who thus reproduce the field and its hierarchies without consciousness of their involvement. It may well be through the habitus that members of a field tap into the rules and resources that Giddens described as the tissue connecting agency and structure (see Figure 4.4).

Taking a different approach, American sociologists Mustafa Emirbayer and Ann Mische presented a version of structuration theory that is more temporally sensitive than either Giddens's or Bourdieu's approach, though, like Giddens, these theorists emphasized agency.[18] Emirbayer and Mische claimed that the key processes by which agents produce structure are: iteration (repetition of past behavior), practical evaluation (as the basis for taking action in the present) and projection (into the future). In the iterative process, agents reactivate their prior patterns of behavior as routines that reproduce existing structures. Practical evaluation allows agents to make informed judgments relevant to their ever changing circumstances and these judgments influence their behavior in ways that either reproduce or change existing structures. Finally, through projection, the possibilities of the future signal creative options that allow for the intentional or even planned reconfiguration of existing structure. Taken together, these three processes help to set structuration in motion by permitting agents to reach both backward and forward in time to structure their present activities.

One thing structuration theory brings home to me is the endless refinement that modernist theorizing begets. I am reminded of the story by the Argentinean writer Jorge Luis Borges about the mapmaker who kept refining his map, making it ever more detailed, until one day his map completely covered the territory he was mapping because only in this way could he reach his goal of making the perfect map. The trouble is, too many refinements to a theory reduce its practical value of summarizing and encapsulating knowledge in useable chunks. In other words, when the map becomes as complex as the territory, who needs the map? Nonetheless, in its attempt to cross the boundary between individual and organizational levels of analysis, and to reconcile the symbolic and material aspects of social relationships, structuration theory makes a bold theoretical move that sets the stage for thinking about structure as process—a way of thinking that symbolic-interpretivists have so far developed to a greater extent than have modernists.

Symbolic-Interpretive Approaches: Social Practices, Institutional Logics and Community

Imagine the buildings of an organization containing only desks, machines, computers, raw materials and documents, but empty of people. Does the organization have a social structure? Modernist organizational theorists, drawing from objectivist ontology, would say that organizations are social structural objects consisting of elements such as hierarchy, lines of authority and accountability along with various integrating mechanisms. From a positivist epistemology, you need only analyze such things as organization charts, policies, rules and technology to draw conclusions about an organization's social structure and to confirm its existence. Symbolic-interpretivists disagree, arguing from subjectivist ontology that an organization's social structure does not exist independently of human consciousness and social interaction. They claim that organizational realities emerge as people work and interact with each other and with the material resources surrounding them. From this perspective the study of organizational structure looks completely different from the structural characteristics invoked by taking the modernist perspective.

The difference between modernist and symbolic-interpretive perspectives can be summarized in this way: modernist organization theorists see structures as things, entities, objects and elements, while symbolic-interpretivists see structures as human creations, they are dynamic works-in-progress that emerge from social interaction and collective meaning-making. In this regard, Weick argued that there are no organizations, there is only organiz*ing*. Along with Giddens's theory of structuration, Weick's insight turns our attention away from understanding social structures as systems for designing and controlling interaction and social relationships, and toward interest in how the everyday practices of organizational members construct the very patterns of organizing that guide their actions. Below I will introduce you to two practices that figure strongly in theorizing the dynamics of social structure from the symbolic-interpretive perspective: routine and improvisation.

It is important to note two major points of divergence from modernism in the symbolic-interpretive approach. First, because meaningful interactions are context-specific, you cannot form generalizations that will apply across different organizations the way you can using modernist dimensions of social structure such as formalization or differentiation. However, it is possible to study *how* organizing emerges by participating in and observing the coordinated activities of organizational members. Our discussion of routines and improvisation below will suggest how an organization's activities are constructed, maintained and changed through the interactions of their members. Second, subjectivist ontology and interpretive epistemology prompt most symbolic-interpretivists to study organizations from a cultural rather than a structural perspective. Much of what interests these scholars will be taken up in Chapter 6, however, in this section we will examine two culturally sensitive theories of organizational social structure: institutional logic and communities of practice.

Two Social Practices: Routine and Improvisation

In the first years of its alliance, Nissan senior assembly-line workers and engineers wrote standard operating procedures (SOPs) to help transfer knowledge about effective work practices to its alliance partner Renault. For example, Nissan gave Renault's dashboard assembly-line workers directions that included hand drawn sketches showing the exact order in which dashboard wires were to be connected, what tools to use and how to reach the wires.[19] **Routines** like this have long been regarded an important fact of organizational life.[20] As routines build up, a stable organizational social structure emerges. Routines are found everywhere in organizations, from techniques associated with the use of production tools and factory equipment, to management practices including hiring and firing employees, strategic planning cycles, annual performance evaluations, quarterly reporting and budget reviews. These and many other routines preserve and transfer organizational knowledge and capabilities so that work can be successfully accomplished and coordinated.[21]

Modernist organization theorists have likened routines like Nissan's dashboard wiring process to organizational habits, programs and genetic codes, metaphoric representations that emphasize their stabilizing influence on the organization.[22] However, as Martha Feldman argued, routines contain the seeds of change as well as offering stability and creating inertia. Feldman defined routines as flows of connected ideas, actions and outcomes and suggested that they emerge as organizational members try to understand what to do in particular work contexts.[23] Routines are created and then endlessly re-created because people do not reproduce actions and behaviors in exactly the same way every time they engage in them. For example, a police officer or social worker dealing with an incident of domestic violence knows the expected routine for dealing with the situation because they have been trained in organizational procedures and have developed particular ways of dealing with these situations from their own experience. However, such routines can be used in a variety of combinations and contexts to construct different ways of dealing with the specific circumstances of domestic violence. In this way changes are introduced to routines and subsequently maintained and spread within the organization or even across organizations (e.g., via institutional mimesis), or they may die out through lack of repetition.

The idea of changing a routine comes close to the concept of organizational **improvisation**.[24] Karl Weick, who has written extensively about improvisation in organizations, proposed viewing organizational structure as an emergent and unfolding process of routines and improvisations operating more like recipes than blueprints.[25] In performing routine activities, organizational members reinforce existing interaction patterns and thereby reproduce organizational social structures to give them a degree of stability. However, acting improvisationally, organizational members will, at times, interact outside established pathways and perform in the gaps that exist in the current version of a social structure. In doing so they behave like jazz musicians who refuse to play what has been played before and thus deliberately step into new territory. Organizational improvisations may help the organization to react to a threat or take advantage of an opportunity.[26] Improvisations will either disappear once they have served their immediate purpose, or be used as templates for new interaction patterns. Once institutionalized through repetition and widespread acceptance, an improvisation becomes routine.

In an article that examined how the structuring of jazz performance applies to organizations, I argued that social structures always have coordination gaps due to the impossibility of structurally interrelating all organizational activities at once.[27] In order to minimize the problems created by these structural gaps, organizational members might want to adopt some of the techniques jazz musicians use for the purpose of improvising on their structures. For example, jazz tunes are performed in successive waves of improvisation that begin with the playing of the head of a selected tune in a recognizable and often routine way (e.g., think of the first chorus of 'I've Got Rhythm'). The head provides the musicians with a basic structure of melody, harmony and rhythm to use as a departure point for their playing. As the performance of the tune unfolds, each soloing musician in turn attempts to lead the band away from the originating structure by playing in the empty spaces in that structure (beats not played and the spaces between beats are two rhythmic examples). Different musicians, taking turns soloing, will improvise differently and each successive musician can build on ideas introduced by the others until, collectively, a unique playing of the tune is achieved that nonetheless retains a relationship to its origin in the head. This relationship between old and new is demonstrated at the conclusion of the tune when the musicians replay the head, embellishing it with some of the best ideas their improvising produced. In this way a structure and its empty spaces are combined to create a performance, whether it be of a jazz tune or an organizational process.

The article offered jazz as a metaphor organizations can use to talk about the ever-present limits of structuring that all organizations face. It also suggested literally using the same practices jazz musicians use to bring structural stability and flexibility into direct connection. Doing the organizational equivalent of playing jazz could continually renew the social structure by offering new options for organizing even while it maintains some existing routines and practices.

Social Structures as Institutionalized Practices and Logics

Institutional theorists who are interested in the processes by which institutions emerge in the wake of new social practices have compared the dynamics of institutionalization to the formation of social movements. For example, Michael Lounsbury, Marc Ventresca and Paul Hirsch used this approach to explain the emergence of recycling as an institution in the United States around which the recycling industry developed.[28] They discovered the dynamics of institutionalization when they studied historical developments within the recycling movement. Their work can be related to that of another group of institutional theorists who proposed that organizational structures are embedded in institutional logics. **Institutional logics** are constituted by mindsets, cognitive frames of reference and mental models that configure thought, compel argument and organize systems.[29] As logic is abstract and communicated only through symbols, the idea of institutional logics forming the context for organizations connects objective behavior with subjective (symbolic) meaning. Thus the social structure that connects and coordinates organizational members has both behavioral and symbolic (objective and subjective) implications. According to organization theorists Robert Drazin, Mary Ann Glynn and Robert Kazanjian: 'Structures can become invested with socially shared meanings, and thus, in addition to their "objective" functions, can serve to communicate information about the organization to both internal and external audiences.'[30] Institutional theorists often mix modernist and symbolic-interpretive perspectives. For instance, Drazin and his co-authors used objectivist ontology when they assumed that structures are objects that can be invested with meaning, as opposed to being momentarily constructed social realities; yet by emphasizing institutional logics for understanding organizations they employed interpretive epistemological assumptions such as that organizational meaning is shaped by its institutional context and all knowledge of it must therefore be context-specific. The study by Lounsbury and his co-authors showed similar sensitivity to context by using historical methods to study the recycling movement.

Social Structures as Communities

The idea of community emphasizes intersubjectively shared knowledge and values as well as voluntary social action. Whereas modernist scholars might view a community in objective terms, such as the occupational statuses it confers, symbolic-interpretivists have focused on organizations as communities of practice and as language communities. Both approaches explore how shared understandings of organizational realities are constructed and maintained through the recurring interaction of organizational members. The focus on interpreting patterns of interaction is what makes the concept of organizations as communities a symbolic-interpretive theory of social structure.

Communities of practice are based on the idea of self-organization through coordinated activity. They are formed when groups of people share ideas and knowledge that allow them to develop new practices as they learn together. The idea of organizations as communities of practice was first suggested by educational theorists Etienne Wenger and Jean Lave who were interested in how learning occurs through social interaction.[31] Wenger and Lave defined a community of practice as a group of people informally bound together by common interests and shared repertoires (e.g., routines, vocabularies). They are self-designing and self-managing and their goal is mutual learning and the development of knowledge. Humans belong to many different communities of practice, each having their own ways of talking that create local meanings, identities and a community context. An organization's social structure can consist of many different communities of practice that emerge spontaneously in response to particular interests, needs or problems. Communities of practice can crosscut business units and project teams, hierarchies or any other dimension of social structure. Community members themselves move between different communities to share and broker knowledge. Communities of practice are characterized by connections rather than hierarchical or formalized relationships, and frequently use improvisation to overcome rigid organizational routines and organizational worldviews (prevailing ways of seeing and doing things) to meet the demands of particular tasks or purposes. A manager's role within a community of practice is one of integration rather than authority—managers look for or try to develop coherence to enable organizational action and innovation.[32]

Sometimes communities of practice are treated as a formal type of social structure. For example, IBM Global Services has over 60 groups formally defined as communities of practice. These groups were created to address issues such as e-business, industry sectors (e.g., distribution, health care) and applications development.[33] Even so, communities of practice are based on the symbolic-interpretive idea of organizations as emergent networks of social connection between individuals and groups. Close personal contacts are believed to create community and this benefits members when they collaborate on tasks. Thus an interesting question is whether institutionalizing communities of practice undermines their effectiveness, both from the perspective of the organization and from their members' perspectives. The concept of community may well offer a complement or alternative to formal social structure as a means of explaining how people organize their work. This possibility will be given further attention in Chapter 6 where you will learn about organizational cutlure.

Using the concept of language communities, organization theorists explore how organizational members talk about their organization; whether there are identifiable, distinct organizational discourses or language games (shared ways of talking that can be distinguished from those of other groups or organizations); and what speech reveals about how organizational members coordinate and organize their actions.[34] Another theory that uses the assumption that organizations are communities draws on the Wittgensteinian concept of language games and on Foucault's concept of discourse as rules influencing what can be said (see Chapter 2). In **language communities** work is structured through the way words are used in the context of member's everyday lives. Organizational members develop shared vocabularies that include rhetorical styles, root metaphors and other distinctive forms of self-expression. These concepts are related to the idea of organizations as language communities because they imply that organizational members will have particular and shared ways of talking about their organizational experience and will create and maintain features of their organization's social structure within their everyday conversations. Activities form around these features and are coordinated through conversations and interactions.

You can see how language communities work by considering differences in the words that organizational theorists use to construct the different perspectives of organization theory you have been studying. Modernist organization theorists talk about causes and effects or structures and outcomes, whereas symbolic-interpretivists use the language of meanings, processes and understandings. Contrast these ways of speaking with the language of postmodernism, which includes words like fragmentation, deconstruction and discourse. The words that you use to talk about your knowledge can give you a sense of objectivity because they create (enable) and stabilize (constrain) particular features of your reality around which you communicate with others, act and interact, but according to the theory of language communities, this objectivity is a product of intersubjectively constructed interpretation that is shaped by the way language is used. The idea that organizational social structures are constructed in the conversations that take place between organizational members lies at the very heart of social constructionism.[35] However, the links to Wittgenstein and Foucault cause this theory to straddle symbolic-interpretive and postmodern perspectives, to which we now turn.

Postmodern Approaches to Social Structure: De-differentiation, Feminist Organizations and Anti-administration

Postmodernism embraces poststructuralist suppositions such as that there are no structures underlying human existence. Instead, many postmodernists believe the world is formless, fragmented and intertextual: there is no hidden order, what you see on the surface is all that there is. Postmodernists also challenge grand narratives of Truth like the Progress Myth that lurk within scientific and technical rationality. As you might imagine, postmodernists are extremely skeptical of the principles of hierarchy, centralization, control and integration that are so dear to modernists, insisting that these are not real underlying orders but merely words used to legitimize those who hold power. They suggest deconstructing any concepts, structures and management practices that presuppose order, rationality or the need for managerial control because these all privilege some groups while exploiting and/or marginalizing others.

Postmodernists suspect the very notion of structure and they therefore put structural thinking under intense scrutiny wherever they find it. Bureaucracy particularly comes under attack. Recall that Weber himself discussed the dark side of bureaucracy, how the drive for rationality, calculation and control may increase efficiency but also traps us in an iron cage that stifles diversity, creativity and free will. A number of critical theorists have used Weber's metaphor of the iron cage to examine how social life is colonized and subverted by rationalistic ideologies, structures and control mechanisms, a theme to which we will return in Chapter 8.

In an influential series of articles, British organization theorists Gibson Burrell and Robert Cooper assessed the implications of postmodernism for organizational analysis. They suggested that modernist organization theory is generally concerned with formal organization and the drive to create order out of disorder. Burrell and Cooper associated the term 'formal' with words like unity, distance, routine and rational. They claimed these associations define a modernist moral code and argued that modernist organization theory fails to recognize that formal organization, while trying to suppress disorder (e.g., the informal, local, spontaneous and irrational), is actually created out of the tensions between the privileged term (organization) and its opposite (disorganization).[36] Thus, while these postmodern organization theorists were interested in many of the same elements of

structure that modernists study, they deconstructed them in order to explore the organizational implications hidden by the silences and repression modernist theorizing produces.

Postmodernists often claim that structural elements do not already exist in the world
but are created by organizational theorists as they attempt to explain organizations and
organizing. This is why many deconstructionists do not specify alternative constructions—
they believe these would only impose other grand narratives. Nonetheless, some suggest
that by deconstructing taken-for-granted ideologies and practices, a space for new organizing possibilities opens. They find some of these new possibilities in organizational forms
that are de-differentiated. De-differentiation, feminist organizations and anti-administration
theory will give you a taste of the ways postmodernists confront and provoke organizational
social structures and those who theorize them.

De-differentiation

According to modernists Lawrence and Lorsch, differentiation consists of the division of
the organization into different hierarchical levels and specialized departments. This
produces a need for integration which, in turn, creates more differentiation and so on, thus
locking an organization into a continuous developmental trajectory such as those
described by Greiner or Katz and Kahn. In opposition to these views of social structure,
postmodernists adopt the concept of **de-differentiation**. British sociologist Scott Lash
claimed de-differentiation marks the defining moment of postmodernism in that it
reverses the modernist progression of ever greater specialization and separation, for
example of rich and poor, weak and powerful, right and wrong.

Borrowing Lash's idea, Stewart Clegg, an Australian organization theorist suggested
that organizations today are over-differentiated and this leads their members to experience
them as incoherent, a state that can render them overly dependant on the most powerful
members of the hierarchy. Such organizations, Clegg claimed, need to de-differentiate,
which is different from integration.[37] Integration implies the coordination of differentiated activities whereas de-differentiation reverses the very conditions of differentiation
that created the need for integration in the first place. In de-differentiation, organizations
integrate activities, not through hierarchical or structural elaboration, but by allowing
people to self-manage and coordinate their own activities. De-differentiation satisfies the
emancipatory interests of critical postmodernists by undermining the controlling mindset
that they believe dominates modernist thinking.

The self-organizing or semi-autonomous team concept from socio-technical systems
theory offers an example of de-differentiation. Workgroups organized as semi-
autonomous teams are given responsibility for a broadly defined set of tasks; they schedule
their own time and monitor, assess and correct their performance, including quality. For
example, in Volvo's Kalmar Plant in Sweden, entire automobiles are assembled start to
finish by teams of self-managing workers. Examples like Kalmar suggest that integration
can be achieved independently of hierarchy. Thus de-differentiation makes it easier to
imagine democratic organizations in which integration and coordination are the
responsibility of everyone and not just management's concern. This is the idea behind
labor-managed firms such as United Airlines or the John Lewis Partnership that operates

department stores in the United Kingdom, both of which are owned and operated by employees. However, some postmodernists warn that these types of organization will turn out to be just another servant of managerial interests, one that projects an image of democracy, autonomy and self-management, but that merely disguises the power struggle by dressing it in new clothes. We will return to this issue in Chapter 8 where you will read more about power and control in organizations.

Feminist Organizations

You may remember from Chapter 2 that the notion of *différance* challenges the modernist focus on presence (things we take to be entities and objects) suggesting instead that meaning resides in the continuous movement between what is present and what is absent in our language. This means that we can use oppositional logic to deconstruct the assumptions and practices associated with modernist ideas of structure as presence and thereby expose and examine its absences. For example, feminist scholars have deconstructed bureaucracy to show that it is a male-gendered and typically white male-dominated form of organization.[38] They claim that bureaucracies privilege hierarchy and justify it by claiming that power and position are based on objective and rational criteria associated with technical competence, yet these organizations define terms like objective and rational from a white male-centered viewpoint that results in the domination of women, people of color and minorities. These gender and race-based structures are reinforced through unspoken assumptions and taken-for-granted objectifications that exist within and are supported by modernist organizational discourses. In modernist discourse, individual performance is generally evaluated against formal criteria such as decisiveness and the possession of leadership qualities. Feminists claim that criteria like these favor the male gender. In contrast, feminist organizations (e.g., women's health centers, domestic violence shelters) evidence more equitable and flexible structures, participatory decision making, cooperative action and community ideals. In **feminist organizations** like these men and women, people of different ethnicities, young and old experience greater equality than do members of traditional (modernist) bureaucracies.

One hybrid form based on postmodern and feminist theories is Karen Lee Ashcraft's idea of **feminist bureaucracy**.[39] Critics have challenged both bureaucratic and feminist forms, in particular the dominating tendencies of the former, and the sustainability of the latter when faced with growth and demands for formalization by funding organizations. Ashcraft's hybrid keeps the seemingly incompatible elements of bureaucratic and feminist characteristics in simultaneous play as organizational members do their work. For example, tasks will be both formal and informal, specialized and general, and hierarchy and centralization will exist but constantly be challenged by egalitarian and decentralized practices. Ashcraft's research in a non-profit organization concerned with domestic violence studied the interplay of bureaucratic elements and necessities (a hierarchical organization chart) with feminist ideals of ethical communication (the right to express views and emotions and to be heard). This hybrid employed the tensions between its contradictory elements to help it cope with paradoxical pressures (e.g., bureaucratic conditions associated with getting external funding and the need to stay small, flexible and responsive to individual clients) to achieve its goal to serve abused women.

Anti-administration Theory

David Farmer, a philosopher and economist, suggested that we can surface and counteract the logic of bureaucratic administration by juxtaposing it with **anti-administration**.[40] Government bureaucracies serve their political masters and enforce justice by privileging hierarchy, efficiency and technical expertise. Anti-administration theorists deconstruct this view and surface its oppositions. Farmer did not advocate anarchy, instead he argued that anti-administration is part of the administrative act, a part that involves radical skepticism toward its ends, means and hierarchical rationality. By engaging in anti-administration, administrators reflect on presence and absence in their policies, procedures and actions to deepen their understanding of the implications of their administrative actions. Bureaucratic justice is normally equated with the rationality and efficiency of actions—what happens if we juxtapose it with postmodern notions that justice involves considering moral relationship with our others? Instead of imposing justice based on rationality, administrators would concentrate on removing injustice.

SUMMARY

Every organization consists of social elements including people, their positions within the organization and the groups or units to which they belong. Three types of relationship among people, positions and units have been used by modernist organization theorists to define social structure: hierarchy, division of labor and coordination mechanisms. The division of labor indicates who does what in terms of task assignments. Task assignments in turn create expectations about who is dependent upon whom. The hierarchy of authority defines formal reporting relationships, but these only account for some of the interactions necessary to support an organization. Coordination mechanisms, ranging from formal rules and procedures to spontaneous hallway conversations, further define and support the social structure of the organization. Classical dimensions of social structure that continue to interest modernist organ-ization scholars include complexity, centralization and formalization. These dimensions offer a means of distinguishing between mechanistic, organic and bureaucratic organizations.

Contingency theory offers a way to combine empirical findings about multiple dimensions of social structure. For example, contingency theory has demonstrated that small organizations operating in stable environments are best organized as simple structures with minimal hierarchy and highly centralized decision making. However, as organizations grow in size (number of employees), they differentiate thereby increasing the number of hierarchical levels and departments, which causes them to add integrative mechanisms such as rules, liaison roles and/or cross-functional teams. Formalization will come along with the increased routineness of work tasks that is likely to accompany the specialization introduced by the greater division of labor in large organizations. Unstable environments and internal differentiation mean that organizational structures will require decentralization so that decisions do not overburden the hierarchy and can be made at the point of knowledge. And on it goes. As new contingencies are discovered, new webs of relationships can be spun out from the findings of contingency research.

Symbolic-interpretivists see social structure as emerging from relationships that form through human interaction. Individuals interact and over time these interactions stabilize into recognizable relationships that define the social structure and contribute to the ways that work is accomplished. These relationships link the formal hierarchical positions into groups and the groups into departments and divisions. However, although structure serves to direct and constrain deviations from expected patterns of behavior, structuration theory reminds us that these constraints are nothing more than our willingness to do things in routine ways. Structuration theory stresses that social structure both influences and is influenced by the everyday interactions of the members of the organization.

Postmodernism and network organizations challenge many modernist ways of looking at social structure, focusing research attention instead on processes and relationships. Symbolic-interpretive and postmodern perspectives remind us that organizations have other resources beyond the social structure to aid in the integration of differentiated activities, as you will see in the following chapters on technology, organizational culture, physical structure and power.

KEY TERMS

bureaucracy
division of labor
departmentalization
hierarchy
formalization
horizontal differentiation
vertical differentiation
flat and tall organizational structures
mechanistic and organic organizations
differentiation and integration
centralization
specialization
size
organizational lifecycle
 entrepreneurial stage
 leadership crisis
 collectivity stage
 autonomy crisis
 delegation stage
 crisis of control
 formalization stage

crisis of red tape
collaboration stage
crisis of renewal
decline
open systems model
 support activities
 maintenance activities
 adaptive activities
structuration theory
 duality of structure and agency
 field
 habitus
routines
improvisation
institutional logics
communities of practice
language communities
de-differentiation
feminist organizations
anti-administration theory

ENDNOTES

1. See Weber (1946, 1947).

2. http://www.sco.ca.gov/ppsd/empinfo/demo/index.shtml, accessed October 23, 2003.

3. Hage (1974), Rousseau (1978).

4. Donaldson (1996: 57).

5. Pugh and Hickson (1979).

6. The link to communication was established later by Galbraith (1973).

7. Pugh, Hickson, Hinings and Turner (1968).

8. Grinyer and Yasai-Ardekani (1980).

9. Blau and Schoenherr (1971), Pugh et al. (1968, 1969), Mansfield (1973).

10. McDonalds website http://www.McDonalds. com, accessed April 2005.

11. http://www.mcdonalds.com/corp/values/socialrespons/sr_report.html, accessed April 2005.

12. Mintzberg (1983).

13. McKelvey (1982).

14. Greiner (1972).

15. Katz and Kahn (1966).

16. Giddens (1979, 1984); see also Ranson, Hinings and Greenwood (1980), Riley (1983), Barley and Tolbert (1997).

17. Bourdieu (1980/1990).

18. Emirbayer and Mische (1998).

19. Yoshino and Fagan (2003: 9).

20. See, for example, Stene (1940) and Cyert and March (1963).

21. March (1991), Argote (1999).

22. Huber (1991); Stene (1940) used the metaphor of habits; March and Simon (1958) suggested the metaphor of programs; the metaphor of genetic material was introduced by Nelson and Winter (1982).

23. Feldman (2000); see also Feldman and Pentland (2003).

24. See Kamoche, Cunha and da Cunha (2002) for a recent selection of important articles on organizational improvisation.

25. Weick (1998).

26. Moorman and Miner (1998a, b) described the role improvisation plays in aiding new product development teams.

27. Hatch (1993).

28. Lounsbury, Ventresca and Hirsch (forthcoming).

29. Drazin, Glynn and Kazanjian (2004).

30. Drazin, Glynn and Kazanjian (2004:162).

31. Lave and Wenger (1991).

32. Brown and Duguid (1991).

33. Gongla and Rizzuto (2001).

34. Examples include Meyer and Rowan (1977), Hirsch (1986), Grant, Keenoy and Oswick (1998), Cunliffe (2001), deHolan and Phillips (forthcoming).

35. Shotter (1993).

36. Cooper and Burrell (1988).

37. Clegg (1990).

38. Eisenstein (1995), Ferguson (1984), Gherardi (1995), Martin (1990).

39. Ashcraft (2001).

40. Farmer (1997).

REFERENCES

Argote, Linda (1999). *Organizational learning: Creating, retaining and transferring knowledge.* Boston: Kluwer Academic Press.

Ashcraft, Karen L. (2001). Organized dissonance: Feminist bureaucracy as hybrid form. *Academy of Management Journal*, 44/6: 1301–22.

Barley, Stephen R., and Tolbert, Pamela (1997). Institutionalization and structuration: Studying the links between action and institution. *Organization Studies*, 18: 93–117.

Blau, Peter M., and Schoenherr, Richard A. (1971). *The structure of organizations*. New York: Basic Books.

Bourdieu, Pierre (1990). *The logic of practice.* Cambridge: Polity Press (first published in 1980).

Brown, J. S., and Duguid, P. (1991). Organizational learning and communities of practice: Towards a unified view of working, learning, and innovation. *Organization Science*, 2/1: 40–57.

Burns, Tom, and Stalker, George M. (1961). *The management of innovation*. London: Tavistock Publications.

Clegg, Stewart (1990). *Modern organizations: Organization studies in the postmodern world.* London: Sage.

Cooper, Robert, and Burrell, Gibson (1988). Modernism, postmodernism and organizational analysis: An introduction. *Organization Studies*, 9/1: 91–112.

Cunliffe, Ann L. (2001). Managers as practical authors: Reconstructing our understanding of management practice. *Journal of Management Studies*, 38/3: 351–71.

Cyert, Richard M., and March, James G. (1963). *A behavioral theory of the firm*. Englewood Cliffs, NJ: Prentice Hall.

de Holan, Martin, and Phillips, Nelson (forthcoming). Managing in transition: A case study of institutional management and organizational change in Cuba. *Journal of Management Inquiry*.

Donaldson, Lex (1996). The normal science of structural contingency theory. In S. R. Clegg, C. Hardy and W. R. Nord (eds.), *Handbook of organization studies*. London: Sage, 57–76.

Drazin, Robert, Glynn, Mary Ann, and Kazanjian, Robert K. (2004). Dynamics of structural change. In M. S. Poole and A. H. Van de Ven (eds.), *Handbook of organizational change and innovation*. New York: Oxford University Press, 161–89.

Eisenstein. H. (1995). The Australian femocratic experiment: A feminist case for bureaucracy. In M. M. Ferree and P. Y. Martin (eds.), *Feminist organizations: Harvest of the new women's movement*. Philadelphia: Temple University Press, 69–83.

Emirbayer, Mustafa, and Mische, Ann (1998). What is agency? *American Journal of Sociology*, 103/4: 962–1023.

Farmer, David. J. (1997). The postmodern turn and the Socratic gadfly. In H. T. Miller and C. J. Fox (eds.), *Postmodernism, 'reality' & public administration*. Burke, Virginia: Chatelaine Press, 105–17.

Feldman, Martha (2000). Organizational routines as a source of continuous change. *Organization Science*, 11: 611–29.

—— and Pentland, Brian T. (2003). Reconceptualizing organizational routines as source of flexibility and change. *Administrative Science Quarterly*, 48: 94–118.

Ferguson, Kathy E. (1984). *The feminist case against bureaucracy*. Philadelphia: Temple University Press.

Galbraith, Jay (1973). *Designing complex organizations*. Reading, Mass.: Addison-Wesley.

Gherardi, S. (1995). *Gender, symbolism, and organization cultures*. Newbury Park, Calif.: Sage.

Giddens, Anthony (1979). *Central problems in social theory: Action, structure and contradiction in social analysis*. Berkeley: University of California Press.

—— (1984). *The constitution of society*. Berkeley: University of California Press.

Gongla, P., and Rizzuto, C. R. (2001). Evolving communities of practice: IBM Global Services experience. *IBM Systems Journal*, 40/4. http://www.research.ibm.com/journal/sj/404/gongla.html (accessed 10.23.2003)

Grant, David, Keenoy, Thomas, and Oswick, Cliff (eds.) (1998). *Discourse + organization*. London: Sage.

Greiner, Larry (1972). Evolution and revolution as organizations grow. *Harvard Business Review*, 50: 37–46.

Grinyer, P. H., and Yasai-Ardekani, M. (1980). Dimensions of organizational structure: A critical replication. *Academy of Management Journal*, 23: 405–21.

Hage, Jerald (1974). *Communication and organizational control: Cybernetics in health and welfare settings*. New York: John Wiley.

Hatch, Mary Jo (1993). The empty spaces of organizing: How improvisational jazz helps redescribe organizational structure. *Organization Studies*, 20: 75–100.

Hirsch, Paul (1986). From ambushes to golden parachutes: Corporate takeovers as an instance of cultural framing and institutional integration. *American Journal of Sociology*, 91: 800–37.

Huber, George (1991). Organizational learning: The contributing processes and the literatures. *Organization Science*, 2: 88–115.

Kamoche, Kenneth, Cunha, Miguel P., and da Cunha, J. V. (2002) (eds.). *Organizational improvisation*. London: Routledge.

Katz, Daniel, and Kahn, Robert L. (1966). *The social psychology of organizations*. New York: John Wiley & Sons.

Lave, J., and Wenger, E. (1991). *Situated learning: Legitimate peripheral participation*. Cambridge: Cambridge University Press.

Lawrence, Paul R., and Lorsch, Jay W. (1967). *Organization and environment: Managing differentiation and integration*. Boston: Division of Research, Graduate School of Business Administration, Harvard University.

Lounsbury, Michael, Ventresca, Marc J., and Hirsch, Paul M. (forthcoming). Social movements, field frames and industry emergence: A cultural-political perspective on US recycling. *Socioeconomic Review*.

Mansfield, Roger (1973). Bureaucracy and centralization: An examination of organizational structure. *Administrative Science Quarterly*, 18: 77–88.

March, James G. (1991). Exploration and exploitation in organizational learning. *Organization Science* 2: 71–87.

March, James G., and Simon, Herbert A. (1958) *Organizations*. New York: Wiley.

Martin, Joanne (1990) Deconstructing organizational taboos: The suppression of gender conflict in organizations. *Organization Science* 1: 339–59.

McKelvey, William (1982). *Organizational systematics*. Berkeley: University of California Press.

Meyer, John W., and Rowan, Brian (1977). Institutionalized organizations: Formal structure as myth and ceremony. *American Journal of Sociology*, 83: 340–63.

Mintzberg, Henry (1981). Organizational design: Fashion or fit? *Harvard Business Review* 59(1): 103–16.

—— (1983). *Structure in fives: Designing effective organizations*. Englewood Cliffs, NJ: Prentice Hall.

Moorman, Christine, and Miner, Anne S. (1998a). The convergence of planning and execution: Improvisation in new product development. *Journal of Marketing*, 61: 1–20.

—— —— (1998b). Organizational improvisation and organizational memory. *Academy of Management Review*, 23: 698–723.

Nelson, R. R., and Winter, Stanley G. (1982). *An evolutionary theory of economic change*. Cambridge, Mass.: Harvard University Press.

Parsons, Talcott (1947). *The theory of social and economic organization*. Glencoe, Ill.: Free Press.

Pugh, Derek S., and Hickson, D. J. (1979). *Organizational structure in context*. Westmead, Farnborough, Hants: Saxon House.

—— —— and Hinings, C. R. (1969). An empirical taxonomy of structures of work organizations. *Administrative Science Quarterly*, 14: 115–26.

—— —— —— and Turner, C. (1968). Dimensions of organization structure. *Administrative Science Quarterly*, 13: 65–105.

Ranson, Stewart, Hinings, Robert, and Greenwood, Royston (1980). The structuring of organizational structures. *Administrative Science Quarterly*, 25: 1–17.

Riley, Patricia (1983). A structurationist account of political culture. *Administrative Science Quarterly*, 28: 414–37.

Rousseau, Denise (1978). Characteristics of departments, positions, and individuals: Contexts for attitudes and behaviors. *Administrative Science Quarterly*, 23: 521–40.

Scott, W. Richard (1992). *Organizations: Rational, natural, and open systems* (3rd edn.). Englewood Cliffs, NJ: Prentice Hall.

Shotter, John (1993). *Conversational realities: Constructing life through language*. Thousand Oaks, Calif.: Sage.

Stene, E. (1940). An approach to the science of administration. *American Political Science Review*, 34: 1124–37.

Weber, Max (1946). *From Max Weber: Essays in sociology* (ed. Hans H. Gerth and C. Wright Mills). New York: Oxford University Press (translation of original published 1906–24).

—— (1947). *The theory of social and economic organization* (ed. A. H. Henderson and Talcott Parsons). Glencoe, Ill.: Free Press (translation of original published 1924).

Weick, Karl (1998). Improvisation as a mindset for organizational analysis. *Organization Science*, 9: 543–55.

Yoshino, Michael Y., and Fagan, Perry L. (2003). The Renault–Nissan Alliance, HBS case 9-3-30023.

FURTHER READING

Adler, Nancy J. (1991). *International dimensions of organizational behavior*. Boston: PWS-Kent.

Bacharach, Samuel B., and Aiken, Michael (1977). Communication in administrative bureaucracies. *Academy of Management Journal*, 20: 356–77.

Bouchikhi, H., Kilduff, M. K., and Whittington, R. (forthcoming) (eds.). *Action, structure and organizations*. Coventry, UK: Warwick Business School Research Bureau.

Braun, P. (2002). Digital knowledge networks: Linking communities of practice with innovation. *Journal of Business Strategies*, 19: 43–54.

Chia, Robert (1996). *Organizational analysis as deconstructive practice*. Berlin: de Gruyter.

Cohen, Michael D., and Bacdayan, P. (1994). Organizational routines are stored as procedural memory: Evidence from a laboratory study. *Organization Science*, 5: 554–68.

Doz, Yves (1988). Technology partnerships between larger and smaller firms: Some critical issues. *International Studies of Management and Organization*, 17/4: 31–57.

Galbraith, Jay R. (1995). *Designing organizations: An executive briefing on strategy, structure and process.* San Francisco: Jossey-Bass.

Gergen, K. J. (1992). Organization theory in the postmodern era. In M. Reed and M. Hughes (eds.), *Rethinking organization: New directions in organization theory and analysis.* London: Sage.

Ghoshal, Sumantra, and Bartlett, Christopher A. (1990). The multinational corporation as an interorganizational network. *Academy of Management Review*, 15: 603–25.

Hage, Jerald, Aiken, Michael, and Marrett, C. B. (1971). Organization structure and communications. *American Sociological Review*, 36: 860–71.

Jablin, Fredric M. (1988). Formal organization structure. In F. M. Jablin, L. L. Putnam, K. H. Roberts, and L. W. Porter (eds.), *Handbook of organizational communication: An interdisciplinary perspective.* Newbury Park, Calif.: Sage.

Jaques, E. (1990). In praise of hierarchy. *Harvard Business Review*, Jan.–Feb.: 127–33.

Koh, Sarah (1992). Corporate globalization: A new trend. *Academy of Management Executive*, 6: 89–96.

Mintzberg, Henry (1979). *The structuring of organizations: A synthesis of the research.* Englewood Cliffs, NJ: Prentice-Hall.

Parker, Barbara (1996). Evolution and revolution: From international business to globalization. In S. R. Clegg, C. Hardy, and W. Nord (eds.), *Handbook of organization studies*, 484–506.

Parsons, Talcott (1947). *The theory of social and economic organization.* Glencoe, Ill.: Free Press.

Perrow, Charles (1986). *Complex organizations: A critical essay* (3rd edn.). New York: Random House.

Powell, Walter W. (1990). Neither market nor hierarchy: Network forms of organization. *Research in Organizational Behavior*, 12: 295–336.

Scott, W. Richard (1975). Organizational structure. *Annual Review of Sociology*, 1: 1–20.

Swan, J., Scarbrough, H., and Robertson, M. (2002). The construction of 'communities of practice' in the management of innovation. *Management Learning*, 33: 477–96.

Tosi, Henry L. (1974). The human effects of budgeting systems on management. *MSU Business Topics*, Autumn: 53–63.

Windeler, Arnold, and Sydow, J. (2001). Project networks and changing industry practices— collaborative content production in the German television industry. *Organization Studies*, 22/6: 1035–60.

5

Technology

Techne is the Greek root of our modern words technical and technology but, in contrast to contemporary meanings, ancient Greeks used this term to refer to the skill of the artist. Of course en route from artists in ancient Greece to modern times, the meaning of *techne* was shaped by artisans in the Middle Ages, craft workers in the preindustrial era, and then production specialists in the industrial age. Today, modern applications of science to engineering and manufacturing have largely overshadowed the ancient link between technology and art due to modernist tendencies to equate technology with its most objective features—the tools, equipment, machines and procedures through which work is accomplished. Nonetheless, recent changes in the economies of postindustrial nations are moving many organizations away from easily objectified technologies back in the direction of their ancient artistic roots. For example, Nissan, like many other manufacturing companies, recently placed marketing at the heart of its product design process to ensure that every aspect of the cars it builds is artfully infused with the Nissan brand.

Modernists generally think of technology in terms of the means organizations use to convert raw material inputs into finished outputs regardless of whether these outputs are products or services (see Figure 5.1). Objectivist ontology and positivist epistemology reveal themselves in modernist typologies of technology, and in the deterministic perspective taken when contingency theorists show that different technology types suit different environments, require different social structures and affect human action differently.

In contrast to the modernist focus on the technical aspects of how goods and services are produced, symbolic-interpretivists study how technologies are themselves shaped by processes of social construction. Symbolic-interpretivists argue that technologies both shape and are shaped by cultural norms, power relations and aspects of the organization's physical structure. To give just one example, although Beta-Max videotape technology was widely considered superior to VHS, the VHS format prevailed in part because its open access allowed organizations to avoid the costs of licensing the rights to use Beta from SONY and thus the values underpinning competitive capitalism won out over the value for purely technical product quality.

Some postmodernists suggest that technology's popularity with modernists derives from its ability to mask the ways employees are monitored and controlled by those in authority. These critics argue that technologies impose discipline on those who use them and that their demands for certain behaviors are built right into the production system. They further claim that technical design choices and their consequences reflect the imbalance of power in

Figure 5.1 The organization as a technical system for transforming inputs into outputs

From this modernist perspective the organization is a technology for transforming inputs into outputs that are consumed by the environment and thus transformed into revenue to purchase further inputs.

organizational relationships—managers and designers control workers but not the other way around. Other postmodernists offer the opinion that technology undermines hierarchy and creates a more democratic world. They maintain, for example, that developments in communication technology enable people across the globe to organize, lobby and take action. Still others extend cyborg theory to the organizational level of analysis to argue that technology and organization are increasingly fusing into cyborganization.

This chapter presents ideas about technology drawn from each of the three perspectives of organization theory, beginning with the modernist approaches from which most of our definitions and typologies of technology are derived. The social construction of technology will be presented next, followed by discussion of how postmodernists use the technology concept.

Modernist Definitions and Three Typologies

When they speak about organizations, macro economists generally focus on production, seeing organizations as the technologies a society uses to provide its members with the things that they need and desire. For example, electronics firms are a means to design and manufacture semiconductors, hospitals are a means to care for people who are ill, and universities are a means to provide citizens with education. From their environmental vantage point, an economy is a vast set of organizations that collectively produces a nation's gross domestic product (GDP) or total output of goods and services, and technology is how they do it.

In contrast to macro economists, modernist organization theorists view technology from closer quarters. You can make the concept of technology more explicit when you take up a position inside an organization because you can observe how things actually get done. At the organizational level of analysis, the technology concept refers to the methods and the knowledge with which objects are produced and services rendered, as well as the tools and equipment used. The modernist conception of organizational technology derives from the fields of micro economics, engineering, manufacturing and operations research, fields that look for ways to minimize inputs to and/or maximize outputs from a given production system. In this sense, technology provides one means by which businesses increase their profits and government agencies and not-for-profit organizations decrease their need for outside funding.

In addition to macro-economic and organizational levels of analysis, the concept of technology can be applied to more micro levels, including the unit and task. For instance, at the unit level, you can locate different technologies in the marketing, accounting, personnel, finance, sales and engineering departments of an organization. The task level of analysis reveals even more complexity; at this level you are focused on the variety of tasks in which organizational members engage and the knowledge and methods used to perform them. Here you might describe technologies for maintaining machinery, assembling products, handling complaints, planning budgets or producing reports, to name only a few of the numerous possibilities. Studying technology at different levels of analysis shows you that many technologies operate simultaneously within every organization.

Take the example of a university department (unit level). The technology employed to provide instruction to students includes: (1) physical objects such as classrooms, libraries, instructors, desks, chairs, photocopiers, computers and video projection systems; (2) activities and processes such as reading, lecture, discussion, experiential exercise, group work and examination; and (3) the knowledge of an academic discipline and of how students learn that discipline. In addition to teaching, university departments produce research which involves other technologies that can be analyzed at the unit level. Each activity associated with a unit-level technology can, in turn, be analyzed at the task level. For example, the technology for writing exams that I use involves: (1) physical objects and equipment including a computer, a printer, paper, and a photocopying machine; (2) activities such as formulating questions and typing them into the computer, pretesting the questions by answering them myself and seeking feedback from colleagues, composing and formatting the exam, proofreading, printing and photocopying; and (3) knowledge of concepts and theories and about testing for mastery as well as for the extent to which students can apply what they have learned. Then there is another task level technology I use for grading exams!

At the organizational level, images of technology at lower levels of analysis can be aggregated into a conception of the total technology of the organization. In the example given above, the university's organizational technology might be described as research and education or simply knowledge production. However, a rich image of this technology can only be formed by separately analyzing how this is done across the various departments and in each classroom, research laboratory and administrative office that constitutes the university. In this sense the concept of technology encourages you to imagine the organization as the product of many different objects, activities and knowledge bases operating and interacting at once.

Definitions

The term 'technology' can generate confusion if you do not carefully define your level of analysis. But there are other meanings of the term in common use that can create trouble as well. Below I describe some of the other uses of the term that are likely to trip you up, namely: core technology, high technology and service (vs. manufacturing) technology.

Core Technology

Due to its application at the unit and task levels of analysis, the term 'technology' not only refers to technologies that contribute directly to production (e.g., machines and equipment) but also to technologies that indirectly maintain the production processes (e.g., purchasing, sales, accounting, internal communication), and to technologies for adapting the organization to its environment (e.g., economic analysis, market research, strategic planning, external communication). Review Katz and Kahn's model in the previous chapter (see Figure 4.3) and think about the technologies of support, maintenance and adaptation that buffer the organization's core transformation process. To avoid confusion, organization theorists developed the term **core technology** to mean the transformation processes directly involved in producing the organization's products and services. For example, the core technology of a manufacturing company is its manufacturing process while a retail store's core technology involves buying, displaying, and selling goods and an estate (or real estate) agency's is brokering the sale and purchase of residential and commercial properties.

Comparing core technologies makes it possible to study the differences between, for example, providing education, governing a state and assembling automobiles. It also allows modernists to group organizations by the similarity of their technologies in order to study the relationship between technology type and other aspects of the organization such as the dimensions of social structure or conditions in the organizational environment.

Some organizations employ two or more different core technologies. Many examples of this can be found among conglomerate organizations, like GE or Tyco, that combine several unrelated businesses. An analysis of firms with multiple-core technologies requires separate analysis of each core technology, plus an analysis of the relationships between them (or lack thereof).

High Technology

Some people confuse the concept of organizational technology with the popular term **high technology**. The latter is related to, but certainly not identical with, the technology concept as it is used in organization theory. High technology has been used loosely to describe many different aspects of computer-based technologies such as microelectronics, fiber optics, satellite communications, lasers, expert systems, robotics and multimedia. Sometimes it refers to products that use these technologies (e.g., computers, cellular telephone) and sometimes to transformation processes that rely upon one or more of them (e.g., computer-aided design and manufacturing, also known as CAD-CAM). At other times high technology refers to any business in which technology is changing rapidly or to one that is considered to be technologically innovative. High technology sometimes merely refers to the demands for computer literacy that high technologies place on workers.

Service Technologies

Additional confusion concerning the concept of technology is sometimes created by contrasting manufacturing and service technologies. Organization theorists define **service**

technology in terms of three main characteristics, according to which services:

- are consumed as they are produced
- are intangible
- cannot be stored in inventory

Consider the example of a news organization whose service involves providing its customers with access to information. Information is produced through communication of messages so that it is consumed at the same moment that it is produced. Information has no tangible form and its news value dissipates so rapidly that, if it is to result in a profit through exchange, it cannot be held for long. These characteristics clearly place the technology of news organizations into the service category.

Now consider a typical manufacturing technology—an automobile assembly process. Certainly the products of this technology are tangible, they are not consumed as they are produced, but rather can be stored for months or years without losing much of their value—they can be sold and resold years after their date of manufacture. Nonetheless, many aspects of the product of an automobile manufacturing technology are similar to those of a service technology. For example, the value of the style and design of the automobile dissipates rapidly with the introduction of new models. Another example is the warranty that accompanies newly manufactured automobiles—a warranty is a promise of service that has become a large part of many automotive products.

The point made here is that the distinction between service and manufacturing technologies is difficult to maintain beyond a superficial categorization of particular types of businesses (e.g., by SEC codes that reflect traditional industrial groupings). When you undertake a more detailed analysis of an organization's technology you will notice that the outputs of most technologies have both service and manufacturing characteristics. It is because of this convergence that manufacturing firms can use the concepts developed for service sector firms, and vice versa, to improve their performance. Banks, for instance, often describe their services as if they were tangible products. This encourages them to focus their attention on packaging and other concerns typically associated with manufactured goods. For their part, numerous manufacturing firms have become obsessed with the customer, a strategy adopted from the service sector. The effectiveness of this cross-fertilization of ideas between the domains of service and manufacturing indicates that the distinction so often made between them is not a clean one. Nonetheless, in modernist organization theory, research on these different sectors continues to inform economists and managers about industry and competitive trends.

Typologies of Technology

Early modernists who studied technology focused on the variety of core technologies in use in their day and on the implications of this variety for discovering the best way of organizing. The typologies of technology they produced extended contingency theory by showing that social structure was contingent on the choice of production methods as well as on conditions in the environment. In this section of the chapter you will learn how to use the typologies of three organization theorists: Joan Woodward, James Thompson and Charles Perrow. Try all three of them out by analyzing the core technology, unit and task technologies of any organization with which you are familiar.

Woodward's Typology

Joan Woodward, a British sociologist, was among the first organization theorists to draw attention to the importance of technology, yet her initial research question did not concern technology at all. Modernist organization theory was embryonic at the time that Woodward designed her study and the legacy of the classical management school—the desire to find a single best way to organize—dominated thinking in the field. Differences of opinion over which of the proposed ways of organizing was best captured the imaginations of researchers and, in this context, Woodward decided to design a scientific study to find out once and for all which organizational arrangements produce the highest levels of performance.[1]

Woodward surveyed 100 manufacturing organizations operating in the vicinity of South Essex, England. She measured their relative levels of performance (above average, average, and below average for their industry) as well as span of control, the number of management levels, degree of centralization in decision-making practices and management style. Woodward expected to find that one pattern of these classical management variables was consistently related to higher levels of performance, thus she was quite surprised when her analysis of the data revealed no significant relationships.

Such an unexpected result could not be presented without explanation so Woodward sought an answer by trying different approaches to her data. At one point she grouped companies according to their level of **technical complexity**, which she defined as the degree of mechanization in the manufacturing process. This move revealed the pattern that made Woodward a famous organization theorist. Her analysis showed that structure was related to performance after all, but only when the type of core technology used by the organization was taken into account. That is, the best structure for an organization (i.e., one associated with high performance) depended upon the core technology employed. The typology Woodward used is shown in Figure 5.2 alongside her scale of technological complexity.

For ease of use, Woodward's technical complexity scale is usually condensed into three core technology types:

- unit or small batch
- large batch or mass production
- continuous processing

Unit and small batch technologies produce one item at a time or a few items all at once. A small amount of product is produced from start to finish and then the process begins again. Custom clothing, such as a tailored suit or theatrical costume, is usually the product of unit production technology. Other products typically produced in this way

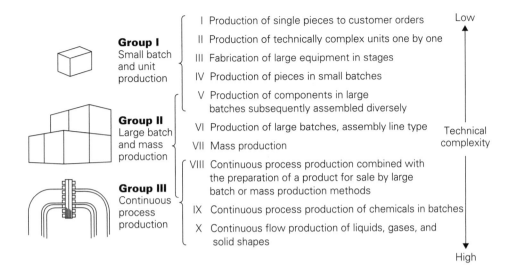

Figure 5.2 Woodward's original typology showing how she arrived at the technical complexity scale

Source: Woodward (1958). Crown copyright is reproduced with the permission of the Controller of HMSO.

include original works of art, designer glassware, commercial building projects and engineering prototypes. The production of wine uses small batch technology—a quantity of the wine is produced in one lot. Small batch technologies are also found in traditional bakeries and most college classrooms. In both unit and small batch technologies workers typically participate in the whole production process start to finish and so have a fairly complete understanding of the technology being used. Woodward's study showed that organizations that use unit and small batch technologies are more successful when they have smaller spans of control, fewer levels of management and when they practice decentralized decision making—characteristics associated with organic organizational forms.

Large batch or mass production technologies produce great quantities of identical products using highly routinized and often mechanized procedures. These technologies involve breaking the total production process into many discrete steps that can be performed either by machine or by human hands. An automobile assembly line is an example of mass production technology while steel production is an example of large batch technology. In large batch and mass production technologies workers repetitively perform a subset of the tasks involved in producing output. For instance, mass production workers are often physically located in positions adjacent to those whose activities are sequentially related to their own—the person on one side of them performs the task that precedes theirs and the person on their other side performs the task that follows theirs. Woodward's study showed that organizations using large batch and mass production technologies are more successful when their managers have larger spans of control and when they practice centralized decision making—characteristics associated with mechanistic forms of organizing.

Whereas mass production is a series of discrete tasks performed sequentially, **continuous processing** is a series of non-discrete transformations occurring in a sequence. Consider the examples of oil refining and waste treatment. In these cases, raw material (crude oil, raw sewage) is fed into one end of the process and, as it flows continuously through the system, contaminants and other unwanted substances are removed until the desired degree of refinement is reached (refined oil, treated sewage). In continuous processing, humans tend equipment that affects the transformation automatically, whereas in mass production humans directly perform at least some of the tasks by hand. Woodward's study showed that the patterns of organizing in successful continuous processing organizations were similar to those for unit and small batch technologies in that they had smaller spans of control and decentralized decision making; however, they required more levels of management than either small batch or mass production technologies.

In general, Woodward found that the highest levels of performance among her firms were achieved when mass production technologies were combined with mechanistic organizational forms, and when small batch or continuous processing technologies were combined with organic forms (these and other findings from her study are summarized in Table 5.1). However, subsequent studies have shown that Woodward's typology was limited in two ways. First, her study examined mainly small and medium-sized organizations and the moderating relationship she found between technology and the structure–performance link proved to be less important when organizations are large and therefore more complex. We will return to this issue later in the chapter. For now, let us turn our attention to the second limitation of Woodward's study, namely that it ignored nonmanufacturing firms.

Thompson's Typology

In the late 1960s James Thompson introduced significant advances in organization theory by stretching his typology of technology to include both manufacturing and service sector

Table 5.1 Findings from Woodward's study linking technology to social structure

Structural dimension	Technology		
	Unit production	Mass production	Continuous process
Levels of management	3	4	6
Span of control	23	48	15
Ratio of direct to indirect labor	9:1	4:1	1:1
Administrative ratio	low	medium	high
Formalization (written communication)	low	high	low
Centralization	low	high	low
Verbal communication	high	low	high
Skill level of workers	high	low	high
Overall structure	organic	mechanistic	organic

Source: Woodward (1965). By permission of Oxford University Press.

organizations.[2] Like Woodward, Thompson developed his theory of technology around three general types:

- long-linked
- mediating
- intensive

Long-linked technologies generally fit into either the mass production or continuous processing categories that Woodward defined. Thus automobile assembly lines as well as technologies for producing chemicals and generating electrical power fit the category of long-linked technology. Thompson used the descriptive term 'long-linked' because all of the technologies of this type involve linear transformation processes that have inputs entering at one end of a long series of sequential steps from which products emerge at the other.

Mediating technologies serve clients or customers by bringing them together in an exchange or other transaction. Banks, brokerage firms and insurance companies all operate using mediating technology. In general, these technologies link partners in a potential exchange by helping them locate one another and conduct their transactions, often without ever having to physically meet. For example, banks use mediating technology to bring together savers who want to invest money and borrowers who want to take out loans. Banking technology mediates between savers and borrowers by providing a location for both types of customers, and by providing standardized procedures to facilitate their mutual benefit, in this case, interest payments for savers and funds for borrowers. Thompson used the term 'mediating' because organizations using these technologies act as go-betweens in bringing together the interests of two or more different parties to a transaction.

Intensive technology occurs in hospital emergency rooms, research laboratories and in project organizations such as engineering design or construction work. Intensive technologies require coordinating the specialized abilities of two or more experts in the transformation of a usually unique input into a customized output. Each use of intensive technology requires on-the-spot development and application of specialized knowledge to new problems or unique circumstances.

Thompson's typology was grounded in the open systems model of organization according to which a core technology is open to its environment on both the input and output sides (see Figure 3.1). This openness alerted Thompson to the importance of the materials that were fed into the technical process and the outputs that the system produced. For example, some inputs and outputs are highly standardized (e.g., traditional mass production automobile manufacturing assembles nearly identical parts into nearly identical automobiles) while other technologies use unstandardized inputs to produce unstandardized outputs (e.g., hospital emergency rooms transform diseased or injured individuals into stabilized patients ready to be discharged or to accept other hospital services).

Thompson also recognized that technologies differed substantially depending upon their transformation processes. He noticed that some technologies were characterized by

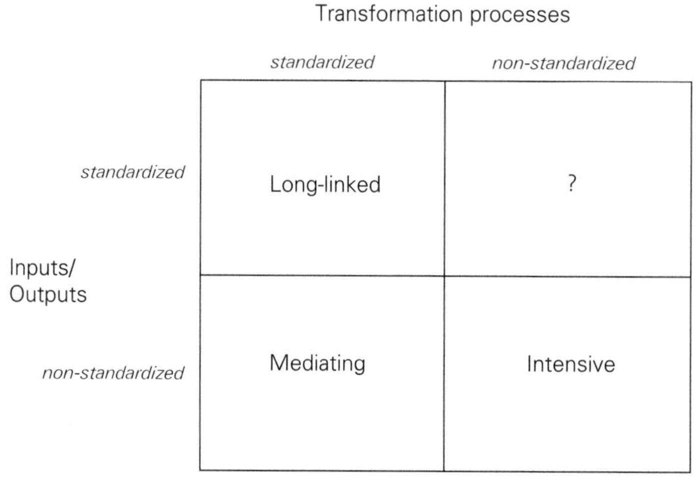

Transformation processes

	standardized	non-standardized
standardized	Long-linked	?
non-standardized	Mediating	Intensive

Inputs/Outputs

Figure 5.3 Two-by-two matrix showing Thompson's typology of technologies
Based on: Thompson (1967).

extreme standardization in their processing of inputs into outputs (e.g., automobile assembly workers perform the same tasks repeatedly), while other technologies seemed to have very little standardization of processes (e.g., emergency room personnel must respond to the unique needs of each patient as they come through the door).

Thompson's typology can be easily visualized in terms of a two-by-two matrix (see Figure 5.3). Using Thompson's two-by-two, you can classify any organization as producing either highly standardized outputs from highly standardized inputs *or* unstandardized outputs from unstandardized inputs, and as either using standardized or unstandardized transformation processes. The four cells of the matrix present Thompson's three alternative types of organizational technologies plus an extra one: (1) standardized inputs/outputs with standardized transformation processes describe long-linked technologies, (2) unstandardized inputs/outputs with standardized transformation processes describe mediating technologies, (3) unstandardized inputs/outputs with unstandardized transformation processes describe intensive technologies, and (4) standardized inputs/outputs with unstandardized transformation processes.

It is interesting to speculate about why Thompson ignored the fourth alternative in his matrix—standardized inputs/outputs with unstandardized transformation processes. The absence of a description of this category is probably due to the enormous inefficiency Thompson would have associated with such a technology. Imagine producing a standard product with standard inputs, and doing so in a different way every time. While such technologies exist (e.g., building prototypes for the design of manufacturing processes), Thompson, who was obsessed with applying norms of rationality, may have deliberately ignored this cell in his typology.

Perrow's Typology

Whereas Woodward and Thompson treated organizations as if they had only one dominant technology, Charles Perrow theorized technology by focusing on the task level of analysis.[3] He began by defining the variability and analyzability of tasks and then created measures that assessed these two dimensions (see Figure 5.4). **Task variability** is measured by counting the number of exceptions to standard procedures encountered in the application of a given technology. **Task analyzability** is measured as the extent to which, when an exception is encountered, there are known analytical methods for dealing with it. Although Perrow created his measures of task variability and task analyzability for organizational units, the same measurement technique can be used to create an aggregated score for a whole organization. Arraying task variability and task analyzability in a two-by-two matrix gave Perrow four technology types that he named:

- routine
- craft
- engineering
- nonroutine

   Routine technologies are characterized by low task variability and high task analyzability. The traditional automobile assembly line of Thompson's long-linked technology and Woodward's mass production category is also an example of Perrow's routine technology. Clerical work is another example. Filing clerks, for instance, encounter few exceptions to their standard work practices and when they do there is almost always a known method of resolution, such as hierarchical referral (i.e., ask the boss).

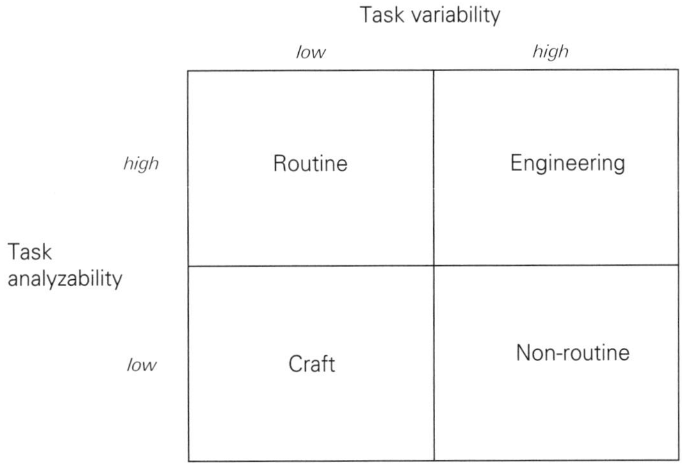

Figure 5.4 Two-by-two matrix showing Perrow's typology of technologies
Based on: Perrow (1967).

Craft technology describes conditions of low task variability and low task analyzability. Construction work is a craft technology. The construction worker encounters few exceptions to standard procedures but when exceptions are encountered, such as mistakes in planning or unavailable materials, a way of dealing with them must be invented. Locating water for drilling wells is another example of craft technology. In this technology intuition and experience become extremely important, as happens when standard geological solutions to finding water fail. Although standard procedures usually work in craft technologies, when exceptions occur (e.g., no water is found using available knowledge), there are few known solutions upon which workers can rely.

Engineering technologies occur where high task variability combines with high task analyzability. The technologies of laboratory technicians, executive secretaries, accountants and, of course, most engineers fit the engineering category (aerospace engineers are the exception, see nonroutine technology below). In engineering technology many exceptions to standard practices arise but employees possess the knowledge needed to solve these problems. Often the knowledge required by engineering technologies comes from advanced and highly specialized training, thus the presence of a great deal of traditional managerial and other professional work usually indicates an engineering technology is in use.

Nonroutine technology was the label Perrow attached to technologies characterized by high task variability and low task analyzability. These technologies occur, for instance, in research and development departments, aerospace engineering firms and prototype laboratories. Perrow's nonroutine category overlaps Woodward's unit and small batch category and has commonalities with Thompson's intensive category as well as his missing category of standardized input/outputs and unstandardized transformation processes. The high number of problems encountered in nonroutine technologies, and the lack of known methods for solving them, place employees in a more or less constant state of uncertainty.

Using the Three Typologies

Even though there are areas of overlap between the three typologies discussed so far, you should always begin a modernist technology analysis by applying all three in order to maximize the information available to you. Using all three will force you to consider the six dimensions that collectively underpin these types: technical complexity, routineness of work, standardization of inputs/outputs, standardization of transformation processes, task variability and task analyzability. Although you may conclude you do not need all of these dimensions to fully describe the technology you are studying, until you try them on your organization you will not know what their usefulness is. Many times I have been surprised by the insight provided when I applied a theory I did not initially think would be helpful.

To see how to apply the typologies, consider a company that manufactures buses. A chassis is brought in at one end of the factory and moves down the assembly line where axels, an engine, the body, interior trim and so on are added. Your initial assessment might be that the core technology at the organizational level of analysis is *long-linked* (Thompson). You discover that it is not large batch, because even though there are 50 buses, at various stages of completion on the assembly line, 10 are for one customer, 5 for another customer, 2 for another . . . and each order has different requirements for heating, air conditioning and internal and external trim; therefore it is a *small batch* technology (Woodward). Closer analysis at the unit level reveals that the Chassis and Suspension Department can be characterized by *routine* technology (Perrow) because task variability is low (the only variation is the choice of two chassis lengths) and task analyzability is high (there are standardized methods for positioning and bolting the suspension on the chassis). The Internal Trim Department, however, is characterized by *engineering* technology because task variability is high (different customers want different seating configurations, heaters, handrails, doors, lights, decals, etc., situated in different places) and task analyzability is also high (there are procedures and methods for dealing with these differences).

The bus manufacturing example highlights the complexity of analyzing the technology of an organization and the danger of ignoring one or more levels of analysis. By focusing only on core technology at the organizational level you lose the interesting details of technological diversity at the unit level. The loss can be justified on the grounds of the power of abstraction to make generalized comparisons for statistical analysis, but you should not forget what has been given up in the bargain. It is also important to take great care in clearly stating what your level and focus of analysis are. Whenever you change levels in order to clarify what is going on in a particular core technology, as in the example above, be certain to note that this is what you are doing so that you do not become lost midway through your analysis. Finally, as you focus on the interesting details that appear at the unit or task levels of analysis you will probably want to combine several different types from among the typologies. By encouraging you to think multi-dimensionally this technique will both stretch your imagination and strengthen your ability to perform modernist technology analysis. But remember to take great care with levels of analysis; it is easy to switch levels without being aware that you are doing so. Level switching is often illuminating but if you lose your bearings it will be hard to avoid confusion.

This section of the chapter has only presented modernists definitions and typologies. Later in the chapter you will learn about the ways modernists employ these to theorize about the relationships between technology, social structure and organizational environments.

Technology in the Symbolic-Interpretive Perspective

Symbolic-interpretivists believe that, like every other aspect of organizations, technology is socially constructed. This perspective expands the definition of technology such that technology is:

- not just physical objects and equipment, but symbols (words and images) and root metaphors
- not just task activities, but actions and interactions between people and technology
- not just knowledge, but interpretation

New Technologies

Shoshona Zuboff suggested that new computer-based (high) technology requires more interpretive processes than does traditional technology because data involves symbolic representations rather than tangible objects. Karl Weick's conception of new technology as stochastic, continuous and abstract reinforces this idea. Weick's theorizing began with the observation that computer technology allows us to monitor production, especially continuous process production, without ever seeing or touching the product it produces. To operate new technologies the product is conceptualized in numerical or graphic terms that are then interpreted as a means to perceiving what is happening inside the production process. Weick asserted that new technologies lie on the frontiers of Woodward's conception of technical complexity and beyond the reach of Perrow's category of nonroutineness. Weick described three properties that distinguish new technologies from their more routine and less complex forerunners: stochastic, continuous and abstract.[4]

Stochastic events are unexpected interruptions. While earlier technologies also occasion stochastic events (e.g., boilers sometimes blow up for no apparent reason), users are able to minimize surprises by learning from experience and observation of their machines. The greater stochastic nature of new technologies means that processes and their underlying causes and effects are not well understood by those who operate them. Problems involve dense interactions that slow operators' reaction times as they try to figure out what is happening. Knowledge accumulates slowly because problems are often unique and/or poorly understood. If my computer freezes, I can spend a lot of time trying different ways to unfreeze it. I may be successful without understanding why or even which of my actions resolved the problem. Next time my computer freezes, I go through a similar process of trial and error and hope for a similarly successful resolution, even though I may never understand the computer's seemingly random behavior. As Weick put it, stochastic events propel us toward alchemy!

New technologies are often operated nonstop, which is to say they are **continuous** in a way that was not anticipated by Woodward's and Perrow's typologies. One implication of the continuous property of new technologies is the need for reliability. For example in order to make flight reservations through the Internet 24 hours a day, 7 days a week, 52 weeks a year, data must be processed continuously and, if the data processing system is not reliable, chaos could ensue from double bookings or the reporting of inaccurate flight times or incorrect destinations. The importance of reliability for new technologies is perhaps most evident when continuous technologies are dangerous, such as nuclear power or air traffic control. The need to maintain a continuously reliable process produces great mental workloads for operators who only see blips on a screen. Another implication of the continuous property of new technologies is that those who design them must do so while they are in use. This creates added complexity for both designers and users, making these technologies nonroutine in another way that was not anticipated by Woodward or Perrow.

The greater mental workload associated with new technologies is evident in their third property—**abstractness**. Compared to old technologies where you can see the moving parts of a machine, the working processes of new technology are hidden from view inside computers and other machines. Operating abstract technologies requires inference and imagination on the part of the operator. Take the case of a computer. You do not see the data flowing through computer hardware, nor can you see the point in the computing process where a glitch occurs. Operators working with symbols of processes (computer readouts) as opposed to actual processes work once removed from what the machinery does and thus the potential differences between the two processes (one in the head, the other in the computer) contributes to misunderstanding, error and the possibility of conflicting interpretations of what things mean when the technology malfunctions.

Weick's theory of new technology indicates that new technologies are substantially more complex and nonroutine than was anticipated by Woodward's and Perrow's typologies and therefore these typologies need updating. In addition, Weick told us that the stochastic, continuous and abstract nature of new technologies mean we need to pay more attention to technology as *equivoque* (open to many possible interpretations)—a topic taken up in several symbolic-interpretive studies of technology.

The Social Construction of Technology (SCOT)

Early work by symbolic-interpretive organization theorists interested in technology took on the linear models of technological innovation preferred by modernists. According to modernist theories, technological innovations move through predictable stages from pure science to applied research, development, production, marketing and finally to use. Symbolic-interpretive theorists subscribed to a different view. For example, Wiebe Bijker and John Law, two early proponents of the social construction of technology (SCOT), argued that there is nothing inevitable about the way technologies develop because they mirror complex social trade-offs.[5] In other words, technology is not a pure application of science; it is co-determined by social, cultural, economic and technical factors in the environment that contextualizes it.

Bijker and Trevor Pinch proposed an evolutionary theory of technological innovation in which variations of products are developed, some are selected and retained, and others die. To demonstrate their theory they traced the development of the bicycle, suggesting that certain social groups gave meaning to various designs and used them for different purposes and in different ways. Design changes were made according to the interpretations given to the needs of these users. For example, women cyclists who wore long dresses required modifications to the bicycle frame while other users demanded stability or speed. These sometimes conflicting demands resulted in multiple design variations from which some were selected and others ignored by users. The technology that produced the bicycle we know today resulted from user influence on the success of various designs. Of course, do not forget mutual influence—while social and cultural contexts influence technology, technology influences society and culture. For example, the bicycle helped change attitudes toward women wearing trousers.

While a number of SCOT theorists focused on the macro level of technological inno-vation in society, others examined interpretive processes that influenced the course of technological development within organizations or units of organizations. One such example is Julian Orr's ethnographic study of the work of photocopier repair technicians at Xerox.[6] In order to explore how meaning is negotiated around technology, Orr immersed himself in a community of Xerox photocopier repair technicians. He and the technicians attended classes at repair school, hung out at lunch and went on service visits; all the while Orr audio taped their interactions and kept field notes. He also studied customers/users, their organizations and the copy machines they used. On the basis of his study, Orr concluded that copy machines have both a technical and a social presence. Their technical presence—which is built into the machines—is constituted by mechanical and electronic technologies that require specific behavioral responses from their technicians and users. However, individual machines also have their own histories and ways of behaving, for example, some have a history of breakdowns, others make unique noises. This means that users and technicians often become attuned to the way they experience a particular machine and, even though they have an operations manual, they often need to improvise when interacting with these machines.

Orr discovered the social presence of technology by observing the conversations that revolved around copiers. For example, he observed technicians and customers negotiating the meaning of technical problems and the appropriate use of the technology the machines offered. Furthermore, Orr noted that technicians discussed their work among themselves, sharing knowledge and constructing their identities as competent technicians by showing off their skill in handling problems and carrying out successful repairs. Their regularized interactions resulted in the development of a community of practice (see Chapter 4) and a subculture (see Chapter 6). Thus Orr's study not only highlighted the socially constructed and situated nature of technical work and technology but also showed that the concepts of technology, social structure and organizational culture influence each other.

You should recognize that the socially constructed nature of technology may be hidden from its users. Although much face-to-face collaboration took place in the work setting of a major computer technology manufacturing company, employees believed that most of their communication was mediated by their computers.[7] All employees of the company were linked through an intranet and everything they emailed to one another was documented by computer programs. However much of the sharing and interpretation of information concerning work improvements and problem solving took place in largely informal, spontaneous face-to-face gatherings. The implications of these findings are profound because they indicate that managing technology (old or new) is not just about the technology itself but also about the interactions and interpretations made by people using the technology. Furthermore those involved may be unaware of the interpretations they make. The meaning we give technology and the interpretations we offer when resolving technological problems have just as much influence on the effectiveness of technology as do physical machine parts or techniques for using machines. You will see that the idea of the social construction of technology carried over into the postmodern perspective is discussed next.

Postmodernism and Technology

The study of technology from a postmodern perspective reveals how the most powerful members of an organization are able to structure the means of production around the ends they desire. German philosopher Martin Heidegger raised provocative questions about the relationship between technology and the self. As an existential phenomenologist, Heidegger's work falls broadly into the symbolic-interpretive perspective, yet postmodernists were the ones to build on his ideas in the field of organization theory. In a book entitled *The Question Concerning Technology*, Heidegger claimed that the essence of technology lies in the manner in which it is used (particularly how we unlock its potential) and how we allow it to shape who we are.[8] Heidegger saw grave danger in technology because, while it offers many possibilities, it can also imprison us if we allow ourselves to become subservient to its needs. Be sure to notice the parallel to Weber's warning that bureaucracy might become an iron cage.[9]

It is the danger and Heidegger's call for reflexivity in the face of it that drew postmodernists into the study of technology in organizations. A number of postmodernists study technologies of representation and control to show how technology controls behavior and serves as a means of disciplining organizational members and reinforcing managerial authority. Others are interested in the liberating potential of technology and its ability to transform the world into a global marketplace or a global village tied together by strong social bonds that work in spite of geographical separation.[10] Many combine the forbidding and liberating aspects of technology, perhaps none more so than those who have been inspired by the cyborg myth portrayed in science fiction. All these themes will be discussed below.

Technologies of Representation

Those who study **technologies of representation** are interested in the way reality, organizations and actions are made visible by our use of symbolism and imagery. Computer technology can be used not only to provide three-dimensional virtual realities and sensory experiences, but also for remote control and surveillance. A modernist conception of computer technology focuses on the computer's ability to improve production, research and service processes. For example, we can create models to test equipment or products before they are built or after they are in service, and we can create computer simulations to project the outcomes of different scenarios or to train equipment operators such as airline pilots. In contrast to this approach, postmodernists, especially those inclined toward critical theory, focus greater attention on the dark side, in particular the seductive and pernicious nature of technology. Recall the film *The Matrix* (discussed in Chapter 2) in which human immersion in computer images causes the loss of a sense of what is real.

Technologies of representation are all ways of managing organizations by remote control through the representation of humans and work processes by bits of electronic data processed by computers. Robert Cooper says that organization theorists and managers often underestimate the impact of technologies of representation on the development of administration and management.[11] Take the case of the unquestioned use of balance sheets and organization charts in most modern organizations and in modernist organization theory. Or consider how federal, state and many city administrations in the United States are governed by a merit system that dictates hiring, evaluation and promotion decisions for government employees based on their qualifications, ability and performance. The merit system consists of extensive regulations and written documents that govern the management of personnel. A complex position classification system describes, evaluates, grades and ranks all jobs so that staffing, job performance, pay and other personnel activities can be monitored and controlled. The hiring process centers around competitive examinations held prior to interviewing that are based on multiple choice questions. Exams scored by computer determine whether a candidate moves on to the next stage of the hiring process. A candidate's suitability for a position is thereby decided without any need for anyone to talk to the person. It is not much of a leap of imagination from these technologies of representation to the cinematic nightmare of technologically imprisoned lives portrayed by futuristic films like *Blade Runner*, *Minority Report* and *The Bourne Identity*.

Technologies of Control

While most postmodernists portray technology as a form of overt control, some also comment on its ability to addict us to mass consumption. We are bombarded daily by media and Internet images selling lifestyles and identities we are encouraged to consume and then communicate to others, enticing them to do the same. In *The Postmodern Condition*, Lyotard stated that technology is an integral part of the discourse of power and social control and consequently the destruction of human social bonds. He argued that postindustrial capitalism, and in particular its associated technology, has shifted social values from those of truth and justice to efficiency, that is, to attaining optimal performance by minimizing the amount of energy expended to achieve the maximum output. Social control is exercised when decisions about the value of a person, department or institution are based primarily on their ability to contribute to the efficiency of the system. The more efficient and knowledgeable the organization, technology or person, the more powerful they become, but also the more they become imprisoned within the system that defines and grants their power.

Lyotard also portrayed technology as the root of all radical change in society. For instance, he claimed that the computerization of society changes the nature of knowledge, turning it into a commodity as opposed to being the hallmark of an educated mind. He predicted that in the future the only knowledge that will be acceptable will be that which can be translated into information for analysis and dissemination by computers. The rest will be abandoned. Power struggles will occur, not over geopolitical territory as in the past, but over control of what is to be regarded as information. Lyotard ends *The Postmodern Condition* by predicting that the computerization of society will either lead to control of the market system and the production of knowledge by terrorism, or to greater justice. He warned that the path to greater justice will only be opened by free public access to information.

To many postmodernists, the realization of Lyotard's vision seems to be in evidence today. His vision can be seen in the scrolling of information across our TV and computer screens and in the flurry of activity that can result as we watch the Dow Jones or the *Financial Times* indexes fluctuate sharply. We can sell or buy shares over the Internet through virtual transactions without actually touching any cash. The terror of this vision can be seen in the growth of cyberveillance—computer programs that can track every keystroke you make, every website you access and can open your email. Postmodernists acknowledge, however, that computer technology also encourages democracy and is a useful tool of economic, environmental and political resistance. Social movements can provide information to mobilize and organize people across the globe. The Greenpeace website, for example, carries information about current campaigns and calls for volunteers, including a cyberactivist community page with e-cards that can be sent to government officials and corporations with one keystroke. In the first week of a campaign against genetically modified foods, 11,000 protest cards were emailed to the Bush Administration.[12]

British organizational researchers Rod Coombs, David Knights and Hugh Willmott have equated information technology (IT) with managerial control.[13] These researchers argued that IT is a means to direct thought and action in organizations and to discipline members for noncompliance with the desires or expectations of managers. They argued that the seeming objectivity of performance data conceals the fact that the categories into which data are collected and from which they are reported impose values on those who work within the system. For example, data reporting the number of patients served per day in a hospital imposes a value for speedy processing, as opposed to a value for quality of care, on the doctors, nurses, and administrators who feel pressured by the desire to keep their jobs and their self-esteem. The critical view recognizes that nonmanagerial employees are not powerless, they can resist control via sabotage (e.g., entering false data into the information system), nonresponsiveness (e.g., refusing to react to feedback from the system), and even joking (e.g., as a psychological defense against changing their values). However, the critique emphasizes the alignment between most technology theories and the interests of management and thus contributes to the postmodern debate about silence and voice.

Cyborganization

Have you ever lost data on your hard drive by making a mistake when closing a file, suffered the crash of a hard drive, or had your computer stolen? If so you are probably acutely aware of the extent to which your memory extends beyond your brain. Now think about the many other forms of technology you rely upon every day—your refrigerator, microwave oven, clock and automobile. Without these technologies many people could not eat or get to work.

Technology researchers are typically fascinated by human dependence on technology and increasingly with the points of contact between humans and machines. A few have adopted the postmodernist approach of disappearing the boundary between humans and machines and have proposed using the idea of the cyborg, popularized in science fiction by films like *The Terminator* and *Robocop*. British organization theorists Martin Parker and Robert Cooper proposed extending cyborg theory to organizations by formulating the concept of **cyborganization**.

The term 'cyborg' was coined by Manfred Clynes, a space scientist who researched ways to free astronauts from routine maintenance tasks in space, but it was American feminist Donna Haraway who wrote about cyborgs in a way that caught the attention of postmodern organization theorists. Haraway proposed using the cyborg myth, not in a bipolar or dichotomizing way, but in the full postmodern sense of a hybrid—something at once human and machine, simultaneously natural and artificial, a complete postmodern blend of dichotomizing polarities. In *Simians, Cyborgs, and Women: The Reinvention of Nature*, she dissolved the boundaries between technology and humans using the myth of the cyborg—a post-gender hybrid of human and machine. She defined cyborgs as 'a kind of disassembled and reassembled, postmodern collective and personal self'.[14] She used cyborg as a metaphor for the relationship between the body, social order, and historical and political repression to show how the human body embodies its context. While the world of the cyborg is one of ambiguity, partial connections and simulated consciousness, not to mention exploitation, domination and social and genetic engineering, Haraway offered an alternative interpretation of the cyborg as a materialization of the dualisms that shape our life—mind/body, male/female, public/private, to name only a few. By being embodied in one creature these dualisms break down permitting old, stale social-political standoffs to be reconfigured. Haraway interpreted cyborg imagery to mean exploring alternative realities, embracing contradiction, constructing and deconstructing boundaries and opening new connections—all of which mark the positive contributions made by the postmodern perspective and in particular the role that feminist technoscience plays in specifying the implications of high-tech culture for humankind.

According to Martin and Cooper, cyborganization is a contraction of cybernetic organization as well as an extension of Haraway's cyborg myth. You will recall from Chapter 2 that cybernetics is a branch of systems theory that focuses on communication and control in humans and machines. It is an organizational science in the sense that patterns of information or activity create organization. One of the primary contributions of cybernetics to science has been its insistence on viewing organization as the outcome of bipolar forces of stability/instability and order/disorder. Cyberneticists not only acknowledge the complexity of bipolarity but introduce the notion of complicity, which refers to partnering, for example humans combined with machines. Man–machine hybrids are, of course, cyborgs.

Cooper related Haraway's cyborg myth to developments in information theory suggested by cyberneticist Norbert Weiner: 'A piece of information, in order to contribute to the general information of a community, must say something substantially different from the community's previous stock of information.'[15] The implication of Weiner's insight, according to Cooper, is that information systems thrive on their openness to novelty and surprise. If we are cyborgs, then we are in a position to thrive on new information. Perhaps this is an explanation for the rise of the power of the media in postindustrial society—cyborgs eat information and the media provide an unlimited supply! Turning this reasoning on organizations, it becomes clear that organizations are even more bound to their technologies than humans are, not just in their core production processes but through and through. Think of all the computers, video equipment, photocopiers, communication and transportation devices, manufacturing gear and so on that make up most organizations. This is cyborganization.[16]

Combining Technology with Social Structure and Environment

Much of the most recent work on technology addresses the impact of new technologies on the design and management of organizations. Modernist organization theorists examine the impact of new technology on social structure, claiming that computer technologies and communication networks have transformed classical conceptualizations of work design. New technologies have reduced the need for physical proximity, hierarchical controls, and direct integrating mechanisms (e.g., supervision, liaison roles, face-to-face task groups) and have enabled the work of virtual organizations and teams. New technologies can also lead to greater decentralization of decision making because data is more readily available—integration occurs through electronic linking, increased spans of control and decreased hierarchical levels as individuals deal with more information. Software programs correct errors and make the exchange of information easier and faster.[17] But the relationship between social structure, technology and the environment has a history that predates new technologies. In this final section of the chapter we will review some of this important theory, starting with the story of how technology came to be added to contingency theory.

The Technological Imperative

Joan Woodward's influential study of technology ushered in the idea that technology determines which sort of organizational structure is most effective. Belief in this idea came to be known as the **technological imperative**—the belief that choosing a technology determines other aspects of the organization, like its structure. While some organization theorists focused on replicating and extending Woodward's study, others found evidence that substantially altered beliefs in the technological imperative. For example, the Aston Group found empirical evidence that the influence of technology on structure depended on the size of the organization; the smaller the organization the greater the significance of technology for the structure–performance relationship.[18]

The explanation provided by the Aston researchers was that, when organizations consist of little beyond their core technology, as was the case for the relatively small organizations studied by Woodward, then technology has a significant and possibly determining effect on social structure. But as the organization becomes more complex this relationship disappears. Another way to interpret the findings of the Aston studies is to recognize that social structures relate to the technology that is being used, which for some units and their employees will not be the core technology of the organization, but the technology of their unit. In small organizations most employees are directly involved with the core technology, for example a small welding company will employ mainly welders with perhaps one staff person. In large organizations many employees are involved in technologies that are not directly related to the core (see Figure 4.3 for examples). Thus, the overall characteristics of social structures in larger organizations reflect the greater differentiation and integration of a wider array of technologies than do social structures in small organizations. In other words, in large organizations the relationship between the core technology and the general characteristics of the complex social structure are diluted. Technology and structure are still significantly related, but the relationship is vastly more complicated in large organizations than it is in small ones.

Technical Complexity, Uncertainty and Routineness

You should remember that Woodward distinguished technologies by their technical complexity, measuring this variable as the extent to which machines perform core transformation processes. In relating technical complexity to structural arrangements, Woodward noticed that technologies at both extremes of her scale (unit and continuous processing technologies) were best served by organic structures, while technologies in the middle range (large batch, mass production) performed better with a mechanistic structure. Woodward's explanation for this pattern was the **routineness of work** performed by people using the various technologies. Woodward noticed that both unit and continuous processing technologies involved work that was nonroutine, while the work associated with mass production was highly routine. Unit and continuous process technologies are better suited to organic structures, she reasoned, because they are more compatible with nonroutine work. On the other hand, mass production technologies are better suited to mechanistic structures because these structures encourage and support routine work.

Compare a small graphics design organization working on a variety of client projects ranging from simple web pages for individual customers to complex corporate websites (unit/small batch), with a manufacturer of standardized electrical components whose raw materials and manufacturing processes vary little across time (mass production/large batch). The graphics design firm needs to be much more responsive to client needs and flexible in relation to how work is accomplished than does the manufacturing company. Now compare both of these to a nuclear power plant where most of the work done by humans consists of monitoring machines. It may help you to remember the relationship between the routineness of work and technical complexity if you see it as the inverted U-shaped curve shown in Figure 5.5. In the figure, graphic designers are classed as artists because their work is nonroutine, creative and driven by unique customer requirements, thus their organization is more likely to be successful if it has organic characteristics. In the manufacturing organization the opposite holds true and so a mechanistic structure is more appropriate. Although most work in a nuclear power plant is highly routine, when the equipment malfunctions workers must be ready for anything so they must maintain flexibility in their structures due to the occasional bout of extremely nonroutine activity.

Although Perrow categorized technologies on a different basis than did Woodward, he too noted the importance of routineness. In fact Perrow's two-by-two matrix is often collapsed onto a one-dimensional scale. Mathematically this involves projecting points in Perrow's two-dimensional space onto a line formed by the diagonal that runs through the routine and nonroutine quadrants (see Figure 5.6). The points, representing technologies located within the

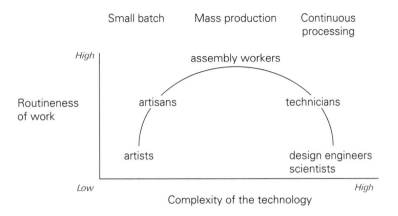

Figure 5.5 The relationship between the routineness of work and technical complexity

Woodward's findings indicate that both unit and continuous processing technologies are associated with low routineness, while mass production technologies have high routineness. Thus, the relationship between routineness of work and technical complexity takes the form of an inverted U.

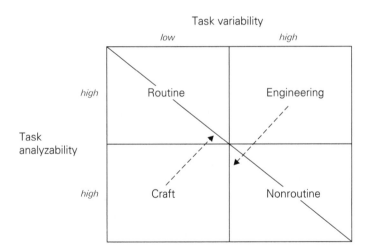

Figure 5.6 Projection of Perrow's two-dimensional typology of technologies onto the single dimension of routineness

quadrants, are plotted on this line according to their level of routineness such that craft and engineering technologies will generally fall between the two extremes of routine and nonroutine work. The relationship between Perrow's and Woodward's conceptualizations of the routineness of work is that Perrow defined two subdimensions of routineness by elaborating on the occurrence of exceptions to work routines involving nonanalyzable problems.

Perrow's interest in nonroutineness led him to focus on technology as a determinant of uncertainty in organizations. According to Perrow, technology contributes to uncertainty either through variations in the quality or availability of inputs to the transformation process or through the variable nature of the transformation process itself. When uncertainty is high it becomes difficult to structure the activities of the organization because the activities that are required are not always known in advance.

Perrow's and Woodward's discussions of the effects of technology are like two sides of a single coin. Both explain the links between technology and social structure in terms of the routineness and nonroutineness of work. However, whereas Woodward was the first to propose the relationship between technology and social structure, Perrow sought a more thorough explanation for it. Like Perrow, Thompson looked for deeper understanding of the links between technology and social structure, but in contrast to Perrow, did so with greater emphasis on social structure. You can see positivist accumulation of knowledge at work here—first Woodward discovered the importance of technology in understanding how organizational structure and performance are related, then Thompson added service technologies to those of manufacturing, and finally Perrow elaborated the differences between technology types when they are viewed from the unit and task levels of analysis.

Task Interdependence and Mechanisms of Coordination

Following Woodward and Perrow's emphasis on variability in the routineness of work, Thompson recognized that the work processes associated with a technology vary in the extent to which they are interrelated. He called this variable **task interdependence** to emphasize the issue of dependence on others for the accomplishment of tasks. Thompson related the task interdependence created by technology to different possible coordination mechanisms that could be designed into an organization's social structure. His work on task interdependence identified links between different forms of coordination and the mediating, long-linked and intensive technologies framed by his typology.

In a mediating technology a number of offices or officials perform their work tasks almost independently of one another, at least so far as actual work flows between units is concerned. Therefore, little direct contact is needed between units (or individuals). Thompson used the term **pooled task interdependence** to refer to cases in which the output of the organization is primarily the sum of the efforts of each unit (see Figure 5.7). Take banking as an example. Banks employ a mediating technology in the sense that they mediate between borrowers and savers or investors. Mediation can be accomplished simultaneously by several bank branches that operate almost independently of one another. Day and night shifts on an assembly line, franchised restaurants and the different departments of a university or a large retail store are additional examples of organizational units that typically operate using pooled task interdependence.

According to Thompson, groups operating with pooled task interdependence demand very little in the way of coordination. The coordination required to achieve a coherent organizational identity or to ensure that services are consistent across units can, for the most part, be accomplished through the use of **rules and standard procedures** for

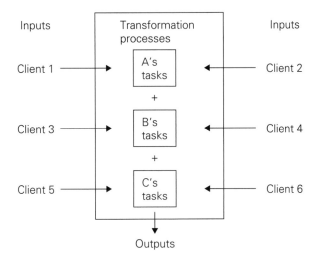

Figure 5.7 Mediating technologies generate pooled interdependence

Notice that A, B and C's joint product forms the output of the organization, yet they can operate more or less independently of one another.

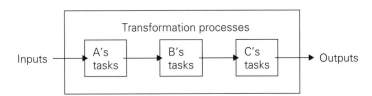

Figure 5.8 Long-linked technologies are associated with sequential task interdependence

This type of technology generates an unbalanced relationship where A experiences the least dependence and C the most, with B's dependence being less than C's but more than A's.

routine operations. For example, rules and standard procedures for tasks such as opening bank accounts, investing in certificates of deposit or mutual funds, and applying for and approving loans and lines of credit produce sufficient coordination for a bank to integrate the activities of its branches.

Long-linked technology involves both pooled and **sequential task interdependence**. For instance, several assembly lines can operate at once in a manner that leaves them practically independent of one another; in this regard the different lines are pooled in the sense that their outputs are aggregated into the total output of the organization. However, within each line interdependence is more complex because each worker is dependent on the work of others located at positions prior to theirs on the line. If workers early in the process are not performing their tasks properly, then the work of those further down the line suffers. This is called sequential task interdependence because the work tasks are performed in a fixed sequence (Figure 5.8).

In long-linked technologies, the sequential nature of task interdependence requires more **planning and scheduling** than does pooled interdependence. Again consider the assembly line as an example. All work tasks must be designed and workers assigned and scheduled to work together in order for the assembly line operation to function properly. Because any break in the line can interrupt production, careful planning of tasks and scheduling of workers is imperative. Of course, in addition to coordination by plans and schedules, rules about coming to work on time and procedures to follow when something on the line has created a problem are also part of coordinating this type of technology.

The scope of the task within an intensive technology is too large for one individual to perform the transformation alone, so there is need for an exchange of information between workers during the performance of their tasks. Thompson describes this as **reciprocal task interdependence**. In a restaurant, for example, the kitchen staff and the wait staff have reciprocal interdependence because the kitchen is dependent upon the wait staff to provide orders, and the wait staff is dependent upon the kitchen staff to provide meals prepared to the customer's satisfaction. The primary difference between sequential and reciprocal task interdependence is that, where long-linked technologies involve work flows that move in one direction only, intensive technologies involve reciprocal work flows (see Figure 5.9).

Coordinating the tasks central to the operation of an intensive technology requires **mutual adjustment** on the part of the individuals or units involved due to the reciprocal nature of their task interdependence. When intensive technologies involve immediate reciprocal coordination, mutual adjustment takes the extreme form of teamwork. In **teamwork**, work inputs to the transformation process are acted upon simultaneously by members of the work team, rather than passing inputs back and forth as is the case for less intensive forms of reciprocal task interdependence. Take the case of an emergency room surgical operation. A surgeon needs to be able to continuously exchange information with

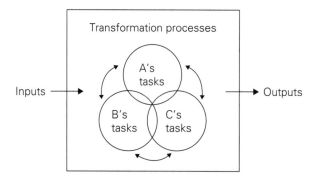

Figure 5.9 Intensive technologies create reciprocal task interdependence

A, B and C are mutually dependent, thus this type of technology generates the highest levels of task interdependence.

Table 5.2 Guttman scale of relationships between types of task interdependence and coordination mechanisms

Task interdependence	Rules and procedures	Schedules and plans	Mutual adjustment
Pooled	x		
Sequential	x	x	
Reciprocal	x	x	x

Based on: Thompson (1967).

the anesthesiologist, assisting doctors and nurses during the performance of the operation. Thus, intensive technologies require joint decision making and either physical co-location or a direct channel of communication such as a satellite link or other instantaneous communication device.

Be sure to notice that intensive technology also involves pooled and sequential task interdependence. Mutual adjustment, planning, scheduling, rules and procedures all contribute to the ability of experts to perform when and where their services are required. For example, emergency room doctors have scheduled work hours and rules to follow, ranging from established surgical procedures to wearing a beeper when they are on call. Notice how, as task interdependence increases from pooled to sequential to reciprocal, mechanisms of coordination get added to the organization. Pooled interdependence only requires rules and procedures, but sequential interdependence uses rules, procedures and scheduling, while reciprocal interdependence uses all these forms of coordination plus mutual adjustment. Such situations are described with a cumulative scale named after Louis Guttman, the sociologist who defined it.[19] In a **Guttman scale**, each level of a variable implies all the correlates of lower levels of the same variable. Table 5.2 illustrates the Guttman scale for task interdependence and the coordination mechanisms that are related to the three levels of task interdependence discussed by Thompson.

Information Processing and New Technologies

Jay Galbraith, an American organization theorist, proposed that complexity, uncertainty and interdependence place demands on an organization to process information in order to coordinate activities.[20] Galbraith claimed that it is demands for communication that shape the structure of the organization. He argued that technical complexity leads to structural complexity, uncertainty promotes organic forms, and interdependence increases demands for coordination *because* these factors increase the communication load carried by an organization. It is this communication load that directly affects how people interact and thus the organization's social structure. According to Galbraith, the effects of technology and the environment on social structure are mediated by

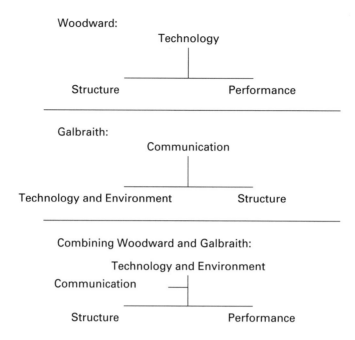

Figure 5.10 How modernist theories are elaborated

Woodward's investigation of structure–performance relationships led to her discovery of the important role of technology for theories of organization. Subsequent studies of the technology–structure relationship led to the discovery of other issues such as uncertainty and task interdependence. For instance, Galbraith proposed that communication mediates the relationship between technology and social structure.

communication. Notice the similarity between Galbraith's reasoning and Woodward's theory. Just as Woodward identified technology as a mediating factor in the structure–performance relationship, Galbraith argued communication mediates the relationships between technology and structure, and environment and structure (see Figure 5.10). This progressive elaboration and refinement of distinctions and relationships within relationships is a good example of how modernist organization theorists develop new contingency theories.

Technology and Structuration

As we saw in Chapter 4, Giddens's structuration theory showed that structure and human action are intimately interwoven, each producing the other. You may recall that while modernists take social structure to be an objective entity, symbolic-interpretivists treat it as the objectification of patterns of relationship arising from recurrent interactions and social practices. Although Giddens believed that each explanation is valid, organizational theorists studying technology as structuration, debate this issue. Some suggest social structure is embedded in the material properties of technology such that we are forced to behave in ways that are predetermined by our equipment. For example, the physical components of a computer force us to sit in front of a screen for hours on end. Others suggest that social structures are not embedded in technology, but emerge as we interact with technology—technology and social structure are co-determinants. For example, our need to be mobile yet connected causes computers to adapt, taking the form of laptops, Blackberries and other portable electronic devices.

The idea that social structures emerge as we interact with and use technology is known as **adaptive structuration theory**.[21] Instead of focusing only on technology (as with modernist conceptions of technology), adaptive structuration theorists examine **technologies-in-practice**. They focus on the recurring social practices and enactment of routines and improvisation associated with technology. American organization theorist Wanda Orlikowski suggested that individuals use technology in different ways. For example, a graphic artist will use different software programs than will an accountant; some people type with two fingers, others with ten. Individuals create and use different technologies-in-practice as they identify and choose different features and develop their own style of interacting with technology and base their sensemaking on it. In this way, we give meaning to and shape technology as it shapes us.[22]

Technologies-in-practice may be resistant to change as we develop habits and then attribute them to the system, but they may change as we modify the technology or improvise new practices. For example, Orlikowski studied how different groups in a multinational consulting firm used a software program called Notes. She found that technology staff used Notes extensively and also customized it to their own needs—the routines they enacted around the Notes technology included electronic discussions, information sharing, and cooperative troubleshooting—a collaborative technology-in-practice. Most of the consultants used the software minimally—they enacted a limited-use technology-in-practice. These users had little knowledge about the system and were skeptical about its value in helping them do their jobs. So, even though the technology was technically the same for both groups of users, practices varied across contexts depending upon the users' levels of interest in using the technology and the practical, institutional and interpretive limits of the technology they perceived.

Structuration theory highlights a different perspective on the relationship between technology and social structure than does the technological imperative. With technologies-in-practice, structure emerges from both the physical properties of technology and the ways we interact with that technology. This can be seen in the field of information technology and in the practices of dotcoms and e-commerce, where technology and social structure take shape as people improvise their use of technology. In these types of organizations, the product is not necessarily a concrete object, but may be a database, website or information-processing routine. In this situation, the means of production is interwoven with the end product as people use the technology for their own purposes. For example, you might use a computer to download music (a product) but also use the sounds within the computer to synthesize virtual instruments to create your own music, perhaps accompanied by visual effects.

SUMMARY

From the modernist perspective, technology is typically defined in terms of its:

- objects—products, services and the tools and equipment used in their production
- task activities or processes—the methods of production
- knowledge needed to develop and apply equipment, tools, and methods to produce a particular product or service

Organizational theorists working from the modernist perspective begin with the premise that organizations have technologies for transforming inputs into outputs. These technologies consist of physical objects, activities, processes and knowledge, all of which are brought to bear on raw materials, labor and capital inputs during a transformation process. The core technology is that set of productive components most directly associated with the primary transformation process used by the organization, for example, production and/or assembly in a manufacturing firm, or service delivery in a service organization. Of course large diversified organizations often have multiple core technologies, but every form of work has a technology that can be defined at the unit or task level. Thus, from a modernist technological perspective, the organization can be imagined as a set of interacting and interdependent technologies.

Although modernist theories give us an image of technology, especially core technology, as lying inside the organization while environment is outside, these two concerns of management are closely connected in the modernist perspective. First of all, the knowledge needed to operate a technology is normally produced outside the organization's boundary and imported, except when basic research is conducted internally, as is sometimes done in R & D departments. Second, tools and many production processes are imported in the form of hardware, software and skilled or educated employees. The environment provides the technological ingredients of an organization just as it provides the material resources upon which the organization depends for its survival. Technology and other resources are scattered about in a more or less random fashion until a portion of the environment becomes organized, that is, until resources and technologies are combined by organizations to provide outputs to satisfy the environment's needs or demands.

A different image of technology is provided by those who adopt the symbolic-interpretive perspective. Drawing on subjectivist ontology, symbolic-interpretive organizational theorists study how technology is constructed within a socio-cultural context of symbolic interaction and meaning making. While some engage in ethnographic studies, social construction of technology (SCOT) theorists theorize the social, cultural and economic context within which resources and technological innovations become linked. Both provide views of how the social organization of society influences the shape of technology and its products. This raises the question of how society, in its turn, is shaped by technology. The theme of society being shaped by technology is taken up in postmodern theories of technology, such as those that promote seeing management systems as technologies of control, and radical ideas like cyborganization.

KEY TERMS

core technology	mediating technology
high technology	intensive technology
service technology	task variability
technical complexity	task analyzability
unit and small batch production	routine technology
large batch or mass production	craft technology
continuous processing	engineering technology
long-linked technology	nonroutine technology

properties of new technologies
  stochastic
  continuous
  abstract
technologies of representation
cyborganization
technological imperative
routineness of work
pooled task interdependence

rules and standard procedures
sequential task interdependence
planning and scheduling
reciprocal task interdependence
mutual adjustment
teamwork
Guttman scale
adaptive structuration theory
technologies-in-practice

ENDNOTES

1. Woodward (1965).

2. Thompson (1967).

3. Perrow (1967, 1986).

4. Weick (1990).

5. Bijker and Law (1992: 3).

6. Orr (1996).

7. Mangrum, Fairley, and Weider (2001).

8. Heidegger (1993: 341).

9. In spite of the threat technology poses, Heidegger believed that the closer we come to the danger, the more likely we are to ask critical questions that will allow us to avoid disaster. Furthermore, by questioning its effects, we not only avoid the shackles of technology and its potential to imprison us, but we open up new horizons.

10. McLuhan and Powers (1989).

11. Cooper (1992); see also Zuboff (1988).

12. http://www.greenpeace.org

13. Combs, Knights and Willmott (1992).

14. Haraway (1991: 163).

15. Weiner (1954), cited in Parker and Cooper (1998: 214).

16. Cooper and Law (1995: 268, cited in Parker and Cooper 1998: 219–20).

17. Huber (1990), Lucas and Baroudi (1994).

18. Pugh, Hickson, Hinings, MacDonald, Turner, and Lupton (1963).

19. Guttman (1944).

20. Galbraith (1973).

21. DeSanctis and Poole (1994), Griffith (1999).

22. Orlikowski (2000).

REFERENCES

Bijker, Wiebe E., and Law, John (1992) (eds.). *Shaping technology/Building society: Studies in sociotechnical change*. Cambridge, Mass.: MIT Press.

Coombs, Rod, Knights, David, and Willmott, Hugh (1992). Culture control and competition: Towards a conceptual framework for the study of information technology in organizations. *Organization Studies*, 13: 51–72.

Cooper, R. (1992). Formal organization as representation. In M. Reed and M. Hughes (eds.), *Rethinking organization: New directions in organization theory and analysis*. London: Sage, 254–72.

DeSanctis, G., and Poole, M. (1994). Capturing the complexity in advanced technology use: Adaptive structuration theory. *Organization Science*, 5: 121–47.

Galbraith, Jay (1973). *Designing complex organizations*. Reading, Mass.: Addison-Wesley.

Griffiths, T. L. (1999). Technology features as triggers for sensemaking. *Academy of Management Review*, 24/3: 472–88.

Guttman, Louis (1944). A basis for scaling qualitative data. *American Sociological Review*, 9: 139–50.

Haraway, D. J. (1991). *Simians, cyborgs and women: The reinvention of nature*. New York: Routledge.

Heidegger, M. (1993). The question concerning technology. In *Martin Heidegger: Basic Writings from Being and Time (1927) to the Task of Thinking (1964)*, ed. D. F. Krell. London: Routledge, Kegan and Paul, 307–41.

Huber, G. (1990). A theory of the effects of advanced information technologies on organizational design, intelligence, and decision making. *Academy of Management Review*, 15/1: 47–71.

Lucas, H. C., and Baroudi, J. (1994). The role of information technology in organizational design. *Journal of Management Information Systems*, 10/4: 9–24.

Lyotard, Jean-François (1979). *The postmodern condition: A report on knowledge*. Minneapolis: University of Minnesota Press.

Mangrum, S., Fairley, D., and Weider, L. (2001). Informal problem solving in the technology-mediated workplace. *Journal of Business Communication*, 38/3: 315–36.

McLuhan, M., and Powers, B. R. (1989). *The global village: Transformations in world life and media in the twenty-first century*. New York: Oxford University Press.

Orlikowski, W. J. (2000). Using technology and constituting structures: A practice lens for studying technology in organization. *Organization Science*, 11/4: 404–28.

Orr, J. E. (1996). *Talking about machines: An ethnography of a modern job*. Ithaca, NY: Cornell University Press.

Parker, Martin, and Cooper, Robert (1998). Cyborganization: Cinema as nervous system. In

J. Hassard and R. Holliday (eds.), *Organization representation: Work and organizations in popular culture*. London: Sage, 201–28.

Perrow, Charles (1967). A framework for comparative organizational analysis. *American Sociological Review*, 32/2: 194–208.

Perrow, Charles (1986). *Complex organizations: A critical essay* (3rd edn.). New York: Random House.

Pugh, D. S., Hickson, D. J., Hinings, C. R., MacDonald, K. M., Turner, C., and Lupton, T. (1963). A conceptual scheme for organizational analysis. *Administrative Science Quarterly*, 8: 289–315.

Thompson, James (1967). *Organizations in action*. New York: McGraw-Hill.

Weick, Karl E. (1990). Technology as equivoque: Sensemaking in new technologies. In Paul S. Goodman, Lee S. Sproull, and Associates (eds.), *Technology and organizations*. San Francisco: Jossey-Bass, 1–44.

Woodward, Joan (1958). *Management and technology*. London: Her Majesty's Stationery Office.

—— (1965). *Industrial organization: Theory and practice*. London: Oxford University Press.

Zuboff, S. (1988). *In the age of the smart machine: The future of work and power*. New York: Basic Books.

FURTHER READING

Bijker, Wiebe E., Hughes, Thomas P., and Pinch, Trevor (1987) (eds.). *The social construction of technological systems: New directions in the sociology and history of technology*. Cambridge, Mass.: MIT Press.

Coyne, R. (1995). *Designing information technology in the postmodern age*. Cambridge, Mass.: MIT Press.

De Laet, M., and Mol, A. (2000). The Zimbabwe bush pump: Mechanics of a fluid technology. *Social Studies of Science*, 30: 225–63.

Haraway, D. J. (1997). *Modest-Witness@Second-Millennium.FemaleMan-Meets-Oncomouse: Feminism and technoscience*. New York and London: Routledge.

Law, J. (1991) (ed.). *A sociology of monsters: Essays on power, technology and domination*. London: Routledge.

MacKenzie, D., and Wajcman, J. (1985) (eds.). *The social shaping of technology*. Milton Keynes: Open University Press.

Perrow, Charles (1984). *Normal accidents: Living with high-risk technologies*. New York: Basic Books.

Pinch, Trevor J., and Bijker, Wiebe E. (1987). The social construction of facts and artifacts: Or how the sociology of science and the sociology of technology might benefit each other. In Wiebe E. Bijker, Thomas P. Hughes, and Trevor Pinch (eds.), *The social construction of technological systems: New directions in the sociology and history of technology*. Cambridge, Mass.: MIT Press, 17–50.

Scott, W. Richard (1990). Technology and structure: An organizational-level perspective. In Paul S. Goodman, Lee S. Sproull, and Associates (eds.), *Technology and*

organizations. San Francisco: Jossey-Bass, 109–43.

Zeleny, Milan (1990). High technology management. In H. Noori and R. E. Radford (eds.), *Readings and cases in the management of new technology: An operations perspective*. Englewood Cliffs, NJ: Prentice-Hall, 14–22.

Organizational Culture

Global organizations like Unilever and Nissan operate differently from country to country due to national cultural influences, yet these companies also express their own unique organizational styles in ways that are recognizable around the world. Think of Southwest Airlines where pilots pitch in at the ticket counter and flight crews improvise with their passengers. Or compare Virgin Atlantic's manicures and massages with British Airways' traditional English tea service. Southwest, Virgin and British Airways each have unique styles that distinguish them from other companies and this uniqueness expresses their organizational cultures.

Organizational cultures have complex relationships with the environments in which they operate and from which they recruit their members. Employees join an organization having already been socialized by cultural institutions such as family, community, church and school. Once they become organizational members, their culturally influenced values, identities and skills meld with those of the organization thereby carrying aspects of national as well as regional, industrial, occupational and professional cultures into the organization.[1] Although the effect is typically not as strong, an organizational, professional or industrial culture can also influence the local, regional or national environment. For example an influx of young, wealthy GenX techies during the dot.com boom of the 1990s changed the culture of California's Silicon Valley by reshaping its business environment and corporate architecture along with many other aspects of the local community.

Sometimes an organizational culture clashes with the regional or national culture of a place where the company locates. The problems surrounding the controversial opening of a new Disneyland theme park in France highlighted the difficulties organizations may face when operating in cultural settings that are new to them. Before construction of the park even got underway, EuroDisneyland was criticized as an assault on French culture. It was attacked as a symbol of the American way of life that French critics feared would Americanize their children. Then, as French employees were recruited and trained, labor unions protested against Disney's strict dress code claiming that it undermined French individualism. They accused Disney of indoctrinating cast members, pointing to the company's rules regarding smiling and appearing to be sincere all day. Eventually Disney adapted the park somewhat to better accommodate French culture. For instance, female employees were allowed to wear bright red lipstick to work and wine was served in EuroDisneyland's many restaurants. Later the theme park was renamed Disneyland, Paris.

Although the Disneyland, Paris example clearly shows the effects of national culture on an organization, an ironic twist to this story shows just how interwoven an organizational culture becomes with its environment. When Disneyland, Paris was threatened with bankruptcy in 2005, instead of rejoicing at the failure of this widely resisted American icon, the French government offered Disney a substantial loan to keep the theme park open in order to avoid the loss of 35,000 French jobs.

Just as you can analyze an organizational culture as a subsystem of much larger cultural contexts, you can examine an organizational culture as the context within which subcultures develop. When companies are large and/or diverse like Disney, their cultures can become quite complex, frequently spawning subcultures such as that of Disneyland, Paris whose French influences give this subculture of the Disney Corporation a style that differs from the organization's many other subcultures.

A **subculture** is a subset of an organization's members that identify themselves as a distinct group within the organization and routinely take action on the basis of their unique collective understandings. According to John Van Maanen and Stephen Barley, subcultures may form around similar interests within an organization and may reflect shared professional, gendered, racial, ethnic or occupational identities as well as national or regional cultural influences. Alternatively, subcultures can form on the basis of the familiarity that develops when employees interact frequently, as they often do when they share territory or equipment (e.g., a region in a factory, office building or cafeteria, coffee machines, photocopiers, toilets).[2]

Because they belong to the same organization, subcultures have relationships with one another. Caren Siehl and Joanne Martin argued that subcultures react to each other in one of four ways: dominating, enhancing, orthogonal or countercultural. Typically the dominant subculture in an organization is put forward by top management and for this reason it is often referred to as the **corporate culture**, though it might be more correct to call it the corporate subculture.

Siehl and Martin defined the possible relationships between the organizational subcultures and the corporate culture as follows: **enhancing subcultures** enthusiastically support the corporate culture, **orthogonal subcultures** hold independent values and beliefs that neither interfere with nor celebrate the dominant subculture, and **countercultures** hold values and beliefs that actively challenge corporate culture. As an example of counterculture, Siehl and Martin cited John De Lorean who in the 1960s headed up a division of General Motors that refused to play by the company's rules yet was tolerated because it was profitable and brought an edge to GM's otherwise conservative line of cars.[3] Indeed, De Lorean himself was so admired by other executives at GM that prior to leaving to start his own company he was promoted to VP of all car and truck divisions and was being considered as a serious candidate for CEO.

As can be seen in the case of the De Lorean led counterculture at GM, subcultures are neither good nor bad per se. Their value to the organization depends on the influence they exercise within the organization. One common subcultural influence that executives readily complain about is known metaphorically as silos. A silo is a tall, cylindrical, self-contained storage unit that farmers use to preserve their harvested corn. Applied to organizations, the **silo metaphor** is used to describe the distinctive norms, values, routines and discourses that develop within an organization's subcultures in such a way as to make coordination and collaboration between them difficult or impossible.

The concept of **strong culture** helps clarify the problem of organizational silos. Jennifer Chatman and Sandra Cha defined strong culture as agreement about what is valued and the intensity with which these values are held. Strong cultures are marked by both high agreement and high intensity. While organizations with silos may have high intensity within their subcultures, the various subcultures do not agree on what matters most.[4]

Table 6.1 shows some of the most widely used definitions of organizational culture. Be sure to notice that these definitions apply equally well at the organizational and subcultural levels of analysis. This is because culture is a particular way of life among a people or community and organizations are communities that sometimes grow to be complex enough to sustain smaller communities or subcultures. Notice too that all of the definitions in Table 6.1 refer to something held in common among group members described variously as shared meanings, beliefs, assumptions, understandings, norms, values and knowledge.

Table 6.1 Selected definitions of organizational culture

Elliott Jaques (1952: 251)	'The culture of the factory is its customary and traditional way of thinking and doing of things, which is shared to a greater or lesser degree by all its members, and which new members must learn, and at least partially accept, in order to be accepted into service in the firm.'
Andrew Pettigrew (1979: 574)	'Culture is a system of publicly and collectively accepted meanings operating for a given group at a given time. This system of terms, forms, categories, and images interprets a people's own situation to themselves.'
Meryl Reis Louis (1983: 39)	'Organizations [are] culture-bearing milieux, that is, [they are] distinctive social units possessed of a set of common understandings for organizing action (e.g., what we're doing together in this particular group, appropriate ways of doing in and among members of the group) and languages and other symbolic vehicles for expressing common understandings.'
Edgar Schein (1985: 6)	'The pattern of basic assumptions that a given group has invented, discovered, or developed in learning to cope with its problems of external adaptation and internal integration, and that have worked well enough to be considered valid, and, therefore, to be taught to new members as the correct way to perceive, think, and feel in relation to these problems.'
John Van Maanen (1988: 3)	'Culture refers to the knowledge members of a given group are thought to more or less share; knowledge of the sort that is said to inform, embed, shape, and account for the routine and not-so-routine activities of the members of the culture.... A culture is expressed (or constituted) only through the actions and words of its members and must be interpreted by, not given to, a fieldworker.... Culture is not itself visible, but is made visible only through its representation.'
Harrison Trice and Janice Beyer (1993: 2)	'Cultures are collective phenomena that embody people's responses to the uncertainties and chaos that are inevitable in human experience. These responses fall into two major categories. The first is the substance of a culture—shared, emotionally charged belief systems that we call ideologies. The second is cultural forms—observable entities, including actions, through which members of a culture express, affirm, and communicate the substance of their culture to one another.'

Sharing is an interesting phenomenon in that it does not mean only that culture involves agreement among its members, the term also embraces differences. Think of sharing a meal with your friends or family—you may prepare the meal together using common ingredients and cooking tools, yet you each eat different portions and enjoy the experience in your own unique way. Cultures allow for similarity and agreement on some matters but also rely upon differences and in some cases make it safe to disagree. Cultures integrate human diversity with a shared sense of belonging that can be expressed in a multitude of ways, only a few of which are likely to be acknowledged by every cultural member. In this sense sharing culture is paradoxical, being at once universal and particular, tangible and intangible, integrated and fragmented, and relying upon both community and diversity.

This chapter begins with a history of the culture concept that explains how organizational culture came to be a part of organization theory. The next three sections of the chapter examine organizational culture from the perspectives of modernism, symbolic-interpretivism and postmodernism. Following this I will conclude the chapter by discussing the practical matters of cultural change and whether or not culture can be managed.

What Is Organizational Culture and How Did It Become Part of Organization Theory?

According to British sociologist Chris Jenks, the concept of culture originally referred to the cultivation of crops. It was extended to include the cultivation of human beings when the academic disciplines of anthropology and sociology were created sometime during the nineteenth century.[5] These disciplines shared an ambition to apply the techniques of science to the study and improvement of humans and the human condition. Often located in the same university departments, anthropologists and sociologists worried a great deal over whose territory was whose and eventually worked out an agreement—sociology would study all phenomena having to do with human society while anthropology would explain the cultural origins and development of the human species. In spite of their ongoing efforts to differentiate themselves, their similar interests and close association show up time and again in the overlapping of anthropological and sociological concepts and theories about culture.[6]

Early cultural anthropologists were primarily concerned with explaining the differences between humans and other animals (culture and nature) in order to provide a foundation for the social sciences that was distinguishable from that of the natural sciences on which they were modeled. In this regard the earliest definitions of culture identified characteristics that distinguished humans from other species. For instance in 1871 British social anthropologist E. B. Tylor defined culture as 'that complex whole which includes knowledge, belief, art, morals, law, custom, and any other capabilities and habits acquired by man as a member of society'.[7]

Along with early cultural anthropologists, early sociologists applied the then novel and very popular theory of evolution to legitimate their study of culture. They reasoned that, if humans develop along some sort of evolutionary continuum as other animal species do, then culture provides an explanation for the distinctiveness of human development. From this theory emerged the belief that different societies could be ordered according to their stage of development, from primitive on one end of the scale to advanced on the other.

Anthropologists then went in search of culture's origins by living with primitive tribes for extended periods of time, learning to speak their languages and documenting various aspects of their members' lives in the hope of learning how advanced cultures lived earlier in their own developmental cycles. However, as their evidence accumulated, the idea that primitive cultures were inferior to advanced cultures became difficult to sustain. It gradually became obvious that cultures described as primitive were in some ways more sophisticated than those from which the anthropologists had come and that so-called advanced cultures were barbaric in certain respects when compared to what had previously been labeled primitive.

As anthropologists pursued their empirical studies in tribal communities throughout the world, culture came to be associated with the particular groups of people studied, and comparisons between these groups took place. This association between groups and cultures (plural rather than singular) shifted the focus of anthropology from the general understanding of humankind as a species, to the distinctive characteristics of particular groups and thus to cultural differences. This shift can be seen by comparing Tylor's definition of culture with the definition offered three-quarters of a century later by American cultural anthropologist Melville Herskowitz: 'a construct describing the total body of belief, behavior, knowledge, sanctions, values, and goals that make up the way of life *of a people*'.[8] Since organizations are groups, the shift of attention onto the cultures of groups opened the door to organizational culture.

With the publication of his book *The Changing Culture of a Factory* in 1952, Elliott Jaques became one of the first to conceptualize organizational culture. Jaques argued that focusing on structure had led organizational researchers to ignore the human and emotional elements of organizational life, which he intended to rectify by applying the concept of culture to organizations. His work inspired organizational scholars like Barry Turner and Andrew Pettigrew in the United Kingdom, who were soon joined by Pasquale Gagliardi in Italy, Gareth Morgan and Peter Frost in Canada, and Lou Pondy and Linda Smircich in the United States, among others. Together these scholars began making a case for studying organizational symbolism and at the same time started to form their own subculture within the internationalizing field of organizational studies.

At first, no one in the mainstream of modernist organization theory took much notice of organizational symbolism. Then in the late 1970s and early 1980s several books on organizational culture appeared on bestseller lists in the United States including William Ouchi's *Theory Z* and Terrence Deal and Allan Kennedy's *Corporate Cultures: The Rites and Rituals of Corporate Life*. Tom Peters and Robert Waterman's *In Search of Excellence*, the most successful of them all, topped the *New York Times* bestseller list for months following its release. The wide appeal of these books stunned and seduced much of the academic community, which, up until this time, had never seen one of its concepts attract so much public attention. Peters and Waterman were even made the stars of a television series documenting the practices of companies they touted as having excellent cultures. As a result of the popular acclaim, academics interested in organizational culture read and studied these materials, along with Edgar Schein's more academic book *Organizational Culture and Leadership* that appeared around the same time.[9]

The most popular books described organizational culture as something to be managed and used to enhance organizational effectiveness and competitiveness. For example, Peters and Waterman promoted the idea that strong cultures breed excellence, while Ouchi made the case for culture as a desirable alternative to both market mechanisms and bureaucratic control systems. Most academic culture researchers were pessimistic about the ease with which organizational cultures might be manipulated to managerial ends, particularly those who had cut their teeth on the symbolic approach to understanding organizations and who now joined forces with researchers who had caught the wave of interest in culture.

The whole thing began quietly enough, with a few small conferences on organizational symbolism held in Europe and the United States attracting a curious mix of scholars from fields as diverse as psychoanalysis, folklore and organization theory. However, a movement soon got underway. Special issues devoted to organizational culture appeared in mainstream academic journals and the fledgling Standing Conference on Organizational Symbolism (SCOS) soon dwarfed its parent organization the European Group for Organization Studies (EGOS), one of Europe's prestigious professional associations.

Many SCOS members and other researchers interested in organizational culture turned to qualitative methods to conduct empirical studies. At that time the method most commonly used was **ethnography**—a combination of participant observation and in-depth interviewing. Organizational culture researchers hoped that ethnography and its proven value in cultural anthropology and interpretive sociology would satisfy the demands for rigor coming from critics and journal reviewers. Most modernists prefer the quantitative methods of the natural sciences and at the time were highly suspicious of ethnography with its origins in the humanistic social sciences. Battle lines were drawn and a war ensued, fought primarily over the legitimacy of using qualitative methods to conduct rigorous organizational research.[10]

The war was waged in the editorial offices of academic journals, during faculty meetings where tenure was decided, and, most publicly, at conferences. Symbolic-interpretive researchers eventually forged a base of support from which to convince their modernist colleagues that they had a right to publish their ideas and to seek and receive tenure. Although the modernists initially had most of the power on their side, the volume of qualitative research conducted began to open the way for the first representatives of symbolic-interpretive organization theory to get their work published and win tenure. It was thus largely through research on organizational culture that the symbolic-interpretive perspective established itself within organization theory. This did not mean that modernists ignored the subject of culture, however. Some of the earliest theories to achieve widespread recognition, not surprisingly, were rooted in this still dominant perspective.

Modernist Approaches to Organizational Culture

This section of the chapter examines the theories of Dutch organization theorist Geert Hofstede and American social psychologist Edgar Schein, two of the modernist organization theorists whose influence helped to establish organizational culture as a legitimate topic within organization theory. Hofstede explored national influences on organizational culture through differences he first discovered in the international subsidiaries of IBM. Schein's theory of organizational culture was built from his fusion of anthropology with clinical psychology in his management consulting practice. Some additional examples of modernist organizational culture research will be described, following presentations of Hofstede's and Schein's ideas.

National Cultural Influences on Organizations

Hofstede's approach to organizational culture is derivative of the idea that organizations are subcultures of larger cultural systems and in the late 1970s Hofstede studied the influence of national cultures on IBM.[11] At the time of the study IBM operated in seventy countries, the forty largest of which Hofstede used for his study. The data came from IBM annual employee surveys conducted from 1967 through 1973. Hofstede used the data to construct measures of work-related values that he then compared across countries. He found distinctive patterns of national cultural differences among IBM's subcultures that, after further analysis, revealed four dimensions of national cultural difference operating within IBM's organizational culture: power distance, uncertainty avoidance, individualism vs. collectivism, and masculinity vs. femininity (see Figures 6.1 and 6.2). The findings supporting these dimensions have been replicated in additional studies that included populations other than IBM employees (e.g., commercial airline pilots, civil service managers, consumers) and that expanded Hofstede's research to include fifty countries and three regions.[12]

Power distance refers to the extent to which the members of a culture are willing to accept an unequal distribution of power, wealth and prestige. Hofstede's data showed that low power distance characterized countries like Denmark where such inequalities are difficult to accept. For instance the Danish Jante Law (pronounced yenta) proclaims that no individual should have more than, or stand out in any noticeable way from, other Danes. Their unwillingness to accept an unequal distribution of wealth can be seen in the exceptionally high income tax paid by Danish citizens. Another indicator is that when Danes try to put themselves forward as more prestigious or powerful than others they are quickly reprimanded and thus reminded of the inherent equality of all.

Organizations from high power distance cultures (like Brazil, Singapore and the Arabic countries) rely heavily on hierarchy, which involves the unequal distribution of authority accompanied by lack of upward mobility. When organizations from higher power distance cultures attempt to impose their authority structures on subsidiaries from lower power distance cultures like Denmark, difficulties generally follow. Similar difficulties confront

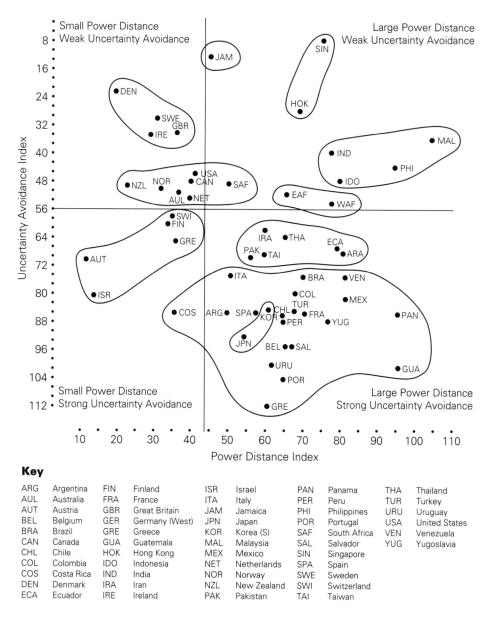

Figure 6.1 Position of countries on Hofstede's uncertainty avoidance and power distance

Source: Hofstede (2001: 152). Reprinted by kind permission of Geert Hofstede.

Danish managers who attempt to use distinctively Danish leadership practices to control international subsidiaries in countries noted for higher power distance. Such difficulties, according to Hofstede, are the result of differences in cultural expectations. In high power distance cultures subordinates expect to be told what to do; for them hierarchy is an existential inequality. In low power distance cultures, hierarchy is considered an inequality

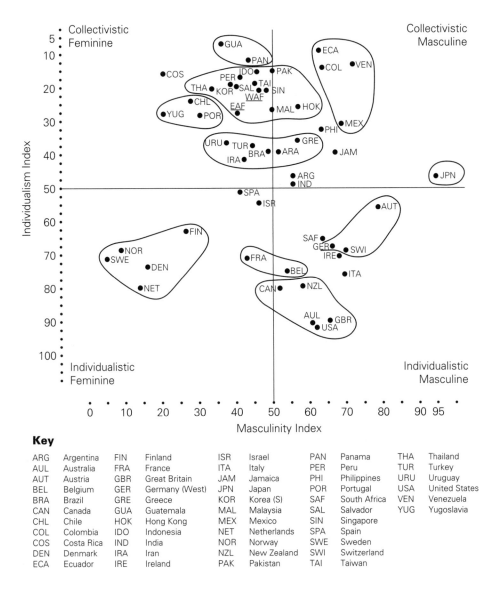

Figure 6.2 Position of countries on Hofstede's individualism scales and masculinity dimensions

Source: Hofstede (2001: 294). Reprinted by kind permission of Geert Hofstede.

of roles created for convenience rather than reflecting essential differences between people, thus subordinates in these cultures expect to be consulted by their superiors. As a consequence of these contradictory expectations, the ideal boss in a low power distance culture is a resourceful democrat, whereas in a high power distance culture the best boss is a benevolent autocrat.

Uncertainty avoidance involves the ways in which human societies have learned to cope with uncertainty and ambiguity. For instance, technology is often used to defend against uncertainties caused by nature (e.g., the use of reinforced building structures in earthquake prone areas) while law defends against uncertainties produced by antisocial behavior (e.g., laws against thievery, brutality, fraud). Religion, on the other hand, is a cultural means to help us accept uncertainties that we cannot defend against. Hofstede argued that different societies have different levels of tolerance for uncertainty and that these differences can be defined as the degree to which members of a culture feel threatened by ambiguity and risk.

In low uncertainty avoidance cultures, people are more accepting of innovative ideas, differences of opinion and eccentric or deviant behavior, whereas in cultures with high uncertainty avoidance these things are resisted or even legislated against. Rules, regulations and control are all more acceptable in high than in low uncertainty avoidance cultures and Hofstede claimed that organizations in these cultures have more formalization and standardization, whereas organizations in cultures with weak uncertainty avoidance dislike rules and resist formalization and standardization. In his original study Hofstede found that uncertainty avoidance was highest in the IBM employees from Greece, Portugal and Japan, while it was lowest in those from Singapore, Hong Kong and Sweden. You can contrast this with the results of his later study (see Figure 6.2) in which Greece, Portugal and Guatemala topped the list, while Singapore, Jamaica and Denmark anchored the low end of the scale.

Individualism versus collectivism involves the degree to which individuals in a culture are expected to act independently of other members of the society. In highly individualistic cultures, individual rights are paramount. You will find evidence of individualism versus collectivism in the ways in which people live together (e.g., alone, in shifting partnerships, tribes or nuclear families) and in their religious beliefs (e.g., whether or not an individual can have a personal relationship with the supernatural). Hofstede pointed out that in cultures such as the United States individualism is seen as a source of well-being, whereas in others like Chinese or Mexican cultures, it is seen as undesirable and alienating. Relationships between members of individualistic cultures are loose and individuals are expected to take care of themselves. By contrast, in collectivist cultures cohesive groups (e.g., extended families) give individuals their sense of identity and belonging, demanding considerable loyalty in return for the sense of security that such loyalty imparts. Hofstede claimed that tasks take precedence over relationships in organizations from individualistic cultures, whereas relationships prevail over tasks in organizations from collectivist cultures. You can imagine the sort of difficulties that are created when an organization from the United States attempts to impose its task-focused control systems on acquisitions located in collectivist cultures.

Masculine versus feminine refers to the degree of separation between gender roles in a society. In highly masculine cultures such as Japan, Austria and Venezuela, men are expected to be more assertive and women more nurturing. In Sweden, Denmark, Norway and the Netherlands, cultures that score high on the feminine dimension, gender differences are less pronounced. The highly masculine cultures in Hofstede's studies tended to place emphasis on work goals having to do with career advancement and earnings, and their members valued assertiveness, decisiveness and selling oneself. The feminine cultures in Hofstede's studies favored work goals concerning interpersonal relationships, service and preserving the physical environment, their members valued quality of life and intuition. Furthermore, members of organizations in feminine cultures were likely to ridicule assertiveness and to undersell themselves. Not surprisingly Hofstede found that women held more professional and technical jobs and were treated more equally in highly feminine cultures than in cultures high on the masculinity scale.

In later research, conducted with students in twenty-three countries, Hofstede and Bond demonstrated the presence of a fifth dimension of national cultural difference: **long-term versus short-term orientation**.[13] This dimension describes cultural differences in predilections for thrift and perseverance as well as respect for tradition. According to Hofstede a high long-term orientation scores indicate belief that hard work will lead to long-term rewards and also that it may take longer to develop business in these countries, particularly for foreigners. Traditions and commitments represent fewer challenges to change in organizations from cultures that are characterized by a short-term orientation. The addition of this dimension provides evidence that there are potentially many more ways to define national cultural differences yet to be explored.

The importance of Hofstede's work is not only that it identified specific, measurable, national cultural differences but also that it showed that organizational culture is a portal through which society influences organizations. The national cultural traits identified by Hofstede can be seen as part of the web of meaning that provides context for organizational culture. In this way, Hofstede's dimensions of cultural difference supply information about some of the core beliefs and assumptions that define organizational cultures, a topic addressed by Schein's theory of organizational culture.

Schein's Theory of Organizational Culture

In contrast to Hofstede, Schein focused strictly on culture at the organizational level of analysis. According to Schein, the essence of culture is its core of basic assumptions (see Figure 6.3). This core manifests as values and behavioral norms that are recognized, responded to and maintained by members of the culture who, in turn, use them to make choices and take action. Finally, culturally guided choice and action produce artifacts.

Basic **assumptions** represent truth, or what members of a culture believe to be their reality. They are typically taken for granted. Try to imagine what a fish thinks about water and you get an idea of the level of awareness cultural members usually have of their basic assumptions. Even though they are beneath ordinary awareness these unquestioned aspects of culture penetrate every part of cultural life and color all forms of human experience. As Schein said, they influence what cultural members perceive and how they think and feel.

Their unquestioned yet all pervasive character is why it is likely that you will only become aware of cultural assumptions when you live for an extended period in a culture that is foreign to your own. Living in a foreign culture will spur consciousness of your own cultural assumptions when your assumptions lead you to engage in inappropriate behavior

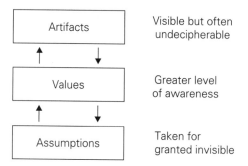

Figure 6.3 Schein's three levels of culture

or to misinterpret someone else's behavior as inappropriate. Because you are using the wrong assumptions to explain what is going on, experiencing some act as inappropriate will encourage you to observe more attentively and ask questions. If your investigation renders you able to release yourself from your native cultural assumptions and try on those of your host culture, you will slowly make your way toward being able to explain the differences and this will lead you not only to function more effectively in the culture you are visiting but to understand your native culture more deeply as well. Even though it may still be difficult to describe cultural assumptions accurately, you will nonetheless become savvy about culture and better at moving between cultures without causing trouble to yourself or to others—unless you choose to do so.

According to Schein, a culture's deep assumptions pervade the next level of culture—cultural values. **Values** are the social principles, goals and standards that cultural members believe have intrinsic worth. They define what the members of a culture care about most and are revealed by their priorities. Because they also guide cultural members in their evaluations of what is right and what is wrong, a culture's values are sometimes equated with its moral code.

Although values are more accessible to consciousness than basic assumptions they are not always on the top of members' minds. Nonetheless, members of an organization are able to recognize their values fairly easily and they become particularly sensitive to them when someone challenges their culture in some fundamental way, such as breaking with convention. When organizational values are challenged, the challenge most often comes from marginal members of the organization such as newcomers or revolutionaries (see Figure 6.4) or from outsiders like a new CEO hired by a board of directors to shake things up. A great deal of modernist research has been devoted to specifying the values that various organizational cultures hold (e.g., value for customers or employees, ethical values), but according to Schein the more important issue is the influence cultural assumptions and values, taken as a whole, have on perceptions, behavior and emotional states. One significant influence that values exercise on cultural members takes place through defining norms for behavior.

Figure 6.4 Challenges to cultural values most often come from marginal members of the culture such as newcomers, revolutionaries or outsiders

In the 1960s, being marginal and challenging mainstream cultural values was a normal part of the youth subculture which in the United States was known as the 'hippie' subculture. The stereotypical hippy drove a VW bus, preferably old, adorned with provocative bumper stickers symbolizing membership of this subculture.

Norms are expressions of values. They are the unwritten rules that allow members of a culture to know what is expected of them in a wide variety of situations including how to coordinate their behavior with that of others. Norms communicate expectations regarding many types of social behavior such as talking in movie theaters, cutting in line, and standing at football games. Business norms communicate important information such as when you should inform your boss of potential problems, what sort of clothing you should wear to work, and when it is appropriate to display emotion. While in some organizations these matters are spelled out by formal rules and regulations (a point of overlap between culture and social structure), in most organizations they are left unstated and communicated informally via normative pressures such as disapproving looks or, in some cultures, by looking away.

While values specify what is important to the members of a culture, norms establish what sorts of behavior to expect from one another. In short, values define what is valued, while norms make clear what it takes to be considered normal or abnormal. The link between values and norms is that the behaviors that norms sanction (either through rewards or punishments) can be traced to outcomes that are valued. For example, norms about not talking in movie theaters or cutting in line might be traced to a cultural value for courtesy to others. Norms about wearing business suits and not displaying any emotion while at work might indicate a value for self-discipline. However, even though values underpin norms, any given norm can be ambiguous relative to its underlying values. For example, a norm for wearing suits at work could indicate a value for self-discipline or for fashion consciousness. This ambiguity of interpretation extends to artifacts.

According to Schein's theory, members of a culture hold values and conform to cultural norms because their underlying assumptions nurture and support these norms and values. The norms and values, in turn, encourage activities that produce cultural artifacts. **Artifacts** are manifestations or expressions of the same cultural core that produces and maintains the values and norms; however, their further distance from the core can make it even more difficult to interpret their cultural significance unambiguously.

A sign displayed in the foyer of a new neighborhood cinema in the United States informed patrons that, in contrast to other cinemas they may have frequented, talking during the screening of a film was permitted in this establishment. The cinema attracted a clientele that liked to express their reactions to movies vocally, and thus they violated the dominant American cultural norm of silence during movies. The sign—an artifact produced by the organization—named an otherwise unspoken dominant cultural norm and, by doing so, drew a symbolic boundary around this counterculture that encouraged those who entered to recognize and accept the countercultural norm.

Although artifacts like the cinema sign are tangible indicators of cultural norms, values and assumptions, you need to study many artifacts before you will be able to recognize the cultural patterns that reveal the deeper layers of culture. To gain access to these deeper levels, you must train yourself to observe a culture's artifacts and the ways its members use them. Categories of artifacts to include in your observations consist of objects, verbal expressions and activities. Table 6.2 shows several examples of each category. A good exercise is to think of an organizational culture you know well and list examples of as many of each type of artifact as you can.

Modernist Methods Applied to Organizational Culture

Irene Lurie and Norma Riccucci adopted Schein's framework to analyze the impact of welfare reform on the culture of Welfare Agencies in four states in the United States: Georgia, Michigan, New York and Texas.[14] Based on analysis of interviews with employees, written documents and observations, they concluded that changes in artifacts were used to reinforce organizational changes. The organizational changes they documented included new client orientation programs and job searches, changes in job titles (e.g., from Payment Worker to Family Independence Specialist), and the hanging of posters in Agency offices bearing slogans like 'Life Works if you Work First'. In addition to these and other artifacts, they found overt expressions of values for high employment rates, having careers (versus jobs), self-sufficiency and accuracy (e.g., in determining eligibility for benefits). At the level of assumptions they discovered that while Agency leaders believed in the reform and worked to change Agency structure and artifacts, many employees believed the change would not be implemented and questioned the effectiveness of welfare reform. The researchers

Table 6.2 Artifacts of organizational culture

Category	Examples
Objects	Art/design/logo Architecture/décor/furnishings Dress/appearance/costume/uniform Products/equipment/tools Displays of posters/photos/memorabilia/cartoons Signage
Verbal expressions	Jargon/names/nicknames Explanations/theories Stories/myths/legends and their heroes and villains Superstitions/rumors Humor/jokes Metaphors/proverbs/slogans Speeches/rhetoric/oratory
Activities	Ceremonies/rituals/rites of passage Meetings/retreats/parties Communication patterns Traditions/customs/social routines Gestures Play/recreation/games Rewards/punishments

Based on: Dandridge, Mitroff and Joyce (1980), Schultz (1995), Jones (1996).

concluded that the level of assumptions in these organizations was highly resistant to cultural change thus supporting Schein's claim that, only when members of the culture can see some benefit in them, will new values become taken for granted and absorbed into unconscious assumptions.

Adopting a more typically quantitative modernist approach, American researchers John Kotter, James Heskett and Dan Denison investigated the effect of cultural strength on organizational performance. Kotter and Heskett measured the cultural strength of over 200 corporations by contacting financial analysts and managers of firms that were in competition with the organizations they wanted to study and asking them to rate the cultural strength of their sample firms.[15] They formulated an average score for each firm and correlated this measure with indicators of organizational performance, including average yearly return on investment and the average yearly changes in net income and the firm's market capitalization. They found that although cultural strength was significantly related to organizational performance overall, when cultural values supported organizational adaptation to the environment, the relationship became much stronger. More explicitly they found that culture significantly influenced organizational performance when it either helped the organization to anticipate or adapt to environmental change or interfered with its adaptation. In other words, when cultures do not support adaptation, cultural strength can interfere with performance but when culture and the need for adaptation are aligned, cultural strength boosts performance.

Denison reasoned that, not only do the relationships between strategy and culture need to be aligned, but both of these must be aligned with the environment as well.[16] Based on the findings of his research Denison claimed that organizations operating in rapidly changing environments will perform best if they either value flexibility and change (Denison called this an adaptability culture) or participation and high levels of organizational commitment (which he called an involvement culture). In stable environments, Denison argued, successful organizations either possess a shared vision of the future (a mission culture) or have strong values for tradition and conformity (a consistency culture). You will recognize Denison's approach as a contingency model that claims the appropriate type of culture depends on the rate of change in its environment and the focus of the organization's strategy and management practices. Adaptability and mission cultures according to Denison's scheme are externally focused, while involvement and consistency cultures focus internally.

Other methods for studying organizational culture have been devised that allow researchers to profile organizational cultures using measures that assess them on a variety of quantifiable dimensions. One widely used approach is the Organizational Culture Instrument (OCI). Robert Cooke and J. C. Lafferty developed the OCI in the early 1980s as a means to measure the extent to which an organizational culture is supported by each of twelve different norms. Analysis of the survey responses provided by organizational members from a variety of organizations revealed the profiles of three distinct organizational culture types: constructive cultures (achievement, self-actualizing, humanistic-encouraging and affiliative norms), passive-defensive cultures (approval, conventional, dependent and avoidance norms) and aggressive-defensive cultures (oppositional, power, competitive and perfectionistic norms).

Studies employing the OCI and relating its dimensions to other variables of organizational interest have yielded significant correlations between the three culture types and a variety of outcomes. For example, data show that constructive cultures are significantly and positively correlated with employee motivation and job satisfaction, teamwork and the quality of customer service, whereas passive-defensive cultures are negatively correlated with these variables. Aggressive-defensive cultures yield few significant correlations with the same measures but show significantly positive correlations with stress levels and negative correlations with quality of work relations and customer service.[17]

Although modernist studies of culture provide knowledge that is readily translatable into prescriptions for management, they are limited by their objectivity to studying dimensions of organizational culture that are predefined by the researcher. Modernist studies are therefore unlikely to present the surprises that occur when a researcher confronts his or her own cultural assumptions via the subjective experience of living in and adapting to another culture. This is where symbolic-interpretive researchers believe they have an advantage over modernist researchers—they can personally enter cultural territory and speak from their subjective knowledge, while modernists keep more distant from the phenomena they study by the measurement tools they use.

A Technique You Can Try

Danish organizational culture researcher Majken Schultz developed a technique that starts off in an objectivist way but then becomes more interpretive. To feel the difference between these approaches to studying culture, try this technique out on a culture to which you have access but of which you are not a member (e.g., someone else's social group, church or family).[18] To use Schultz's technique you first must describe many artifacts of your chosen culture (Table 6.2 will help you to make certain you do not leave anything important out). I like to start with at least fifty artifacts, one hundred is better. This part of the technique is modernist because collecting artifacts is a fairly objective task. What follows, however, involves interpretation.

Once you have a large number of artifacts to analyze, begin by choosing any artifact you like from your collection and then select others that intuitively seem to you to relate to the first one (Schultz recommended choosing at least one from each category; go for about four or five in all). Repeat this step several times, each time starting with a different artifact until you have exhausted either your imagination or your pool of artifacts. It is fine to include the same artifact on several spirals so long as you do not overdo it. Also try to use lots of different artifacts, but do not feel you have to use them all.

Next, take a sheet of paper and draw as many spirals as you have artifact groupings. Array each group of artifacts around its own spiral by writing brief artifact descriptions along the line you have drawn. Leave the center of the spiral open until you are finished, locating the artifacts from all your groupings. Look at each spiral in turn and try to figure out what this particular set of artifacts is trying to tell you about the culture. Write a few key words or a phrase suggestive of this theme in the center of the spiral. When you are done interpreting all the spirals, take a red pen and draw a circle around each central theme and connect these circles with a line. Try to describe the logic of the red thread connecting your spirals and this should lead you to one or more hypotheses about what matters in the culture.

Beware of the tendency many people have to impose their own cultural values on those of the group they are studying. Learning to separate the values of your own cultural context from those of the culture you want to understand will take some time. It will help if, as you proceed with your analysis, you talk to cultural members and ask them to help you develop and challenge your hypotheses until gradually you gain deeper understanding. One way you will know you are making headway is when the data you are collecting and analyzing surprises you. Surprises indicate that you are getting beneath the surface of the artifacts by learning how cultural members understand their world. Doing this analysis will help you to better appreciate the culture you are studying. It will also serve as a means of understanding your own culture and the concept of culture in general.

Symbolic-Interpretive Organizational Culture Research

In the early 1960s, Anselm Strauss and his research team studied hospitals using participant observation.[19] They learned that professionals and patients negotiated patient care regimens and in doing so created and maintained a sense of order. Strauss's team called this phenomenon the **negotiated order** and noted that, although the hospital's rules and hierarchies needed to be considered, emergent patterns of understanding were more important in accounting for the way hospital work actually got done.

American cognitive sociologist Harold Garfinkel was another important figure in the development of the interpretive foundation of culture studies. In his 1967 book *Studies in Ethnomethodology*, Garfinkel reported the results of field experiments that he and his students carried out. Garfinkel instructed his students to violate the commonsense expectations of everyday life such as how to shop in a department store or eat a family dinner. The students would first violate prevailing norms and then observe and document what happened, including their own feelings and responses. You can try this out for yourself. Next time a friend reports going on a blind date or having a flat tire, pretend not to know what a blind date is or what it means to have a flat tire and carry out the interaction accordingly. It is important that you maintain a position of innocence as you do this. It will not be easy and you should take care to notice and later document your own feelings in the situation. Do not simply assume you know how this will work out—go for the surprise.

In explaining the results of his experiments on cultural expectations, Garfinkel argued that engaging in deliberately inappropriate behavior denies the taken-for-grantedness of shared understanding and catapults participants out of their everyday frameworks for interpreting experience. The students reported that the experiments caused confusion, discomfort and occasional bouts of offence, yet although a great deal of nonsense was produced in the process, the prevailing social order never collapsed. Instead, participants renewed their efforts to reestablish or retain their sense of things-as-usual, for example by saying: 'You are just kidding around, right?' or 'Why don't you come back when you are ready to behave like a normal human being?' Based on these experiments, Garfinkel concluded that whatever sense everyday social life makes, its sensibility is a social accomplishment, that is, people conspire to achieve and maintain the taken-for-grantedness of their lives, even if they do so unwittingly.

You can see that the concepts of negotiated order and social life-as-accomplishment parallel those of enactment and the social construction of reality. You will remember from Chapter 2 that social construction refers to the theory that reality is not formed by conditions in the physical world as much as it is defined through shared experiences and attributed meanings. In this sense cultures are constructed as interacting individuals interpret what is going on around them and thereby collectively create meaning. Thus meaning produces culture even as it is the product of symbolic behavior.

Organization theorists working within the symbolic-interpretive perspective assume subjective ontology and interpretive epistemology and focus on how organizational members make meaning and the role that meaning-making plays in the workplace. Symbolic-interpretivists argue that meaning is dependent on the **context** in which artifacts and symbols are encountered and this context is what they refer to as culture. You have probably had the experience of having your words taken out of context, for example when someone uses something you have said against you in an argument. Similarly, you have probably heard politicians make this claim in defending themselves against charges made by the press or other politicians. The act of moving cultural symbols out of one context and into another changes their meaning. Thus, when symbolic-interpretivists talk about **contextualizing** they advocate studying artifacts and symbols in the situations and locations in which they naturally occur, allowing organizational members to use and speak about them as they ordinarily do. The goal of symbolic-interpretive culture researchers is to experience the contextualizing effects of organizational culture on themselves and to witness these effects on others in order to understand culture from the inside, as its members do.

Symbols, Symbolism and Symbolic Behavior

According to American sociologist Abner Cohen: 'Symbols are objects, acts, relationships or linguistic formations that stand ambiguously for a multiplicity of meanings, evoke emotions and impel men to action.'[20] **Symbols** denote or stand for something, as when a corporate logo stands for a company. The **denotative meanings** of symbols refer to their instrumental use as signifiers, for example, holding up a white flag to indicate your desire to surrender. But symbols also carry **connotative meanings** that refer to their expressive uses as when an American flag is burned or a logo is transformed into a means of ridiculing the company it signifies. For example, the Canadian magazine *Adbusters* published an altered photo of professional golfer and Nike ambassador Tiger Woods that made his wide smile appear in the form of the Nike Swoosh.

Because symbols like the Swoosh logo can be made to carry multiple meanings, symbolic meaning remains open and therefore ambiguous. Symbolic-interpretivists place less emphasis on the specific meanings that symbols take on and more on the activity or processes by which that meaning is constructed. According to John Van Maanen: 'To study symbolism is to learn how the meanings on which people base actions are created, communicated, contested, and sometimes changed.'[21]

There is a theoretical relationship between cultural symbols and artifacts. Artifacts can become symbols, but not all artifacts do so.[22] According to organization theorists Gareth Morgan, Peter Frost and Lou Pondy: 'Symbols are created and recreated whenever human beings vest elements of their world with a pattern of meaning and significance which extends beyond its intrinsic content.'[23] For instance, we can see that a national flag is a symbol by the responses given to it by members of the culture that it represents. It can be used symbolically at one moment (saluting it, flying it over your home, painting it on your face, burning it in protest) and not at the next (when the flag is tucked away in a drawer or you wash the paint from your face). As these examples show, what makes an artifact a symbol is its use to make and communicate meaning.

Notice that recognizing that an artifact is being used as a symbol does not necessarily equate with knowing its meaning. Discovering the meaning of a symbol involves interpretation within the appropriate cultural context. I remember being mildly alarmed by the number of Danish national flags I saw on display when I moved to Denmark in 1990. In the U.S. culture, where I grew up, such behavior typically indicates aggressive levels of nationalism. When I encountered these symbols displayed not only outside houses and public buildings, but inside homes and offices and even on birthday cakes, I wondered what was going on. Yet my Danish friends seemed puzzled when I asked them about their flag waving (my term). They told me the Danish flag was a normal part of their everyday life and would be a matter for comment for them only if it was absent. This and many similar surprises taught me that members of a culture may or may not be aware of symbolic uses of their culture's artifacts, but the artifacts themselves can be directly observed by anyone. Furthermore, whereas artifacts may be the most accessible elements of culture because they appear in tangible forms, you need to remember that they lie furthest from the cultural core and can be easily misinterpreted by those who are culturally naïve, especially culture researchers when they enter a new culture! Symbolic-interpretive researchers interested in studying cultural meaning need to be sensitive to misunderstandings, like my encounter with the display of flags in Denmark, as these can lead them to profound cultural insights.

Symbolic-interpretive organization theorists are concerned less with the tangible or artifactual aspects of symbols and more with symbolic meaning and even more with meaning making (interpretation) processes. They believe that meaning does not reside in the symbol itself but is constructed around symbols when people interact. Thus while symbols are often shared, their interpretations may, and usually do, differ. In fact, the potential for multiple and even contradictory meanings is a part of what makes symbolism and culture both so rich and so difficult to control. For those who produce an artifact with a symbolic purpose in mind meaning may be clear and direct, but once others adopt the artifact and thus make it their symbol, they will express their own meanings with it. Consider the Mercedes logo. Intended by its maker to symbolize prestige, it can also be (re)interpreted as a sign of overindulgence or to symbolize the injustice of being poor. While executives can exercise considerable control over the design and display of corporate artifacts, the symbolic meanings with which these artifacts become associated are far less easy to control and often are unpredictable. Recognizing the limitations to predicting and controlling the multiplicity of symbolic meaning is important for successfully applying the symbolic approach to management. Celebrating the multiplicity of meaning and human expressiveness was the next step. American cultural anthropologist Clifford Geertz's method of thick description led the way.

Thick Description

In the early 1980s, Geertz's highly acclaimed book *The Interpretation of Cultures* carried symbolic-interpretive cultural anthropology into the mainstream of organization theory. Organizational researchers who were disenchanted with positivist methods used Geertz's success to legitimize their interests and his methodology to guide their research activities. One particular quotation from this book is widely cited because it concisely and evocatively describes the conceptual foundation of the symbolic-interpretive approach and differentiates it from positivism: 'Believing, with Max Weber, that man is an animal suspended in webs of significance he himself has spun, I take culture to be those webs, and the analysis of it to be therefore not an experimental science in search of law but an interpretive one in search of meaning.'[24]

The method of **thick description** Geertz advocated is a form of ethnography that is extremely sensitive to symbols, their context and how cultural members interpret them. The term 'thick description' was coined by the British philosopher Gilbert Ryle. Geertz used Ryle's distinction between a wink and a twitch to explain the difference between symbolic and non-symbolic behavior. Both a wink and a twitch are contractions of the eyelid, but a wink means something (e.g., I like you or I acknowledge our conspiracy) while a twitch is involuntary. The difference lies in the use of symbolism by the winker. To get at the wink's significance requires digging beneath the surface of behavior to the inferences and implications made by those who give and receive winks or otherwise use artifacts as symbols. Thick description is all about digging beneath surfaces to discover symbolic meaning in order to show culture at work.

A famous story from one of Geertz's ethnographies will give you a taste of thick description. In this story Geertz explained how he and his wife, recently arrived in Bali to study its culture, gained acceptance by the normally aloof Balinese who typically treated strangers as if they were invisible. The Geertz's were no exception, until:

> ten days or so after our arrival, a large cockfight was held in the public square to raise money for a new school.... Of course, like drinking during Prohibition or, today, smoking marihuana, cockfights, being a part of 'The Balinese Way of Life', nonetheless go on happening, and with extraordinary frequency. And, as with Prohibition or marihuana, from time to time the police (who, in 1958 at least, were almost all not Balinese but Javanese) feel called upon to make a raid, confiscate the cocks and spurs, fine a few people, and even now and then expose some of them in the tropical sun for a day as object lessons which never, somehow, get learned, even though occasionally, quite occasionally, the object dies.
>
> As a result, the fights are usually held in a secluded corner of a village in semisecrecy, a fact which tends to slow the action a little—not very much, but the Balinese do not care to have it slowed at all. In this case, however, perhaps because they were raising money for a school that the government was unable to give them, perhaps because raids had been few recently, perhaps, as I gathered from subsequent discussion, there was a notion that the necessary bribes had been paid, they thought they could take a chance on the central square and draw a larger and more enthusiastic crowd without attracting the attention of the law.
>
> They were wrong. In the midst of the third match, with hundreds of people, including, still transparent, myself and my wife, fused into a single body around the ring, a superorganism in the literal sense, a truck full of policemen armed with machine guns roared up. Amid great screeching cries of 'pulisi! pulisi!' from the crowd, the policemen jumped out, and springing into the center of the ring, began to swing their guns around like gangsters in a motion picture, though not going so far as actually to fire them. The superorganism came instantly apart as its components scattered in all directions. People raced down the road, disappeared headfirst over walls, scrambled under platforms, folded themselves behind wicker screens, scuttled up coconut trees. Cocks armed with steel spurs sharp enough to cut off a finger or run a hole through a foot were running wildly around. Everything was dust and panic.
>
> On the established anthropological principle, 'When in Rome', my wife and I decided, only slightly less instantaneously than everyone else, that the thing to do was run too. We ran down the main village street, northward, away from where we were living, for we were on that side of the ring. About halfway down another fugitive ducked suddenly into a compound—his own, it turned out—and we, seeing nothing ahead of us but rice fields, open country, and a very high volcano, followed him. As the three of us came tumbling into the courtyard, his wife, who had apparently been through this sort of thing before, whipped out a table, a tablecloth, three chairs, and three cups of tea, and we all, without any explicit communication whatsoever, sat down, commenced to sip tea, and sought to compose ourselves.

A few moments later, one of the policemen marched importantly into the yard, looking for the village chief. (The chief had not only been at the fight, he had arranged it. When the truck drove up he ran to the river, stripped off his sarong, and plunged in so he could say, when at length they found him sitting there pouring water over his head, that he had been away bathing when the whole affair had occurred and was ignorant of it. They did not believe him and fined him three hundred rupiah, which the village raised collectively.) Seeing me and my wife, 'White Men', there in the yard, the policeman performed a classic double take. When he found his voice again he asked, approximately, what in the devil did we think we were doing there. Our host of five minutes leaped instantly to our defense, producing an impassioned description of who and what we were, so detailed and so accurate that it was my turn, having barely communicated with a living human being save my landlord and the village chief for more than a week, to be astonished. We had a perfect right to be there, he said, looking the Javanese upstart in the eye. We were American professors; the government had cleared us; we were there to study culture; we were going to write a book to tell Americans about Bali. And we had been there drinking tea and talking about cultural matters all afternoon and did not know anything about any cockfight. Moreover, we had not seen the village chief all day; he must have gone to town. The policeman retreated in rather total disarray. And, after a decent interval, bewildered but relieved to have survived and stayed out of jail, so did we.

The next morning the village was a completely different world for us. Not only were we no longer invisible, we were suddenly the center of all attention, the object of a great outpouring of warmth, interest, and most especially, amusement. Everyone in the village knew we had fled like everyone else. They asked us about it again and again (I must have told the story, small detail by small detail, fifty times by the end of the day), gently, affectionately, but quite insistently teasing us: 'Why didn't you just stand there and tell the police who you were?' 'Why didn't you just say you were only watching and not betting?' 'Were you really afraid of those little guns?' As always, kinesthetically minded and even when fleeing for their lives (or, as happened eight years later, surrendering them), the world's most poised people, they gleefully mimicked, also over and over again, our graceless style of running and what they claimed were our panic-stricken facial expressions. But above all, everyone was extremely pleased and even more surprised that we had not simply 'pulled out our papers' (they knew about those too) and asserted our Distinguished Visitor status, but had instead demonstrated our solidarity with what were now our covillagers. (What we had actually demonstrated was our cowardice, but there is fellowship in that too.) Even the Brahmana priest, an old, grave, halfway-to-heaven type who because of its associations with the underworld would never be involved, even distantly, in a cockfight, and was difficult to approach even to other Balinese, had us called into his courtyard to ask us about what had happened, chuckling happily at the sheer extraordinariness of it all.

In Bali, to be teased is to be accepted. It was the turning point so far as our relationship to the community was concerned, and we were quite literally 'in'. The whole village opened up to us, probably more than it ever would have otherwise (I might actually never have gotten to that priest, and our accidental host became one of my best informants), and certainly very much faster. Getting caught, or almost caught, in a vice raid is perhaps not a very generalizable recipe for achieving that mysterious necessity of anthropological field work, rapport, but for me it worked very well.[25]

Geertz's story illustrates many of the tenets of thick description including contextualizing, using vivid detail, documenting unexpected events or surprising plot twists, directly quoting sources, comparing and contrasting the reader's assumptions and beliefs with those of the culture being described, and presenting the interpretations that cultural members give to objects and events. Perhaps the most important aspect that Geertz's story reveals is the narrative nature of ethnography, or, for that matter, of any other type of research.

Organizational Stories, Narratives and Narrating

Narrative approaches to the study of organizational culture are related to thick description by their emphasis on the lived details of organizational life. The simplest way of defining **organizational narrative** is as a story of real events with a plot and characters that, when analyzed, will tell us about the organization's culture and distinctive practices. Stories have been a long-standing interest for symbolic-interpretive organization theorists. For example, in 1983 Joanne Martin, Martha Feldman, Sim Sitkin and I challenged claims that organizational cultures are unique on the basis of our analysis of corporate biographies.[26] We found that, paradoxically, although members often illustrated the uniqueness of their organizational cultures by telling stories, all organizations used variants of the same seven stories to express their uniqueness. The seven stories were about: What do I do when a higher status person breaks a rule? Is the big boss human? Can a little person rise to the top? Will I get fired? Will the organization help me when I have to move? How will the boss react to mistakes? How will the organization deal with obstacles?

As American folklorist Michael Owen Jones pointed out, taking a narrative approach to culture demands more than just collecting and analyzing the content of stories—it involves the process of **storytelling**.[27] The cultural significance of stories lies as much in the teller's art as in the message the story relays. As Jones explained it:

> During 'narrating' . . . a speaker communicates not only through linguistic channels (words) but also through paralinguistic and kinesic ones (intonation, change in pitch, body language). Moreover, the speaker responds to listener feedback by digressing, explaining, repeating, emphasizing, elaborating, abbreviating, dramatizing, and so on . . . Participants in a narrating event infer multiple, even quite different meanings from the varied cues; much depends on their experiences, feelings, and concerns in the present circumstances (the situational context that makes this narrating a 'situated event'). Therefore, it is misleading to refer to 'a story' or 'the story' as if it has an independent existence. It is inadequate to document 'stories' as linguistic entities with no regard for other channels of communication that convey information and affect responses. And it is misguided to assume that the event has a single meaning for participants.[28]

The uniqueness paradox study was vulnerable to all the criticisms Jones raised. David Boje overcame these problems when he observed a U.S. office supply company where storytelling was an integral part of everyday work life. One of the surprises Boje's study revealed was that storytelling is often abbreviated when participants share a common history of working together. Much like the story about the prisoners who know each other's jokes so well they simply call out a number and everyone laughs, **terse stories** mean that outsiders may not realize the extent to which storytelling is rampant in an organization. On the basis of his study Boje defined the storytelling organization as a 'collective storytelling system in which the performance of stories is a key part of members' sense making and a means to supplanting individuals with institutional memory.'[29]

According to social constructionists, the members of a culture socially construct their realities by narrating. Alasdair MacIntyre, a British moral philosopher, claimed that all social life is narrated and that we are each subjects in self-identifying narratives that form our life story. MacIntyre claimed that the narrative that links our birth, life and death is a story with a beginning, middle and end, or plot. Our individual narratives give meaning to and even construct our lives, yet, because we live our lives within social and historical contexts, they are intertwined with organizational, social, and historical narratives.[30] It is thus that narrative can be regarded as epistemic, that is, as a way of knowing that includes knowing ourselves. Using **narrative epistemology** means believing that humans develop knowledge by listening and telling stories to one another and themselves and that we can learn about organizations and organizational identities by studying the stories and accounts of experience that organizational members tell.

In addition to conceptualizing organizations as narratives, symbolic-interpretive organizational culture researchers use narrative epistemology to study their own theorizing as a narrative act. This approach was first developed by American organization theorist John Van Maanen. His book *Tales of the Field* encouraged organizational researchers to be more reflexive about their own narrative practices and attentive to the influence their narrative choices have on the stories they tell—the theories and research reports they write.[31] For example, Van Maanen called modernist research reports realist tales because they are written as objective reports of social facts that tell us what really goes on in organizations. Calling them realist tales encourages us to see how modernist researchers rhetorically construct subjective experience as objective fact, while hiding the identity of the researcher/narrator. Confessional tales are usually relegated to ethnographic appendices and are used to divulge the researcher's biases as the author confesses prejudices, preconceptualizations and mistakes made along the way. Impressionist tales, such as Geertz's story about the Balinese cockfight, are personal accounts that incorporate both realist and confessional writing. They are designed to put readers in the context of the culture and allow them to vicariously appreciate the ethnographer's experiences.

American communication scholar Ellen O'Connor's study of the start-up of a high tech research organization in Silicon Valley offers one example of an impressionist tale.[32] She spent the better part of a year immersed in daily organizational life, attending meetings and discussions, talking to organizational members and reading memos and emails. Based on her experiences, O'Connor suggested that the success of the start-up depended on the narrative competence of its founder, that is, his ability to weave together plot and character to create a coherent and persuasive story shared and acted upon by other organizational members. She also identified three different types of narratives used within the organization:

- personal narratives including the life history, dreams and visions of the founder
- generic narratives that create the company, for example, business plans and strategy
- situational narratives or histories of critical events that explain why things are done in certain ways within the organization

Table 6.3 Aristotle's typology of stories

	Comic	Tragic	Epic	Romantic
Protagonist	Deserving victim, fool	Undeserving victim	Hero	Love object
Other characters	Trickster	Villain, helper	Rescue object, assistant, villain	Gift-giver, lover, injured or sick person
Plot focus	Misfortune or deserved chastisement	Undeserved misfortune, trauma	Achievement, noble victory, success	Love triumphant, love conquers misfortune
Predicament	Accident, mistake, coincidence, the unexpected or unpredictable	Crime, accident, insult, injury, loss, mistake, repetition, mis-recognition	Contest, challenge, trial, test, mission, quest, sacrifice	Gift, romantic fantasy, falling in love, reciprocation, recognition
Emotions	Mirth, aggression, scorn	Sorrow, pity, fear, anger, pathos	Pride, admiration, nostalgia	Love, care, kindness, generosity, gratitude
Function in business	Amusement	Catharsis	Inspiration	Compassion

Source: Hatch, Kostera and Koźmiński (2005), based on Gabriel (2000).

O'Connor's observation about the narrative competence of entrepreneurial founders was corroborated by an interpretive study of the CEO interviews *Harvard Business Review* publishes. Whereas nearly all the CEOs in a sample of thirty interviews showed signs of narrative competence, the interviews of those who founded a company were constructed almost entirely of personal narratives. Like all the CEOs in the sample, the entrepreneur/ founders relied heavily on the epic form of storytelling, but they also demonstrated considerable skill using other story types including those identified by Aristotle (see Table 6.3).

To illustrate the application of the Aristotelian approach, consider the following story told by Masayoshi Son, founder and CEO of Japan's Softbank:

> When I first started the company, I only had two part-time workers and a small office. I got two apple boxes, and I stood up on them in the morning as if I was giving a speech. In a loud voice, I said to my two workers, 'You guys have to listen to me, because I am the president of this company.' I said, 'In five years, I'm going to have $75 million in sales. In five years, I will be supplying 1,000 dealer outlets, and we'll be number one in PC software distribution.' And I said it very loudly.
>
> Those two guys opened their mouths. They stood up and opened wide their eyes and mouths, and they thought, this guy must be crazy. And they both quit.
>
> That was in 1981. About a year and a half later, we were supplying 200 dealer outlets. Now we supply 15,000. In ten years, we've gone from two part-time employees doing software distribution

and making about $12,000 to 570 employees doing software distribution, book and magazine publishing, telephone least cost routing, system integration, network computing, and CAD-CAM and making about $350 million.[33]

Son's story combines comedy with epic. The comedic element of this story arises from Son's self-positioning as the deserving victim of the misfortune of losing his first two employees. To generate the epic effect, Son positioned himself as heroically enduring the trials of starting up a company and achieving success. According to Aristotle, the story should produce an interesting combination of scorn and admiration that encourages amusement but also inspires you.

The Theater Metaphor: Dramaturgy and Performativity

Perhaps Shakespeare's famous metaphor, 'All the world's a stage/And all the men and women merely players', will come to mind when I tell you that Erving Goffman, a Canadian sociologist, borrowed from drama theory to explain how individuals shape their social realities.[34] Goffman developed his approach while studying how individuals in a mental hospital conformed and adapted to their formal organizational roles. He discovered that the social order of the hospital depended upon doctors, nurses and patients acting their parts within the institutional performance.

Dramaturgy is concerned with the theatrical elements of a performance such as acting, costumes, staging, masks, props, scenery and so on. It is closely related to the notion of **performativity**. In his book *How to Do Things with Words*, linguist John L. Austin defined a performative as a set of words, the utterance of which performs an action as opposed to simply conveying information (e.g., 'I thee wed' or 'You're fired!').[35] The concept of performativity emphasizes the fact that dramatic performance involves taking action.

Applications of dramaturgy and performativity to the study of organizations build on similarities between organizations and the theater and therefore are sometimes referred to as the **theater metaphor**. For example, both acting and organizing require the playing of roles and both troupes of actors and businesses are known as companies. Performance features prominently in the discourses of both theater and organization as in references to the performance of an actor or of a play, and to individual or organizational performance.

The theater metaphor can be broken down in many ways by using its various components to describe organizational phenomena. To give just one example, organizations can be metaphorically described as having a front stage where their members present the organization's public face and where they manage the impressions of others through appearance, language and so on. This is where actors and their audiences (stakeholders) co-construct an organizational performance and conspire to maintain it. Back stage, organizational members are less publicly available. There they can shed their costumes and masks, relax and prepare for the next show. Applying dramaturgy, organizations are analyzed as social dramas or theaters consisting of many different performances that are directed at achieving organizational goals.

Michael Rosen used dramaturgy to analyze the cultural ritual of an American advertising agency's annual corporate breakfast.[36] Rosen described the symbols, dress, language and pictures on display at the restaurant where the breakfast was held, and how different groups and individuals manipulated these symbols to communicate meanings that reinforced their individual and organizational identities and enacted the organization's hierarchy. For example, Rosen observed that different groups of employees dressed differently for the occasion—whereas clerical workers and creative people did not appear to be restricted by a dress code, employees looking for promotion and rewards wore suits of a particular type. Speeches were made by senior executives (all wearing the right suits) and their remarks reinforced images of control and benevolence, as when the Chairman of the Board talked about how some employees' attitudes caused problems requiring changes in personnel, and then presented ten-year service awards to loyal employees. Rosen claimed that, juxtaposed in this way, the awards symbolized conformity to company rules and reinforced the agency's hierarchical values.

British organization theorist Heather Höpfl, a former stage manager for a theater in the United Kingdom, pointed out many similarities between the actors' subjective experience of their craft and the world of work. Her studies examining the dramaturgical and performative aspects of customer service in airline crews and employment agencies showed that when customer service employees embody corporate values, they set aside a part of themselves in order to perform their roles, just as dramatic actors do.[37] On the basis of this denial of the whole person at work, Höpfl critiqued organizational practices and procedures governing customer experience performances. She argued that the costs of role performance, for dramatic and corporate actors alike, must be measured in terms of the hypocrisy, degradation, stress and emotional burnout that performing demands.

Höpfl quoted from the radical eighteenth-century French philosopher Denis Diderot to make her point. Diderot compared an actor to a prostitute, saying that the actor is like 'the whore who feels nothing for the man she is with, but lets herself go in his arms anyway as a demonstration of her professional competence.'[38] According to Höpfl: 'Diderot's actor is an instrument or an empty vessel, capable of playing any or all characters precisely because his/her own character is eradicated and sensibilities obliterated in the pursuit of professional craft.' She goes on to consider the implications for those who manage organizations for whom 'the achievement of a flexible and well-rehearsed work force which can move easily between a variety of roles with skill is considered to be a desirable accomplishment.'[39] It is this attitude on the part of management, she claimed, that both exploits and masks the actor's pain.

To demonstrate that performing in the theatrical sense is a familiar aspect of many service jobs, and to give an example of the pain customer service inflicts on organizational performers, Höpfl described a group of employees she observed in the act of overplaying their roles.

> In 1998, on a scheduled flight from Warsaw to Heathrow, I witnessed an extraordinary performance by the cabin crew that resembled a sixth-form review. The cabin crew donned the duty free articles they were selling and one of the male cabin crew members pushed his trolley up the aisle in an ostentatiously camp manner, wearing a silk headscarf and Rayban sunglasses, with a small teddy bear mascot waving from his breast pocket. The female member of the crew who accompanied him gestured and pointed like a magician's assistant. I have never seen anything like it in many years of flying. Another cabin crew member announced that this was the floorshow and

the passengers broke into spontaneous and sustained applause. At the end of the performance, the crew took their bows. I was struck by the inevitable logic of the performance requirement of the organization which takes performance to this extreme. Without doubt, these crew members were acting beyond the call of their roles. This example provides an insight into what occurs to a lesser degree in everyday organizational performance in a less immediate and obvious way. Its significance lies in what is revealed by the extreme variant. This has much in common with the notion of the theatre of the absurd in which the production of the action is made transparent in its performance.[40]

Höpfl's last point about performance rendering the production of action transparent illustrates what is meant by performativity. Students of organizational performativity aim to expose the theatrical means by which organizations perform their production tasks. In a service economy they do so in large measure through the playing of dramatic roles. The concept of performativity also reveals that organizational theater goes beyond metaphor—it is a literal description of customer service and with this literal reading comes the realization that acting roles exacts a price from the actor. Thus Höpfl's work moves in the direction of postmodernism by raising the critical question: Why isn't the whole person accepted into the workplace?

Postmodernism and Organizational Culture

Postmodernists rely heavily on the metaphor of the text. For example, they regard narrative as a textual space where multiple voices (writers and readers) and their language systems combine to construct meaning. Bulgarian-born French linguist Julia Kristeva introduced the term **intertextuality** to suggest that no text exists in isolation, all texts are interwoven with other texts to which they refer (e.g., by quotation, allusion, description, inscription) and that provide some of their meaning.[41] Thus each text takes part in a larger discourse that itself is open to alteration by future texts and readings. In this postmodern perspective the question of the original meaning of a text as intended by its author is nonsense because, over time, texts are written and rewritten repeatedly by many different authors and readers. In this sense discourses produce and are produced by many texts whose multiple authors and readers continuously (re)read and (re)write them.

The application of intertextuality to organizations suggests treating culture, identities, organizational members, symbols and actions as interwoven texts that create one another via mutual ongoing referencing.[42] Barbara Czarniawska compared organizational narratives to sagas, serials and soap operas, providing a vivid image of the never-ending intertextual construction of complex plot lines and multiple characters that weave in and out of always unfinished organizational lives.[43] She studied several public sector organizations in Sweden and the organizational narratives she documented demonstrated the suitability of soap opera as a framework for reading and writing organizational narratives. She provided examples of privatization and computerization, each of which were presented as stories told by multiple voices and broken into episodes with no clear ending in sight. However, although Czarniawska's organizational soap operas offer a non-linear, open-ended version of storytelling, her narratives remain coherent enough to be understood. Postmoderism leads others to more radical uses of narrative that involve abandoning meaningful coherence and undermining all traces of understanding.

Culture as Fragmentation

Some culture researchers assume neither consistency nor stability but focus on the ways in which organizational cultures are inconsistent, ambiguous, multiplicitous and in a constant state of flux. In this view alliances or coalitions never stabilize into subcultures and certainly not into an integrated culture because discourse and its focal issues are always changing. In this spirit Debra Meyerson and Joanne Martin provided an image of organizational culture as **fragmentation** to offset what they regarded as overly consensual views of organizational culture.[44] Researchers who assume a fragmentation view of culture claim there can be no unity of understanding and that any consensus or affinity, even within a subculture, is temporary because interpretations shift incessantly. Martin explained that because race, ethnicity, gender, occupation, hierarchical position and other identifying characteristics co-exist within each member of an organization, allegiances that others might call subcultures constantly shift in response to the ever-changing issues that appear in an organizational discourse. The organizational issues in play at one moment of time will draw out one configuration of a member's identity, while at the next moment a different configuration may be called upon. As Martin put it:

> when two cultural members agree (or disagree) on a particular interpretation of, say, a ritual, this is likely to be a temporary and issue-specific congruence (or incongruence). It may well not reflect agreement or disagreement on other issues, at other times. Subcultures, then, are reconceptualized as fleeting, issue-specific coalitions that may or may not have a similar configuration in the future. This is not simply a failure to achieve subcultural consensus in a particular context; from the Fragmentation perspective this is the most consensus possible in any context.[45]

While fragmentation studies have much in common with postmodernism, Martin claimed that postmodern cultural studies often go beyond the fragmentation assumption to assert that reality (and therefore culture) is an illusion—an arena of competing truth claims and stories that aim to suppress and marginalize those who do not accept and support the dominant view the illusion hides.[46] In spite of this difference with postmodernists, Martin agreed with critical cultural scholars who believe that organizational culture is just one more way for those in power to mask their manipulation and control of others. It is the desire to unmask the power relations hidden behind the illusions of culture that drove many postmodernist organizational culture researchers to deconstruction.

Deconstructing Organizational Culture

Postmodern organizational theorists challenge grand narrative in organizations and organization theory by criticizing the ideological function of modernist organizational narratives and stories (including modernist theory and modernist writing styles). As you have seen, modernists consider stories to be expressions of organizational unity and ways of socializing and controlling members. Postmodernist communication scholar Dennis Mumby used this definition to suggest that narratives lead to a systematic distortion of organizational culture because they reproduce and maintain particular meanings that support relationships of dependence and domination.[47] He proposed deconstructing organizational stories so as to expose their ideological nature—how they privilege particular groups and exclude others.

Joanne Martin deconstructed a story told by the CEO of a multinational corporation who claimed that his story showed how concerned the company was for the welfare of its female employees.[48] In the story a young woman arranged her Caesarean section around the launch of a new product she had been instrumental in developing. The company provided a closed circuit television by her bed so she could watch the launch event. Martin argued that the primary beneficiary of this act was not the woman but the company because the woman's continued involvement in the launch enhanced the company's productivity rather than the woman's well-being or that of her child. Martin went further by suggesting that what the CEO referred to as the company's culture of concern actually controlled and supported gender discrimination by blurring the boundary between public and private life, thus enabling the organization to appropriate some of the time the woman otherwise would have given to her newborn child.

Other interpretations of the story told by the CEO are possible, of course, including that of the mother/employee. For example, the woman in the story might claim to have seen herself giving birth to two progeny at the same time—one her child and the other the new product—hence she may have welcomed having access to both events from her hospital room. A critical reader might counter that the mother's version gives evidence of false consciousness. These opposing interpretations point to the potential of deconstructive readings to reveal the possibilities of dominance and other forms of power (such as the woman's creative power to give birth and to help develop a new product) without the necessity to settle the matter of which interpretation wins the struggle for supremacy. While one version of a story may be triumphant in one setting, another version may carry more weight in another. The point of deconstruction is not to settle these matters once and for all, but to sensitize you to the ongoing struggle over meaning within which everyday organizational life is constituted.

Another approach to deconstructing culture relates to the way culture is conceptualized and operationalized in the form of values and performance. In Chapter 2 you read about Baudrillard's notion of **simulacra**, a concept that stands for no reality. If we relate this idea to organizational culture, then there is no organizational culture to study, instead organizational members are only engaged in simulations, images and interactive performances. Postmodern organization theorists deconstruct the notion that culture is linked to underlying values, beliefs and systems of meaning, claiming that any idea of a unifying and cohesive culture is merely an illusion created by hollow and ambiguous rituals and symbols that support many different interpretations. For example, meetings can be interpreted by various participants at various times as struggles for power, theatres of the absurd or as symbols of commitment.[49] Rituals are an important part of the simulacrum because they are so obviously performative and often involve acts of imitation (e.g., parroting the characteristics Peters and Waterman equated with excellent cultures) that seduce members into conformity with organizational culture and ideology.

A number of scholars studying culture as a simulacrum claim that cultures of empower-ment (team work, quality circles, etc.) are ways of manipulating work performance and worker identities, an issue we will discuss further in Chapter 8. Douglas Ezzy, an Australian sociologist, suggested that organizational cultures have created a simulacrum of trust and family that is contradicted by rewards for individual achievement rather than cooperation, and by layoffs during hard times.[50] Workers who trust and invest themselves in an organ-izational culture that controls and then abandons them have been manipulated by a simulacrum. In his ethnographic study of the Engineering Division of a U.S. electronics company, Gideon Kunda found that workers complained it was difficult to maintain a boundary between their 'organizational' and 'true' selves. They found themselves working long hours developing innovative technologies in a culture of fun that they themselves produced at the expense of their personal lives, which led many of them to suffer burn out. Thus, paradoxically, the simulacrum of organizational autonomy represses and controls workers who believe in it.[51]

Mikhail Bakhtin: Culture as Polyphony and Dialogue

Russian literary theorist Mikhail Bakhtin believed that language is a byproduct of human communication and therefore its use implies dialogue with others, or in other words, language is dialogic. Bakhtin's theory was that, even when we use it to think when we are alone, language places us in dialogue with others. Organization theorists have used Bakhtin's theory to describe the ways in which a **dialogic organization** is constructed in and by dialogue.[52]

Polyphony, another of Bakhtin's concepts, is used to account for the many discourses in which organizational dialogue takes place—between organizations and their environ-ments and stakeholders, between units of an organization and between the people who work in them. Bakhtin borrowed the term **polyphony** from orchestral music theory where it refers to the many voices or sounds made by the symphonic instruments: violin, cello, French horn, and so on. When applied to organizations, polyphony means that, like orchestras, organizations are composed of multiple voices speaking simultaneously. Confronting the dialogic and polyphonic aspects of organizations urges researchers and managers to *hear* organizing, not only to attend to the content of organizational dialogue, but to listen for its rhythms, harmonies and dissonance.

Storytelling researcher David Boje offered an example of polyphony combined with dramaturgy.[53] In the play *Tamara*, audience members choose which characters they will follow across the multiple stages on which this play is enacted.[54] Each actor literally has their own following and as they perform their roles on the different stages (often different rooms in a house) with various other actors, audiences merge and separate, constituting and reconstituting themselves continuously. This means that there is the potential for each member of the audience to leave the play having constructed a different story and each actor can conceivably play to many different audiences during a single performance, thus no two actors or audience members are likely to have the same experience of a *Tamara* play. Boje claimed that organizations are like *Tamara*, because organizational members are forever creating, telling and negotiating stories with different people, at different times and in different places. In this sense *Tamara* offers a vivid description of polyphony with its multiple dialogic threads.

Boje's postmodern reading of organizations that behave like *Tamara* is that there is no coherent or completed storyline or plot because people continually chase and retell the stories they hear. No collective organizational memory or even subculture is possible (notice the similarity with the concept of culture as fragmentation). While you may think it is impossible to study organizational culture defined by this much fragmentation, Boje suggested that, if you study the various narratives and plotlines created by particular groups and individuals along with their assumptions, rationalizations and biases, then you have a chance to trace their intertextual linkages across time. For example, you might chronicle initial narratives and counter-narratives, their interpretations and responses, struggles over whose plot takes precedence and how various stories interweave to construct the discourse of the organization, as Czarniawska did with her organizational soap operas.

Irony

Sanford Ehrlich and I took another approach to organizational dialogue. By studying the dialogue of a middle-management team in a mainframe computer company in the late 1980s we discovered a pattern of joking and laughter that revealed fear and other negative emotional reactions provoked by organizational change. The team's business was purchasing and inventory management and thus the corporation's decision to adopt just-in-time inventory delivery threatened the team's existence. The managers openly interpreted their role as putting themselves out of business and they used gallows humor and irony to offset negative emotions while confronting the contradictions inherent in their situation. For example, one of the contradictions involved having to terminate the employment of loyal subordinates and then do the same to themselves. While discussing a corporate request for yet another headcount reduction, one of the managers was greeted with laughter when he quipped: 'Last one out, turn out the light!'[55] Putting their local humor in the context of the larger corporate discourse about needed change (the mainframe computer industry was undergoing massive restructuring at the time due to the competitive threat from personal computers) made listening polyphonically to their organizational dialogue a bittersweet experience. This is just one illustration of how Bakhtin's ideas sensitize you to the emotional content of everyday organizational life and give you the chance to hear the intermingling of harmony and discord as you take part in its pathos and irony.

Irony takes on a particularly important role in postmodernism because it denies the possibility of the unequivocal authoritative narratives to which Lyotard so strenuously objected.[56] As sociologist Richard Harvey Brown put it: irony 'constitutes itself on the awareness of the impossibility of literally "telling it like it is".'[57]

Changing Culture

Managers often want to know how to change their organization's culture. The question of whether or not cultures can be managed is largely a modernist concern that has provoked long and at times heated debates among organization theorists. For those who believe that culture can be managed, organizational culture holds the promise of new forms of managerial influence and control. Modernists reason that, if culture influences behavior via norms and values, then it should be possible to manage the norms and values of the organization in such a way that desired behaviors and other organizational performances are more or less guaranteed. Such control might come, for instance, through recruiting and hiring practices aimed at finding value-compatible employees, through socialization and training that inculcates organizationally preferred values and introduces desired norms, and through rewards that reinforce conformity.[58] Those who oppose the idea that culture can be managed argue that the possibilities for managing culture are severely limited by norms and values grounded in deeply rooted basic assumptions, unquestioned beliefs, everyday understandings, routines and informal social relationships. Furthermore, they warn, trying to control culture risks transforming its delicately negotiated web of meaning into an inflexible set of institutionalized rules and entrenched power relationships more likely to motivate cynicism than loyalty.[59] More productive, they argue, is to consider how organizational culture creates an interpretive context that frames the meaning of change programs initiated by executives.

One assumption organizational culture researchers almost all make is that top managers are the most influential members of an organizational culture. Because of their relatively high visibility to other organizational members and because power structures favor giving them attention, their behavior provides a model for others, their words are more likely to be heard and their directives obeyed. This opportunity to influence, however, does not necessarily guarantee that the expressions and actions of top executives will be understood as intended or that they will have the desired effects on other members of the culture. This dilemma lies at the heart of the culture as control debate. Those who believe culture can be used as a mechanism of control are accused by those who do not of being unrealistic about the potential to control the interpretations of employees. Others, including some postmodernists, agree that culture is a controlling influence, but either question the managerial ethics of using culture to control others, or promote the benefits of relinquishing managerial control (e.g., innovation, freedom, democracy).

The symbolic-interpretive approach to culture theory offers a way to carve out a middle ground in this debate. From this perspective it can be argued that managers have the potential to become powerful symbols within their organizations but that this potential can only be realized by others. As symbols, managers represent the meanings that other employees associate with the organization and therefore successful leadership rests on a leader's ability to adapt to the symbolism of organizational culture.[60] This argument recognizes that managers are themselves part of their cultures and are managed *by* cultural influences even while they are trying to manage culture. In this framework a manger is an artifact who would like to be a symbol.

Two theories of organizational culture change provide examples of this symbolic-interpretive perspective on change, and both build on Schein's theory. Italian organizational theorist Pasquale Gagliardi offered a theory of the relationship between culture and strategy that he used to explain both how culture affects change and how change affects culture. My own model of the dynamics of organizational culture explains both change and stability in everyday organizational life in terms of the cultural processes that link assumptions, values, artifacts and symbols.

Culture as Strategy and Organizational Identity

Gagliardi began with Schein's notion of assumptions and values as the core of an organizational culture and then argued that every organization's primary strategy is to protect the organizational identity that these assumptions and values create and maintain (see Figure 6.5). In service to the primary strategy, Gagliardi argued, organizations develop and implement a range of secondary strategies. These secondary strategies can be either instrumental or expressive. **Instrumental strategies** are operational in nature; they direct attention to the attainment of specific measurable objectives. **Expressive strategies** operate in the symbolic realm and protect the stability and coherence of shared meanings by enabling group members to maintain a lively awareness of their collective self and offer a recognizable identity to the outside world.[61]

Of course secondary strategies can be both expressive and instrumental. For example, an advertising campaign can be designed to present the organizational identity to its external audiences (expressive) at the same time that it helps to sell the company's

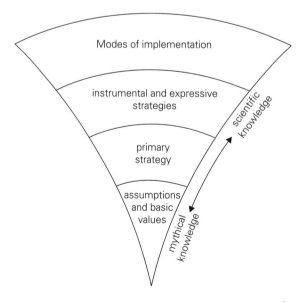

Figure 6.5 Gagliardi's fan model of culture in relation to strategy
Source: Gagliardi (1986).

products (instrumental). Similarly a move to an open plan office may reflect a strategy to improve communication efficiency (instrumental) and to symbolize a reduction in the importance of hierarchy (expressive). Changes in behavior, technology, symbols and structures occur through implementation of secondary strategies. In Gagliardi's view strategy is grounded in and limited by cultural assumptions and values. The most effective strategies in his view are identity laden expressions of culture.

How then does culture change ever occur? Gagliardi described three types of change. One type, **apparent change**, occurs within culture but does not change it in any significant way. That is, new problems are confronted by choosing from the range of secondary strategies permitted by organizational culture and identity. Implementation of these secondary strategies produces changes at the level of cultural artifacts, but these cultural changes are superficial; the organization only adapts within the confines of its existing identity.

In **revolutionary change**, a strategy incompatible with cultural assumptions and values is imposed upon the organization, usually through the entry of outsiders who destroy old symbols and create new ones. This can occur, for example, when the founder of an organization is succeeded, or when a company is merged or acquired. But in these cases, Gagliardi argued, it is 'more correct to say that the old firm dies and that a new firm, which has little in common with the first, was born'.[62]

Gagliardi's third type of cultural change, **incremental change**, is the only type that reaches the deep level of cultural values and assumptions. In this case, a strategy that implies different, but not incompatible, values stretches the organizational culture to include new values alongside its old ones (see Figure 6.6). As Schein argued, if the new strategy meets with success, then the change it brings about will be incorporated into the

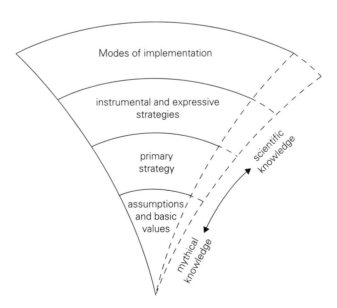

Figure 6.6 The fan model stretched to include new cultural assumptions and values
Source: Gagliardi (1986).

organization's taken-for-granted assumptions. Gagliardi added that this transformation of values, assumptions and identity is more likely if the success is celebrated with storytelling and mythmaking.

Gagliardi's model suggests that different strategic moves have different effects on organizational culture. When strategies align with organizational assumptions and values, cultures do not change. When strategies are in conflict with assumptions and values, culture is either overthrown by being replaced or destroyed, or the strategy is resisted and never implemented. When a strategy is different but not incompatible with assumptions and values, the culture is extended by the new assumptions and values carried by the new strategy. What Gagliardi's model does not explain is how strategies, or strategists for that matter, are absorbed within or act upon the organizational culture. To be more specific about the processes by which organizational cultural change occurs, I will now present my own theory of the dynamics of organizational culture.

The Dynamics of Organizational Culture

Like Gagliardi's model, the cultural dynamics model was built on Schein's theory of culture as assumptions, values and artifacts.[63] Cultural dynamics theory, however, focused not on the elements of assumptions, values and artifacts, but on the processes connecting them. These processes were represented in Schein's model by the two pairs of arrows linking assumptions with values, and values with artifacts (see Figure 6.3). The cultural dynamics model flipped Schein's diagram onto its side, split the two sets of arrows and inserted symbols into the bottom half of the resulting model (see Figure 6.7). Turning the diagram on its side overthrew the hierarchy suggested by Schein's original formulation by making artifacts and symbols equal in importance with assumptions and values, a move that highlights

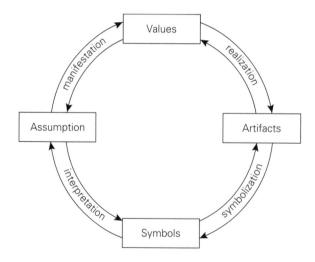

Figure 6.7 Hatch's cultural dynamics model shows interrelated processes of cultural stability and change

Source: Hatch (1993). Permission granted by Academy of Management.

the interactions between these aspects of culture. Adding symbols made Schein's theory more compatible with the assumptions of the symbolic-interpretive perspective.

The cultural dynamics model explains how a change in artifacts, values, symbols or assumptions can affect the other elements (though it may not). In the first half of the cultural dynamics model, assumptions and values create expectations about the world that produce images to guide action. This process is called **manifestation**:

> Consider the assumption that humans are lazy. According to the cultural dynamics perspective, this assumption produces expectations of laziness, which lead to perceptions of lazy acts. These perceptions, in combination with other manifesting assumptions, color thoughts and feelings about these acts. For instance, in an organization that assumes that success depends upon sustained effort, laziness is likely to be considered in a negative light, and perceptions of laziness along with negative thoughts and feelings about it can easily develop into a value for controlling laziness. Meanwhile the laziness assumption also works to inhibit expectations of industrious acts (because humans are lazy, why would they act in this way?), and perceptions, thoughts, and feelings about these acts will be constrained. This inhibition suppresses a value for autonomy (because giving lazy people autonomy will almost certainly lead to little or no effort being exerted), which further supports the value for control by eliminating a potentially competing force from the value set. That is, although autonomy would be compatible with an assumption that organizational success depends upon effort, the laziness assumption interferes with an effort/autonomy value set and supports an effort/control value set.[64]

Once culture influences action by manifesting values, value-based action produces cultural artifacts (e.g., objects, events, verbal statements, texts). The production of artifacts is referred to as the **realization** process because it is by this process that images grounded in assumptions and values are given tangible forms (i.e., made real). To carry on with the laziness example from above:

> An assumption that the organization is filled with laggards contributes to a value for control that enhances the likelihood that certain social and material forms will appear. For instance, time clocks, daily productivity reports, performance reviews, and visually accessible offices are acceptable ideas in a culture that values controlling laziness. Proactive realization is the process by which manifest expectations are made tangible in activity. Thus, time clocks might be installed, daily activity reports requested and filed, performance assessed, and visually accessible offices built, all as partial means of realizing the expectation of 'how it should be' in an organization assumed to be filled with laggards.[65]

The top half of the cultural dynamics model shown in Figure 6.7 describes the manifestation and realization processes by which artifacts are created; the bottom half describes what happens once artifacts are made part of the organization's cultural inventory and become available for symbolization and interpretation. In the upper half of the model, assumptions and values shape activity such that artifacts of these influences are created and maintained within the culture. In the lower half of the model, organizational members choose some (but not all) of the artifacts available to them and use the selected artifacts to symbolize their meanings in communication with others.

The process by which symbols are fashioned from artifacts is called **symbolization**. For example, an organization's beautiful new open office building might be used by members of top management to communicate an image of the organization as participative and inclusive. Meanwhile, at lower levels in the hierarchy, time clocks, daily activity reports and the behavior of managers tell employees that they are not trusted and lead to feelings of resentment and exclusion. Interpretations invested in the selected symbols then influence what people believe and assume about the organization. However, the interpretation process works in two directions. It uses assumptions to help determine the meaning of symbols, but allows symbols to either maintain or challenge existing assumptions. Maintenance of assumptions (stability) occurs when interpretations support what is already expected, but interpretations sometimes run counter to expectations.

The possibility of cultural change comes when assumptions are symbolically challenged within the **interpretation** process. For instance, in a culture that assumes laziness the appearance of an obviously hardworking individual challenges the basic assumption and brings the possibility of new meaning into the culture. Of course it may happen that the symbol of the hardworking individual is simply reinterpreted to fit into existing assumptions, for instance, by making an excuse for the aberration ('his twin daughters are ready for college and he really needs a promotion so he is kissing up to the boss'). But change is also possible, and when it occurs it is by the mechanism of confrontation with symbols that do not fit the assumed reality. For example, suppose the same hardworking individual wins a $50,000,000 lottery and keeps on working. In this case the assumption of laziness is opened a little, and now people start to assume that at least some workers have initiative. This leads to a desire to distinguish lazy and hardworking individuals and perhaps to a new employee selection process that changes the artifact pool, and so on, round and round the model.

The processes described by the cultural dynamics model are ongoing and interrelated. Active attempts by managers to change organizations would therefore also be described as a part of these processes. An attempt to intentionally introduce change usually begins with the processes of realization and symbolization when management or contact with another culture introduces a new idea through language and other artifacts that are new to the culture (do not forget that physical objects and behavioral manifestations are also powerful communicators) which then may be symbolized and interpreted by those who will either carry the change forward or deny it any influence. If the symbols made are in alignment with existing organizational assumptions and values, change should be relatively easy but not very deep (this is Gagliardi's notion of apparent change). However, change in line with existing assumptions and values may not be what management wants. Some change may involve introducing foreign ideas into the system. Cultural processes of absorption then come into play, and change initiators must recognize that their control over cultural processes will diminish as others confront the new artifacts, construct symbols with them and make their own interpretations of the meaning of the change and the intent of the change agent. This is how cultural dynamics theory places the manager within the organizational culture model. It suggests that much of the power attributed to leaders lies in their sensitivity to their own symbolic meaning within the cultural contexts in which it is produced and maintained. Leaders have tremendous influence within organizations, but their ability to effectively mobilize this influence depends upon their knowledge of, and relationship with, the culture and their openness to and respect for the interpretive acts of others.[66]

SUMMARY

An organization can be viewed as a culture in its own right, as a set of subcultures, or as a subculture of an even larger culture, as shown by Hofstede's study of IBM. We have examined examples of each of these levels of analysis in this chapter, but it is important to bear in mind the many ways these analytical levels work together. For example if you only pay attention to cultural forces at the environmental level, and do not consider culture at the level of the organization, you will miss much of what makes an organization distinctive and differentiates it from other organizations—its organizational culture. Likewise, if you only focus on the organizational culture and ignore its subcultures, you may miss the tensions and contradictions organizational members confront in trying to understand and manage their organizations.

Members share their culture in the dual senses of similarity and difference. The elements upon which cultural sharing is based include artifacts, norms, values, beliefs and assumptions (from Schein's perspective), and physical, behavioral and linguistic symbols (from the symbolic point of view). These cultural elements interweave forming a web of meanings described as a set of core assumptions (modernist) or a worldview (symbolic-interpretive) that is accessible to all members of the culture or subculture, depending on your level of analysis.

Modernists follow symbolic-interpretivists in believing that assumptions and values influence behavior through their expression in norms and values and that culture is communicated through artifacts including stories, symbols, tradition and customs. The difference between the two perspectives on organizational culture comes from the way their proponents define knowing and what counts as knowledge about culture. Symbolic-interpretivists define culture as a context for meaning making and interpretation. In their view, cultural understanding permits you to know yourself in relation to others and what is meant by the various uses made of objects, behavior and verbal language. Modernists, on the other hand, interpret knowledge about culture as a tool of management, and culture itself as a variable to be manipulated to enhance the likelihood of achieving desired levels of organizational performance.[68]

According to symbolic-interpretivists the worldview is a socially constructed reality that aids members in coordinating their activities and in making sense of their organizational experiences. This context, to which organizational members routinely orient their identity, experience and activity, is what symbolic-interpretivists refer to as organizational culture. Cultural dynamics theory explains cultural stability and change using the same ongoing processes of manifestation, realization, symbolization and interpretation.

Postmodernists find numerous ways to challenge the notion that organizations have or are cultures. Some use postmodern literary theories like polyphony and intertextuality to suggest that the idea of shared understanding is an illusion and therefore so is organizational culture. Others spend their research energy deconstructing organizational narratives to unmask the power struggles that they believe explain organizational life. Still others develop metaphoric forms of analysis based in literature and drama to describe the performativity of organizing and to extend the boundaries of organization theory beyond both the natural and the social sciences.

KEY TERMS

subculture
   enhancing
   orthogonal
   countercultural
corporate culture
silo metaphor

strong culture
ethnography
dimensions of national cultural differences
   power distance
   uncertainty avoidance
   individualism vs. collectivism

masculine vs. feminine
long-term vs. short-term orientation
assumptions
values
norms
artifacts
negotiated order
context
contextualizing
symbols
  denotative meaning
  connotative meaning
  symbolic behavior
thick description
organizational narrative
  storytelling
  terse stories
  narrative epistemology

theater metaphor
  dramaturgy
  performativity
intertextuality
fragmentation
dialogic organization
polyphony
irony
instrumental vs. expressive strategy
Gagliardi's culture change theory
  apparent change
  revolutionary change
  incremental change
Hatch's cultural dynamics theory
  manifestation
  realization
  symbolization
  interpretation

ENDNOTES

1. Phillips, Goodman, and Sackmann (1992).
2. Van Maanen and Barley (1984).
3. Siehl and Martin (1984), Martin and Siehl (1983); see also De Lorean and Wright (1979).
4. Chatman and Cha (2003).
5. Jenks (1993).
6. For example, one of the newest subfields of sociology labels itself cultural sociology, a term that evokes the ire of sociologists of culture who believe that, while it is appropriate to investigate cultures sociologically, it is wholly unacceptable to allow a cultural perspective to infiltrate sociology. See Alexander (2003).
7. Tylor (1871\1958: 1).
8. Herskowitz (1948: 625).
9. Schein (1985); see also Schein (1983, 1991, 1992, 1996, 2000).
10. Martin and Frost (1996); see also Hatch and Yanow (2003).
11. Hofstede (1997, 2000, 2001).
12. Hofstede (2001).
13. Hofstede and Bond (1988).
14. Lurie and Riccucci (2003).
15. Kotter and Heskett (1992).
16. Denison (1990).
17. Cooke and Szumal (2000: 157–59).
18. Schultz (1994).
19. Strauss, Schatzman, Ehrlich, Bucher and Sabshin (1963, 1964).
20. Cohen (1976: 23).
21. Van Maanen (2005: 383).
22. Ortner (1973).
23. Morgan, Frost and Pondy (1983: 4–5).
24. Geertz (1973: 5).
25. Geertz (1973: 413–16). Used with permission of the author.
26. Martin, Feldman, Hatch and Sitkin (1983).
27. Jones (1996). A similar critique was raised by Boland and Tenkasi (1995).
28. Jones (1996: 7).
29. Boje (1991).
30. MacIntyre (1984: 205).
31. Van Maanen (1988); see also Sandelands and Drazin (1989), Golden-Biddle and Locke (1993, 1997), Czarniawska (1999) and Hatch (1996).
32. O'Connor (2000).

33. Webber (1992: 93–94), in Hatch, Kostera and Koźmiński (2005).

34. Goffman (1959).

35. Austin (1962).

36. Rosen (1985).

37. Höpfl (2002: 262).

38. Diderot (1773) cited in Höpfl (2002: 255, 258).

39. Höpfl (2002: 262).

40. Höpfl (2002: 258–59).

41. Kristeva (1984).

42. Notice the similarity to Derrida's use of the term 'différance' to explain the fluid meaning of words (see Chapter 2); by a similar logic, intertextuality explains the fluid meaning of texts.

43. Czarniawska (1997).

44. Meyerson and Martin (1987), Martin (1992, 2002).

45. Martin (1992: 138).

46. See Schultz (1992) for discussion of some of the ways in which organization theorists and others have presented organizational culture as an illusion.

47. Mumby (1988).

48. Martin (1990).

49. Schultz (1992).

50. Ezzy (2001).

51. Kunda (1996).

52. Roberts (2002), Schein (1993), Isaacs (1993).

53. Boje (1995).

54. Boje (2001).

55. Hatch and Ehrlich (1993, 2002), Hatch (1997).

56. To read more about research on irony in organizations, see Johansson and Woodilla (2005).

57. Brown (1987: 26).

58. Kilmann, Saxton and Serpa (1986), O'Reilly (1989), O'Reilly, Chatman and Caldwell (1991).

59. Chatman and Cha (2003).

60. Max Weber made this argument in his theory of the routinization of charismatic leadership; see Hatch (2000) for a discussion of Weber's theory and an application of it to organizational culture theory.

61. Gagliardi (1986: 125).

62. Ibid. 130.

63. Hatch (1993, 2000, 2004).

64. Hatch (1993: 662).

65. Hatch (1993: 667).

66. See especially Hatch (2000) where a link between the cultural dynamics model and Weber's notion of charismatic leadership and organizational influence is explored.

REFERENCES

Alexander, Jeffrey (ed.) (2003). *The meanings of social life: A cultural sociology*. Oxford: Oxford University Press

Austin, J. L. (1962). *How to do things with words*. New York: Oxford.

Boje, David (1991). The storytelling organization: A study of story performance in an office-supply firm. *Administrative Science Quarterly*, 36: 106–26.

—— (1995). Stories of the storytelling organization: A postmodern analysis of Disney as Tamara-land. *Academy of Management Journal*, 38: 997–1035.

—— (2001). *Narrative methods for organizational and communication research*. London: Sage.

Boland, Richard J., Jr, and Tenkasi, Ramkrishnan V. (1995). Perspective making and perspective taking in communities of knowing. *Organization Science*, 6/4: 350–73.

Brown, Richard Harvey (1987). *Society as text: Essays on rhetoric, reason and reality*. Chicago: University of Chicago Press.

Chatman, Jennifer A., and Cha, Sandra Eunyoung (2003). Leading by leveraging culture. *California Management Review*, 45/4: 20–66.

Cohen, Abner (1976). *Two dimensional man: An essay on the anthropology of power and symbolism in complex society*. Berkeley: University of California Press.

Cooke, Robert A., and Szumal, Janet L. (2000). Using the organizational culture inventory to understand the operating cultures of organizations. In N. Ashkanasy, C. Wilderom and M. Peterson (eds.), *Handbook of organizational culture and climate*. Thousand Oaks, Calif.: Sage, 147–62.

Czarniawska, Barbara (1997). *Narrating the organization: Dramas of institutional identity*. Chicago: University of Chicago Press.

—— (1999). *Writing management: Organization theory as a literary genre*. Oxford: Oxford University Press.

Dandridge, Thomas C., Mitroff, Ian, and Joyce, William F. (1980). Organizational symbolism: A topic to expand organizational analysis. *Academy of Management Review*, 5: 77–82.

Deal, Terrence E., and Kennedy, Allan A. (1982). *Corporate cultures: The rites and rituals of corporate life*. Reading, Mass.: Addison-Wesley.

De Lorean, John Z., and Wright, J. Patrick (1979). *On a clear day you can see General Motors*. Grosse Pointe, Mich.: Wright Enterprises.

Denison, Daniel R. (1990). *Corporate culture and organizational effectiveness*. New York: John Wiley & Sons.

Ezzy, D. (2001). A simulacrum of workplace community: Individualism and engineered culture. *Sociology*, 35: 631–50.

Gagliardi, Pasquale (1986). The creation and change of organizational cultures: A conceptual framework. *Organization Studies*, 7: 117–34.

Geertz, Clifford (1973). *Interpretation of cultures*. New York: Basic Books.

Goffman, Erving (1959). *The presentation of self in everyday life*. Garden City, NY: Doubleday.

Golden-Biddle, Karen, and Locke, Karen (1993). Appealing work: An investigation of how ethnographic texts convince. *Organization Science*, 4: 595–616.

—— —— (1997). *Composing qualitative research*. Thousand Oaks, Calif.: Sage.

Hatch, Mary Jo (1993). The dynamics of organizational culture. *Academy of Management Review*, 18/4: 657–63.

—— (1996). The role of the researcher: An analysis of narrative position in organization theory. *Journal of Management Inquiry*, 5: 359–74.

—— (1997). Irony and the social construction of contradiction in the humor of a management team. *Organization Science*, 8: 275–88.

—— (2000). The cultural dynamics of organizing and change. In N. Ashkanasy, C. Wilderom and M. Peterson (eds.), *Handbook of organizational culture and climate*. Thousand Oaks, Calif.: Sage, 245–60.

—— (2004). Dynamics in organizational culture. In M. S. Poole and A. Van de Ven (eds.), *Handbook of Organizational Change and Innovation*. Oxford: Oxford University Press, 190–211.

—— and Ehrlich, S. B. (1993). Spontaneous humor as an indicator of paradox and ambiguity in organizations. *Organizational Studies*, 14/4: 539–60.

—— —— (2002). The dialogic organization and the language of organizational change. In Nancy C. Roberts (ed.), *The transformative power of dialogue*. New York: JAI/Elsevier, 107–31.

—— Kostera, M., and Koźmiński, A. K. (2005). *The Three Faces of Leadership: Manager, Artist, Priest*. London: Blackwell.

Herskowitz, Melville J. (1948). *Man and his works: The science of cultural anthropology*. New York: Alfred A. Knopf.

Hofstede, Geert (1997). *Cultures and organizations: Software of the mind* (rev. edn.). New York: McGraw-Hill.

—— (2001). *Culture's consequences: Comparing values, behaviors, institutions and organizations across nations* (2nd edn.). Thousand Oaks, Calif.: Sage.

—— and Bond, M. H. (1988). The Confucius connection: From cultural roots to economic growth. *Organizational Dynamics*, 16/4: 4–21.

Höpfl, Heather (2002). Playing the part: Reflections on aspects of mere performance in the customer–client relationship. *Journal of Management Studies*, 39: 255–67.

Issacs, William N. (1993). Taking flight: Dialogue, collective thinking, and organizational learning. *Organizational Dynamics*, 22/2: 24–39.

Jaques, Elliott (1952). *The changing culture of a factory*. New York: Dryden Press.

Jenks, Chris (1993). *Culture*. London: Routledge.

Johansson, Ulla, and Woodilla, Jill (2005) (eds.). *Irony and organizations*. Liber, Sweden: Copenhagen Business School Press.

Jones, Michael Owen (1996). *Studying organizational symbolism*. Thousand Oaks, Calif.: Sage.

Kilmann, R., Saxton, M., and Serpa, R. (1986). *Gaining control of the corporate culture*. San Francisco: Jossey-Bass.

Kotter, John P., and Heskett, James L. (1992). *Corporate culture and performance*. New York: Free Press.

Kristeva, Julia (1984). *Revolution in poetic language*. Translated by Margaret Waller. New York: Columbia University Press.

Kunda, G. (1996). *Engineering Culture*. Philadelphia: Temple University Press.

Louis, Meryl Reis (1983). Organizations as culture-bearing milieux. In L. Pondy, P. Frost, G. Morgan, and T. Dandridge (eds.), *Organizational culture*. Greenwich, Conn.: JAI Press, 39–54.

Lurie, Irene, and Riccucci, Norma M. (2003). Changing the 'culture' of welfare offices: From vision to the front lines. *Administration & Society*, 34/6: 653–77.

MacIntyre, Alasdair (1984). *After virtue: A study in moral theory*. Notre Dame, Ind.: University of Notre Dame Press.

Martin, Joanne (1990). Deconstructing organizational taboos: The suppression of gender conflict in organizations. *Organization Science*, 1: 1–22.

——— (1992). *Cultures in organizations: Three perspectives*. New York: Oxford University Press.

——— (2002). *Organizational culture: Mapping the terrain*. Thousand Oaks, Calif.: Sage.

——— and Frost, Peter (1996). The organization culture war games: A struggle for intellectual dominance. In S. R. Clegg and C. Hardy (eds.), *Studying organization: Theory and method*. London: Sage, 345–67.

——— and Siehl, Caren (1983). Organizational culture and counterculture: An uneasy symbiosis. *Organizational Dynamics*, Autumn: 52–64.

——— Feldman, Martha, Hatch, Mary Jo, and Sitkin, Sim (1983). The uniqueness paradox in organizational stories. *Administrative Science Quarterly*, 28: 438–53.

Meyerson, Debra, and Martin, Joanne (1987). Cultural change: An integration of three different views. *Journal of Management Studies*, 24: 623–47.

Morgan, Gareth, Frost, Peter J., and Pondy, Louis R. (1983). Organizational symbolism. In L. R. Pondy, P. J. Frost, G. Morgan and T. C. Dandridge (eds.), *Organizational symbolism*. Greenwich, Conn.: JAI Press, 3–35.

Mumby, Dennis K. (1988). *Communication and power in organization: Discourse, ideology and domination*. Norwood, NJ: Ablex Publishing.

O'Connor, Ellen S. (2000). Plotting the organization: The embedded narrative as a construct for studying change. *Journal of Applied Behavioral Science*, 36/2: 174–93.

O'Reilly, Charles (1989). Corporations, culture, and commitment: Motivation and social control in organizations. *California Management Review*, 31: 9–25.

——— Chatman, Jennifer, and Caldwell, David (1991). People and organizational culture: A Q-sort approach to assessing person–organization fit. *Academy of Management Journal*, 16: 285–303.

Ortner, S. B. (1973). On key symbols. *American Anthropologist*, 75: 1338–46.

Ouchi, William (1981). *Theory Z: How American business can meet the Japanese challenge*. Reading, Mass.: Addison-Wesley.

Peters, Thomas J., and Waterman, R. H. (1982). *In search of excellence: Lessons from America's best run companies*. New York: Harper & Row.

Pettigrew, Andrew (1979). On studying organizational culture. *Administrative Science Quarterly*, 24: 570–81.

Phillips, Margaret E., Goodman, Richard A., and Sackmann, Sonja A. (1992). Exploring the complex cultural milieu of project teams. *Pmnetwork*, 6/8: 20–26.

Roberts, Nancy (2002) (ed.). *The transformative power of dialogue*. Research in Public Policy analysis and Management, Vol. 12. Amsterdam: Elsevier.

Rosen, Michael (1985). Breakfast at Spiros: Dramaturgy and dominance. *Journal of Management*, 11: 31–48.

——— (1991). Organizational culture. *American Psychologist*, 45: 109–19.

——— (1992/1985). *Organizational culture and leadership* (2nd edn.). San Francisco: Jossey-Bass.

——— (1993). On dialogue, culture and organizational learning. *Organizational Dynamics*, 22 (Autumn): 40–51.

——— (1996). Culture: The missing concept in organization studies. *Administrative Science Quarterly*, 41: 229–40.

——— (2000). Sense and nonsense about culture and climate. In N. M. Ashkanasy, C. P. M. Wilderom and M. F. Peterson (eds.), *Handbook of organizational culture and climate*. Thousand Oaks, Calif.: Sage, xxiii–xxx.

Sandelands, Lloyd, and Drazin, Robert (1989). On the language of organization theory. *Organization Studies*, 10/4: 457–78.

Schultz, Majken (1992). Postmodern pictures of culture: A postmodern reflection on the 'Modern notion' of corporate culture. *International Studies of Management and Organization*, 22: 15–36.

—— (1995). *On studying organizational cultures: Diagnosis and understanding*. Berlin: Walter de Gruyter.

Siehl, Caren, and Martin, Joanne (1984). The role of symbolic management: How can managers effectively transmit organizational culture? In J. D. Hunt, D. Hosking, C. Schriesheim and R. Steward (eds.), *Leaders and managers: International perspectives on managerial behavior and leadership*. New York: Pergamon, 227–39.

Strauss, Anselm, Schatzman, Leonard, Ehrlich, Danuta, Bucher, Rue, and Sabshin, Melvin (1963). The hospital and its negotiated order. In Eliot Friedson (ed.), *The hospital in modern society*. London: Free Press of Glencoe, 147–69.

—— —— —— —— —— (1964). *Psychiatric ideologies and institutions*. New York: Free Press.

Trice, Harrison M., and Beyer, Janice M. (1993). *The cultures of work organizations*. Englewood Cliffs, NJ: Prentice-Hall.

Tylor, Edward Burnett (1958). *Primitive culture: Researches into the development of mythology, philosophy, religion, art and custom*. Gloucester, Mass.: Smith (first published in 1871).

Van Maanen, John (1988). *Tales of the field: On writing ethnography*. Chicago: University of Chicago Press.

—— (2005). Symbolism. In N. Nicholson, P. G. Audia and M. M. Pillutla (eds.), *The Blackwell Encyclopedia of management* (2nd edn.), 383. London: Blackwell.

—— and Barley, Stephen R. (1984). Occupational communities: Culture and control in organizations. In B. M. Staw and L. L. Cummings (eds.), *Research in organizational behavior*. Greenwich, Conn.: JAI Press, vi. 287–366.

Webber, A. M. (1992). Japanese-style entrepreneurship: An interview with SOFTBANK's CEO, Masayoshi Son. *Harvard Business Review*, Jan.–Feb.: 93–103.

FURTHER READING

Alvesson, Matts, and Berg, Per Olaf (1992). *Corporate culture and organizational symbolism: An overview*. New York: Walter de Gruyter.

Ashkanasy, Neal M., Wilderom, Celeste P. M. and Peterson, Mark F. (2000) (eds.). *Handbook of organizational culture and climate*. Thousand Oaks, Calif.: Sage.

Dandridge, Thomas C., Mitroff, Ian, and Joyce, W. F. (1980). Organizational symbolism: A topic to expand organizational analysis. *Academy of Management Review*, 5: 77–82.

Eisenberg, Eric M., and Riley, Patricia (1988). Organizational symbols and sense-making. In G. M. Goldhaber and G. A. Barnett (eds.), *Handbook of Organizational Communication*. Norwood, NJ: Ablex.

England, G. W. (1975). *The manager and his values*. New York: Ballinger.

Frost, P., Moore, L., Louis, M., Lundberg, C., and Martin, J. (1985) (eds.). *Organizational culture*. Beverly Hills, Calif.: Sage.

—— —— —— —— —— (1991) (eds.). *Reframing organizational culture*. Newbury Park, Calif.: Sage.

Gabriel, Yiannis (2000). *Storytelling in organizations: Facts, fictions, and fantasies*. Oxford: Oxford University Press.

—— (2004) (ed.). *Myths, stories and organizations: Premodern narratives for our times*. Oxford: Oxford University Press.

Gagliardi, Pasquale (1990) (ed.). *Symbols and artifacts: Views of the corporate landscape*. Berlin: Walter de Gruyter.

Hatch, M. J. and Yanow, D. (2003). Organization theory as an interpretive science. In C. Knudsen and H. Tsoukas (eds.), *The Oxford Handbook of Organization Theory: Meta-theoretical Perspectives*. Oxford: Oxford University Press, 61–87.

Isaacs, W. (1993). Taking flight: Dialogue, collective thinking, and organizational learning. *Organizational Dynamics*, 22/2: 24–39.

Linstead, Stephen, and Grafton-Small, Robert (1992). On reading organizational culture. *Organization Studies*, 13: 331–56.

Mangham, I. L., and Overington, M. A. (1987). *Organizations as theater: Social psychology and dramatic performance*. Chichester: Wiley.

Martin, Joanne (1982). Stories and scripts in organizational settings. In A. Hastorf and A. Isen (eds.), *Cognitive and social psychology*. London: Routledge, 255–305.

Pfeffer, Jeffrey (1981). Management as symbolic action: The creation and maintenance of organizational paradigms. In L. L. Cummings and B. M. Staw (eds.), *Research in Organizational Behavior*, 3: 1–52.

Pondy, Lou, Frost, Peter, Morgan, Gareth, and Dandridge, Tom (1983). *Organizational symbolism*. Greenwich, Conn.: JAI Press.

Schein, Edgar H. (1999). *The corporate culture survival guide*. San Francisco: Jossey-Bass.

Smircich, Linda, and Calas, Marta (1987). Organizational culture, a critical assessment. In F. Jablin, L. Putnam, K. Roberts, and L. Porter (eds.), *The handbook of organizational communication*. Beverly Hills, Calif.: Sage, 228–63.

Turner, Barry A. (1990) (ed.). *Organizational symbolism*. Berlin: Walter de Gruyter.

Williams, Raymond (1983). *Keywords: A vocabulary of culture and society* (rev. edn.). New York: Oxford University Press.

Young, Ed (1989). On naming the rose: Interests and multiple meanings as elements of organizational change. *Organizational Studies*, 10: 187–206.

The Physical Structure of Organizations

Interest in the physical structure of organizations is generally traced to a series of studies carried out at the Hawthorne Works of Western Electric in the late 1920s and early 1930s.[1] The Hawthorne researchers, led by Harvard University professor Elton Mayo, set out to perform a series of field observations and experiments to learn how changes in the physical setting of work affected worker productivity. To set up one of the experiments, workers were moved into an enclosed space so that illumination levels could be precisely controlled. Inside this room the workers performed their normal tasks while the researchers systematically increased the amount of available light and measured the workers' output. As anticipated, the study showed that productivity increased with illumination.

In order to check the effectiveness of the experimental manipulation, the researchers then reduced illumination levels, expecting productivity to drop. To everyone's surprise productivity continued to increase—even when the workers were operating in almost total darkness. Apparently the workers had interpreted the special room and all the attention the researchers lavished upon them as managerial interest in their work. This special attention gave the workers elevated social status among co-workers who were not part of the study. The researchers concluded that the observed increases in productivity were due to these social effects, and therefore they abandoned their initial hypothesis that the physical conditions of work explain productivity in favor of exploring social influences on performance.

Because they revealed the potency of social influences on worker productivity, the Hawthorne studies are often credited with inspiring the field of organizational behavior. But for our purposes it is important to recognize that the initial interpretations given to the Hawthorne studies also marginalized physical structure as a research topic within organization theory by making the effects of physical structure seem relatively insignificant. However, as American sociologist George Homans astutely observed, the so-called **Hawthorne effect** was triggered by a change in physical structure—the workers were moved to a separate space away from the surveillance of their supervisors. In a book called *The Human Group*, published in 1950, Homans reinterpreted the Hawthorne effect arguing that the new physical setting symbolized management concern for and trust in these particular workers and marked their special social status.[2] Thus, it could be claimed that the symbolic message of changes to the physical structure set the social dynamics of the Hawthorne effect in motion.

In spite of Homan's efforts to reclaim it, the topic of physical structure remained a theoretical backwater until the 1970s and 1980s when environmental psychologists revived this line of research and a few modernist organization theorists followed their lead. Today symbolic-interpretive and postmodern organization theorists who study the physical structure of organizations turn for inspiration to the relatively new field of cultural geography and to architecture theory, both of which have been strongly influenced by symbolic-interpretive and postmodern perspectives.

Because the physical structures of organizations make organizational phenomena like culture and power seem more tangible, much of what has been said about symbolic-interpretive and postmodern aspects of organizations will seem more obvious when applied to the concept of physical structure. One effect of this tangibility is that you may start to think that the three perspectives of organization theory are not all that different. While it is true that proponents of the three perspectives have fewer points of disagreement when they study physical structures, this does not mean that the distinctions between their philosophical positions can be disregarded. In this chapter particularly you must be wary of the urge to reduce the three perspectives to one objectivized point of view. Just because physical structures are tangible does not mean the interpretations given to them are obvious, and even though physical structures can be literally deconstructed, critical readings of built spaces are still appropriate.

Some modernist organization theorists argue that the reason modernist and symbolic-interpretive perspectives live more peaceably in the domain of physical structure than they do in organizational culture theory is because the theoretical stakes are so low. They claim that, because it is centered in the realm of the concrete and particular rather than the abstract, physical structure has no theoretical importance at all. This point of view does not stop them from looking for empirical relationships between physical structure and behavior. For nearly all modernists, the importance of physical structure is that organizing takes place in a physical domain. Physicality gives organizations objective spatial dimensions that can be measured and correlated with outcomes such as efficiency and performance to determine which physical structures are best for given work situations.

Symbolic-interpretivists, on the other hand, see nothing atheoretical about the physical substance of signs and symbols, and they cite the long tradition for studying material culture in anthropology in support of their claims to theoretical validity and relevance. For them, movement in space causes humans to associate certain experiences with particular places which, in turn, allows physical structures (built spaces) to evoke meaning for their occupants. Through these interpretive associations physical structures become important organizational symbols capable of imbuing social relations with their significance. Consider the added meaning a meeting between two lovers derives from a rendezvous in the place where the couple first met, or in some romanticized locale such as atop the Eiffel Tower or in front of the Taj Mahal.

Postmodernists accept the modernist argument that physical structures are non-abstract but reverse the implications of this assumption. They interpret non-abstraction as a reason to make physical structure a part of organization theory rather than to exclude it from theoretical discourse. By contrast with symbolic-interpretivists who emphasize that built spaces are cultural artifacts capable of expressing all sorts of organizational meaning, most postmodernists hold the view that they are material expressions of the power relations embedded within them (e.g., executives occupy the most desirable spaces in their organizations) and it is this link with power that they claim gives built spaces theoretical importance. Reading built spaces like texts and deconstructing them to reveal the power relations they materialize is one way postmodern organization theorists approach the topic of organizational physical structures, but this can be difficult to separate from symbolic-interpretive treatments because symbolic-interpretivists also treat built spaces as texts. Postmodernists refer to the spatial embeddedness of human life as **spatiality** and criticize the vast majority of organization theorists whose explanations of organizations and organizing are a-spatial (disembedded and disembodied).[3]

This chapter begins by defining basic elements forming the physical structures of organizations: organizational geography, layout, landscaping, design and decor. Each of these elements will be discussed from modernist, symbolic-interpretive and postmodern perspectives. Following this I will present some theories that combine physical structure with other core concepts from Part II. First you will read about how physical structures influence and are influenced by social structure and technology, and then I will present some ideas about the relationship between physical structure, organizational culture and identity.

Elements of Physical Structure

Just as relationships between the social elements of an organization define its social structure (e.g., hierarchy of authority, division of labor and coordination mechanisms), relationships between the physical elements of an organization define its physical structure. The physical elements of organizing to which organization theorists have given the most attention are organizational geography, layout, landscaping, design and décor.

Organizational Geography

It is becoming increasingly common for organizations to operate in more than one location. You can no doubt think of numerous examples such as multinationals, conglomerates, joint ventures, franchises, retail or fast food chains, organizations with branch offices or service centers, and firms with regional warehouses, distribution centers, or field sales offices. Although the importance of organizational geography is more obvious in cases involving multiple locations, all organizations, no matter how small or spatially self-contained, confront issues associated with their geography. This is because the concept of organizational geography focuses attention not only on the extent of the organization's spatial distribution but also on features of the locations where it operates.

An organization has a physical presence that exists in both space and time. In modernist terms, the space an organization occupies can be represented as a set of interconnected

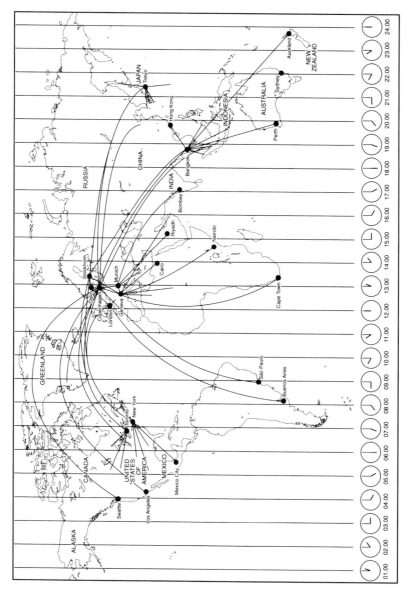

Figure 7.1 Airline route map showing the geographical distribution of organizational activities

locations that you might describe with reference to an ordinary map. An airline route map, for example, depicts the collection of destinations (airport locations) and the well-traveled paths connecting them (see Figure 7.1).

As you can see in the airline example, an organization's geographic distribution consists of all those points on the planet where the organization conducts its business, including not only the locations of facilities owned or operated by the organization but also locations regularly visited by organization members, such as the facilities of customers, suppliers, partners or other influential stakeholders. In a way analyzing the geographic distribution of an organization involves superimposing an interorganizational network analysis on a map of the world—or of outer space if the organization you are analyzing involves space travel, as do NASA and telecommunications companies that make use of orbiting satellites. On the basis of this spatial map you can compute the **geographic extent** of the organization. The more widely its activities are distributed, the greater its geographic extent, and by implication the more time it will take organizational members to communicate and coordinate the organization's multisite activities.

Consider another example. Julie is a student studying business in Chicago. Her parents are retired and live in Monterey, California, and her brother studies jazz in Boston. In terms of its spatial distribution, Julie's family is divided into three locations that reach across the continental United States. The organization of Julie's family is much more spatially disbursed than is that of her roommate, Marta, who grew up in Chicago and whose entire family lives in the area (see Figure 7.2). Julie plans to make a career in international business and hopes to work in South America after graduation; her brother intends to tour Europe. Notice how these plans will further extend Julie's family geography if they are realized. Marta's acceptance of a position as a loan officer in a Chicago bank, on the other hand, will not introduce as much change into the geographic configuration of her family. You can imagine that Marta's family geography will remain more stable for a longer period of time than will Julie's and will enable greater face-to-face communication, whereas Julie's family will probably come to depend even more than they already do on telephone and other electronic media for their communication and coordination needs (or lose touch!).

Geographic extent poses both problems and opportunities for organizations. In the case of Julie's and Marta's families, different problems and opportunities include, for example, the cost of transportation and phone calls, availability for mutual support in times of crisis, coordinating across time zones, exposure to different cultural influences and economic opportunities, and coping with change. The same is true for other organizations, each of which faces different circumstances associated with its geography and geographic extent.

In addition to organizational communication and information sharing, geographic extent relates to the logistics of supplying the organization with raw materials and delivering output to customers. Access to various modes of transportation (domestic and international airports, waterways, etc.), distance to markets (including labor, supply and consumer markets), and the speed and cost of communication, transportation and travel are but a few of the logistical concerns related to spatial distribution. Additionally, locations near to influential stakeholders (e.g., regulatory agencies, funding institutions, universities engaged in relevant basic research) offer an organization advantages in terms of managing critical environmental dependencies but also increase its geographic extent.

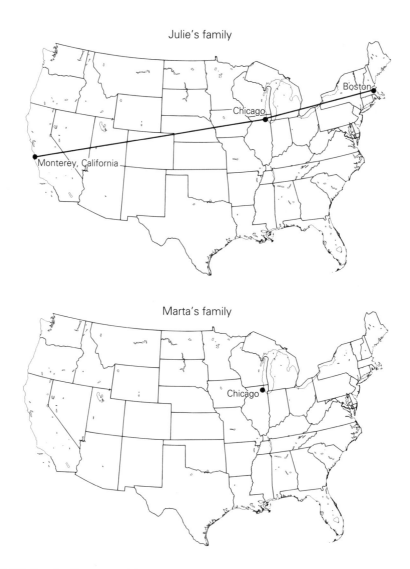

Figure 7.2 Two family geographies

In addition to mapping an organization's geography you will want to analyze the **geographic features** of each of its locations including climate, terrain and natural resources. Population density, industrialization, urbanization and the presence (or absence) of different races or ethnic minorities are features of human geography that are useful for describing the locations in which an organization operates. The geographic features of an organization's locations can affect many aspects of doing business. Success with recruiting is just one example. Consider how proximity to lakes, mountains or an ocean or to the varied attractions of a large urban center influence the lifestyles of organizational members and how the lure of the organization's location will help to define the types of employees the organization can hire. For instance, compare the lifestyles of employees of firms operating in Madrid, Johannesburg, Moscow, São Paulo, San Francisco and Beijing, or compare any of these to the lifestyle offered by a firm in a rural location far from any large metropolitan or industrialized area. Lifestyle is just one implication of organizational geography. Other aspects of an organization likely to be related to geographic features include corporate image and organizational identity, issues we will discuss later in this chapter.

As the examples above illustrate, geographic locations acquire reputations and are associated with images that affect their attractiveness for different individuals and organizations. Symbolic-interpretive geographers refer to this aspect of geography with the distinction of **place vs. space**. Place involves the experiences of and interpretations given to regions of space.[4] Places are sometimes compared to a stage on which life's drama is played out. Like the theatrical stage, a place provides more than a backdrop, it becomes a character in the play.[5] Most people have emotional reactions to familiar place images. For example, consider your reaction when, while watching a film, you recognize a place where you have lived or visited.

The concept of place used by symbolic-interpretivists and postmodernists crosses the boundaries between organizational geography and layout, landscaping, design and décor because the emotional and aesthetic qualities of place cannot easily be contained by these conceptual categories. For example, postmodernists say that physical structure encodes power in a spatial language that speaks unobtrusively about those who do and do not belong in certain places. Think of the difference in your level of comfort when you enter a church of your own versus one of someone else's faith. Precisely because physical environments are material, they can be made into symbolic expressions of meanings and values that the dominant members of society or particular cultures want to reinforce. Take the practice of building monuments. Monuments are typically designed to the specifications of politicians who choose designs that reinforce their own images and ideologies, hence the practice of toppling the monuments of a prior regime during political revolutions (e.g., statues of Lenin were destroyed throughout post-Cold War Eastern Europe and those of Saddam Hussein were pulled down following the war in Iraq). Be sure to notice that there are textual and mythological elements to place as well as political and behavioral elements. Like novels and poems, the meanings embedded in places can be read by others who come in contact with the cultural context that spatial perception and appreciation help to construct. The mysterious and grand pyramids of Egypt offer just one example of the symbolic significance architectural constructions can produce and maintain for extensive periods of time. People invest meaning in the relationships they form with their surroundings and so, as with other texts, you can learn to read the meanings others make by paying attention to how they interpret their built spaces.

Layout

Layout refers to the spatial arrangement of physical objects and human activities. Within a specific building, layout involves the internal placement of objects, especially walls, large pieces of furniture, equipment and employees. These spatial arrangements carve up and help to define the interior spaces of a building. When a particular location has more than one building, the orientation of the on-site buildings to each other is another aspect of the layout of the organization. For example, employees of large high technology organizations are often distributed throughout a group of buildings arranged to look like a college campus. Such campus arrangements consist of several buildings visually tied together by the design of walkways and/or landscaped areas. Presumably many of those who work in these environments attended college and the familiarity of the campus layout offers them intellectual and emotional support as well as aesthetic inspiration.

The assignment of people to specific locations and groups to particular spatial regions are key aspects of the internal layout of a building. For instance, office and workstation assignments and locations of shared facilities such as cafeterias, drinking fountains, restrooms and meeting rooms all contribute to internal layout. So does the spatial grouping of similar forms of work activity such as by project teams or by organizational function (e.g., R & D, marketing, manufacturing, accounting). Figure 7.3 shows a functional layout designed for a geophysics firm.

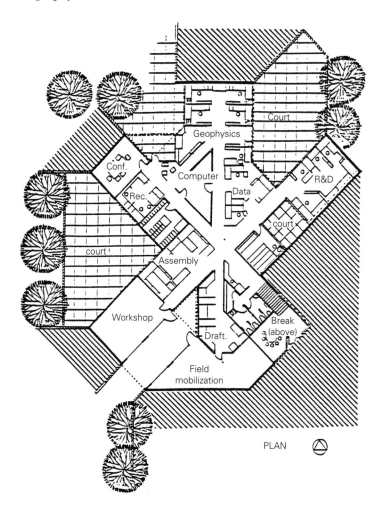

Figure 7.3 Layout of activity regions in a geophysics firm

Source: Doxtater (1990: 121, Fig. 2). By permission of Walter de Gruyter.

Modernists measure many aspects of organizational layout including: proximity, openness, accessibility, and privacy. **Proximity** is a measure of the distance between the assigned regions of individuals and work groups, with less distance equating to greater proximity. The most common way of making distinctions like openness, accessibility and privacy is to contrast open with private offices. Open offices have either low partitions with no doors, or use such things as file cabinets, bookcases or tropical plants to visually separate work areas. Private offices have floor-to-ceiling walls, usually with a door to allow their occupants full enclosure which allows for the greatest amount of **privacy**. **Openness** refers to the lack of physical boundaries within the work area, while **accessibility**, which is positively related to openness and negatively related to privacy, is a measure of how easy it is for others to interact with the person in their assigned work area. Occupants of bullpen offices have the greatest degree of accessibility to one another and the least privacy, as bullpens are typically enclosed spaces that have no physical barriers between workstations whatsoever. Modernist studies show that layout affects the way that individuals and groups communicate and coordinate their work efforts. For instance, office location affects amount and type of information processed by organizational members and is related to the development of informal channels of communication such as grapevines and rumor mills.[6]

The most obvious example of the relationship between layout and coordination is the automated assembly line where individuals and their tools are located at fixed positions along a moving line of partly assembled products. Locating work stations at fixed points along the assembly line not only allows for precise planning of the manufacturing process but permits easy surveillance of workers by management (it is easy to spot an empty station). In the case of an assembly line, layout involves matching locations with task requirements. Many inefficiencies and inconveniences will be introduced into the manufacturing process if layout is poorly conceived. This physical aspect of assembly line work should help you to visualize a relationship that is common to many other types of work; whenever workers perform sequential or reciprocally interdependent tasks, their ability to coordinate their activities will be affected by the location and layout of the workspaces they occupy. Although it is easier to visualize in the case of assembly line work, this is true for employees doing other sorts of work, including management.

Symbolic-interpretivists look for meaning associated with the physical features of the workplace as they tend to see accessibility, privacy and proximity as expressive of organizational values and the identity and status of occupants. Postmodernists partial to critical theory see spatial arrangements as objectifications of power used to dominate and control the weak or the powerless. To see this effect, contrast large classrooms where the teacher stands in front and student must face forward because their chairs are bolted to the floor, with small seminar style classrooms where teacher and students sit around a circular conference table.

Be careful in your interpretation of the meanings of built space when you are working in cultures that are foreign to your own. For example, in Western cultures the vertical dimension of space is interpreted as higher is better, but some non-Western cultures support a different interpretation. American public administration professor Dvora Yanow described how, in India, executive offices are more likely to be located on lower rather than upper floors of office buildings because problems with electricity and unpredictable or nonexistent elevators make accessibility by foot an attractive feature of lower floor locations. Yanow also noted the possibility that this cultural preference is related to Hindu traditions that place the soul in the center of the body (rather than the head, as in many Western philosophies), making the location of executive offices at the heights of buildings less attractive than they are in the West.[7]

One of the dilemmas faced by all organizations is choosing whether to locate managers' offices close to their subordinates or to group them for ease of communication between departments or divisions. The typical choice is to co-locate top executives at corporate headquarters along with key staff personnel, and then place other managers' offices as close to those they manage as possible. This means that executives must travel whenever they require face-to-face contact with their subordinates or they must ask their subordinates to do so. With greater organizational size and geographic extent, more organization members must commit to more travel to connect distributed parts of the organization. This need to travel is compounded by the need to meet stakeholders at their sites.

The demands of near continuous travel by some executives as well as many technical professionals who routinely visit sites away from their home offices have produced an innovation in office design known as hot desking. With hot desking, permanent assignments of office space are sacrificed for the flexibility and cost savings introduced by assigning workspace on an as needed basis. Some companies operate a reception desk similar to that used in hotels to handle allocation of office space, meeting room scheduling and coordination of services including secretarial and computer support. One advantage of hot desking is that the expenses of building and maintaining office space are minimized. The possibility to temporarily co-locate entire groups of employees who are working together as a team is another advantage. Of course hot desking is also an aspect of the fluidity to which postmodernists point when trying to convince others of the revolutionary nature of recent changes in organizing practices. In their view hot desking is but one indicator of the impermanence and fluidity of organizations. Hot desking also shows that, as was the case for structuration, physical structures are dynamic phenomena whose structural aspects influence and are influenced by agency, a consideration to which we will return shortly.

Landscaping, Design and Décor

When you hear the words landscaping, design and décor, you probably think of the artistic side of architecture and the decoration of an organization's buildings and grounds. Façade, focal points, furnishings, lighting fixtures, ceiling and wall treatments, floor coverings, use of color and form, displays (e.g., of foliage, art, advertising or technology) and countless other details contribute to the landscaping, design and décor of an organization's physical structure. Temperature, air quality, illumination, noise levels and smells are effects of landscaping, design and décor that modernists measure (e.g., the Hawthorne studies).

You might want to consider the physical bodies of employees and their dress to be part of organizational design and décor.[8] For example, at Disneyland all the employees who work in public view are subject to rules concerning dress and grooming, and body type and looks are used to determine their work assignments.[9] This does not violate anti-discrimination laws because Disney uses body types and personal appearance for theatrical effect when providing service to their customers. Thus, for example, those assigned to play the part of pirates in the Pirates of the Caribbean attraction need to look like pirates. Similarly, to convey a desired image, some organizations insist on certain forms of dress. IBM used to be known for their dark suits and white shirts while UPS insists that all delivery personnel dress in brown uniforms. The white coats worn by medical professionals, police uniforms and even the casual attire of Apple employees all communicate the organizational or occupational identities of these workers.

Architectural critic and professor of urbanism, Witold Rybczynski, gave three reasons for the link between dress and décor as follows:

> The first is technical. Décor, like dress, incorporates fabrics . . . [and] . . . architecture sometimes directly mimics dress. The garlands in eighteenth-century buildings are sculpted or painted versions of the sashes and flowered ornaments worn by men and women. The ancient Greeks incorporated elements of dress in temple architecture . . . . Ancient authors likened the vertical flutes [of Greek colonnades] to the folds in a chiton, or tunic.
>
> The second connection between dress and décor is social . . . . Since homes and clothes are timeworn ways in which to convey status, there is a conformity in the types of materials and symbols used to convey social standing. If family coats of arms are displayed, they will be seen on wall medallions as well as on blazer buttons. If gold is treasured, the wealthy will wear gold braid and surround themselves with gilt moldings. If this is considered too flashy, other materials can convey status: stainless steel kitchen appliances and stainless steel watch bracelets. . . . . In a more general sense—and this has nothing to do with conspicuous consumption—both homes and clothes convey values.
>
> The third connection between dress and décor concerns perception. Architecture, interior decorations, and fashion design are three distinct fields, yet we experience them with the same eye. Whether we look at dress or décor, we bring the same visual bias, the same sensibility, the same taste. This sensibility is not constant. Sometimes we appreciate simplicity, sometimes complexity.[10]

Be sure to consider both the exteriors and the interiors of factories, offices, and other workplaces when analyzing an organization's landscaping, design and décor. Focus not only on the architecturally designed features of the organization's built spaces but also pay attention to the unplanned and emergent aspects of the appearance of buildings and grounds and the meanings they are given by organizational members and other stakeholders. For example, I once toured a newly opened office building with the building's architect and an executive who had been involved with the building design. As we moved through the space we came upon a large golf umbrella hung at a precarious but alluring angle in a large atrium designed to be the focal point for the building. The umbrella was both a colorful addition to a relatively bland interior and a means to block a beam of sunlight that hit a worker's desktop nearly every afternoon, which is the reason he gave for hanging the umbrella. The umbrella, in turn, provoked multiple reactions. The architect greeted the umbrella with delight that the occupants of the building were beginning to treat the space as their own, while the executive bemoaned the loss of the pristine look of the building (and presumably his sense of control over its use).

Both symbolic-interpretive and postmodern organization theorists point to the symbolism of built space in organizations and how its occupants interpret and use it.

Shaped in a giant pyramid, the headquarters building of one German insurance company located in Dusseldorf is an obvious example. Scandinavian symbolic-interpretivists Kristian Kreiner and P. O. Berg emphasized the hierarchical symbolism of this design and linked it to the value this culture holds for working one's way up in the organization.[11] They might also have interviewed the building's architects to learn that the executives who commissioned the building wanted to communicate the importance of corporate success to company employees and other stakeholders. Postmodernists, on the other hand, are likely to emphasize the ways in which built spaces conceal the hegemonic interests of capitalism and the personal interests of the powerful by embedding them in physical forms that, once taken-for-granted, leave no traces of the alternative forms that might have been built to express other interests and support different interpretations of power.

Both postmodernists and symbolic-interpretivists are more likely than modernists to lead you to the aesthetic appreciations of a building's occupants. Notice that the landscaping, design and décor of physical structures can range from being ugly to being nondescript, tolerable, pleasing, beautiful and inspiring. However even when an organization's physical structure has nothing to recommend it aesthetically, physical elements associated with landscaping, design and décor offer important clues to the organization's culture and its image to outsiders. Take the example of an organization that occupies low-rent facilities and furnishes its offices minimally and inexpensively. Such an organization may be communicating its commitment to a low-cost strategy and/or telling you that the organization is unaware or unconcerned about its physical appearance. Keep in mind, however, that landscaping, design and décor preferences are heavily influenced by personal taste. For the purposes of organizational analysis your personal preferences are less important than your sensitivity to the fact that organizations evoke aesthetic responses that are open to the interpretations of employees and other members of the organizational community. Remember that it is the judgments of organization members and other stakeholders that matter in understanding the aesthetic effects of physical structure on the organization and the inhabitants of its spaces.

Linking Technology, Social and Physical Structure

Space and hierarchy are closely connected showing one way in which social structure and physical structure co-exist in mutual support. Typically, as you are promoted through the ranks in an organization, the spaces you occupy will communicate your progress. From smaller, less well-appointed spaces, you will move to offices with more floor space, better views outside and possibly with privileges such as choosing your own furniture and décor. In addition, depending upon your level of authorization, you will have more or less access to the spaces others occupy, the highest level of access permitting you to stroll into the offices of other employees—even senior executives—unannounced. The organizational allocation of space and rules or norms governing access to it thus mirror the hierarchical pyramid of senior executives, managers, workers (permanent over temporary) and visitors.

There is a close connection between technology and physical structure in most organizations because the technologies an organization uses often necessitate proximity between machines and/or individuals. You have already seen that assembly-line technology creates demands for the placement of people and equipment, but technology designs are also tightly linked to decisions about physical structure such that physical properties of the organization can influence decisions about what technologies to use or how to use them. Take the case of outsourcing work to units of the organization located overseas. The decision to increase the organization's geographic extent is likely to demand new transportation equipment (e.g., corporate jets) and changes in communication technologies (e.g., additions of video links and electronic boardrooms).

The Modernist Perspective

When you look at physical structure from the modernist perspective, you will see that it provides opportunities for and constraints upon the communication of information and ideas, and upon the coordination of interdependent activities. The focus of most modernist studies or physical structure has been on the relationship between the physical form an organization adopts and the behavior of individuals performing their work activities within these spaces. The basic idea is that, since humans cannot walk through walls or see through floors, their behavior is shaped by the geography and layout of the physical structures they occupy.[12]

In general the more distance separating people the fewer will be the opportunities for direct interaction and the more time such activities will consume. While it is true that new methods of electronic communication, such as email, fax machines, teleconferencing and faster modes of transportation, have considerably reduced the limitations imposed by geographic distance on interaction capabilities, these limitations are far from being entirely overcome. Face-to-face interaction is still considered superior to all other forms of communication and spatial layout and proximity are likely to be as important in encouraging face-to-face contact as are task interdependence or hierarchy.[13] For example, John Kotter observed that top executives and office workers interacted spontaneously with those whose offices were close to theirs, something they were much less likely to do with those whose offices were distant from their own.[14] The need for proximity, for example that imposed by task interdependence, makes the greatest demands on spatial configuration because there are physical limits to how many people can be located close together (e.g., a traditional office has no more than two adjacent offices).[15]

One way to assess the relationship between internal layout and interaction involves measuring the distance from one employee's assigned workspace to another. Research has shown a negative correlation between this measure of distance and the likelihood that two employees will engage in interaction, especially interaction involving face-to-face encounters.[16] That is, all other factors being equal, the more distance between the workstations of two individuals, the less likely they are to share information or to form a relationship. Separation by assignment to different floors or to different buildings decreases the likelihood of interaction even further.[17]

Keep in mind that formal reporting structures, similar cultural backgrounds and task interdependence also help to explain information-sharing and relationship patterns in organizations. However, physical distance will usually create problems for information exchange and relationship formation because, when potential partners are far apart, they must take the trouble to arrange their meetings. When locations are close and/or equipment is shared, relationships can form through interactions that occur spontaneously, for instance, in the hallway, in a restroom, around the coffee machine or in areas designated for smoking or relaxing. In a ten-year long study of R & D organizations, Thomas Allen found that performance was increased by chance encounters between members of different project teams who shared washrooms, libraries, coffee machines or photocopy equipment.[18]

While distance between employees has been shown to interfere with informal interaction, other physical barriers such as movable partitions and fixed walls have been found to be positively related to some forms of interaction. In particular meetings, brief interruptions, confidential conversations and working together occur significantly more often, and for longer periods of time, when co-workers occupy enclosed spaces.[19] However, even though modernist studies show that these forms of interaction are more likely to occur in closed than in open offices, many people continue to believe that open office settings with few or no physical barriers encourage interaction and communication.

One explanation for the belief that open offices encourage communication is found at the group-level of analysis. Some groups, especially innovative design teams, claim that the intimate sharing of their workspaces stimulates creativity and supports teamwork. However, enclosure rather than openness seems the most likely causal factor in these cases, since the groups in question generally had some sort of physical barrier literally and symbolically separating them from the rest of the organization. A second explanation for the link between open physical arrangements and the impression of greater (more open) communication is purely symbolic.[20] That is, at least in some situations, the openness of offices symbolizes open communication. Both of these explanations focus on the meaning of physical structures, which takes us into the symbolic-interpretive perspective.

The Symbolic-Interpretive Perspective

What may appear to be a fairly straightforward matter of understanding physical structure in terms of behavior becomes considerably more complicated when the symbolic aspects of physical structure are brought into focus. Consider for instance how the following places evoke emotion and act as common symbols for members of their cultures: Ellis Island (United States), Red Square (Russia), Tiananmen Square (China), the Acropolis (Greece). The study of organizational culture has taught us that managers should not overlook the importance of meanings associated with organizational symbolism and many aspects of an organization's physical structure serve in a symbolic capacity. The most obvious examples are found in the communicative power of architecture.

Over time buildings come to represent their organizations and have the effect of helping people construct what they think and feel about it.[21] Consider how the Mia Hamm building on the campus of Nike Corporation communicates respect for the first U.S. women's soccer team member to achieve international celebrity (partly through her endorsement of Nike products!). Semiotic interpretations of buildings provide other examples of the symbolic power of buildings. For instance, the Italian semiotician Umberto Eco stated: 'The colonnade by Bernini in St. Peter's Square in Rome can be interpreted as an immense pair of arms, open to embrace all the faithful.'[22] You may recall Eco as the author of the popular novel *The Name of the Rose* whose climactic moment was set in a labyrinthine library building that symbolized, among other meanings, the convoluted logic contemporary historians believe typified the Middle Ages in Europe.

British Prime Minister Winston Churchill once famously observed that 'We shape our buildings and afterward our buildings shape us.' American sociologist Thomas Gieryn used this idea as inspiration for his study of a newly constructed biotechnology research building located on the Cornell University campus in Ithaca, New York. Gieryn explained:

> The social structure of biotechnology [at Cornell] is shaped by choices made during the design of the building—for example, what people and functional activities are included or excluded, and how are these allocated in architectural space. The finished and occupied building measures a reorganized set of institutional arrangements, interpersonal relations and research practices now routinized and normalized into a more stable, enduring and constraining form. Still, from the day its doors opened, Cornell's Biotechnology Building has become something other than what its designers envisaged and something more than what got built—as users and visitors see in those walls a diverse range of significations.[23]

To explain the link between physical and social structures that he observed, Gieryn combined Giddens's structuration theory with a theory proposed by French sociologist Pierre Bourdieu. Bourdieu theorized that buildings are objectified histories in the sense of being 'systems of classifications, hierarchies and oppositions inscribed in the durability of wood, mud and brick.'[24]

In the course of his study of the African Berber tribe known as the Kabyle (located in Morocco, Libya, Tunisia and Algeria), Bourdieu came to believe that social relations between men and women in this society were built into their houses. The Kabyle divided their residences into two sections separated only by a 'small openwork wall half as high as the house'. Bourdieu reported that one section was larger and higher than the other and was paved with clay and cow dung that the women polished to a high sheen. This space was regarded as male and used for human activities like eating and entertaining guests. The smaller space, where animals were kept, was regarded as female. It had a loft where the women and children slept and where tools and animal fodder were stored. According to Bourdieu the Kabyle associated the male space with concepts such as high, light, cooked, dry culture, whereas they associated female space with low, dark, raw, wet nature.

In theorizing the relationship between structure and agency, Gieryn contrasted Giddens's more agency-oriented view (social structure is produced, maintained and changed by human interaction) with Bourdieu's structuralist theory that the social and physical structures surrounding us define who we are and organize our behavior. To investigate *how* agency and structure impinge on one another, Gieryn analyzed the evolution of Cornell University's biotechnology building and its meanings during the phases of design, construction and occupation. Gieryn defined three phases and described the relationships between agency and structure that he observed within each of them as follows:

> Design is both the planning of material things and the resolution of sometimes competing social interests . . . [wherein] . . . the interests of powerful voices in the design process are etched into the artifact itself . . . the enrollment of investors, patrons, consumers, managers, eager publics, regulators and vendors is accomplished through the design process [during which] an evolving artifact is shaped to fit the wants and needs of those who must be on board to move it off the drawing board.[25]

Following design, Gieryn explained:

> Some designs get built. What once was a malleable plan—an unsettled thing pushed in different directions by competing interests during negotiation and compromise—now attains stability.[26]

Then, during occupation:

> Once unleashed by designers and builders, artifacts become available for later reconfiguration as they are returned to the hands of human agents for more or less creative redefinition, reevaluation and even re-(or de-)construction.[27]

Through analysis of his observations and interview data, Gieryn discerned that agency played a predominant role in the design phase but that the building's physical structure became the dominant force once the building was completed and occupied, that is, as the new occupants adapted their behavior to the buildings rigid contours. However at some point after occupation the dominance of physical structure gave way once more to the influence of human agency, as Gieryn put it: 'agency returns to people when the building is narrated and reinterpreted—discursively made anew.'[28]

Although structuration theory, and in particular Giddens's notion of instantiation (structure is reproduced moment by moment or instantiated), suggests that the interplay of structure and agency occurs moment-to-moment, Gieryn looked at how structure and agency intermingled over the course of the two years covered by his study. Contrasting Gieryn's theory to those of Giddens and Bourdieu, you begin to suspect that their different understandings of structuration processes are embedded in different **temporal orders**. You see different elements and relationships when you pay attention to what happens over seconds, minutes or hours than you see if you attend to what happens weekly, monthly or annually, and different again if you track events over decades or millennia. When Giddens theorized structuration processes on the order of instants, he saw more agency than structure, whereas Bourdieu's longer historical view made structure seem to dominate agency. Gieryn's approach, midway between these two, was organized around events that transpired over weeks and months, and this permitted him to analyze (1) structure emerging from agency (design and construction of a building), (2) agents being constrained by their structures (the built space influencing the behavior of the building's occupants), and (3) agents (e.g., occupants, visitors, critics) reconfiguring those structures and their effects via interpretations and meanings.

Existing physical arrangements make it difficult to imagine other arrangements—we just start taking for granted that things like privacy or accessibility are determined by built spaces and unconsciously deal with their implications. For example, in noting that buildings conceal as well as reveal, Gieryn commented upon the human tendency to take the commonplace for granted:

> Buildings insist on particular paths that our bodies move along every day, and the predictable convergence or divergence of these paths with those of others is (in a sense) what we mean by *structured* social relations. If buildings silently steer us into associations or away from them, we hardly notice how (or question the rightness of it all) . . . buildings emplace sociations and practices.[29]

Both symbolic-interpretivists and postmodernists make us aware that, because built space often appears to be a natural part of the social world, its behavioral effects and socially constructed meanings are generally taken for granted. But many postmodernists go beyond being reflexive about how power and dominance are naturalized in physical structures. They demand that we learn to control or resist their reproduction so that we can free ourselves of unwanted influence. Resistance calls for demystification of the processes by which meanings get built into (constructed along with) physical structures. They argue that only through the deconstruction of built space (literary not literal!) can misuses and abuses by the powerful be exposed.

The Postmodernism Perspective

Neo-Marxist and postmodernist geographers such as Henri Lefebvre, David Harvey and Edward Soja criticized social theorists for marginalizing spatial concerns in explanations of social interaction and human relationships. These critics accused Durkheim, Marx, Weber and their followers of ignoring space to the detriment of their theorizing about social processes and institutions. As the vast majority of modernist organization theorists followed the lead of Durkheim, Marx and Weber, postmodernist organization theorists follow the post-modern geographers in accusing modernists of spatial ignorance. This critique opens social theory to spatial reconstruction, thus British postmodern geographer Derek Gregory claimed that 'social structures cannot be practiced without spatial structures, and vice versa.'[30]

A similar argument has been made about the relationship between physical structure and technology. The assembly line invented by Henry Ford is a favorite target of deconstruction for many postmodern organization theorists. Deconstruction of Ford's technology (sometimes referred to as Fordism) typically begins with the assertion that belief in the factory owners' right to control how work is done (labor) is built into technol-ogy. Thus, they argue, the assembly line has ideological content that privileges owners and managers over workers but hides their inherent conflicted interests within the machinery. This is because, once it is installed, the physical presence of line machinery precludes discussion of the right of management to organize work as a mass production process—the choice has already been made. Although the assembly line seems to be ideologically neutral, it is not because, once workers take machines and their layout for granted, the workers silently, and in most cases unreflexively, accept the ideology of management control. As American economist Richard Edwards described the situation:

> Struggle between workers and bosses over the transformation of labor power into labor was no longer a simple and direct *personal* confrontation; now the conflict was mediated by the production

technology itself. Workers had to oppose the pace of the *line*, not the (direct) tyranny of their bosses. The line thus established a technically based and technologically repressive mechanism that kept workers at their tasks.[31]

At the point at which workers accept the mechanized assembly line, the physical structure of the production process organizes social relations of dominance and submission within the hierarchy of owners and workers. Each time the machinery is turned on, it reconstitutes the status quo and suppresses resistance to it.

Interpretations of the effects of physical structures on social relations are not always so sinister. Some postmodern architects and critics, for example, see in built space the possibility of reconstructing the symbolic world we inhabit in any way we choose and postmodern architecture worked to reestablish the symbolic power of built space and the possibility of exploiting it (for good or for evil). Heinrich Klotz, former director of the German Architecture Museum in Frankfort, explained modernist architecture this way:

> For many decades we were indifferent to the meanings of architectural forms, either because we were totally opposed to them or because we could afford to ignore them. The structural aspects of a building and the functional values in terms of cost economisation and optimisation of use were the main objects of interest. The fact that a form could mean one thing or another was not a topic for official discussions, and it remained outside the range of debatable questions for architectural theory. To consciously consider the form of architecture a vehicle of meaning was an exceptional thing to do.[32]

But, Klotz continued, with postmodernist hindsight:

> Whether architects like it or not, a building acts as a vehicle of meaning even if it is supposed to be meaningless. One way or another, it presents a visual aspect. Even the vulgar postwar functionalism that cut the characteristic features of a building to a minimum produced buildings that, as they entered one's visual field, acquired a meaning: An apparently neutral and monotonous uniformity.

Klotz then explained the 'new possibilities of architectural symbolisation' that postmodern architecture offers:

> In contrast to the kind of architecture that consciously renounced any symbolic effect since by its own definition in terms of functional efficiency any consideration of meaning was too much, the new trends in architecture are predominantly marked by attempts to draw attention to other contents besides the functional qualities of a building—to contents referring to nonarchitectural as well as architectural contexts.[33]

Postmodern architectural theory thus points to the possibility of using built space to refer to organizational contexts of meaning. This is not to say that these possibilities did not exist before postmodernists commented upon them, it is only to say that modernists have ignored them. Furthermore the reflexivity about meaning and context that postmodernism requires introduced irony into architectural design, making buildings more playful and sometimes humorous. The Disney headquarters building designed by American architect Michael Graves, for example, offers the viewer a façade on which the Seven Dwarfs are frozen into columns supporting the roof. Are they there to cartoonishly invite employees to whistle while they work, or is the façade a comment on Disney's treatment of its workers?

The French postmodern geographer Henri Lefebvre pointed out many ways that space has been appropriated by the powerful to maintain their superiority over others. Starting with art in the Renaissance, modern thought came under the influence of perspectivalism, a way of knowing space that situates the viewer to take a vantage point from above. This preferred spatial orientation, Lefebvre claimed, gives hierarchy and other hegemonic practices the character of being part of the natural order. Resistance to this depiction of nature is one way of interpreting art that turns away from singular perspectives. Think about the art of multiple perspectives that Pablo Picasso and George Braque introduced with Cubist painting in which the artist moves around their subject, overlaying on one canvas the many different images they see from different angles.

Postmodernists like to make centers visible in order to contest their dominance. The very notion of a center as opposed to margins is but one of several spatial paradoxes that postmodernists use to explain how power is embedded in our language. Other binary constructions that involve spatial thinking are exclusion/inclusion, private/public, local/global and, perhaps basic to all of these: interior/exterior. For example the binary opposition inclusion/exclusion is communicated via the built spaces of gated communities, or in a different way, by the construction of ghettos, slums and favelas. These examples help to show that built space is socially produced through relations of power, but social power is practiced and reproduced through the uses of space.[34] For an organizational example consider how some executives erect office buildings with executive suites and then use this spatial distinction to symbolically reinforce their dominance in the hierarchy.

Physical Structure, Organizational Culture and Identity

All of us use symbolic cues provided by mundane aspects of physical structure to define our identity and guide our actions. Think about how you instantly know by your physical surroundings whether you are at home or at work, in your own office or in someone else's. What is more, knowing where you are triggers specific memories and behavioral routines.[35] For example members of the Catholic Church know how to behave in the presence of the altar because kneeling and making the sign of the cross have been conditioned to this element of the physical structure.[36] These responses are so automatic for a practitioner of the Catholic faith that the mere sight of the church altar provokes the expected behavior, often ushering in memories of past religious experiences and the emotions associated with them. Because the stimulus to which the behavior and emotional responses have been conditioned is a symbol, this sort of conditioning is referred to as **symbolic conditioning**. Similar evidence of symbolic conditioning can be observed in business organizations. For instance, consider responses to the counter of a McDonald's restaurant where customers have been conditioned to queue up to receive service from employees who know they are supposed to stand behind the counter and wait on customers in sequential order

Figure 7.4 Fast food resaurant customers have been symbolically conditioned to line up for service

Notice how when you enter such an establishment you automatically engage in the desired behavior. What signals the appropriate response may be the other customers lined up waiting to be served, or, over time, the counter itself may act as the signal.

(see Figure 7.4). Other places to look for symbolically conditioned responses include outside closed office doors and in and around reception desks, libraries and meeting rooms.

The importance of the idea of symbolically conditioned behavior lies in the unconscious link between physical structure and the normal routines that make up so much of daily life in organizations. For instance the habit of responding to others in an impersonal way is typical of many business cultures and can become symbolically conditioned to the physical surroundings of the workplace. As a result it is not uncommon to find people meeting outside office settings from time to time in order to interact with each other in more personal ways. Or consider the example of the employee who works at home but finds it necessary to dress up and say goodbye to family members before going to work in the next room in order to overcome the effects of symbolic conditioning to being at home and to send a signal to family members not to interrupt work activity.

The matter of symbolic conditioning may not be purely symbolic, it may have physiological implications as well. French anthropologist Claude Levi-Strauss discovered that the Bororo tribe in the Amazon built their village along both a North–South axis and an East-West axis that paralleled a river. The tribe used the axes to divide individuals into groups that were expected to follow rules governing who could marry whom (e.g., marriage partners needed to be from different groups), where people could reside (e.g., the married couple were to live in the group of the male partner) and other aspects of their social structure. When missionaries arrived they moved the villagers to another place where the houses were built in rows that did not conform to the axes of the former village. According to Levi-Strauss,

> Disoriented with regard to the cardinal points, deprived of a disposition that gave meaning to their knowledge, the natives rapidly [lost] their sense of traditions as though their social and

religious systems were too complex to function without the design made obvious by the disposition of the village.[37]

In organizations that undergo merger or acquisition it is not uncommon for the expected benefits of the partnership to go unrealized. Many explain this unfortunate outcome as cultural incompatibility; however, the study of the Bororo suggests that there are spatial forces in operation too. Consider that, as companies implement a decision to merge, members of one or both organizations are likely to change their physical locations and surroundings. Without familiar orienting cues to support their values, their organizational cultures are threatened with extinction and, to the extent that this creates stress, it affects productive behavior and consequently the economic value of the merged partners is eroded or even destroyed.

Other evidence of the physiological nature of space includes navigation habits that allow you to drive to work or school by the same route everyday without any conscious awareness of your actions, and the ability to pour a cup of coffee without spilling a drop or lifting your eyes from your newspaper. That the body knows its way around so you do not need to pay attention to what you are doing shows that humans have a preconscious capacity that is both spatial and physiological. Epistemologists sometimes refer to physical-spatial knowledge as **embodied knowledge**.[38] You can find evidence for embodied knowledge in the ways in which you use language. For example, it probably does not seem strange at all to think in terms of up–down, forward–backward, in–out, here–there, east–west, near–far, and numerous other spatial orientations because your body continuously orients you to your surrounding space. Our capacity for metaphor leads us to further spatialize life: happy is up, depressed is down; accepted is in, rejected is out, and so on.[39]

In addition to the symbolic conditioning of behavior, spatial elements (buildings, furniture, color schemes) and spatial relations (geography, layout, design and décor) play a significant role in producing and shaping individual, group and organizational identities. Consider the symbolic significance of a Wall Street address for an investment bank doing business in the United States, or imagine the symbolic value of being assigned to a luxurious private office next to the office of a high-ranking executive. These examples illustrate how physical structure symbolically communicates as well as constructs the identity of the organization and its members.

You have already seen how elements of physical structure contain cues and communicate messages capable of reminding people, not only of where they are and how they should behave, but of who they are in terms of their individual, group and organizational identities. We will now discuss relationships between physical structure and identity in terms of three issues: status, group boundaries, and corporate image.

Status and Individual Identity

Quality of furnishings, amount of floor space, privacy, a privileged location and the right to personalize one's office space are consistently associated with high status for employees of many organizations around the world.[40] Organizational and national cultures support these interpretations and the associations between space and status make it possible for the physical structure of an organization to support its social hierarchy and communicate its values using the language of spatial distances and physical objects. Of course there are always behavioral and physiological **status indicators**. For example, privacy not only indicates status but also allows an occupant to limit distractions and interruptions and to communicate without being overheard. It is in these ways that physical structures shape behavior and imbue it with cultural meaning.

You can learn a great deal about an organization's status hierarchy by carefully observing status indicators within its physical structure. Try noting the relative size and location of spaces occupied by individuals, or assessing the style and value of furnishings and decorations (e.g., artwork and other objects on display). You will also observe differences in the accessibility of a given organization member both to more and less important members of the organization (access to more important figures communicates higher status than does access to less important people, the latter being the case for many middle managers), to support facilities and equipment (e.g., copiers, fax machines, personal computers, laser printers) and to conveniences (e.g., restrooms, coffee machines, parking spaces). Attempts by workers to personalize their work spaces are often read by postmodernist organization theorists as efforts to regain lost control over self-identity usurped by modernist organizations.[41]

Be alert to status markers that may not match your preconceived expectations. In the absence of traditional status indicators, organizations having high power distance cultures may improvise symbols of distinction. In one such case the location of cheap coat racks, initially purchased because the building designers neglected to install closets in the organization's new building, served to identify the most powerful members of the organization. When the coat racks were first introduced they were made available to anyone who wanted them on a first come, first served basis. Over the course of only a few weeks, however, the coat racks migrated into the cubicles of those with the greatest status. In another case, the purchase of work group coffee pots became an informal indicator of status; however, this time the migration was to the offices of lower status clerical employees whose offices were next to those with the greatest status. On the other hand, in organizations with low power distance cultures, high ranking individuals may choose to personally and symbolically underscore the value for equality by foregoing status markers and other privileges. In these organizations you will have to be sensitive to the lack of status markers and to other symbols of equality such as the absence of reserved parking spaces.

Territorial Boundaries and Group Identity

Workspaces are territories in that they become physically and symbolically associated with the people and processes that inhabit them; they are the physical domain of social life and as such they will be defended by any individuals and groups who feel ownership over them. As is true for other animals, humans engage in dominating behavior when they are inside their own territory. When organizations are divided into multiple territories to accommodate the activities carried out within them, the occupants of the various territories are likely to become territorial about their spaces.

Territorial boundaries may be marked by a wide variety of physical elements—walls, doors, different buildings or locations, or by decorating schemes or other discriminating spatial features. Individuals physically mark their organizational territories with displays of personal belongings, signs, decorative style or other visual expressions of identification and ownership. The marking of territories within physical structures creates visible cues that become symbolically associated with the groups and individuals who occupy these spaces. Typical interpretations given to physical territories include information about inclusion and exclusion (i.e., who can enter freely and who cannot), what the group wants to be known for (e.g., look at what is hung on walls or otherwise displayed, the style of furnishings and the décor) and who shares the boundary.

Although there has not been much empirical investigation of the phenomenon, the available evidence suggests that the physical marking of group boundaries is associated with strong group identity in organizations.[42] J. D. Wineman found evidence that the presence of physical barriers around groups (e.g., walls, partitions, furniture) influenced group cohesiveness and interpersonal relationships.[43] He also found that prior cohesiveness compensated for the negative effects of an inadequate physical environment, underscoring the interconnection of the physical and social dimensions of organization structures. In *Street Corner Society* William Foote Whyte noted that the emergence of street gang subcultures coincided with the marking of territories.[44] What is not known is whether boundaries give groups their strong sense of identity or whether groups in the process of forming a strong identity tend to construct visible boundaries. It is possible of course that both forces are simultaneously in play, as structuration theory might suggest. Remember too that strong group identity can interfere with inter-group cooperation—no expressed value for strong versus weak group identity is implied by the discussion here. The link with physical structure primarily gives you a way of examining existing group identities and may provide a source of inspiration concerning what to do if a change is desired.

Corporate Image and Organizational Identity

You can see some of the same forces that make territorial boundaries significant for group identity formation on a grander scale in the phenomenon of organizational identity. Whereas group identity forms in association with a particular place within an organization, the organization itself is associated with a more general notion of place. A sense of place is derived from experiences of places that congeal in perception and memory into an emotionally and aesthetically charged image.[45] An example might be the feeling of danger many people associate with Rio de Janeiro, Brazil. The film *City of God* played on this sense of place, adding to the problems faced by the tourism industry in that city—in addition to needing to keep tourists safe, after the film appeared tour guides needed to cope with additional images of danger created by the film.

A sense of place is often dramatized symbolically by the design of a building or other physical feature such as a piece of sculpture, fountain or some aspect of landscaping. Architects and designers claim that having a singular and unique visual reference point to which all members can orient themselves is a key component of establishing and maintaining a sense of place and through it of enhancing organizational prestige.[46]

Organizational identity refers to members' experiences of and beliefs about the organization as a whole. It is influenced by past actions as well as aspirations for the organization's future. Identity should be distinguished from a closely related term that is also important to the discussion—**corporate image**. Organizational identity, though carried and communicated by organizational members, is influenced by images of the organization formed by its other stakeholders. Images reflect the various impressions that an organization makes on its many audiences, while organizational identity is the product of the mutual influences of image and culture on organizational self-definitions.[47] More will be said about organizational identity, corporate image and organizational culture in Chapter 10.

Because the physical appearance of an organization is a potent medium in which to create a lasting impression, some top managers attempt to influence organizational identity and corporate image by focusing on elements of their organization's appearance. Physical elements with particular potential to represent organizational identity or to influence corporate image include: dramatic architectural features (façade, roofline, lighting effects, office interiors, decorating themes), product design, company logos, corporate literature (e.g., annual reports, brochures) and styles of dress (uniforms, dress codes). Corporate identity consultant Wally Olins claimed that, when they are carefully designed to complement each other, these elements influence impressions of organizational credibility and character and symbolically reinforce strategic vision.[48] Olins's link to strategic vision suggests further that specific messages can be communicated via architectural design; for example, a very tall building might be used to symbolize an intention to push the organization to higher levels of performance or, in the case of an aerospace engineering firm, to reach for the stars.

In your enthusiasm to unleash the forces of organizational appearance you must not forget that the images an organization's stakeholders put forth cannot avoid contributing to the identity the organization maintains.[49] Furthermore, the interpretations of both corporate image and organizational identity that will be reflected in a physical structure can be numerous. For example, an exquisite new corporate headquarters building may favorably impress investors ('they must be generating great wealth to afford such a wonderful facility'), customers ('this kind of opulence indicates real staying power'), and community leaders ('what a marvelous aesthetic complement to the community'), while simultaneously being viewed as irresponsible by union leaders ('that money could have gone into better wage packets') and environmentalists ('a little less squandering on executive perks and more environmental projects might have been possible'). Never assume that the intended meaning designers and executives use to create their architectural designs are the only meanings their designs allow.

An excellent example of the unplanned interpretation of architecture is provided by Notre Dame University in South Bend, Indiana. Notre Dame is famous for the many championship football teams it has contributed to college athletics in the United States. Some years ago, the university built a large new library building intended to be an architectural focal point for the entire campus. To symbolize the religious heritage of this Roman Catholic institution, the building was adorned with a beautiful mosaic featuring Jesus

Figure 7.5 Notre Dame library mosaic

Photograph by Joseph C. Fross.

Christ, his arms outstretched and raised toward heaven (see Figure 7.5). Coincidentally, in American football when one team scores a goal, called a touchdown, the official in charge indicates the accomplishment by raising his outstretched arms in a gesture similar to the one depicted in the mosaic. What is crystal clear in retrospect, but apparently no one foresaw while designing the mosaic, is the connection between the two most important symbols of campus culture: Christ and football. The Notre Dame culture produced the now obvious name for the mosaic: Touchdown Jesus.

I would like to make one last point about the issue of multiple meanings and it is that organizations can send symbolically mixed signals with the physical design and structure of their workplaces. For instance, I once studied an organization in the personal computer business that claimed to be innovative but did not provide its employees with physical symbols of innovation (e.g., the latest design tools or even their own computers). This situation prompted its employees to question corporate commitment to innovation and their attitudes toward the company damaged its relationship with some of its customers who likewise were shocked to learn that those selling them computers did not have much opportunity to work with these company products.[50] What you have learned about analyzing the meanings given to an organization's cultural artifacts will serve you well in appreciating the many meanings built spaces carry.

SUMMARY

An organization is a designed and decorated physical entity with geographic extent and a layout of workspaces, equipment and employees. These physical elements of organizational structure and their relationships have important implications for the behavior of people who are associated with the organization including managers, employees, customers, suppliers, members of the local community and others who interact with or within the organization. The physical features of an organization also have symbolic importance. The most obvious symbolic message that an organization's physical structure delivers is the impression it makes with its buildings and grounds, particularly when they are architecturally designed to communicate a strong visual statement that reinforces corporate vision and signals corporate priorities and values. But physical structures deliver more subtle symbolic messages such as those communicated by what is *not* built or by interpretations that were unintended by architects or building planners. Both designed and the undesigned features, and intended and unintended meanings of an organization's physical structure offer useful clues to the culture of an organization and can help you to visualize organizational identity (e.g., status symbols, group boundaries, and corporate image) as well as provide insight into many features of organizational social structure (e.g., the relative placement of people and status symbols provides insight into hierarchy and the distribution of power) and technology (e.g., the layout of equipment and machines provide insight into work flows).

KEY TERMS

Hawthorne effect
spatiality
organizational geography
  geographic extent
  geographic features
  place vs. space
layout
proximity
privacy
openness

  accessibility
landscaping, design and décor
temporal orders
symbolic conditioning
embodied knowledge
status indicators
territorial boundaries and group identity
organizational identity
corporate image

ENDNOTES

1. Roethlisberger and Dickson (1939), Mayo (1945).

2. Homans (1950).

3. See Yanow (in press) for a thorough discussion of how built spaces mean and a nice summary of Casey's work on the relations between human embodiment and spatial orientation.

4. See Casey (1993, 2002).

5. Godkin (1980).

6. Davis (1984), Allen (1977).

7. Yanow (1993).

8. Rafaeli and Pratt (1993), Rafaeli, Dutton, Harquail and Lewis (1997).

9. Van Maanen (1991).

10. Rybczynski (2001: 21–25).

11. Steele (1973), Berg and Kreiner (1990).

12. Pfeffer (1982).

13. Conrath (1973).

14. Kotter (1983).

15. Daft and Lengel (1984).

16. Gullahorn (1952), Wells (1965), Gerstberger and Allen (1968), Allen and Gerstberger (1973), Conrath (1973), Szilagyi and Holland (1980).

17. Festinger, Schacter and Back (1950), Estabrook and Sommer (1972), Parsons (1976).

18. Allen (1977).

19. Oldham and Brass (1979), BOSTI (1981), Oldham and Rotchford (1983), Hatch (1987).

20. Hatch (1990).

21. Urry (1991), Yanow (1993).

22. Eco (1986: 297).

23. Gieryn (2002: 36).

24. Bourdieu (1981: 305–6) cited in Gieryn (2002: 39).

25. Gieryn (2002: 42).

26. Gieryn (2002: 43).

27. Gieryn (2002: 44).

28. Gieryn (2002: 53).

29. Gieryn (2002: 61).

30. Gregory (1978: 121).

31. Edwards (1979: 118).

32. Klotz (1992: 235).

33. Ibid. 235–36.

34. Lefebvre (1991).

35. Giddens (1987).

36. Berg and Kreiner (1990).

37. Levi-Strauss (1955), cited in Fischer (1997: 24–5).

38. Seamon (1980).

39. Lakoff and Johnson (1980).

40. Louis Harris and Associates (1978), BOSTI (1981), Konar et al. (1982).

41. Baldry (1999).

42. Richards and Dobyns (1957), Wells (1965).

43. Wineman (1982).

44. Whyte (1943).

45. Steele (1981).

46. Olins (1989).

47. Alvesson (1990), Hatch and Schultz (1997, 2002, 2003), Hatch (2005).

48. Olins (1989, 2003).

49. Dutton and Dukerich (1991), Ginzel, Kramer and Sutton (1993), Elsbach and Kramer (1996), Christensen and Cheney (2001).

50. For examples of gaps between image, organizational culture and strategic vision that threaten organizational identity, see Hatch and Schultz (2003) and Schultz and Hatch (2003) who discuss the cases of British Airways and LEGO Company, respectively.

REFERENCES

Allen, T. (1977). *Managing the flow of technology: Technology transfer and the dissemination of technological information within the R&D organization*. Cambridge, Mass.: MIT Press.

—— and Gerstberger, P. (1973). A field experiment to improve communications in a product engineering department: The nonterritorial office. *Human Factors*, 15: 487–98.

Alvesson, Mats (1990). Organization: From substance to image? *Organization Studies*, 11: 373–94.

Baldry, Chris (1999). Space—the final frontier. *Sociology*, 33/3: 535–53.

Berg, Per Olof, and Kreiner, Kristian (1990). Corporate architecture: Turning physical settings into symbolic resources. In Pasquale Gagliardi (ed.), *Symbols and artifacts: Views of the corporate landscape*. Berlin: Walter de Gruyter, 41–67.

BOSTI (Buffalo Organization for Social and Technological Innovation) (1981). *The impact of office environment on productivity and quality of working life: Comprehensive findings*. Buffalo: Buffalo Organization for Social and Technological Innovation.

Bourdieu, Pierre (1981). Men and machines. In Karin Knorr-Cetina and Aaron Cicourel (eds.), *Advances in social theory and methodology*. London: Routledge, 304–18.

Casey, Edward S. (1993). *Getting back into place*. Bloomington: Indiana University Press.

—— (2002). *Representing place*. Minneapolis: University of Minneapolis Press.

Cheney, George, and Christensen, Lars T. (2001). Organizational identity: Linkages between internal and external communication. In F. M. Jablin and L. L. Putnam (eds.), *New handbook of organizational communication*. Thousand Oaks, CA: Sage, 231–69.

Conrath, C. W. (1973). Communication patterns, organizational structure, and man: Some relationships. *Human Factors*, 15: 459–70.

Daft and Lengal (1984). Information richness: A new approach to managerial behavior and organization design. In B. M. Staw and L. L. Cummings (eds.), *Research in organizational behavior*. Greenwich, Conn: JAI Press, 6: 191–233.

Davis, T. M. R. (1984). The influence of the physical environment of offices. *Academy of Management Review*, 9: 271–83.

Doxtater, Dennis (1990). Meaning of the workplace: Using ideas of ritual space in design. In Pasquale Gagliardi (ed.), *Symbols and artifacts: Views of the corporate landscape*. Berlin: Walter de Gruyter, 107–27.

Dutton, J., and Dukerich, J. (1991). Keeping an eye on the mirror: Image and identity in organizational adaptation. *Academy of Management Journal*, 34: 517–54.

——— and Harquail, Celia V. (1994). Organizational images and member identification. *Administrative Science Quarterly*, 39: 239–63.

Eco, Umberto (1986). *Travels in hyper reality*. San Diego: Harcourt Brace Jovanovich.

Edwards, Richard (1979). *Contested terrain: The transformation of the workplace in the twentieth century*. New York: Basic Books.

Elsbach, Kimberly D., and Kramer, Roderick, M. (1996). Members' responses to organizational identity threats: Encountering and countering the *Business Week* rankings. *Administrative Science Quarterly*, 41: 442–76.

Estabrook, M., and Sommer, R. (1972). Social rank and acquaintanceship in two academic buildings. In W. Graham and K. H. Roberts (eds.), *Comparative studies in organizational behavior*. New York: Holt, Rhinehart & Winston, 122–28.

Festinger, Leon S., Schacter, Stanley, and Back, Kurt (1950). *Social pressures in informal groups*. Stanford, Calif.: Stanford University Press.

Fischer, Gustave-Nicolas (1997). *Individuals and environment: A psychosocial approach to workspace* (trans. Ruth Atkin-Etienne). Berlin: Walter de Gruyter.

Gerstberger, Peter G., and Allen, Thomas J. (1968). Criteria used by research and development engineers in the selection of an information source. *Journal of Applied Psychology*, 52: 272–9.

Giddens, Anthony (1987). Structuralism, poststructuralism and the production of culture. In A. Giddens and J. Turner (eds.), *Social theory today*. Stanford, Calif.: Stanford University Press, 195–223.

Gieryn, Thomas F. (2002). What buildings do. *Theory and Society*, 31: 35–74.

Ginzel, Linda E., Kramer, Roderick M., and Sutton, Robert I. (1993). Organizational impression management as a reciprocal influence process: The neglected role of the organizational audience. *Research in Organizational Behavior*, 15: 227–66.

Godkin, Michael A. (1980). Identity and place: Clinical applications based on notions of rootedness and uprootedness. In A. Buttimer and D. Seamon (eds.), *The human experience of space and place*. New York: St. Martin's Press, 73–85.

Gregory, Derek (1978). *Ideology, science and human geography*. London: Hutchinson.

Gullahorn, J. T. (1952). Distance and friendship as factors in the gross interaction matrix. *Sociometry*, 15: 123–34.

Hatch, Mary Jo (1987). Physical barriers, task characteristics, and interaction activity in research and development firms. *Administrative Science Quarterly*, 32: 387–99.

—— (1990). The symbolics of office design: An empirical exploration. In Pasquale Gagliardi (ed.), *Symbols and artifacts: Views of the corporate landscape*. Berlin: Walter de Gruyter, 129–46.

—— (2005). Identity, organizational. In N. Nicholson, P. G. Audia, and M. Pillutla (eds.), *The Blackwell encyclopedia of management* (2nd edn.). London: Blackwell, 160–1.

—— and Schultz, Majken (1997). Relations between organizational culture, identity and image. *European Journal of Marketing*, 31/5: 356–65.

—— —— (2002). The dynamics of organizational identity. *Human Relations*, 55: 989–1018.

—— —— (2003). Bringing the corporation into corporate branding. *European Journal of Marketing*, 37: 1041–64.

Homans, George (1950). *The human group*. New York: Harcourt Brace & World.

Klotz, Heinrich (1992). Postmodern architecture. In C. Jencks (ed.), *The post-modern reader*. London: St. Martins Press, 234–48.

Konar, E., Sundstrom, E., Brady, C., Mandel, D., and Rice, R. (1982). Status markers in the office. *Environment and Behavior*, 14: 561–80.

Kotter, John P. (1983). *The general managers*. New York: Free Press.

Lakoff, George, and Johnson, Mark (1980). *Metaphors we live by*. Chicago: University of Chicago Press.

Lefebvre, Henri (1991). *The production of space* (trans. D. Nicholson-Smith). Oxford: Blackwell.

Louis Harris and Associates, Inc. (1978). *The steelcase national study of office environments: Do they work?* Grand Rapids, Mich.: Steelcase.

Mayo, Elton (1945). *The social problems of an industrial civilization*. Boston: Graduate School of Business Administration, Harvard University.

Oldham, Greg R., and Brass, Daniel J. (1979). Employee reactions to an open-plan office: A naturally occurring quasi-experiment. *Administrative Science Quarterly*, 24: 267–84.

—— and Rotchford, Nancy L. (1983). Relationships between office characteristics and employee reactions: A study of the physical environment. *Administrative Science Quarterly*, 28: 542–56.

Olins, Wally (1989). *Corporate identity: Making business strategy visible through design*. London: Thames and Hudson.

—— (2003). *Wally Olins: On brand*. London: Thames & Hudson.

Parsons, H. M. (1976). Work environment. In I. Altman and J. F. Wohlwill (eds.), *Human behavior and environment: Advances in theory and research*. New York: Plenum, i: 163–209.

Pfeffer, Jeffrey (1982). Chapter 8: Developing organization theory, Organizations as physical structures. In *Organizations and organization theory*. Boston: Pitman, 260–71.

Rafaeli, Anat, Dutton, Jane, Harquail, C. V., and Mackie-Lewis, Stephanie (1997). Navigating by attire: The use of dress by female administrative employees. *Academy of Management Journal*, 40: 9–45.

—— and Pratt, Michael G. (1993). Tailored meanings. *Academy of Management Review*, 18: 32–55.

Richards, C. B., and Dobyns, H. F. (1957). Topography and culture: The case of the changing cage. *Human Organization*, 16: 16–20.

Roethlisberger, F., and Dickson, W. (1939). *Management and the worker*. Cambridge, Mass.: Harvard University Press.

Rybczynski, Witold (2001). *The look of architecture*. New York: Oxford University Press.

Schultz, M. S., and Hatch, M. J. (2003). The cycles of corporate branding: The case of LEGO Company. *California Management Review*, 46/1: 6–26.

Seamon, David (1980). Body-subject, time-space routines, and place ballets. In A. Buttimer and D. Seamon (eds.), *The human experience of space and place*. New York: St. Martin's Press, 148–65.

Steele, Fred I. (1973). *Physical settings and organization development*. Reading, Mass.: Addison-Wesley.

—— (1981). *The sense of place*. Boston: CBI Publishing Company.

Szilagyi, Andrew D., and Holland, Winford E. (1980). Changes in social density: Relationships with functional interaction and perceptions of job characteristics, role stress, and work satisfaction. *Journal of Applied Psychology*, 65: 28–33.

Urry, John (1991). Time and space in Giddens' social theory. In Christopher G. A. Bryant and David Jary (eds.), *Giddens' theory of structuration: A critical appreciation*. London: Routledge, 160–75.

Van Maanen, John (1991). The Smile Factory: Work at Disneyland. In P. J. Frost, L. F. Moore, M. R. Louis, C. C. Lundberg and J. Martin (eds.), *Reframing Organizational Culture*. Newbury Park, Calif.: Sage Publications, 58–86.

Wells, B. (1965). The psycho-social influence of building environments: Sociometric findings in large and small office spaces. *Building Science*, 1: 153–65.

Whyte, William Foote (1943). *Street corner society*. Chicago: University of Chicago Press.

Wineman, J. D. (1982). Office design and evaluation: An overview. *Environment and Behavior* 14: 271–98.

Yanow, Dvora (1993). Reading policy meanings in organization-scapes. *Journal of Architectural and Planning Research*, 10: 308–27.

—— (in press). How built spaces mean: A semiotics of space. In D. Yanow and P. Schwartz-Shea (eds.), *Interpretation and method: Empirical research methods and the interpretive turn*, ch. 20. Armonk, NY: M E Sharpe.

FURTHER READING

Becker, Franklin D. (1981). *Workspace: Creating environments in organizations*. New York: Praeger.

Buttimer, A., and Seamon, D. (eds.) (1980). *The human experience of space and place*. New York: St. Martin's Press, 148–65.

Casey, Edward S. (2002). *Representing place*. Minneapolis: University of Minneapolis Press.

Fischer, Gustave-Nicolas (1997). *Individuals and environment: A psychosocial approach to workspace* (trans. Ruth Atkin-Etienne). Berlin: Walter de Gruyter.

Gagliardi, Pasquale (1990) (ed.). *Symbols and artifacts: Views of the corporate landscape*. Berlin: Walter de Gruyter.

Giddens, Anthony (1985). Time, space and regionalisation. In D. Gregory and J. Urry (eds.), *Social relations and spatial structures*. New York: St. Martin's Press, 265–95.

Hatch, M. J., and Schultz, M. S. (2004). *Organizational identity: A reader*. Oxford: Oxford University Press.

Jencks, Charles (1977). *The language of post-modern architecture*. London: Academy.

Rappaport, Amos (1982). *The meaning of the built environment*. Beverley Hills, Calif.: Sage.

Schultz, M., Hatch, M. J., and Larsen, M. H. (2000) (eds.). *The expressive organization: Identity, reputation and corporate branding*. Oxford: Oxford University Press.

Soja, Edward W. (1989). *Postmodern geographies: The reassertion of space in critical social theory*. London: Verso.

Sundstrom, Eric (1986). *Work places: The psychology of the physical environment in offices and factories*. Cambridge: Cambridge University Press.

8

Organizational Power, Control and Conflict

As is indicated by the grey color pervading all the circles of Figure 1.2, power is inherent in all the core concepts covered in Part II of the book. Power has been discussed throughout the previous chapters in relation to the core concepts treated there. It is now time to focus on power as a core concept in its own right and to examine the related issues of conflict and control.

One way to think of the relationship between power, conflict and control is that conflict is a manifestation of the continuous struggle over control that power relations imply. You may have noticed in previous chapters that theories dealing with power seem radically different from the others that make up organization theory. This is because power theorists assume that conflict rather than cooperation is the basis of organizing. Their viewpoint traces to Karl Marx whose theory was that conflict keeps society in a state of potentially continuous transformation. Organization theorists who follow Marx's lead have applied this idea to organizations giving rise to theories that diverge from those of the mainstream, particularly those of modernism.

Max Weber and Frederick Taylor also contributed to theories of power and to the practice of managerial control in organizations although, unlike Marx, they were concerned with making the exercise of power and control rational and systematic. For example, Weber assumed that legitimate power is embedded within a hierarchy that gives owners and managers the right to control the means of production and the laborers who employ these means. Similarly Taylor built his Scientific Management principles on the assumption that managers have the power not only to define and control work, but to engineer the physical environment and dictate the location and movements of workers within it. With this foundation most early modernists did not feel any need to reflect on the ethics of using power and control, they simply assumed this to be a managerial prerogative as can be seen in this statement from American sociologist Arnold Tannenbaum:

> Organization implies control. A social organization is an ordered arrangement of individual human interactions. Control processes help circumscribe idiosyncratic behaviors and keep them conformant to the rational plan of the organization. Organizations require a certain amount of conformity as well as the integration of diverse activities.[1]

While most early proponents of the modernist perspective shared Tannenbaum's assumptions, there were some who acknowledged that the authoritative use of control creates resistance and so, by its very nature, lays a foundation for conflict that they believed defines organization. These Marxists and the neo-Marxists who followed them, took power, control and conflict as central concepts in their theories of organization.

I begin this chapter with some modernist theories of power, politics and control, followed by critical and postmodern views on of these phenomena, including feminist theories of gender and power in organizations. At the end of the chapter I will present

Table 8.1 Modern, critical and postmodern conceptions of power, control and conflict

	Modern	**Critical**	**Postmodern**
Locus of power	Authority (hierarchy), knowledge and the ability to resolve critical organizational problems	Social, economic and political structures and ideologies	Everyday social relationships, and discursive and non-discursive practices
Basis of power	The right to control production and know-how	Challenges the owner/shareholder's right to profit; favors democracy of stakeholder interests	Based on disciplinary power embedded in taken for granted, discursive and non-discursive practices
View of organizations	Rational and/or political systems	Systems of exploitation, domination, resistance, and systematically distorted communication	Products and producers of disciplinary power
Goal	To improve organizational efficiency and effectiveness	To emancipate dominated groups and develop democratic and humanistic forms of communication and decision making	To interrogate discursive and nondiscursive practices that lead to self-disciplinary behaviors and the marginalization of groups and individuals
Implications for control	Managerial control exercised by monitoring the performance of employees through the mechanisms of the market, bureaucracy or organizational culture (clan control)	Control exercised through hegemony and systematically distorted communication processes. Employees give active consent to their own exploitation through false consciousness	Control exercised through disciplinary technologies and self-surveillance—a fear of being watched
View of conflict	Conflict is counter-productive and should be managed by those in power to maximize corporate performance	Conflict is an inevitable consequence of capitalism and its resultant social and economic inequalities. Conflict is necessary for resistance, the overthrow of those in power and radical change	Conflict emerges within the network of power relations as groups contest the ability to frame the realities and subjectivities of others

a framework for analyzing how all of the core concepts of organization theory—environment, social structure, technology, culture, physical structure and power/politics/control—contribute to understanding organizational conflict. Although this model originated in modernist thinking, it is broad enough to accommodate multiple perspectives and thus will stand as an example of the potential for integrative theorizing. Remember, however, that the desire to integrate is challenged by postmodernists who suspect a grand narrative at work, and by critical theorists who spy hegemony.

To get an overview of concepts and issues you will study in this chapter, take a look at Table 8.1, which compares modern, critical and postmodern conceptions of power, control and conflict.

Modernist Conceptions of Power, Politics and Control

As you saw in Chapter 3, knowledge and the ability to deal with organizational uncertainty renders some groups within the organization more powerful than others. Modernist theories of the internal distribution of organizational power represent organizations as political arenas. This idea entered organization theory from political science early in its history (take another look at Figure 1.1) but was initially subordinated to the interests of economists and engineers whose values for rationality, authority and legitimacy dominated the discourse of organization theory at that time. As a result, most early modernists considered organizational politics to be inappropriate in business because they undermined rationality and authority and therefore the legitimacy of management. These modernists believed that by asserting the need for rational action, the inefficiencies inherent in political behavior would be eliminated. It was not until observational studies of organizational decision making revealed undeniable evidence of political behavior that theories of power and politics in organizations found their place within modernist organization theory. So transformative was this evidence that by 1980 American sociologists Samuel Bacharach and Edward Lawler were able to state flatly that: 'Survival in an organization is a political act. Corporations, universities, and voluntary associations are arenas for daily political action.'[2]

The transformation of attitudes about organizational power and politics began with American administrative and political scientists Herbert Simon and James March. Their book, *Organizations*, published in 1958 and followed in 1963 by Richard Cyert and March's *A Behavioral Theory of the Firm*, focused attention on the politics of organizational decision-making processes. These organization theorists built on Simon's theory that organizational decision making is rational only under highly restrictive conditions.[3] Simon argued that the rational model ignores the organization's internal politics because it assumes that decision makers agree about organizational goals, use the same decision rules and have no disagreements over the appropriate method for deciding.

Simon pointed out that organizational decision makers are often faced with competing goals, scarce resources, interdependence and other sources of conflict. Under these conditions, those with the most powerful positions tend to dominate decision-making processes via political behavior by individuals. However, when decision makers are aware of this tendency, they can manage or manipulate the decision-making process by aligning their interests with others behind a jointly favored alternative via politics at the group or organizational level. It works this way: decision makers take stock of their relative power positions vis-à-vis other decision makers within the decision-making process and, if their forces are not strong enough to overcome opposition, they join together with others to form a **coalition**. In most cases coalition formation requires behind-the-scenes negotiations to ensure that the interests of all coalition members are considered. This causes decision-making processes to diverge from the rational ideal, often leading to suboptimal decision outcomes. The suboptimality of coalitional decision making is explained at least in part by the negotiated nature of the process—the give and take required from individual members to reach agreement. What is traded for the sake of making a deal is not always or even often beneficial to the overall organization and so, while suboptimality seems to occur, deals are beneficial in the sense that they enable decision makers to break deadlocks and take action.

Following the work of Simon, March and Cyert, power and political processes became much more common research subjects in organization theory. Two major modernist theories that explicitly considered power appeared in the 1970s and 1980s: strategic contingencies and resource dependence theory. Before diving into the political aspects of these theories, let's talk about what the concept of power means.

What is Power?

In 1957 American political scientist Robert Dahl offered this widely cited definition of **power**: 'A has power over B to the extent that he can get B to do something that B would not otherwise do.'[4] In Dahl's definition, A and B can be defined at any level of analysis (individual, group or organization) but, regardless of level, power is always exercised in the context of relationships between actors rather than residing in the actors themselves. This is why you will sometimes hear it said that power is relational.

Organization theorists agree that there are many sources of power. Authority in particular stands out because it is associated with hierarchy, part of the social structure of organizations. In other words, an individual's formal authority derives from their structural position in the hierarchy. But formal authority is only one source of power in organizations; others include: personal characteristics (a charismatic personality), expertise (skills, knowledge, or information needed by others), coercion (the threat or use of force), control of scarce and critical material resources (budgets, raw materials, technology, physical space), ability to apply normative sanctions (informal rules and expectations set up by cultural assumptions and values) and opportunity (access to powerful persons). These additional sources of power do not necessarily follow the organizational hierarchy and, as American sociologist Melville Dalton showed, lower level participants in organizations often enjoy significant power in their relationships with those in positions of authority as the result of drawing on one or more of these sources.[5]

One of the main differences between authority and other forms of power is that the exercise of authority is directed downward in organizations, while the exercise of other forms of power works in other directions as well (upward, laterally, cross-organizationally) and may work in all directions at once. Think about expertise. Even the highest authority (e.g., the Queen, president, CEO) will allow themselves to be influenced by expert advisors in matters pertaining to their expertise. Perhaps for this reason authority is not always easily distinguished from other forms of power. Many theorists argue that authority is any form of power that has become legitimized within the organizational setting, and that the primary difference between authority and other forms of power lies in the way power is perceived within a given relationship. In this view authority occurs when the exercise of power becomes both accepted and expected. In this view, there is an active distribution and redistribution of power among the units and individuals of an organization, but when a particular distribution becomes institutionalized as a normal part of the organization's daily operations, power relations crystallize into an authority structure.

Another important difference between authority and other forms of power is that the exercise of authority has fewer costs. Using one's non-authorized power usually demands an expenditure of resources such as knowledge or personal attention, or by making commitments or concessions in exchange for support on a given issue (i.e., within coalition-building processes). Once expended, these resources cannot be recovered and the power holder must replace them or suffer an eroded power base. By comparison, the exercise of authority, because it is accepted and expected, has fewer costs and in some cases is enhanced through use.

Power and Politics: Strategic Contingencies and Resource Dependence Theories

The **political frame** I am encouraging you to consider in this chapter offers an alternative to structural and rational ways of thinking about organizational power.[6] The political frame is fundamentally pluralistic because it takes into account the interests of the many subcultures, factions and discourses that exist within organizations. When groups disagree over goals or over the preferred means for pursuing them, decision-making processes will be open to the effects of power and politics. As Pfeffer put it: 'Organizational politics involves those activities taken within organizations to acquire, develop, and use power and other resources to obtain one's preferred outcomes in a situation in which there is uncertainty or dissensus about choices.'[7]

Because differing interests are built into organizational structures, each decision represents an opportunity for negotiation and renegotiation in a never-ending stream of political maneuvering that constitutes everyday organizational life. Adopting this perspective, modernist political theories of organization address a number of questions: What determines the power of the various social actors within the organization? What are the conditions under which power is used? What strategies can one use to develop power? How can managers enhance their chances of having their power legitimized? Much of the research devoted to these questions is conducted at the individual level of analysis, and many theorists have suggested how an individual manager can maximize his or her power relative to other actors within the organization (see, for example, Table 8.2).

Table 8.2 Some common strategies for developing and using power within an organization

Develop power by:

Creating dependence in others
- work in areas of high uncertainty
- cultivate centrality by working in critical areas
- develop non-substitutable skills

Coping with uncertainty on behalf of others
- prevention
- forecasting
- absorption

Developing personal networks
Developing and constantly augmenting your expertise

Use power to:

Control information flows to others
Control agendas
- issue definition
- order of issues
- issue exclusion

Control decision-making criteria
- long vs. short term considerations
- return vs. risk
- choose criteria that favor your abilities and contributions

Cooptation and coalition building
- external alliances (e.g., supplier or customer relationships, interlocking boards of directors)
- internal alliances
    promote loyal subordinates
    appoint committees
    gain representation on important committees
Bring in outside experts (consultants) to bolster your position

Organization theorists have been most interested in studying power and politics at the unit (or group) and organizational levels of analysis. Sometimes this involves nothing more than interpreting organizational theories from a political point of view. For example, population ecology and institutional theory can be interpreted as explanations for the distribution of power among organizations. Population ecology concerns the distribution of power based in coercion (physical resources), remuneration (economic resources) and knowledge (technological resources), whereas institutional theory concerns the distribution of power based in institutionalized expectations (cultural resources), social norms (social resources) and regulations (political-legal resources).

Two theories of organization–environment relations that you studied in Chapter 3 were explicit about organizational power and politics: strategic contingencies theory explains how uncertainty predicts who will have power in an organization, while resource dependence theory explains how power derived from managing uncertainty determines the distribution of authority within the organizational hierarchy.

Strategic Contingencies Determine Who Gets Power

Strategic contingencies theory stated that the ability of an actor to protect others from uncertainty determines their power. As Pfeffer explained:

> Uncertainty coping is seen as a critical task or activity within organizations in part because organizations are viewed as social entities in which uncertainty is reduced through the use of standard operating procedures, forecasting, buffering, and other activities that permit the rationalization of organizational activity, while at the same time keeping the organization adaptive to external constraints.[8]

Accordingly, Pfeffer argued, individuals or departments derive power from their ability to provide something that the organization needs, for example, a high level of performance, an irreplaceable skill, an ability to solve critical problems or to obtain scarce resources.

In his study of power among units in an organization, the French sociologist Michel Crozier noted the influence of uncertainty on power relationships in a state-owned cigarette factory in France.[9] Crozier discovered that the organization was completely bureaucratized and faced little uncertainty because it operated a highly routinized technology within a stable environment. However, the maintenance men had an unexpected amount of power because they controlled the repair of broken machinery and thereby managed one of their organization's remaining uncertainties. The power of the maintenance workers derived from the fact that they could cause major problems by delaying repairs of machine breakdowns: production workers lost money because they were paid on a piece-rate system, and managers were also affected because plant productivity was a crucial factor in their performance evaluation. The dependency of these employees on the maintenance workers gave them enough power to negotiate for the right to organize their own work, which they did, and which led to Crozier's observation of their unexpected power in their workplace.

Crozier's research illustrated how handling a critical uncertainty confers power to units able to manage that uncertainty, even if they otherwise have low status in the hierarchy. In this case, maintenance workers obtained and maintained their power politically by hoarding critical information about how the machines operated. Similar findings regarding the ability to handle critical uncertainty have been reported in studies of universities where power accrues to those departments that have the highest levels of enrollment, produce the most grants or otherwise bring outside income into the university.[10] Such groups then use their power to political advantage within the organization, for example, to promote one of their members to a top hierarchical position or to garner control of other areas of critical uncertainty thus further enhancing their power base.

In their explanation of strategic contingencies theory, British organization researchers David Hickson, C. R. Hinings, and their colleagues pointed out that simply being accountable for the handling of uncertainty is not enough. Power is linked to the ability of a subunit or department to deal effectively with sources of uncertainty that otherwise would affect the organization to a significant negative degree.[11] For example, when an organization faces accusations of gender discrimination, the Human Resource (HR) Department should have the knowledge and expertise to deal with the issue on behalf of the organization. The dependence of other units on HR to resolve this critical problem provides HR power if they can effectively handle the uncertainty so that it does not negatively affect the rest of the organization.

Hickson and his colleagues suggested three coping strategies that at least partly determine whether or not uncertainty will translate into power: prevention, forecasting and absorption. In the case of the HR Department, prevention might involve developing anti-discrimination policies and training programs; forecasting could be accomplished by collecting, analyzing and providing information about new legal requirements, recent court decisions, and changes in the definitions of discrimination; and absorption would result from handling discrimination lawsuits arising from the actions of other organizational units. But remember, coping with uncertainty only generates power for a unit when its task is central to operations of the organization and when no other unit can perform the coping activity (that is, the unit's coping capabilities are non-substitutable).

In short, identifying **strategic contingencies for developing power** in an organization means locating the sources of organizational uncertainty. Converting a strategic contingency into power means managing the negative consequences of that contingency on behalf of the organization.

The Politics of Resource Dependence

Resource dependence theory elaborated strategic contingency theory's central claim by explaining that the scarcity of critical resources provokes uncertainty, the management of which, in turn, produces differential subunit power. This power may then be focused on decisions that institutionalize this influence by placing the powerful in positions of formal hierarchical authority. Once changes in authority are implemented, new actions will be taken that then have a feedback effect on the environment which, in turn, creates new strategic contingencies to be managed and so on. In other words, environments give rise to uncertainty, uncertainty creates opportunities for power differentials among organizational units (groups), power differentiations are used to distribute formal authority, those granted authority make key decisions that affect organizational actions that change the environment and so on.

Salancik and Pfeffer suggested that the dynamic set up by resource dependence becomes political when subunits are rewarded for dealing with uncertainty by being given bigger budgets, more resources, higher status positions and so on. The **politics of resource dependence** involves a unit's use of its resources to legitimate and institutionalize its position rather than to perform the organization's core task—the essence of political behavior.[12] Notice that resource dependence theory argues that internal political processes occur somewhat independently of environmental contingencies because different individuals and units within the organization make different uses of opportunities to cope with uncertainty and because already powerful and thus institutionalized units can subvert the resource redeployment and power redistribution attempts of those seeking to use newly acquired power.

In later work, Pfeffer pointed out that language and symbols are important in the exercise of power because, like other resources, they can be appropriated by social actors to support and maintain their power position.[13] These symbols include the location, size, and decor of one's office, the right to call a superior by his or her given name, and the ability to force others to call oneself by title (e.g., General, Detective, Doctor, Professor). Other symbols of authority include reserved parking spaces, luxurious offices, executive dining room privileges, high salaries and other special benefits and considerations. Symbolic forms of power are thus accepted as part of normal organizational life and become institutionalized.

Be sure to notice how many potential power symbols the culture and physical structure of an organization provide (see Chapters 6 and 7). Employees will usually take a keen interest in the physical design of their organizations and thereby politicize architectural design processes because of the potential to gain or lose control of symbols of power. Notice too that people can acquire the symbols of power without having any formal authority. In some organizations the competition over status symbols may be as high, or even higher, than the competition over the formal authority with which these symbols are often confused. The musical comedy *How to Succeed in Business Without Really Trying*, a long-standing favorite among business students, satirized this phenomenon. The story is about a young man who works his way into an organization and then up the corporate ladder by systematically associating himself with the organization's symbols of authority and success (e.g., wearing the right tie, having an office and a secretary). Although believing that symbols are all that is required for power is going too far, it is true that symbols help to establish and maintain power by supporting interpretations of who has power within the organization. Since power is relational, the attribution of power by others can grant power.

The discussion of the **symbols of power**, of course, brings the symbolic-interpretive approach into the study of power. Reviewing the symbolic-interpretive theories in the preceding chapters of Part II using the political frame should give you a variety of examples of ways that symbols can be used politically to reinforce or change established power relations. Similarly, reviewing postmodern theories in earlier chapters will provide you with several examples of resistance to organizational power and managerial control. Other examples will be presented later in this chapter. For now, let me turn your attention to modernist applications of power and political theory to the phenomenon of control in organizations.

Three Modernist Control Theories

Managers of organizations constantly face the problem of divergent interests interfering with organizational strategies and goals. This provides the rationale for managerial control: since organizations are composed of individuals with divergent interests, managers must exercise control. The quote from Tannenbaum at the beginning of this chapter is a case in point. Modern control theorists therefore have sought mechanisms for controlling employees so that self-interest is minimized and organizational interests are served.

In this section I will present three modernist theories of control in organizations. The first deals with performance evaluation and feedback and has much in common with the cybernetic model of general systems theory that you read about in Chapter 2 and the input-output model of the system seen in Figure 3.10. A model of cybernetic theory as it applies to organizations explains how executives can harness the intentions and actions of their subordinates to organizational strategies and goals. The second, agency theory, was developed by behavioral economists and accountants and focuses on controlling the motivation and behavior of executives so that they protect the interests of organizational owners. The third theory subsumes the other two in a way. It provides a framework for comparing markets, bureaucracies, and clans as alternative forms of organizational control. To give you a preview: clan control is based in the controversial idea that culture can be used as a control mechanism (recall the debate about culture as control discussed in Chapter 6). Table 8.3 summarizes the main points of all three of these modernist control theories.

In one way or another, all the theories you will study in this section of the chapter use the conceptual distinction between output and behavioral control. **Output control** focuses on the measurement of work results, such as the number of products completed, customers or clients served, and rejects, errors, or customer complaints. When outputs are not easily measured, for instance in teaching (where the output is student learning) or nursing (where patient health is determined by many factors in addition to nursing), behavioral control can often act as an alternative to output control. **Behavioral control** depends upon knowing which behaviors yield desired performance levels. For example, teaching is evaluated using indicators such as demonstrated knowledge or enthusiasm for the subject matter, whereas nurses can be assessed on the basis of their demeanor with patients and responsiveness to doctors' orders and requests. When indicators such as these are known or believed to relate to desired outcomes, the behaviors associated with high performance can be used as reasonable standards with which to assess individuals.

Table 8.3 Three theories of control

	The cybernetic model	Agency theory	Market, bureaucracy, or clan control
Purpose of control	Identify and adjust for any differences between desired and actual individual and organizational performance	Ensure that managers act in the best interests of owners	Achieve cooperation among individuals
Types of control	Output and Behavioral	Output and Behavioral	Output, Behavioral and Symbolic
Control processes	1. Set organizational goals as part of the overall strategic plan 2. Set work targets or standards at each level of the organization 3. Monitor performance (individual and group) against targets 4. Assess and correct deviations	1. Establish a contract between principals (owners) and agents (managers) 2. Obtain information to ensure agents are meeting their contractual obligations and hence are serving the interests of principals 3. Reward agents for fulfilling the demands of the contract	**Market**—comparison of prices and profit as indicators of economic performance (Output control) **Bureaucracy**—compliance with rules monitored by close supervision (Behavioral control) **Clan**—socializing organizational members in cultural values, norms and expectations (Symbolic control)

Cybernetic Control

Cybernetic control aligns organizational and individual goals using resource allocation, performance evaluation, and feedback and reward mechanisms (see Figure 8.1). Once goals and performance standards are set, means for measuring performance are developed. Take the case of evaluating faculty members. You can find behavioral measures on student evaluation forms and peer teaching review documents (e.g., demonstrated knowledge, enthusiasm, clarity, skill at managing the classroom). Output measures might include the number of research articles published or the amount of grant money generated by research proposals. Some or all of these measures will be combined and used to assess and compare the performance of individual faculty members relative to any established goals and/or to each other. Any negative deviation from the desired or normative level of performance is then used for feedback and punishment (e.g., denial of tenure or promotion, assignment of unpleasant tasks), while positive deviations are rewarded (e.g., praise, research fellowship, teaching award).

Most business organizations and government bureaucracies apply cybernetic control systems to groups as well as individuals. At the group level measures include things like statistical reports on unit output volumes (e.g., number of students or courses taught by department), quality control data (number of rejected items per 1,000 produced by shift), or occupancy rates (e.g., in a hospital, hotel or apartment complex). Data from measures like these are then used to provide feedback to units and individuals about their performance relative to targets or goals, and to determine rewards and punishments. Negative deviations between goals and performance will usually be resolved in one of several ways. First, the goal or its measure can be adjusted if it is determined that the deviation is the result of an error in the control system. Second, the individual or group can decide to change their performance by altering their behavior or output level. Often this is encouraged by management through the use of pay or other incentives made contingent on specified levels of performance. Third, workers or units can be replaced or removed if it is determined that they cannot function as required by the system. Over time, the cybernetic control system is designed to act like the thermostat it emulates—the system can be set to any goals and standards and it will adjust its behavior accordingly.

Agency Theory

Agency theory addresses the problem of how to ensure that managers (agents) act in the best interests of owners (principals). This is typically done by designing contracts that specify goals and measures, and then monitoring and rewarding goal-related performance along the lines described by cybernetic control theory. However, according to agency theorists, the ability of principals to monitor agent performance against outcomes such as profitability depends upon the amount, relevance and quality of information available, which is often easy for managers to manipulate. This situation is known as the **agency problem**.

Whether to choose behavior or outcome controls becomes a question of the costs associated with collecting the information required to minimize the chance that agents will shirk their responsibilities. Behavioral controls can be costly if monitoring behavior

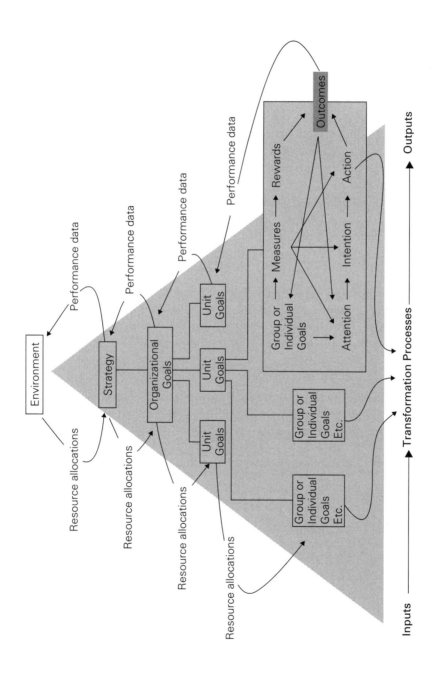

Figure 8.1 Modernist view of control processes

Control processes at individual/group, unit and organizational levels of analysis and how they are aligned with environmental demands and corporate strategy.

requires either the use of added layers of management (e.g., hiring agents to watch other agents) or the development of sophisticated information systems, such as cost accounting, budgeting, and formal reporting. As behavioral control becomes infeasible or too expensive, output control generally becomes more attractive. Output control is least costly when output is readily measured (e.g., number of units shipped); however, if outputs are difficult to measure (e.g., quality or customer satisfaction are as important as production quantities), output control becomes less attractive.

American organization theorist Kathleen Eisenhardt suggested that there are a variety of control strategies available to organizations that face the agency problem.[14] The first alternative is to design a simple, routine job so that behaviors can be easily observed, and to reward based upon the performance of targeted behaviors (i.e., behavioral control). The second alternative is to design a more complex, interesting job and invest in information systems (e.g., budgeting systems, audits, or additional layers of management) as a means of gaining knowledge about behaviors and rewarding performance (a combination of behavior and output controls).

The third alternative is to design more complex and interesting jobs, but use a much simpler evaluation scheme (e.g., corporate profitability, revenues) with rewards based on corporate results. In this strategy, greater but riskier rewards are substituted for measures and precise job design. This alternative is what leads many organizations to base salary increases and/or bonuses (including stock options) on the overall performance of the firm. This alternative means that agents face the same risks as investors do and thus they will be punished for things over which they have no control (market risk, for example). Because they receive rewards for the same outcomes, this alternative aligns the interests of principles and agents and thus reduces the need for monitoring on the assumption that if agents are motivated by the same rewards that principals are, they will choose the same courses of action that the principals would have chosen. However, agents typically must be offered higher inducements under this control system to offset the greater risk that they are forced to accept.

Like alternative three, Eisenhardt's fourth option focused on eliminating the divergent interests of principles and agents, but this time relying on the organization's culture to control behavior. In this option, first described by American organization theorist William Ouchi, selection, training, and socialization offer a radical alternative to cybernetic control systems.

Markets, Hierarchies and Clans

Ouchi proposed markets, bureaucracies and clans as alternative solutions to the problem of 'achieving cooperation among individuals who hold partially divergent objectives'.[15] **Market control** takes place through economic competition. When organizations participate in free markets, prices and profits can be used to evaluate and control their performance. In competition, prices are taken as indicators of economic performance because it is assumed that the comparison of prices and profits among a group of competitors in a free market provides a reasonable means of evaluating their relative efficiency. Market control can also be used at the unit level within organizations by treating the units or divisions of a multi-divisional organization as profit centers. When units within an organization operate as profit centers, top management tracks their revenues and costs in order to compare their relative performance, just as stockholders do when they look at the relative performance of organizations traded on a stock market.

As you can see, market strategies lean heavily on output controls. Market control is only effective when the organization or unit produces products or services that can be defined and priced, and when competition (simulated or real) for these outputs makes prices meaningful. When competition is not present or cannot be effectively simulated another mechanism of control must be found. In an influential book from 1975 called *Markets and Hierarchies*, American institutional economist Oliver Williamson claimed that when markets fail to adequately control organizational performance, organizations turn to bureaucracy.[16]

Bureaucracies rely on a combination of rules, procedures, documentation and behavioral monitoring to achieve control. The focus of bureaucratic systems is on the standardization of behavior and the reward of individuals for compliance with established rules and regulations. **Bureaucratic control** depends upon the existence of a legitimatized hierarchy of authority to administer the bureaucratic mechanisms and to closely supervise and direct subordinates. Rules and procedures generally describe processes to be completed or standards of output and quality to be met, and supervisors and managers assess the extent to which these have been implemented. Bureaucracies so defined rely heavily on behavioral controls.

You may be inclined to associate bureaucratic control with public sector and not-for-profit organizations because these types of organizations do not normally face market competition. However, many public sector and non-profit organizations find ways of incorporating market control mechanisms into their operations. For example, the idea of school choice establishes competition among schools within a community. The process of bidding out contracts to provide city services (e.g., garbage collection) forces external contractors and city departments to compete on price and the range and quality of services they offer. The reason for such moves is the greater efficiency associated with market control mechanisms. Of course, questions emerge in relation to whether one can put a price on some services such as education, and whether a city has a social responsibility to provide a decent salary and benefits to its employees—especially when service contractors in the United States so often employ minority workers on a part-time, no-benefits basis.

Having a choice between market and bureaucratic control will still not meet the control needs of every organization. When environments are complex and rapidly changing, and uncertainty and ambiguity are consequently high, neither market nor bureaucracy is likely to provide an organization enough control for timely adaptation to its environment. Likewise, if the types of behaviors that produce outputs are ambiguous, or it is difficult to assess results, then rational means of control by market or bureaucratic mechanisms will fail. Under these conditions, organizations must rely upon their social systems to keep members focused on organizational objectives and control performance. Ouchi argued that **clan control**—cultural values, norms and expectations that define proper behavior—offers the most effective form of control under these conditions.

Clan control requires that new members be socialized so that they internalize the cultural values, goals, expectations and practices that will drive them to desired levels of performance. Once internalized, implicit understandings help direct and coordinate the activities of organizational members and justify sanctioning any behavior that is not deemed suitable. This form of control represents a fairly high level of commitment to the system by its members who frequently sacrifice some or all of their self-interest to become socialized.

Organizations with large numbers of professionals are particularly good examples of clan control because professionals are highly socialized to the norms and expectations of their profession. Their commitment to preserving and enhancing their professional reputation helps to control their behavior. However, professional commitment can diverge from the interests of the organization and professionals will typically abandon organizational interests if forced to choose between loyalty to the organization and their professional identity. So, while professionalization may be a good model of clan control, simply employing professionals is not equivalent to creating clan control in an organization.

Ouchi observed that all organizations employ a combination of the three control strategies outlined above, but that each organization favors one form of control over the others. He suggested that the type of control an organization prefers predicts the extent to which it will make use of its culture or instead will invest in sophisticated information systems. Clan-controlled organizations require the most highly developed social systems (e.g., Southwest Airlines) while market-controlled organizations require the least (e.g., most small businesses), with bureaucracies falling in between (e.g., IBM, most government organizations and universities). With respect to information systems, Ouchi claimed that the opposite relationship holds—market-controlled organizations demand the most highly evolved information systems for tracking prices and profits, while clan-controlled organizations require much less of this sort of activity. Again, bureaucracies fall into the middle range. Of course, all organizations will have both social and informational systems, but the extent of their reliance upon and development of these systems will vary with the type of control they favor.

Critical Studies of Power and Control

Whereas modernist scholars focused most of their attention on explaining how power gets distributed in organizations, critical and postmodern scholars have been more interested in understanding how networks of power relations are intertwined with knowledge and ideology. In the most general terms, critical and postmodern scholars seek to establish humanistic, ethical, and inclusive organizational decision-making processes as alternatives to the rational ideal held by modernists. Based initially on Marx's definition of power as domination, and employing ideas like manufactured consent and systematically distorted communication, critical theorists maintain something of the modernist stance by assuming that social, economic and political structures determine power relationships. However, by challenging mainstream modernist ideologies and assumptions, particularly those favoring instrumental rationality, they align themselves with postmodernists.

Critical theorists question the institutionalization of power within the organizational hierarchy and the assumption that managers have a legitimate right to control others. The negative connotation they attribute to domination raises the Marxist question: why do dominated groups consent to their own exploitation rather than resist it? Many critical theorists study this phenomenon by analyzing the structural mechanisms and communication processes that maintain exploitative relationships. Their ultimate goal is to create communication and decision-making processes that represent the full range of stakeholder interests—including human rights and environmental protection. Their ambitions will be illustrated by labor process theory, communicative rationality and democratic forms of governance.

Critical theorists typically adopt the grand narrative of progress favored by modernists, although for most critical theorists progress is defined as the emancipation of dominated groups and the establishment of democratic control structures. Several streams of critical studies will be presented below. The first—the critique of ideology—lays the foundation for critical theory by defining power as domination. Labor process theory explains power as control in a way that explicitly applies critical theory to work settings. The concept of communicative rationality, offered as an alternative to instrumental rationality, reveals the hidden forms of power and control that the communicative nature of human existence makes possible. Finally, an antidote to the societal and organizational problems addressed by critical theorists is presented: **workplace democracy**.

The Critique of Ideology

You face **ideology** whenever a group of people systematically expresses belief in a set of ideas (e.g., shared beliefs, values, culture and/or institutionalized structures and practices). Critics of ideology examine how ideologies legitimate the domination of one group over another. Applying this concept to organizations allows critical theorists to claim that managerialist ideology assumes that owners and managers have the right to dominate workers and thus provides the basis for managerial control and the exploitation of workers. Accepting the managerialist ideology is paramount to a failure to resist the owner/shareholder's right to profit or the manager's right to give orders and make judgments about the value of employees to the organization. Accepting these conditions of work—what modernists sometimes refer to as the employment contract—hides the power issues involved behind a neutral vocabulary of normalcy. Putting a political frame around this scenario, Marx argued that when workers participate in their own exploitation by legitimizing their oppressors' right to dominate them they exist in a state of **false consciousness**. In other words, the oppressed willingly consent to their oppression by adopting the managerialist ideology and subordinating their interests to those of their hierarchical superiors.

Hegemony

The question of why employees acquiesce to domination has been addressed in a number of ways. For instance, Italian Marxist theorist Antonio Gramsci used the concept of **hegemony** to explain that dominated groups give their spontaneous and active consent to those who dominate them because institutional and ideological forms of domination become part of their taken-for-granted everyday activities.[17] Hegemony refers to how the practices and values of a culture or institution align with and maintain existing systems of wealth and power. In such a system you are never coerced, but you are subtly and incessantly influenced (e.g., by your parents, educators and the media) to participate in established ways of thinking and talking that seem normal or commonsensical but that privilege the elite. Clan control, total quality management programs, and business process re-engineering have all been described by critical theorists as hegemonic practices used by managers to more or less dictate the actions and decisions of organizational members by articulating their interests and realities for them. Even though hegemonic practices proclaim the value of autonomy or use the velvet language of participation, involvement or empowerment, they are ideologically engineered to benefit only the interests and goals of managers and owners.[18] The fictional phenomenon of Newspeak provides a good example of hegemonic practices. According to the on-line encyclopedia Wikipedia:

> Newspeak is a fictional language in George Orwell's famous novel *Nineteen Eighty-Four*. Orwell included an essay about it in the form of an Appendix after the end of the novel, in which the basic principles of the language are explained. Newspeak is closely based on English but has a greatly reduced and simplified vocabulary and grammar. This suited the totalitarian regime of the Party, whose aim was to make subversive thought ('thoughtcrime') and speech impossible. The Newspeak term for the existing English language was Oldspeak. Oldspeak was supposed to have been completely eclipsed by Newspeak by 2050.[19]

Three Faces of Power

Steven Lukes, a British political and social theorist, claimed that power has three faces: decision making, non decision making, and the ability to shape the preferences and perceptions of others without their awareness.[20] The first face of power involves a forum (e.g., organization, parliament) where various actors or groups fully and equally participate in decision making. The second face involves non decision making. Non decision making occurs when powerful groups prevent those less powerful from being involved in the decision making process, such as when particular individuals and groups manipulate the issues open to decision making by determining what issues make it onto a meeting agenda, by suppressing undesired alternative views during discussion, or interpreting silence as agreement.

Lukes's third face of power is the most radical and it incorporates Gramsci's notion of hegemony in that social practices shape the desires and actions of particular groups in ways that actually work against their interests. The third face of power limits freedoms and oppresses groups because divergent interests, values and practices are not open to discussion so that alternative forms of organizing are never considered. Also, in giving active consent, workers engage in activities that benefit the organization but result in a restriction of personal choice. For example, having greater autonomy at work often leads employees to spend more time at the office and less time with family.

Gramsci suggested that to change power relationships, one needs to understand the process of hegemony and how power is constituted through structures and practices. Acts of resistance do not have to take the form of open rebellion but can be more subtle, such as withdrawing effort or engaging in theft, dishonesty or sabotage. Stories of injustice and oppression, if told and shared by organizational members, can also serve as acts of resistance.[21] The quote below, an excerpt from a research conversation with a female manager in a large US organization, is an example of a linguistic act of resistance to hegemonic practices:

> Issues of diversity are very personal and unless you confront them in a personal way, organizations just aren't going to get anywhere. It's not about how do I get L___ to fit into this white, male oriented organization, because there is going to come a point at which I say 'No, I'm not going to give up who I am to do that'. . . . And in meetings they use baseball and football metaphors— so I thought 'I'm not using any sporting metaphors, I'm creating my own'.[22]

Be sure to notice that the manager in this example recognized her need to confront the hegemonic practice of using male-gendered metaphors to exclude her from the dominant organizational conversation or suppress her unique interests. Her acts of resistance include telling her story and creating her own metaphors.

Labor Process Theory

Within critical theory, managerial control is sometimes defined as the means by which capitalist ideologies and interests dominate. American sociologist Harry Braverman provided a theory based on this understanding of control that is known as **labor process theory**.[23] Braverman suggested that the owners of the means of production (capitalists) control work by systematically **deskilling** labor through job fragmentation and routinization, practices that were introduced by Taylor's scientific management. Deskilling continues until the work is so simple that very little training is required and thus it becomes easy for managers to replace workers who put up any resistance. In this way, control over the labor process shifts from workers to management and the workers' power base is systematically eroded to the point where resistance is futile. Deskilling allows owners to drive down the price of labor, which enhances their profits but also exploits and degrades workers and contributes to alienation from their work and their workplace.

Graham Sewell, an Australian organizational theorist, illustrated labor process control in his study of teams in an electronics organization.[24] Sewell found that control was maintained through electronic quality tests at various stages of an assembly process. The resulting quality data was symbolically displayed over each employee's workstation using traffic lights: red meant the team member had exceeded quality error allowances, amber that he was within an acceptable range of error, and green that he or she had no quality errors. This practice led not only to management control (vertical surveillance) but also to self-discipline and intense peer pressure exerted by members of each autonomous work team (horizontal surveillance). Sewell's study showed that the horizontal control exerted by team members—who expressed their approval or disapproval and rewarded or punished individual performances at daily team meetings—was far more potent than the vertical control exerted by the managers.

Communicative Rationality

German social philosopher Jürgen Habermas claimed that modern society is dominated by institutions that are governed by scientific, technical, and administrative experts who focus on the most technically-efficient and rational way of achieving goals.[25] This techno-cratic ideology invades our everyday life and ignores the ethical and moral aspects of indi-vidual and social development. Defining **instrumental rationality** as achieving goals through efficient means, Habermas argued for the alternative of **communicative ratio-nality**, which he defined as debate, open discussion and consensus. He not only claimed the superiority of communicative rationality but also that instrumental rationality domi-nates and distorts it because of the widespread acceptance of technocratic ideology.

Consider this example. You are invited to a meeting of all departmental employees to discuss how work could be more productive and satisfying. The discussion ranges from streamlining procedures to eliminating the duplication of work that causes uncertainty and conflict between department members. Someone suggests that the department man-ager give an employee-of-the-month award with a bonus for attaining results above targets. Another person suggests weekly meetings to clarify individual responsibilities and share information. Departmental members might be able to come to some consensus about what would make their work life better and feel good about their involvement in the process. However, Habermas would argue that communication was systematically distorted by those in power because in setting the agenda and accepting only particular suggestions, the department manager controlled the behavior of employees and ensured the outcome of the meeting supported the goals of instrumental rationality (recall Lukes's three faces of power).

From a Habermassian perspective, **systematically distorted communication** is an implicit form of manipulation and control because it privileges one meaning and ideology over others; involves deception (of self or other); and precludes sincere and ethically informed conversation. In the example above, the goal of the meeting was not to create a sat-isfying workplace by exploring a range of possibilities through open discussion and mutual understanding (i.e., communicative action), but a way for those in authority to exploit employee ideas and obtain consensus (although false) on how to improve productivity.

Workplace Democracy

In his 1992 book *Democracy in an Age of Corporate Colonization*, Stanley Deetz drew on Gramsci, Habermas and Foucault, arguing that corporations have become extremely pow-erful in the sense that they have colonized and now control the institutions and practices of society as well as individual lives and identities.[26] This colonization is sustained by the commercialization of language, the vocationalization of the education system and the restructuring of family life around the demands of work. Deetz claimed that corporate power is far more insidious than state power because it is inherently non-democratic, per-vades our everyday experience, and is regarded as normal. Systematically distorted com-munication processes within organizations strategically reproduce corporate ideologies by creating false consensus and encouraging employees to actively support corporate inter-ests. Deetz prescribed the antidote of balanced responsiveness, a moral communicative practice in which organizational stakeholders engage in open communication as a means of surfacing and responding to everyday forms of domination and suppressed conflict. Calls for open communication such as this one are typically embedded in some form of workplace democracy.

Worker cooperatives and labor-managed firms (LMFs) are applications of workplace democracy designed to answer the moral questions critical theorists have raised about capitalist ideologies and the concentration of power among the few. Although issues of workplace democracy run the gamut from participation and stock ownership to codetermination and worker-owned and worker-managed firms, it is the latter form of organization that most directly challenges capitalism by embracing democratic principles and promoting collective property ownership.

Cooperatives are independent non-profit groups organized by and for the benefit of their members. They have a long history. For example, Benjamin Franklin formed the Philadelphia Contributionship for the Insurance of Houses from Loss by Fire, over 250 years ago. Other examples include the New Mexico Rural Electric Cooperatives (this cooperative consists of one cooperative that generates electricity and transmits it to nineteen others that handle distribution) and the plywood industry of the Pacific Northwest, which was taken over by several independent cooperatives formed by local workers when the plants became unprofitable.[27] You may be familiar with a food or day care cooperative in your hometown. Numerous communities have formed a variety of cooperatives like these to serve the needs of local families.

A group of British weavers, who formed the Rochdale Equitable Pioneers Society in the United Kingdom, developed seven cooperative principles that underlie most cooperatives in existence today. These principles range from ownership and control by employees rather than investors or shareholders (these are sometimes referred to as governance issues), to decisions reached by the democratic vote of employees, and economic surplus distributed amongst employees in an equitable way depending on pay level or hours worked. Those who promote these democratic governance structures argue that worker ownership leads to more socially and community-responsible decision making and creates a supportive network.

One of the largest and most successful cooperatives in the world is Mondragón founded in the mid-1950s in the Basque region of Northern Spain. The Mondragón cooperative consists of over one hundred industrial, agricultural, housing, educational, financial, and distribution cooperatives.[28] The most notable features of the system include an initial capital contribution by all new members; a restriction on the ratio of pay between the highest and lowest paid workers; and the rule that the cooperative's earnings may be distributed only as wages or pensions—there are no dividends paid as there would be in a corporation.

Feminist and Postmodern Conceptions of Power and Control

The themes of ideology and hegemony are woven throughout both critical and postmodern approaches to the study of power and control, albeit in very different ways. As you saw previously, critical approaches focus on the structural and ideological aspects of conflict and present power and ideology as inseparable because power is used by dominant groups to frame and impose particular assumptions and worldviews on others. This type of domination is reflected in the concept of stratification and by dual labor market theory, two products of critical theory that fed directly into feminist organization theory.

By now you should recognize that postmodern scholars reject the idea of universal truth. If there is no universal truth, then there can be no false state from which to be freed, and so postmodernists diverge from critical theorists around the denial of foundational thinking. Postmodernists believe that to replace one foundational truth or ideology with another merely leads to other forms of domination and oppression, so while postmodernists applaud critical theorists' revelations of hegemony, they do not believe that their efforts will overturn domination and oppression. Perhaps you know the Who's 1960s rock anthem: *Won't Get Fooled Again*. The line 'Meet the new boss / Same as the old boss' is an expression of this idea in popular culture.

Following Michel Foucault's influential theories, postmodernists also reject the idea of a conscious subject in favor of the discursive construction of subjectivities. According to Foucault's followers, human selves are neither self-conscious nor independent beings, they are only positions in discourse. This assumption has significant implications for the way that postmodernists conceptualize and study power, which I will explain below. But first let's consider the relationship of gender to organizing originally studied by feminist organization theorists.

Gender and Organizing

Feminist theory has produced many different approaches to the study of gender. These range from modernist studies (e.g., of differences in the proportions of male and female managers, the conflict between work and family responsibilities, and gender-based discrimination), to applications of critical, psychoanalytical and poststructuralist theory to gender issues.[29] Many feminist organization theorists are inspired by the observation that decision making and leadership in organizations continue to be dominated by men who are served by women both in the office and at home. Take, for example, this statement by American feminist Jane Flax, who argued that **gender stereotypes** 'make it seem natural that women do some kinds of work and not others. In turn the devaluation of the stereotypically female contributes to and reinforces a devaluation of "women's work" and the wages it can command.'[30]

Gendered Stratification and Dual Labor Market Theory

Using labor market analysis, **stratification** theorists have shown considerable evidence of the inequitable distribution of high paying, powerful, and prestigious positions in modern organizations. Numerous studies demonstrate an extreme disproportion of white males in positions of power and authority in capitalistic societies. The most popular explanation for stratification in the labor market was provided by American labor economists Peter Doeringer and Michael Piore, who proposed **dual labor market theory**.

Dual labor market theory argues that the market for labor is composed of two different sectors: the primary and the secondary.[31] High wages and good career opportunities are provided within the primary sector, while the secondary sector is marked by lower wages and by poor conditions of employment (e.g., no job security, limited or no benefits). The reason Doeringer and Piore gave for the discrepancy in opportunities between the primary and secondary sectors is that, to remain competitive, employers must have a steady supply of qualified workers who can maintain the firm's technological advantage in the marketplace. This means that they must pay top wages and provide substantial benefits to employees who have the desired skills and education. Employers then attempt to offset the costs of maintaining this highly skilled and motivated workforce by employing unskilled workers to perform less central tasks for less pay and poorer working conditions.

Dual labor market theory explains stratification, but not the disproportion of white males in the primary sector. This is because dual labor market theory only considers the economic and technological reasons for labor market stratification, the theory ignores important conditions in the cultural, social, physical, legal and political segments of the general environment. It therefore cannot explain why women, ethnic minorities, youth and the elderly are underrepresented in the primary sector because economic and technological reasons do not account for these outcomes. To put it bluntly, it cannot be that only white males are technically qualified for primary sector jobs. Based on empirical evidence, claims of unequal treatment suggest that the divisions that Marx observed between capitalists and workers are not the only bases of class conflict. Class conflict must also be explained along gender, race, ethnicity, and age-related lines and these categories form the bases for many different possible classes of employees in contemporary work organizations (e.g., young African-American females, older white females, young Latino males, young homosexual males). This thinking is found in research into the effects of diversity on organizations, to which we will give more attention in Chapter 9.

Barbara Czarniawska and Guye Sevón looked more deeply into the stratification phenomenon by applying narrative analysis to the biographies of four scientists who were each the first woman in their country of residence to be named to a professorial chair at a university.[32] According to Czarniawska and Sevón, the four biographies illustrate that, in order for women to succeed in a world dominated by males, they need some unique distinction. The women in their study possessed the unique distinction of double strangeness—they were not only non-male but also foreigners. Their appointments in the place of similarly qualified women nationals in Sweden, Poland, Finland and France, convinced Czarniawska and Sevón that the foreignness of these female academics cancelled the negative implications of their womanhood by rending these talented women less threatening to those already in power.

Gender Studies and Organization Theory across Perspectives

A popular feminist position holds that devaluation of the female occurs in the split between public (male) and private (female) life, and is reinforced by the production of knowledge that supports difference: work in private life is characterized by caring and a sense of community (feminine) and in public life by rationality and competitiveness (masculine). A number of feminist scholars have argued that this separation of male and female domains and practices reinforces a binary view of gender that underpins the everyday actions and interactions of both men and women, thus reproducing traditional relations of domination and subordination. Other common linguistic oppositions—rational/emotional, hard/soft, active/passive—are pressed into service to accentuate male/female differences. For example, women are emotional, soft and passive, while men are rational, active and tough.

Calls to overturn the opposition or replace male by female practices do not address the underlying issue of how such differences are reproduced in ongoing and taken-for-granted ways, and so they continue to support the idea of gender difference rather than address the political issues of marginalization, voice and diversity. Although the feminist literature is far from homogeneous, deconstructing and overcoming the gendered nature of organizational life seems to be a common interest of feminist organization theorists, regardless of their philosophical orientation. Gender studies therefore examine the 'systematic forces that generate, maintain, and replicate gendered relations of domination'.[33]

By assuming that gender is not just concerned with biology but is constructed within social, historical, material and discursive practices, some feminist studies of organizational power and politics adopt critical and postmodern perspectives. One such view postulated that gender power relations and organizing are interwoven:

> Gender is constitutive of organizing; it is an omnipresent, defining feature of collective human activity, regardless of whether such activity appears to be about gender. Second, the gendering of organization involves a struggle over meaning, identity, and difference; this ongoing discursive struggle occurs amid, and acts upon, gendered institutional structures. Third, such struggle (re)produces social realities that privilege certain interests.[34]

From this perspective, organizations and organizing are gendered processes that control and marginalize women and other minority groups. We will explore this issue by examining two ideas: organizations are fundamentally gendered, and identities (subjectivities) are constituted within a system of power relations.

Joan Acker, an American Professor of Sociology, has been influential in promoting the idea of **gendered organizations**. Her claims have been reinforced by organizational researchers and theorists who, like managers, 'are part of the relations of ruling'.[35] Building on her work, a number of feminist scholars have argued that organizations are both discursive products and producers of gender-based power relations, and that masculine ways of doing things are inherent in structural, ideological and symbolic aspects of organization as well as in everyday interactions and practices. Some of these authors suggested that masculinity is embedded in bureaucratic forms of organization that focus on hierarchy, impersonality, and the separation of work and private life. For example, hierarchy is premised on the assumption of a masculine elite that depends on a feminized support staff, and careers based on one's continued commitment to the organization.[36] While the argument is often made that women's interests are represented through women's advisory committees, in effect this is unequal representation because such committees are explicitly constructed as outsiders separated from the taken-for-granted, insider male structure. Both scholars and activists have focused on creating alternatives to bureaucracy (thus reinforcing the binary view) that reflect 'women's ways of organizing', especially in areas of health care and domestic violence.

Other scholars explore how gendered organizations are constructed in discursive and non-discursive ways. In her study of female engineers, Joyce Fletcher suggested that definitions of work have a masculine bias that suppresses alternative conceptions. In the high-tech organization she studied, the types of behaviors worthy of promotion were autonomy, technical competence, self-promotion, individual heroics, and being able to quantify issues. Relational practices (which she defined as being associated with feminine belief systems) included preserving the well-being of a project, contributing to programs, mutual empowering and collaborative teams, all of which were undervalued or ignored by organizational members. Fletcher called ignoring relational practices **disappearing**, after a similar concept introduced by Michel Foucault. Disappearing includes referring to relational behaviors as inappropriate for work or as a sign of weakness.[37] Fletcher found that the female engineers themselves, while wanting to work differently, colluded in disappearance by warning their female colleagues about the consequences of engaging in relational behaviors.

Recently, two feminist communication theorists, Karen Ashcraft and Dennis Mumby, articulated a *feminist communicology of organization* that is positioned at the intersection of modern, critical, and postmodern discourse.[38] They suggested that researchers need to explore the dialectical relationship between power, resistance and organizing by focusing on how meanings and identities are created intersubjectively in embodied everyday communication, such as that in which airline pilots engage. The identity of airline pilots has evolved across time and spheres of organizing activity including historical narratives in popular culture, aviation organizations, and through individual pilots. The construction of pilot identity is also tied into various discourses of gender including cultural icons and stories of male fliers (e.g., Superman); stories of romantic ladybird female pilots; the discursive production of the professional, technically capable white masculine pilot by the commercial aviation industry; the severing of professional/commercial pilots and lady-fliers by questioning the ability of women to fulfill their duties because of family obligations or lack of physical strength; and the reconstruction of the masculine pilot as the adventurous, rugged yet civilized professional. Ashcraft and Mumby suggested that all of these discourses weave together over time to produce gendered identity among airline pilots through the unobtrusive exercise of discursive power.

In summary, understanding the politics of gender involves studying the ways in which behavior and language express and maintain dominant cultural understandings of women and men and thereby structure power relationships in organizations and in society in general. The study of the use of language in organizations provides a means for exposing the gendered nature of organizational relationships of power and domination. The argument put forward by feminist theorists is that language itself is gendered because meaning circulates around a network of images that have distinctive male or female associations.[39] For example, American feminist organization theorist Kathy Ferguson argued that:

> Rhetorical and grammatical practices organized around, for example, images of soft and hard, fluid and solid, open and closed, particular and universal, connection and distance, reception and assertion, are gendered in the sense that they ride on an already constituted and widely circulated set of understandings about appropriately feminine and masculine ways of being in the world.[40]

One of the implications of the study of gender relations in organizations is that, if current gender constructions lead to devaluing women's work and to keeping women out of positions of power in organizations and society, then, in the name of justice, these constructions need to be changed. Feminist organization theorists currently pursue several lines of research aimed at creating this change politically. These include:

- giving voice to women in order to articulate feminist viewpoints

- overturning unitary representations of experience to make way for the multiplicity of not only gender, but race, ethnicity, age and class

- promoting and using a reflexive stance with regard to research and writing practices by redefining the subjects of and audiences for research (e.g., changing these from white, male managers, to women, people of color, indigenous people, the working-class, youth and the aged).

Foucault's work offers a link between feminist and postmodern notions of power because his interest in sexuality, the body and subjectivity closely aligns with feminist interest in gendered identity.[41] Foucault suggested that the phenomena of sexuality and the body are socially and historically constructed through the exercise of power. A number of feminist scholars have built on his work to explore the construction of gendered identity in everyday practices and have used Foucault's concept of disciplinary power to examine how the female body is controlled and subjected to prevailing norms of feminine attractiveness.

Disciplinary Power and Surveillance

Foucault used the concept of **disciplinary power** to explain that the anticipation of control causes people to engage in self-surveillance. Building on this idea, a number of organization theorists have suggested that disciplinary power is part of everyday organizational life. One of these, Stan Deetz, argued that 'Disciplinary power resides in every perception, every judgment, every act. . . . It is not just the rule and routine which becomes internalized, but a complex set of practices which provide common-sense, self-evident experience and personal identity.'[42] Postmodernists like Deetz see power and control not as something located in a particular position or possessed by an individual, but as embedded in all social relations and organizational practices, and expressed and reconstructed in day-to-day interactions between people. Consequently, forms of power and control are inescapable and unobtrusive, they arise from the ways in which values, ideals and beliefs are shared and become part of everyday life.

Foucault believed that organizations such as hospitals, prisons, schools and factories are sites of disciplinary power. Disciplinary power differs from the modernist concepts of sovereign power (residing in a person) and hierarchical power (residing in a position), in that it resides in the routine practices of surveillance used in organizations and is regarded as normal by employees. Foucault suggested that disciplinary power is inherent in all social relationships and therefore is part of everyday life. It is exercised constantly in a network or cluster of relationships and shifts from one person to another as it is produced and repro-duced from one moment to the next.[43]

Since power is relational, a manager does not exercise power alone. She may ask a staff member to work on a project, but as they talk about the project they negotiate what will be done, how, and whether collaboration with others is needed. In this way, power relations emerge at every level of the organization: between managers and subordinates, managers and their bosses, and between colleagues in the workplace and on committees. For example, note the complex network of power relations described in the following excerpt from a conversation with the project manager responsible for coordinating a move of 2,000 employees to a centralized location:

> Then on top of which is another layer which is a Site Council.... Here we have layers and layers of managers who believe they have to have a say, and even though I ultimately get my authority from the Site Council and I report to one of the managers—he reports to another one and then there's a third person, the Personnel Manager.... So, that's who we go to when we're running into problems and we need decisions. The problem is, even there, the degree to which those people are listened to by other general managers.

This excerpt illustrates Foucault's notion that power operates constantly in relation-ships, is always shifting and asymmetrical as one group or individual takes an advantaged position in the process. But just as power is everywhere, so is resistance—and resistance also takes multiple forms; it does not have to be expressed as overt resistance or noncompliance, it can also appear as a reduced amount of work effort, lateness, silence or barbed humor.

Foucault believed that disciplinary power is neither inherently good nor bad; it can be productive in creating possibilities for knowledge production, pleasure, and new living conditions. It also creates **economies of power**, control techniques less open to resistance than sovereign forms where individuals are closely monitored by those in power. Autonomous work groups exemplify economies of power because group members make decisions and monitor their performance without the need for managerial control and its associated costs (e.g., manager's wages). When the savings are applied to benefit all organ-izational members, disciplinary power may be tolerable and even desirable, but its tendency to marginalize some and privilege others must be held in check.

Foucault's notion of disciplinary power has particular importance for the critical study of organizations because it highlights disciplinary technologies as forms of **surveil-lance** and self-discipline that are internalized and often taken for granted by organiza-tional members. These technologies not only control performance and behavior but also our bodies and identities. They are designed to make us compliant and efficient, and to punish us when we are deviant. Foucault drew on Jeremy Bentham's (1748–1832) idea of the Panoptican—a single tower in a prison yard situated so that a prison guard could see into every prison cell and monitor every individual's behavior. Because the prisoners can-not see into the tower they do not know when they are being watched. Consequently they conform to the rules and behave in the desired way in case someone is watching them. In this sense they engage in self-surveillance, which is a highly efficient monitoring system. Foucault defined **self-surveillance** as the product of two processes: **the gaze** of inspection (in which managers employ a number of surveillance techniques to set up the expectation of surveillance), and **interiorization** (anticipation of the gaze and self-monitoring).

British organization theorist Barbara Townley argued that many human resource techniques enact the gaze as defined by Foucault.[44] Because they are ways of classifying individuals to make them visible and therefore manageable, tools such as interview protocols, psychological tests, performance appraisals, assessments centers and so forth, are all ways of controlling individuals (e.g., by examining, categorizing, recording and normalizing them). Job descriptions control behavior; performance evaluations reward compliance; training programs alter bodies and minds by specifying what is correct knowledge and what skills and attitudes must be mastered for the job; technology and work processes determine body movements and cause their users to adapt to machines and required procedures. Performance management systems become forms of interiorization and self-surveillance when employees participate in goal setting and are rewarded for goal achievement. All of these techniques (critical theorists call them economies of power) represent ways in which power is made to seem normal and acceptable. Try to locate the taken-for-granted nature of disciplinary power as well as various disciplinary technologies in this quote from a Program Manager working in a large high-tech organization:

> In manufacturing I was a Process Engineering Manager and one of the reasons I was asked to take this job [as Project Manager] was the feeling that product development was lacking some process, and that someone who understood how to apply processes and how to develop processes needed to come in and help. So I was explicitly told coming in that: 'your strength in designing and implementing processes is why we chose you'.... There was a class offered through Corporate on 'Managing Complex Projects' and some textbooks they suggested, so I get a lot of ideas from those and try to apply them to this organization.

In this quote, process training and textbooks are disciplinary technologies used to normalize this manager's knowledge and practice. Process (which in this case involves operating procedures and systems) is the panoptican that encourages interiorization and self-surveillance.

Organizational theorists who build on Foucault's theory examine the micro-practices of power and how these may be influenced by broader strategies of power at an institutional and societal level. For example, Australian organization theorist Stewart Clegg studied the power created through techniques of discipline and production that reinforce the status quo.[45] He concluded that power relations flow through three interdependent circuits: the **episodic** (daily interaction), **dispositional** (socially constructed rules), and **facilitative** (systems and mechanisms including technology, work, rewards). The circuits intersect and can lead to the empowerment or disempowerment of groups: if a group of workers have knowledge about a particular technology on which others depend (facilitative circuit), they will be empowered in relation to other groups and will be able to negotiate outcomes to their advantage within the episodic and dispositional circuits.

A number of studies based on Foucault have uncovered techniques of surveillance used in organizations. They show how information technology, acting as an electronic panoptican, has provided new forms of surveillance that allow individuals to exercise discretion while simultaneously intensifying control. In addition to vertical forms of disciplinary power, self-managed work groups and worker participation programs all encourage self-surveillance. Hegemony operates, not as consent given to dominant ideologies or privileged groups, but as consent to many different forms of power constructed within everyday activities through discursive and nondiscursive practices. For example, wearing a suit to work, changing your eating habits because your doctor tells you to, or participating in self-development activities to enhance your prospects for promotion, all involve engagement with power circuits. However, in contrast to the position held by critical theorists, those following Foucault's line of reasoning suggest we might not want to resist these practices because they give us pleasure.

In a study of control and domination in a knowledge-intensive firm where work was characterized by autonomy and self-management, Deetz found that employees actively limited their autonomy and engaged in self-disciplinary behaviors that were over and above those required by management. They worked long hours, slept at worksites, under-reported the hours they worked, and dealt with aggressive and sometimes abusive clients, all under the umbrella of autonomy. They participated in their own exploitation in order to obtain money and to create and maintain their professional identities as consultants, while believing it was for the good of the company and client.[46] Deetz claimed that consent in this case was based on applying personal autonomy and commitment in the interests of the organization.

Postmodernists argue that we need to open our own scholarly practices to reflexive scrutiny. For example, Gibson Burrell suggested that Foucault's work presents a contradiction for organization theory. Namely if we accept that organizations both reflect and maintain disciplinary power in society, then organization theory itself reproduces a disciplinary society because it offers ways of categorizing, analyzing, and improving efficiency that normalize us.[47]

If you consider the modernist, symbolic-interpretive, and postmodern perspectives, you will see that each has very different interests, beliefs, research methods, and ways of determining what is true—all leading to different ideas and theories based on different ontological and epistemological positions. The reigning truth of the modernist perspective is capitalism, which is based on the idea that profit can be generated through the efficient management of productive resources. Good (modernist) knowledge therefore addresses how the efficiency sought by capitalism can be achieved. Organizational practices in the form of hierarchies, technologies and processes (e.g., training and performance appraisals) are designed to support this truth. Experts who create this knowledge are powerful because they determine what can be done by whom and how, as well as who gets rewarded or punished. As long as modernism prevails in mainstream organization theory, proponents of symbolic-interpretive and postmodern perspectives will be excluded whenever they resist the assumptions and philosophical position of modernist discourse.

Burrell recommended focusing on what is considered the same and what is regarded as different within organizational contexts in order to reveal the disciplinary forces and institutional control that is exerted upon us. In my view, this is where a multiple perspectives approach to organization theory makes its most significant contribution. By reflexively studying the multiple discourses of organization theory you can reveal to yourself and possibly to others the ways in which organizations are embedded in society, how they influence our daily lives in ways that we take for granted, and possible alternative ways of organizing and managing. It is this potential that many postmodernists seek to unleash.

Organizational Conflict in Relation to Environment, Social Structure, Technology, Culture, Physical Structure and Power

Critical theorists and many postmodernists assume that conflict is an inevitable aspect of organizing. For example, conflict is implicit in relations of power and control as discussed already and is revealed by linguistic dichotomies such as powerful/powerless, dominant/submissive, insider/outsider and so on.

As you will see in the model of interunit organizational conflict presented below, conflict can be combined with all the other core concepts of organization theory you have studied in Part II of this book: environment, social and physical structure, technology, culture and power. The model also crosses the multiple levels of analysis with which you are by now familiar—environmental, organizational, group and individual. Although the organizational conflict theories presented below arose from the modernist perspective, with the knowledge you now possess about critical, feminist and postmodern perspectives on power, politics and control, you should be able to adapt these frameworks to embrace these other perspectives. You may even be ready to develop your own theory of conflict or to deconstruct one of these.

Organizational Performance is Contingent on Conflict Levels

Organizational conflict has most often been defined as struggle between two or more groups in an organization, or between two or more organizations. In general, **conflict** is centered on some state or condition that favors one group over others and occurs when the activities of one group are perceived as interfering with the outcomes or efforts of other groups. American social psychologists Daniel Katz and Robert Kahn defined conflict as 'a particular kind of interaction, marked by efforts at hindering, compelling, or injuring and by resistance or retaliation against those efforts'.[48]

One widely accepted modernist theory of organizational conflict proposes that both too little and too much conflict result in poor performance, whereas performance is optimized by an intermediate **level of conflict**; in other words, there is a curvilinear relationship between conflict and organizational performance (see Figure 8.2). Accordingly, conflict should be managed so as to produce the benefits of optimal stimulation of ideas and fresh points of view, and to strengthen intragroup cohesiveness while minimizing the negative effects of uncooperative behavior or open hostility between units or individuals.

Recognize, however, that one of the forces that solidifies group identity and enhances cohesiveness is in conflict with other groups. Because of the benefits of group cohesiveness

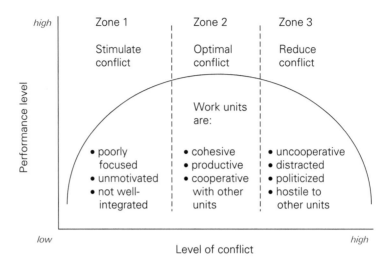

Figure 8.2 The curvilinear relationship between conflict and performance

Strategies for conflict management differ depending on whether the organization is experiencing too little or too much conflict (see Tables 8.4 and 8.5). Characteristics typical of those experiencing conflict in each zone are described beneath the curve.

Table 8.4 Ways to reduce conflict in organizations

Recommended action	Implicit strategy
Physical separation	Avoidance
Increase resources	Avoidance
Repress emotions and opinions	Avoidance
Create superordinate goals	Collaboration
Emphasize similarities	Smoothing
Negotiate	Compromise
Appeal to higher authority	Hierarchical referral
Rotate jobs	Structural change
Physical proximity	Confrontation

Based on: Robbins (1974); Neilsen (1972); Pondy (1967).

in stimulating productivity, some organizations intentionally create competition between units to maximize productivity; however, the price of this extra productivity can be poor cooperation and communication between groups. Therefore the tradeoff between the productive influences of interunit competition must be balanced against the negative effects that conflict can generate. Prescriptions for reducing and encouraging conflict, such as those listed in Tables 8.4 and 8.5, will help you to apply this theory. However, to make effective use of such lists, you must have a clear understanding of the situation you face. This is where a second model of conflict is helpful.

Table 8.5 Ways to stimulate conflict

- Acknowledge repressed conflict
- Role model functional conflict through open disagreement and collaborative responses
- Alter established communication channels
- Hold back information
- Overcommunicate
- Deliver deliberately ambiguous messages
- Differentiate activities or outcomes among subordinates
- Challenge the existing power structure

Based on: Robbins (1974).

The Interunit Conflict Model

Explaining conflict in organizations is tricky because humans employ numerous psychological defense mechanisms and conscious strategies in order to disengage from overt conflict, including avoidance, smoothing, compromise, problem solving, and hierarchical referral (examples are given in Table 8.4). Thus, overt conflict does not occur every time the opportunity for conflict presents itself. You will find that explanations for specific instances of conflict are easily constructed in retrospect, but predicting when overt conflict is going to occur before it actually happens is much more difficult. To aid in predicting and understanding conflict, organization theorists Richard Walton and John Dutton offered a framework for assessing the possible sources of organization conflict in a given situation (see Figure 8.3).[49] Their theory was based on the study of conflicts between sales and production departments in two firms.

Figure 8.3 A model showing the possible sources of interunit conflict

Conflict is seen to be embedded in local conditions which are even more deeply rooted in the environment and organizational context. *Based on:* Walton and Dutton (1969).

At first, you will understand Walton and Dutton's interunit conflict model best if you read Figure 8.3 backwards, that is, from right to left. It may also help you to grasp the value of this model if you think of a specific occurrence of organizational conflict you have experienced. As I work through the various parts of the model, use your example to analyze the immediate or local conditions associated with this instance of conflict. First I will show you how to find the local conditions for your example of conflict, and then how to dig into its deeper sources in the organization and its environment.

Local Conditions for Interunit Conflict

Walton and Dutton began with the observable indices of conflict shown on the right side of Figure 8.3. Observable indices represent what you are likely to see or experience in a conflict situation. This can range from open hostility to complete avoidance of interaction. In between these extremes lie expressions of distrust and disrespect, information distortion, frequent use of 'we–they' rhetoric, or simply the lack of assistance or cooperation.

Be sure to notice that, although they are called observable indices, lack of cooperation and avoidance of interaction can be extremely difficult to observe. These conditions are felt more than seen and require you to be attentive to what is absent from a situation as well as to what is present. I find theories to be extremely useful for recognizing absences. As I attempt to apply the various concepts and models, I become aware that something is missing when a component of a model is not being discussed. As a researcher or consultant, this recognition helps me to ask pertinent questions and to frame problems in new ways. Managers who learn to use theory in this way similarly find that it helps them to understand, communicate about and solve organizational problems, sometimes before they even become problems!

Walton and Dutton traced the observable indices of conflict to nine local conditions, many of which you should now be able to see have been influenced by decisions that are politically charged and/or may be implicated in organizational control systems.

Individual differences

Not all people get along with each other. You will encounter many individual differences in organizations—for example, differences in authoritarianism and sociability, self-esteem, gender, race, ethnicity, age or socioeconomic background—and any of these can become a source of conflict. However, it is far too common for managers to attribute instances of conflict within the organization to individual differences or to simply blame one party or the other by taking sides without considering other factors. Generally speaking, this approach is not likely to be effective, since the vast majority of conflicts in organizations are not simply the result of interpersonal differences, but rather are associated with conditions at the group, organizational or environmental level of analysis. In fact, many people who truly have personality conflicts with one another routinely work together in organizations everywhere. Thus, individual differences rarely provide a complete explanation of conflict in organizations and one or more of the remaining local conditions are likely to be involved.

Group characteristics resulting from differentiation

Each internally differentiated unit of an organization performs a different task and/or copes with a different segment of the environment. These differences become conditions ripe for conflict when units develop distinct discourses, subcultures and identities producing multiple interests with the potential to collide. When the differentiated units are expected to coordinate their activities and share resources and opportunities, the potential for conflict is magnified. If the organization adds layers of management or additional units to bridge relations between conflicted parties, then the opportunities for conflict begin to multiply.

American sociologist William Foote Whyte studied a classic conflict between organizational units—that which occurs in restaurants between wait staff and cooks.[50] Whyte found that these two groups differed markedly in their flexibility, their time horizons, and the results for which they were held accountable. Wait persons followed strict routines in order to be efficient enough to give adequate attention to all of their customers, while cooks remained flexible so they could adapt to the unpredictable flow of customer orders coming into the kitchen. Wait persons generally kept track of time in terms of the stages of a meal, whereas cooks thought in terms of shifts (e.g., lunch, dinner). Wait persons were accountable to the customer for their efficiency, demeanor and accuracy in taking and communicating orders, while cooks were evaluated on their culinary achievements. These differences defined the unique characteristics of the subcultures to which the waitresses and cooks belonged and these group characteristics made communication and coordination between them difficult.

Operative-level goal incompatibility

Goals defined at the highest levels of an organization must be translated and divided between the units and positions of the organization so that a variety of activities will ultimately be performed to achieve them (review Figure 8.1). Once the goals have been translated to the operative level, however, it is often the case that trade-offs are revealed. For instance, marketing departments typically state their goals in terms of sales to customers, which are enhanced by responsiveness to customer demands for services, such as fast delivery or customized product designs. A traditional manufacturing unit, on the other hand, will usually specify its goals in terms of efficiency of production, which is best served by standardizing the product line and producing economically determined lot sizes at a steady rate regardless of the flow of customer orders. While both efficiency in production and service to the customer contribute to the overall performance of the firm, there is plenty of opportunity for disagreement and hostility to develop as each group pursues its key objectives.

Task interdependence

As James Thompson explained (see Chapter 5), there are at least three different forms of task interdependence and each implies different amounts and types of conflict. Pooled task interdependence demands very little in the way of interaction in order for the interdependent units to perform their tasks, which translates into few opportunities for direct conflict because each unit can pursue its own goals and interests more or less independently of the others. Reciprocal task interdependence, on the other hand, demands almost continuous interaction and therefore offers unlimited opportunities for conflict. However, the opportunities for conflict are moderated by mutuality—each group relies upon the other to achieve its objectives so that open conflict hinders both parties simultaneously. Thus reciprocal task interdependence tends to produce periods of non-conflicted interaction punctuated by periods of intense conflict because, when reciprocal interdependence breaks down, there is usually rapid escalation on both sides so that the situation reaches crisis proportions in a hurry. Contrast both pooled and reciprocal task interdependence with sequential task interdependence where one unit is highly dependent on another but the dependency is not reciprocated. The independent unit has little incentive to respond to the interests and demands of the dependent unit and this can set up conditions for chronic conflict between them.

Rewards and performance criteria

When performance criteria and rewards emphasize the distinct performance of separate units, they downplay the combined performance of the entire organization and lead units to ignore the value of cooperation. Consider the problem of giving exams to multiple sections of students taking the same course in a given semester. One way to ensure that students in earlier sections will not give the questions to students in later sections is to inform them that all examinations will be graded on the same standard, and that if students in later sections get the exam questions and improve their own scores it will be at the expense of students who did not have this advantage. Notice how the creation of a conflict of interests between students leads to elimination of cooperation between them. Also be aware that while this strategy may increase fairness in the grading system, such strategies may be counterproductive from the viewpoint of encouraging information-sharing and the formation of cooperative study groups that benefit all students and the classes they attend.

Common resources

Dependence on a common pool of scarce resources will often provoke conflict. The resources can include, for example, operating funds or capital allocations, physical space, shared equipment (e.g., copying machines, computer terminals), and centralized staff services (secretarial, administrative, computer, or other technical support). Also, because the acquisition of resources can indicate power, additional pressure to compete for scarce resources adds to the conflict potential of these situations. Consider how your frustration level increases with the length of the queue for using a shared copy machine or one of the limited number of computer terminals in the library. When two groups each face pressures to work rapidly, claims about their relative need for access to shared resources can quickly escalate into open hostility that can create long-lasting ill-will between them.

Status incongruity

Conflict can occur whenever two groups have significantly different statuses within the organization yet are asked to coordinate their activities. The imbalance of status is not problematic as long as higher status groups influence lower status groups; however, if lower status groups must initiate activities or otherwise directly influence higher status groups, then conflict is more likely to occur than it would without the incongruity. Conflicts of this sort were observed by Whyte in his study of the relations between waitresses and cooks when the waitresses initiated activity for the cooks by giving them customer orders. Similar conflicts were observed where engineers directed a higher status research group to do routine testing.[51] In both cases the inversion of a status hierarchy led to breakdowns in interunit cooperation. You can observe conflict of this sort in required classes on organizational behavior (OB) in business schools. Grades in these classes often invert the status hierarchies of business schools that place the quantitatively gifted on top of those having other abilities, like the people skills that are rewarded in OB classes. This inversion frequently leads to conflicts between finance students and their organizational behavior professors and also contributes to devaluing this subject within groups that are dominated by high-status students.

Jurisdictional ambiguities

Jurisdictional ambiguities occur when there is unclear delineation of responsibility. This condition produces conflict when credit or blame is at stake. Situations in which it is unclear which groups or units deserve credit or blame present an opportunity for the groups to come into conflict as each tries to take credit from, or assign blame to, the other. A lost order in a busy restaurant kitchen is a problem that triggers this sort of conflict when wait staff and cooks each can claim that the other is at fault. Whyte showed that the addition of food servers to buffer communication between wait staff and cooks eased this conflict but only when this new group was given responsibility for tracking all orders, thus eliminating the ambiguity of who was at fault for a lost order.

Communication obstacles

When units speak different languages, they are less likely to agree on issues of mutual concern and more likely to attribute the lack of agreement to intransigence and self-interest by the other party, than to understand it as the result of the two groups looking at things in incommensurable ways. Take the example of resident doctors and hospital administrators. Conflicts between these groups can often be traced, at least in part, to the different ways in which they communicate. Each of their discourses (medical vs. administrative) depends upon language that serves the unique purposes of their group, but as each group uses its preferred terms the other group feels its interests are being marginalized, a situation that can provoke resistance and hostility. Similar communication obstacles are famous sources of conflict between university departments whose faculties are professionally committed to producing well-differentiated (and some would say impenetrable) discourses.

Environment and Organization as Contexts for Interunit Conflict

It is now time to consider the deeper patterns that relate observable conflict and its local conditions to the environment, and to other aspects of organizing we have studied in this book. When you grasp the larger picture you learn how to put conflict in its proper perspective, even when those around you are caught in the grip of negative emotions.

Environment

The principle of isomorphism suggests that organizations attempt to match the complexity and rate of change in their environments by internal differentiation in the form of both vertical and horizontal structural complexity and by adaptation of these structures as necessitated by environmental change. Changing environmental conditions are often experienced as uncertainty within the organization, and groups that develop greater capacities for coping with the uncertainty can then alter organizational power relations between units. Altered power relations can shift control over, as well as need for resources, reward distributions, relative status, jurisdictions and so on. Thus, complexity and change in the environment of an organization can contribute to any or all of the local conditions for conflict reviewed above.

Strategy

A growth strategy for an organization leads to increases in size and differentiation within an organization with effects similar to those just related to environmental complexity and change, including an increase in internal complexity and changes in the existing power structure. Downsizing also contributes to conflict by creating the perception of shrinking resources, which provokes competition over what remains to be divided. When jobs are on the line, competition becomes fierce. Thus, strategies that effect organizational size in either a positive or a negative direction can magnify the effects of some or all of the local conditions for conflict. On the other hand, periods of abundance can mask conflict, so in these periods you may not find it easy to observe conflict even though it exists.

Technology

The organization's tasks are defined in large measure by its choice of technology, and changes in technology mean changes in the tasks assigned to units and individuals. Since the assignment of tasks influences the amount and type of interdependence between units of the organization, technologies set up at least this local condition for organizational conflict. But technology can also influence other local conditions, for example, status incongruity (e.g., when a new technology is introduced technical experts often need to instruct higher level organizational members in its use), reward criteria (new tasks demand different control structures), and even group characteristics (as when computers were new and organizations added information technology specialists to their organization structures).

Social structure

The creation and maintenance of a hierarchy of authority defines the basis for vertical conflict in the organization, while the division of labor separates the organization in a way that presents opportunities for horizontal conflict. Thus, choices about social structure (i.e., organizational design, see Chapter 9) lay a foundation for all the local conditions of conflict.

Organizational culture

Subcultures may develop on the basis of divergence from dominant values in the organization. Divergent values may be interpreted as independent of the dominant culture in which case they are less likely to contribute to conflict, or they may diverge in opposition to dominant values, in which case they are more likely to contribute to conflict. Similarly, divergence in basic assumptions between groups can help to explain the communication obstacles that arise in many organizations. For instance, the assumption that science is a communal activity that requires the sharing of research findings within the scientific community brings research and development scientists into conflict with representatives of corporate legal departments who believe that protecting the patent rights of the company depends upon *not* sharing research findings.

Physical structure

Differentiation of groups, communicated through differences in the quality or style of physical settings, can feed feelings of superiority or inferiority among work units. These conditions can contribute to all the local conditions for conflict or may increase sensitivity to the conflicts inherent in other contextual factors. In addition, physical proximity contributes to conflict when it makes otherwise conflicted groups accessible to one another, while physical distance can reduce opportunities for engaging in conflict behavior but may introduce an obstacle to communication. Layout of physical facilities and the locations of groups and individuals can produce or eliminate communication obstacles and affect the level of conflict that is due to task interdependence.

Applying the Interunit Conflict Model

Once you have grasped the pattern of conflict you should find it easier to read Figure 8.3 from left to right. You can then use the model to help visualize the organization and its environment as a context for group and individual conflict. But remember the lessons of structuration theory—conflict can change organizations and their environments because contexts embed agents whose actions produce and reproduce their contexts. Remember as well that the use of conflict to change organizations is a political act that depends upon the use of power and the ability to control others and that power and control, like conflict itself, may be suppressed and hidden from view. Thus are the themes of power, control and conflict intertwined, and all the perspectives of organization theory brought to bear on them.

SUMMARY

When politics is needed to overcome legitimate differences in preferences for goals or methods, then the coalitional model of decision making is of great value in resolving conflicts and moving organizations forward to take action. Politics loses its organizational usefulness, however, when it is applied to situations in which these conditions do not hold. This does not mean that politics will never be misapplied in organizations. A seasoned organizational politician can create conflict out of nearly any situation and will do so if the stakes are high enough. The bad feelings you may have experienced surrounding political maneuvering in organizations most likely stem from the misapplication of politics within organizational decision-making processes and the consequent counterproductive occurrence of conflict that such behavior can produce. However, you should recognize the useful aspects of political behavior as well as its dangers.

Traditional views suggest that the political process is most effectively managed by seeking a balance between too little and too much political activity, channeling political action into situations where it will be of value, and discouraging it when conditions favor other decision-making activities. However, critical, postmodern and feminist studies should remind you to be self-reflexive about the judgments you make as to what is a useful and what is a disruptive use of political action. If managers only permit political discourse around issues that do not challenge *their* claims to authority and autonomy, then suppression of voices within the organization is likely to occur. Since suppression can affect productivity, particularly where innovation is important, even the most modern of managers will do well to reflect honestly on their motivations concerning political actions—their own and those of other members of the organization. Postmodernism encourages managers to understand that power is part of everyday social relationships and can lead to unintended consequences and repressive practices that dehumanize and mechanize the self. By revealing these practices, along with the gendered nature of organizing and organizations, more ethical and responsive forms of organizing can be created.

For critical and many feminist organizational scholars, power is evident in the domination of one group over another and is reflected in social, economic and class structures. Seen from this perspective, organizations are systems of power relations that exist within broader historical, ideological, economic, and social conditions. The focus of these organization theorists is on the oppression of workers by owners and managers, and how the capitalist ideology is maintained willingly by all members of society. They examine the material differences and injustices associated with the control of one group over another—with control being exercised through the deskilling of work (labor process theory) and by workers giving their active consent to the policies, practices and requirements of management (hegemony and false consciousness). While some critical theorists focus on a theoretical critique, others have carried out empirical studies of how power relationships are produced and maintained in organizational practices and these merge with the perspective of postmodernists who study the effects of voice and other acts of resistance within the context of everyday organization life, often using the ethnographic methods introduced by symbolic-interpretive culture theorists.

Critical theorists have studied taken-for-granted inequalities lying within ideologies, the negative effects of instrumental reasoning on human beings and the planet, false consciousness and systematically distorted communication. By doing this they attempted to ensure that all interests are heard and no one's interest dominates. As you have seen, postmodern scholars use concepts of difference and fragmentation to study conflicts between different constructions of reality and the marginalization of groups of people. They believe that by bringing conflict and resistance into the open, they can reclaim a space for those marginalized voices. Meanwhile, modernist approaches carry on viewing conflict as a manageable tool for leveraging worker and organizational productivity.

KEY TERMS

coalition
power
political frame
strategic contingencies for developing power
politics of resource dependence
symbols of power
output control
behavioral control
cybernetic control
agency theory
agency problem
market control

bureaucratic control
clan control
ideology
false consciousness
hegemony
three faces of power
labor process theory
deskilling
instrumental vs. communicative rationality
systematically distorted communication
workplace democracy
gender stereotypes

stratification
dual labor market theory
gendered organizations
disappearing
disciplinary power
surveillance and self-surveillance
the gaze

interiorization
three circuits of power
   episodic
   dispositional
   facilitative
levels of conflict and performance
interunit conflict model

ENDNOTES

1. Tannenbaum (1968: 3).

2. Bacharach and Lawler (1980: 1).

3. Simon (1957, 1959), March and Simon (1958); see also Cyert and March (1963) and March (1978).

4. Dahl (1957: 203).

5. Dalton (1959); see also Mechanic (1962).

6. Bolman and Deal (2003).

7. Pfeffer (1981b: 7).

8. Pfeffer (1981b: 110).

9. Crozier (1964).

10. Salancik and Pfeffer (1974), Pfeffer and Moore (1980).

11. Hickson et al. (1971).

12. Pfeffer and Salancik (1978).

13. Pfeffer (1981a).

14. Eisenhardt (1985).

15. Ouchi (1979: 845); see also Ouchi and McGuire (1975).

16. Williamson (1975).

17. Gramsci (1971).

18. Alvesson and Willmott (1996: 98).

19. Wikipedia (en.wikipedia.org/wiki/Newspeak, accessed 6-21-2005).

20. Lukes (1974).

21. Gabriel (2000).

22. All following interview excerpts from Cunliffe (1997).

23. Braverman (1974).

24. Sewell (1998).

25. Habermas (1971).

26. Deetz (1992b).

27. Craig and Pencavel (1992).

28. Mondragón has recently deviated from cooperative principles by hiring non-member workers and centralizing decision making (http://www.geo.coop/huet.htm).

29. See Calás and Smircich (1999), Deetz (1992a), Gherardi (1995).

30. Flax (1990: 151–2).

31. Doeringer and Piore (1971).

32. Czarniawska and Sevón (forthcoming).

33. Ibid. 139.

34. Ashcraft and Mumby (2004: xv).

35. Acker (1992: 249). See also Calás and Smircich (1992).

36. For example, see Grant and Tancred (1992) and Martin, Knopoff and Beckman (1998).

37. Fletcher (1998).

38. Ashcraft and Mumby (2004).

39. Ferguson (1994: 90).

40. Ibid. 91.

41. Foucault (1980a).

42. Deetz (1992a: 37).

43. Foucault (1980b).

44. Townley (1994).

45. Clegg (1989).

46. Deetz (1998).

47. Burrell (1988).

48. Katz and Kahn (1966: 615).

49. Walton and Dutton (1969).

50. Whyte (1949).

51. Seiler (1963).

REFERENCES

Acker, Joan (1992). Gendering organizational theory. In A. J. Mills and P. Tancred (eds.), *Gendering organizational theory*. Newbury Park, Calif.: Sage, 248–60.

Alvesson, M., and Willmott, H. (1996). *Making sense of management: A critical introduction*. London: Sage.

Ashcraft, K. L., and Mumby, D. K. (2004). *Reworking gender: A feminist communicology of organization*. Thousand Oaks: Sage.

Bacharach, Samuel B., and Lawler, Edward J. (1980). *Power and politics in organizations*. San Francisco: Jossey-Bass.

Bolman, Lee G., and Deal, Terrece E. (2003). *Reframing organizations: Artistry, choice and leadership* (3rd edn.). San Francisco: Jossey-Bass.

Braverman, Harry (1974). *Labour and monopoly capital: The degradation of work in the twentieth century*. New York: Monthly Review Press.

Burrell, G. (1988). Modernism, post modernism and organizational analysis 2: The contribution of Michel Foucault. *Organization Studies*, 9: 221–35.

Calás, M. B., and Smircich L. (1992). Using the 'F' word: Feminist theories and the social consequences of organizational research. In A. J. Mills and P. Tancred (eds.), *Gendering organizational theory*. Newbury Park, Calif.: Sage, 222–34.

——— (1999). From 'the woman's' point of view: Feminist approaches to organization studies. In S. R. Clegg and C. Hardy (eds.), *Studying organization: Theory and Method*. London: Sage, 212–51.

Clegg, S. R. (1989). *Frameworks of power*. London: Sage.

Craig, B., and Pencavel, J. (1992). The behavior of worker cooperatives: The plywood companies. *American Economic Review*, 82: 1083–1106.

Crozier, Michel (1964). *The bureaucratic phenomenon*. London: Tavistock.

Cunliffe, Ann L. (1997). Managers as practical authors: A social poetics of managing and the implications for management inquiry and learning. Ph.D. Thesis, Lancaster University, UK.

Cyert, Richard M., and March, James G. (1963). *A behavioral theory of the firm*. Englewood Cliffs, NJ: Prentice-Hall.

Czarniawska, Barbara, and Sevón, Guye (forthcoming). *The thin end of the wedge: Foreign women professors as double strangers in academia*. Malmo: Liber.

Dahl, Robert A. (1957). The concept of power. *Behavioral Science*, 2: 201–15.

Dalton, Melville (1959). *Men who manage*. New York: Wiley.

Deetz, Stanley A. (1992a). Disciplinary power in the modern corporation. In M. Alvesson and H. Willmott (eds.), *Critical management studies*. London: Sage, 21–45.

——— (1992b). *Democracy in an age of corporate colonization: Developments in communication and the politics of everyday life*. Albany: State University of New York Press.

——— (1998). Discursive formations, strategized subordination and self-surveillance. In A. McKinlay and K. Starkey (eds.), *Foucault, management and organization theory*. London: Sage, 151–72.

Doeringer, Peter B., and Piore, Michael J. (1971). *Internal labor markets and manpower analysis*. Lexington, Mass.: Heath.

Eisenhardt, Kathleen M. (1985). Control: Organizational and economic approaches. *Management Science*, 31: 134–49.

Ferguson, Kathy E. (1994). On bringing more theory, more voices and more politics to the study of organization. *Organization*, 1: 81–99.

Flax, Jane (1990). *Thinking fragments: Psychoanalysis, feminism and postmodernism in the contemporary West*. Berkeley: University of California Press.

Fletcher, Joyce (1998). Relational practice: A feminist reconstruction of work. *Journal of Management Inquiry*, 7: 163–88.

Foucault, Michel (1980a). *The history of sexuality*, Vol. 1. *An introduction* (trans. R. Hurley). London: Penguin.

——— (1980b). *Power/knowledge: Selected interviews and other writings by Michel Foucault, 1972–1977* (ed. C. Gordon). New York: Pantheon.

Gabriel, Yiannis (2000). *Storytelling in organizations: Facts, fictions and fantasies*. Oxford: Oxford University Press.

Gherardi, Silvia (1995). *Gender, symbolism and organizational culture*. London: Sage.

Gramsci, Antonio (1971). *Selections from the prison notebooks* (trans. Q. Hoare and G. Nowell-Smith). New York: International.

Grant, Judith, and Tancred, P. (1992). A feminist perspective on state bureaucracy. In A. J. Mills and P. Tancred (eds.), *Gendering organizational theory*. Newbury Park, Calif.: Sage, 112–28.

Habermas, Jürgen (1971). *Toward a rational society*. London: Heinemann.

Hickson, David J., Hinings, C. R., Lee, C. A., Schneck, R. E., and Pennings, J. M. (1971). A strategic contingencies theory of intra-organizational power. *Administrative Science Quarterly*, 16: 216–29.

Katz, Daniel, and Kahn, Robert L. (1966). *The social psychology of organizations*. New York: John Wiley & Sons.

Lukes, Steven (1974). *Power: A radical view*. London: MacMillan.

March, James G. (1978). Bounded rationality, ambiguity, and the engineering of choice. *Bell Journal of Economics*, 9: 587–608.

—— and Simon, Herbert A. (1958). *Organizations*. New York: John Wiley.

Martin, Joanne, Knopoff, K. and Beckman, C. (1998). An alternative to bureaucratic impersonality and emotional labor: Bounded emotionality at the Body Shop. *Administrative Science Quarterly*, 43: 429–69.

Mechanic, David (1962). Sources of power of lower participants in complex organizations. *Administrative Science Quarterly*, 7: 349–64.

Neilsen, Eric H. (1972). Understanding and managing conflict. In J. W. Lorsch and P. R. Lawrence (eds.), *Managing group and intergroup relations*. Homewood, Ill.: Irwin and Dorsey.

Ouchi, William G. (1979). A conceptual framework for the design of organizational control mechanisms. *Management Science*, 25: 833–48.

—— and McGuire, Maryann (1975). Organizational control: Two functions. *Administrative Science Quarterly*, 20: 559–69.

Pfeffer, Jeffrey (1978). The micropolitics of organizations. In M. W. Meyer and Associates (eds.), *Environments and organizations*. San Francisco: Jossey-Bass, 29–50.

—— (1981a). Management as symbolic action: The creation and maintenance of organizational paradigms. In B. M. Staw and L. Cummings (eds.), *Research in organizational behavior*. Greenwich, Conn.: JAI Press, 3: 1–52.

—— (1981b). *Power in organizations*. Boston: Pitman.

—— and Moore, William L. (1980). Power in university budgeting: A replication and extension. *Administrative Science Quarterly*, 25: 637–53.

—— and Salancik, Gerald R. (1978). *The external control of organizations: A resource dependence perspective*. New York: Harper & Row.

Pondy, Louis R. (1967). Organizational conflict: Concepts and models. *Administrative Science Quarterly*, 12: 296–320.

Robbins, Stephen P. (1974). *Managing organizational conflict: A nontraditional approach*. Englewood Cliffs, NJ: Prentice-Hall.

Seiler, J. A. (1963). Diagnosing interdepartmental conflict. *Harvard Business Review*, 41: 121–32.

Sewell, G. (1998). The discipline of teams: The control of team-based industrial work through electronic and peer surveillance. *Administrative Science Quarterly*, 43: 397–429.

Simon, Herbert A. (1957). *Models of man*. New York: John Wiley.

—— (1959). Theories of decision-making in economics and behavioral science. *American Economic Review*, 49: 253–83.

Tannenbaum, Arnold S. (1968). *Control in organizations*. New York: McGraw-Hill.

Townley, B. (1994). *Reframing human resource management: Power, ethics and the subject at work*. London: Sage.

Walton, Richard E., and Dutton, John M. (1969). The management of interdepartmental conflict. *Administrative Science Quarterly*, 14: 73–84.

Whyte, William F. (1949). The social structure of the restaurant. *American Journal of Sociology*, 54: 302–10.

Williamson, Oliver E. (1975). *Markets and hierarchies*. New York: Free Press.

FURTHER READING

Burawoy, M. (1979). *Manufacturing consent: Changes in the labor process under monopoly capitalism.* Chicago: University of Chicago Press.

Czarniawska-Joerges, Barbara (1988). Power as an experiential concept. *Scandinavian Journal of Management,* 4: 31–44.

Dahrendorf, R. (1959). *Class and class conflict in industrial society.* London: Routledge and Keegan Paul.

Emerson, R. M. (1962). Power-dependence relations. *American Sociological Review,* 27: 31–40.

French, J. R., Jr., and Raven, B. H. (1959). The bases of social power. In D. Cartwright (ed.), *Studies in social power.* Ann Arbor: University of Michigan Press, 150–67.

Kanter, Rosabeth Moss (1977). *Men and women of the corporation.* New York: Basic Books.

Knights, David, and Roberts, John (1982). The power of organization or the organization of power? *Organization Studies,* 3: 47–63.

March, James G. (1994). *A primer on decision making: How decisions happen.* New York: Free Press.

—— and Olsen, Johan P. (1976). *Ambiguity and choice in organizations.* Bergen, Norway: Universitetsforlaget.

McKinlay, A., and Starkey, K. (1998) (eds.). *Foucault, management and organization theory.* London: Sage.

Mills, Albert J., and Tanered, Peta (1992) (eds.). *Gendering organizational theory.* Newbury Park, Calif.: Sage.

Mumby, Dennis K. (1988). *Communication and power in organizations: Discourse, ideology and domination.* Norwood, NJ: Ablex Publishing.

Pettigrew, Andrew (1973). *The politics of organizational decision-making.* London: Tavistock.

Pondy, Louis R. (1977). The other hand clapping: An information-processing approach to organizational power. In T. H. Hammer and S. B. Bacharach (eds.), *Reward systems and power distribution.* Ithaca, NY: School of Industrial and Labor Relations, Cornell University, 56–91.

Pringle, Rosemary (1988). *Secretaries Talk: Sexuality, Power and Work.* London: Verso.

Salancik, Gerald R., and Pfeffer, Jeffrey (1977). Who gets power—and how they hold on to it: A strategic contingency model of power. *Organizational Dynamics,* 5: 3–21.

Simon, Herbert A. (1979). Rational decision making in business organizations. *American Economic Review,* 69: 493–513.

Wildavsky, Aaron (1979). *The politics of the budgeting process* (3rd edn.). Boston: Little, Brown.

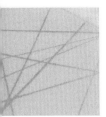

Practical Issues and New Directions in Organization Theory

The conversations and interests of organization theorists have ranged much more broadly than is indicated by the basic concepts and theories described in Part II. In Part III you will confront some of the issues organization theorists grapple with as they apply their theory to practical organizational problems: organizational design and change, knowledge management and organizational learning. You will also learn about ongoing efforts to generate new knowledge about organizations and organizing including: critical realism, complexity theory, network theories, organizational identity and organizational aesthetics. Because the issues to be examined in Part III cut across the perspectives of organization theory and combine many different theories, they provide another, if more complicated, entry point to the study of this field.

The difficulty of keeping concepts and distinctions separate is more acute in Part III than it was in Part II and you will soon discover that Part III synthesizes ideas that were kept separate until now. In a way, the circles of Figure 1.2 will melt together and new lines of demarcation will appear. It is not that the ways of thinking we developed in Part II are wrong, it is that you are now ready to move on to more complex aspects of organization theory and theorizing.

Adding to the complexity in Part III is my assumption that you now know the concepts and theories covered in Part II. In Part III I will chunk these ideas in order to allow greater scope to our discussions. This means that you may need to go back to core concepts and theories covered in earlier chapters to refresh your memory of them. Rereading the earlier material will enrich your concepts and will help you to build associations necessary for theorizing. In the chapters that follow I will indicate some of the connections to material from earlier chapters to help you see how this process works, but you should make your own connections as well. Although it is an inherently messy undertaking, I believe it offers an important step on the road to becoming a theorist. What is more, it is where the fun really begins.

9

Theory in Practice

German-American social psychologist Kurt Lewin once said, 'there is nothing so practical as a good theory.' Generations of organization theorists have clung to this statement for the legitimacy it offers. However, frequently it has proven all too easy to substitute Lewin's pronouncement for doing the hard work of finding the practical contribution theory makes. Nonetheless, just because a theory's relevance is not immediately obvious to you does not mean that it has none. Sometimes to unlock the practical value theory holds you will need to combine several theories, at other times you may find more value in developing your own theory than you will find in the application of existing theories.

In this chapter I invite you to approach theory from the direction of the practical problems managers and other organizational members face. I will show you ways in which organization theory has contributed to understanding and finding solutions to some of these problems. The first issue is a classic: organizational design. As you have seen already, the question of how work can best be organized was on the table at the inception of the field. It remains just as relevant today because globalization and other changes in organizational environments and technology demand new solutions to this perennial problem. Below I will summarize the types of organizational designs that have been proposed over the course of history and then introduce you to two related questions practitioners often ask—how does organizational change occur and how can it be managed? Change is an inherent characteristic of most organizations: environments change, organizations grow, new technologies are introduced, conflicts arise and so on. These changes lead to altered work practices and new personnel, and all of these derail organizational routines and stability.

In regard to approaches to organizational change I will first present the theories proposed by Kurt Lewin and Max Weber. These two theorists provided templates for most of the organizational change models in use today—developmental models and process models. You have seen examples of these two model types already. For example, Greiner's model of evolution and revolution in organizational growth (Chapter 4) traced the development of a typical organization across its lifecycle from birth to death or renewal. My theory of the dynamics of organizational culture (Chapter 6) represents process-based theorizing about organizational change (and stability). Of course there are other approaches to change theory including prescriptive models like those based on modernist thinking such as contingency theory (Chapters 3 and 4). Lewin's model of the stages of planned change (unfreezing—movement—refreezing) represents the most long-standing approach to change management, while Weber's theory of the routinization of charisma describes how the introduction of new ideas or practices by a charismatic authority figure changes individuals and their organizations or societal contexts. Lewin's and Weber's approaches both identify processes that underlie or drive observed changes in behavior and understanding.

The chapter will conclude with some contemporary theories that focus on the relatively new concepts of organizational learning and knowledge management. There I will present some recent empirical studies of organizational change in response to the issues of diversity, corporate social responsibility, sustainability and corporate branding and what they might contribute to the theory of organizational change. These studies all approached theorizing from the direction of observing practice and thus demonstrate how to incorporate practice into theory. But first consider the question of organizational design.

Organizational Design

Theories of **organizational design** are prescriptive by nature in that they seek to address the practical problem of intentionally changing organizational structures and processes to enhance organizational performance. Modernists have traditionally led the way into prescriptive theory, while symbolic-interpretivists typically shy away from prescriptive design specifications due to their descriptive orientation. The main contribution of symbolic-interpretivists has been to urge organizational designers to be sensitive to the culturally embedded meanings that contextualize social orders and to the symbolism of representations like organization charts. Symbolic-interpretive studies of the human consequences of organizational design for everyday experience have aided postmodernists' efforts to bring the interests of those who constitute the organizational structure into focus, along with any processes of hegemony or marginalization. Postmodernists use this research as a basis for prescribing ethically desirable objectives and means for structuring these into organizations.

From a modernist perspective a good organizational design optimizes organizational performance by balancing elements or dimensions of a social structure such as differentiation and integration. Modernists often use criteria such as efficiency and effectiveness to judge organizational designs. For instance, organizational design is **effective** if it guides the attention of employees to the differentiated activities for which they are responsible and promotes ease of integration among all the activities of the organization; it is **efficient** if it minimizes the time, effort and resources needed to achieve organizational goals. Careful analysis of an organizational design will reveal where efficiency and effectiveness are not achieved and organizational design changes can be implemented to address these problems. Bear in mind, however, that every social structure has gaps and conflicts resulting from the practical impossibility of perfectly integrating a differentiated organization. Gaps and conflicts should therefore not automatically be interpreted as bad because they may function in ways that allow an imperfect social structure to work in spite of its imperfections.

Organization theorists and managers alike use organization charts like those introduced in Figure 4.1 to get a quick impression of an organizational design. These charts show some of the main elements of an organizational social structure as well as providing a tool for redesigning an organization. For example, organization charts provide a fairly clear representation of an organization's hierarchy of authority and a general idea of its division of labor. But, be sure to notice that an organization chart does *not* give much information about coordination mechanisms, informal relationships (although some can be represented with dotted lines), or the distribution of power that flows outside the formal hierarchy. An organization chart is a tool for mapping the structure of roles and responsibilities distributed throughout an organization. In the remainder of this section you will find descriptions of generic organizational designs that organization theorists and managers use as templates for designing organizational structures.

Simple Organizational Designs

Extremely small and/or highly organic (flexible, dynamic, de-differentiated, entrepreneurial stage) organizations often appear to have little if any social structure. These cases usually involve **simple designs** characterized by completely flexible relationships with limited differentiation and almost no hierarchy. The members of such organizations can easily carry the organization chart around in their heads so formalization is not required. Attention to tasks is determined by management decree or by mutual agreement and is usually open to direct and informal coordination and supervision that occur as part of the flow of activity with those in authority being constantly available for consultation and instruction. There is little need for delegation, since everyone works, more or less, side-by-side to get the job done. Small size limits specialization in simple organizations because everyone must share in performing tasks as needs arise. Simple organizational designs are characteristic of newly formed organizations (e.g., an entrepreneurial venture) or permanently small organizations (e.g., a traditional, one-dentist dental practice). They also occur within prototype laboratories, product design or project teams, in cross-functional management groups and in many subunits of large organizations.

Functional Organizational Designs

Organizations that grow too complex to be administered using a simple design usually adopt a **functional design** to cope with the increased demands of differentiation. Functional designs are so called because they group activities according to a logic of similarity in work functions (the nature of the work people perform), but functional similarity usually also implies high levels of task interdependence and common goals. For instance, the functions of a typical manufacturing organization include production, sales, purchasing, personnel (or human resource management), accounting, and engineering, and may also include finance, marketing, research and development, public relations and facilities management (Figure 9.1). Within each of these functions, people do similar kinds of related or interdependent work tasks and strive to accomplish a particular set of goals. Functional organizational designs are also common in government organizations, as you can see in the organization chart for the City and County of Honolulu (Figure 9.2).[1]

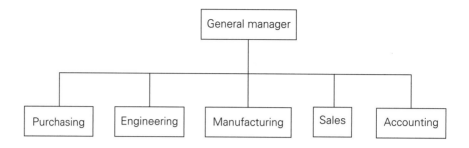

Figure 9.1 An organization chart showing a functional design

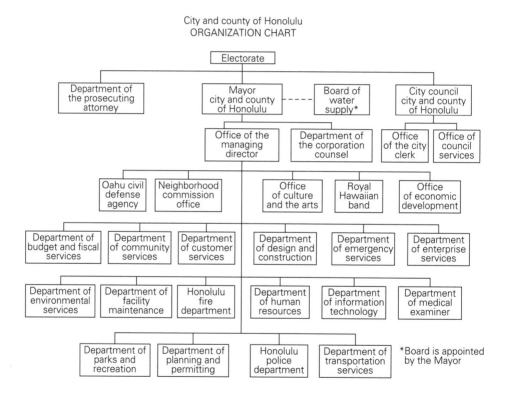

Figure 9.2 Organization chart for the city and county of Honolulu

Functional designs maximize economies of scale resulting from specialization and thus are efficient in the sense that they limit duplication of effort. The logic of functionally designed organizations is highly transparent to employees who can easily recognize the connections between the tasks performed within their function and the tasks others perform (e.g., marketing work is easily differentiated from accounting or manufacturing work).

The downside of this is that employees may develop greater loyalty to their function than to the organization as a whole, leading to the problem of functional silos. Another benefit of functional designs is that they give the top manager in the organization tight control in the sense that this individual is the only person whose position grants them the big picture with respect to what everyone else in the organization is doing. This tight control, however, can also be a major shortcoming because, as the solitary pinnacle of authority, the top manager can easily become overburdened by decision making as the organization grows. Another limitation of functional organization designs is that no one else in the organization has the same breadth of perspective and responsibility, so if the top manager is suddenly lost, no other managers in the organization are well prepared to take over.

Multidivisional Forms

In developmental terms, the organization that outgrows a functional design will often turn to the **multidivisional form** (called M-form, for short) as a means to alleviate overburdened decision makers. The multidivisional form is essentially a set of separate functionally structured units that report to a headquarters staff (see Figure 9.3). Division management of each functionally structured unit is responsible for managing its own day-to-day internal operations (e.g., production scheduling, sales, and marketing), while the headquarters staff take responsibility for financial controls and the long-range strategic development of the firm.

M-form organizations group people, positions, and units in one of three ways, either by similarities in products or production processes, customer type, or geographical region of activity. For example, the NASA Glenn Research Center has four Directorates (Aeronautics, Research and Technology, Space, and Engineering and Technical Services) each of which is subdivided into product divisions.[2] British Telecommunications (BT) is divisionalized by customer type. Its divisions include BT Global Services (worldwide business services and solutions), BT Retail (residential and end-business customers), BT Wholesale (telecommunications networks, sales of network capacity and call terminations

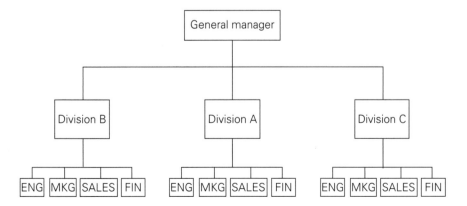

Figure 9.3 An organization chart showing a multidivisional design

to other carriers), BT Exact (network design, telecommunications engineering, IT systems and other services to BT businesses), BT Openworld (international mass-market Internet), all of which are managed by a holding company BT Group plc.[3] The United States Geological Survey (a Department in the US Department of the Interior) is divisionalized on the basis of three geographic regions: Western, Central, and Eastern.[4]

When they are treated as profit centers, multidivisional designs allow for a type of accountability that is not possible in functional designs; each division can be assessed in comparison with its competitors on the basis of its performance in the marketplace, whereas the higher level of interdependence among groups in a functional design makes this type of accountability impossible. However, you should recognize that, within each division of an M-form organization, the problem of functional accountability remains. Nonetheless, M-form organizations are usually able to offer enhanced responsiveness to the needs of customers because the specialization of the organization allows greater focus on the businesses each division operates.

Sometimes companies operate divisions in different industries rather than just divisionalizing products within an industry. Such organizations are known as conglomerates or holding companies. Conglomerates are usually formed by merger or acquisition of other organizations, although not all mergers and acquisitions result in conglomerates. The reasons for forming a conglomerate are generally financial, involving investment opportunities rather than concern for technical economies or market advantages such as are produced by vertical and horizontal integration, which can also be achieved through merger or acquisition. Since the core activities of the conglomerate often consist of unrelated technologies operating in different environments, all information must be reduced to a common denominator in order for top executives to make the comparisons that drive their budgeting decisions. The common denominator is profitability, and therefore concern for profit becomes the driving force within these organizations.

As with other M-forms, strategy at the corporate level of a conglomerate focuses on managing resource flows into divisions. This resource flow management is accomplished via capital investment and budgeting procedures and by creation, acquisition, or divestment of divisions. Business-level strategy and operating decisions are delegated to divisional heads. The main difference between the conglomerate and other M-forms is that top executives of conglomerates come to view their organizations almost entirely in financial terms, rather than in terms of providing goods or services to a particular market or environment. This way of thinking trickles down to the rest of the organization, for example, by creating enormous concern for budgeting decisions, middle managers learn to focus much of their attention on the financial reports that they provide as input to budgeting decisions, sometimes at the expense of other aspects of the business.[5] (Be sure to review Figure 8.1, which shows a modernist control system with resources flowing from the environment downward to all levels of the organization and reporting of how budgeted resources were converted to performance flowing in the opposite direction.)

Most if not all outcomes within the divisions of a conglomerate depend upon decisions concerning how profitability is to be calculated, and arguments over these calculations abound. For example, when divisions sell products to one another, conflicts occur over transfer prices. This is because one division's costs are the other division's revenues. The irony of the multidivisional form is that, for all their emphasis on profit, M-forms generally turn out to be less profitable than their functional equivalents, in part due to the resources diverted to political battles (see below for other reasons).[6] A greater irony is that the financial management model developed within conglomerates has become an institutionalized feature of many organizations that use other design types. In spite of the evidence that the M-form is usually less profitable than other designs, institutional pressures supporting this type of structure cause many managers to prefer the M-form.

One reason that M-form organizations are not as profitable as those using functional designs is that instead of one sales, accounting, production, and purchasing department, the M-form organization has one of each for every division. To the extent that some of the work of these departments is redundant, M-form organizations will be more costly to operate. This redundancy can only be reduced by centralizing some functions (e.g., sales force, supply chain); however, coordination costs are high and the advantages of responsiveness to the market will be lost if the organization moves too far back toward a fully centralized functional design. The costs of integrating multidivisional structures are also greater. Top management must coordinate across several divisions that are often geographically separated. Increased complexity is costly in terms of control loss, travel, and demands for communication.

In spite of the drawbacks, the M-form has several advantages to recommend it. The first of these is size. Multidivisional organizations consistently grow larger than their functional counterparts. Size gives organizations a competitive advantage in that large organizations can have greater influence on their environment and usually occupy more central positions in their interorganizational networks than do small organizations. Larger organizations can typically hire the best executives because most are attracted to the power and influence large organizations command. Furthermore, the resources that are under the control of large organizations give them more opportunities to broaden their competitive activities both domestically and abroad. The multidivisional form also provides better training for future executives than does the functional structure—divisional managers operate with roughly the same perspective and set of responsibilities as would the president of a functionally designed organization, and headquarters staff acquire broad-based experience that is unlikely to be gained within the functional form.

Matrix Designs

The **matrix** was developed with the intention of combining the efficiency of the functional design with the flexibility and responsiveness of the M-form (Figure 9.4). You can think of the matrix organization as having two structures, each of which is the responsibility of a different group of managers. Managers on the functional side of the matrix are responsible for allocating specialists to projects, helping them maintain their skills and acquire new ones, and monitoring their performance with respect to the standards of their functional specialty.

Managers on the project side of the matrix are responsible for overseeing specific projects: planning the project, allocating resources, coordinating work, monitoring task

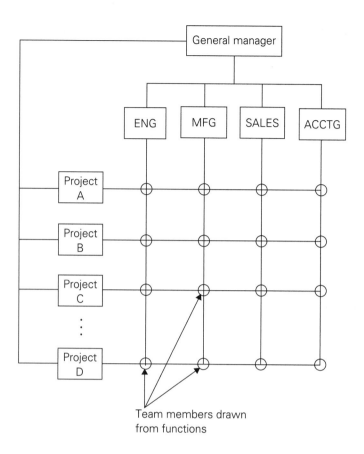

Figure 9.4 An organization chart showing a matrix design

performance, and ensuring project requirements and deadlines are met. The goal of project managers is to bring the project to completion on time and within budget.

The greatest difficulty in using the matrix design lies in managing the conflict built into the dual lines of authority to which employees working inside the matrix are subjected. Functional managers will expect their matrix employees to meet the requirements of their specialty, while project managers want them to adjust to the requirements of the rest of the project team and meet or exceed customer expectations. Thus matrix employees confront the often contradictory expectations of performing complex tasks to high quality specifications while at the same time facing pressure to minimize costs and meet tight schedules. When employees serve on more than one project team, they face the additional pressure of conflicting demands from multiple project leaders. You should recognize, however, that it is this same conflict that provides the primary benefit of the matrix structure; it promotes simultaneous attention to both functional standards and project demands.

Conflict is also built into the jobs of functional chief and project boss. For example, at this level in the matrix conflict frequently emerges over the assignment of persons to projects. Obviously some individuals and some task assignments will be preferred over others and political maneuvering is to be expected in the project team formation process. Another challenge with matrix structures is that the person responsible for the total matrix design will need to balance the functional and project interests to be certain that one side of the matrix does not dominate the other. The result of an imbalance is to lose most of the benefits of using the matrix form, either the flexibility of the M-form or the efficiency of a functional design.

In spite of the considerable difficulties inherent in adapting to the conflicts and pressures of a matrix, this organizational design has offsetting advantages to recommend it. One is enormous flexibility to take on new projects. Within both functional and M-form designs, starting up a new activity generally requires a major structural adjustment (i.e., adding a responsibility to every function or creating a new division), whereas starting a new project is a common event within matrix organizations. Structurally, at least, starting a new project in a matrix organization only entails finding a project manager and recruiting a team. Thus a matrix retains the flexibility of the M-form to provide customer service and respond to opportunities in the environment.

Another advantage of matrix designs derives from their unique ability to maximize the value of expensive specialists. This is because the talents of specialists can be pooled for use among a wide variety of projects, some of which may be otherwise unrelated and thus likely to remain structurally unconnected in the M-form. Although the individual specialist will have to deal with the fragmentation that this disconnectedness implies (e.g., working on two or more unrelated projects for project managers who have little concern for the specialists' competing responsibilities), from the perspective of the organization, the sharing out of specialized capabilities creates the considerable efficiency the functional design offers relative to the multidivisional form. This is because where the M-form would hire potentially redundant specialists for each of its divisions, the matrix can more easily use its specialists to their full capacity.

Hybrid Designs

The organizational designs examined above represent pure types. Organizations will not always conform to one of these. **Hybrid designs** are partly one design type and partly another. Hybrids may occur either because designers deliberately mix forms in an attempt to blend the advantages of two or more different types, or because the organization is changing. For example, a research and development unit may use a matrix, while other units are organized functionally. Most big companies today are hybrids. They are combinations of corporate functions, matrices and divisions that may also embrace joint ventures and alliances, licensing arrangements, supplier contracts and so on (see below).

Many networks (discussed below) also combine forms. Hybrid forms can be confusing in that the basis of relationships changes as you move from one part of the organization to another. On the other hand, the hybrid form allows the organization the flexibility to adopt the design most appropriate to the varied needs of its different subunits.

Strategic Alliances and Joint Ventures

Strategic alliances represent contractual, often long-term, relationships created between different organizations to allow collaboration on new opportunities, such as the development of a new product or technology transfer. Alliances can be formed with or between government organizations or with organizations in the same or different industries and countries, and even between competitors. They can take the form of joint ventures or contracts (e.g., licensing arrangements, supplier and distributor contracts) and involve two or more organizations cooperating to design, produce, and distribute a product or service. In a **joint venture** (JV), a separate organization (the joint venture) is created to manage the relationship, whereas in a contractual alliance there is no new organization, at least not formally speaking. Companies operating within both alliances and joint ventures help their partner organizations utilize their strengths, reduce uncertainty, learn, minimize costs, share risk and facilitate low-cost entry into new markets.

Nissan and Renault exemplify a successful alliance between two global automotive manufacturers, one headquartered in Japan and the other headquartered in France. These organizations are legally separate companies that compete in a few markets but who share manufacturing facilities, automotive designs, and, from time to time, executives. Carlos Ghosn now heads up Renault, but was on loan as Nissan's CEO during its now famous turn-around and continued to hold Nissan's top position even after returning to Renault. Airbus is an example of a joint venture. This European consortium of French, German, Spanish, and UK companies was established in the 1970s to enable the Europeans to share development costs and compete with much larger U.S. aircraft manufacturers. In 2001 Airbus became a single company incorporating the joint stock of EADS and BAE. Based in Toulouse, France, the company is managed by an Executive Committee of ten members and so far has captured about 50 percent of the global aircraft market.[7]

Multinationals and the Global Matrix

The **multinational organization** is involved in activities in two or more countries. With its headquarters located in a single country, its culture and organizational structure will be typical of the expectations and practices of the headquarters location, but it will standardize technologies and organizing processes and policies throughout its domain of operation. Thus nationality is an issue for most people within a multinational organization.

Global organizations establish a worldwide presence in one or more activities, adopt a worldwide strategy, and develop an outlook that is focused on the world as a whole rather than on nations or borders. Although the global organization is likely to maintain a single headquarters, the organization is typically managed by a team whose members live in diverse locations. The top managers of a global organization will spend as much or more time abroad than at home. Its worldly outlook means that the culture of the global organization values diversity and its policies, practices and technologies are likely to be less standardized than those of a nationally dominated multinational organization. Flexibility is essential to global organizations for which changing patterns of opportunities and threats in the world alter the environment ceaselessly. Global organizations develop a worldwide presence and do not hesitate to breech traditional boundaries, particularly those that involve nationalistic thinking. For example, when Brazilian-born French executive Carlos Ghosn took over as CEO of Nissan, he overturned that company's adherence to the Japanese tradition of guaranteeing lifetime employment to its workers. While we typically think of large organizations, firms of any size can be global as interorganizational networks and the Internet allow even extremely small organizations to take advantage of global opportunities.

In these days of increasing international competition, many organizations are strategically positioning themselves to take advantage of opportunities around the world. An organization that desires to move beyond a purely domestic orientation to operate on a multinational or even a global scale will confront the need for structural adaptation. This is because the new orientation will require the organization to engage in new activities that will put differentiation pressures on existing structures. A functionally designed organization that merely wants to market its products or services abroad, or wants to take advantage of low-cost labor to produce products for home markets, will generally form a new department to handle the details of import and export, usually by subcontracting with experts in the markets in which the organization wants to be involved. At this stage the organization is really not multinational in its focus, but rather remains committed to the logic of its domestic business.

As experience with non-domestic markets accumulates, the organization will typically become aware of opportunities abroad and become more experienced at addressing them, at least in one or a few of its foreign locations. At this point many of the activities that were originally subcontracted will be brought in-house and an international division will be formed. Notice that the M-form structure adopted at this stage allows the organization to maintain essentially a multi-domestic orientation. That is, it acts like a firm operating domestically in several national markets at once, similar to the way a conglomerate operates in several industries at the same time.

Finally, the multinational corporation (MNC) appears. This comes about as international sales become the main source of organizational revenues and as suppliers, manufacturers, and distributors from a variety of countries form an interdependent interorganizational network on a truly multinational scale. No longer can the activities of the firm be separated into either domestic or international units, and the international division is replaced by a multinational product or geographic M-form structure in which all units engage in the coordination of international activities. Of course, as with conglomerate M-forms, an organization can achieve a multinational structure either through internal growth, generally progressing through the stages described above, or through joint venture, merger, and/or acquisition.

The multinational product or geographical divisional forms confront the same drawbacks, as do domestic M-form organizations. The desire to be more efficient and flexible leads to matrix structures that move MNC logics into the domain of global thinking (see Figure 9.5). In a global matrix there are managers of geographic regions and of products or product groups such that local units are organized both by interests in corporate effectiveness related to serving a particular region of the world and by interests in developing the corporation's knowledge and efficiency in regard to production across regional markets. Each of the local units can be fully operational companies in their own right, and the array of the units that comprise the MNC may be a hybrid of any of the other designs described above.

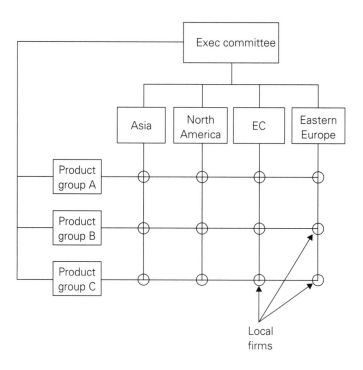

Figure 9.5 The global matrix

Obviously, a major drawback of MNCs and global matrices are their often mind-boggling complexity. Even with electronic communication and rapid transportation between most destinations, the coordination problems of these organizations stretch modernist organization designs to their breaking point. As complexity increases through demands for attention to more than the two or three dimensions that can be represented in an organization chart, the fragmentation and incoherence about which postmodernists write becomes increasingly apparent. Here, an image of fragmented organizations as networks of loosely connected interests operating without grand narratives of overarching corporate strategy overtakes the idyllic images of planning and control offered by modernist organization theory. Here, too, the importance of symbolism becomes hard to deny, as symbols may be the only means to form webs of social relationship between network partners. Think of Benetton's controversial 'United Colors of Benetton' international advertising campaign, for example. The meanings and interpretations of these symbols are unlikely to be controllable worldwide, but they become the focus of network identity around which relationships among network partners cohere.

Organizational Networks and Virtual Organizations

Network organizations are formed by nonhierarchical relationships comprised of human points of contact called nodes. Organizationally, networks link headquarters with subsidiaries and business units with each other, their stakeholders and their employees. They are typically represented by maps showing nodes linked by the number of interactions connecting them (look again at Figure 3.3 and imagine that the circles are business units, teams or individuals within an organization).

Virtual organizations are networks of people whose connections take place primarily or entirely via electronic media, as opposed to face-to-face interaction. For example, the market created on e-bay lets buyers and sellers negotiate exchanges safely, easily and without ever making contact except through the Internet. Wikipedia, an online encyclopedia, is another virtual organization, this one comprised of user volunteers who edit one another's entries and socialize new contributors.[8] Of course, some virtual networks, like on-line dating services, exist to create a means for people to meet non-virtually, so there are hybrid blends of virtual organizations and traditional networks for you to consider.

Networks of organizations are most likely to form when organizations face rapid technological change, shortened product lifecycles, and fragmented, specialized markets. In such a network, needed assets are distributed among several network partners, such that it is not a single organization within the network that produces products or services, but rather the network at large that is the producer or provider. Most, if not all, vertical communication and control relationships are replaced with lateral relationships and partnerships among several organizations in these networks. Networks can result from outsourcing a strategic alliance or from collaboration between small firms whose scale of operations would not allow them to compete in international markets by themselves. Sometimes a network will be formed by spinning off units from an original organization that retains only those activities for which it has a particular competence. All other necessary activities are purchased from other organizations including the spin-offs. When all the task activities are outsourced, you have a virtual organization.

Benetton is an example of a network organization. It is comprised of hundreds of small clothing manufacturers and thousands of franchised sales outlets arrayed around a central distribution channel with a common information and control system. Some of the manufacturers within the Benetton network were spun off the original Benetton operation, while others joined the network because their small size would otherwise have left them out of the international fashion market in which Benetton firms participate. In addition to managing distribution channels (which are also part of the network) Benetton provides its suppliers with technical manufacturing expertise, much of the necessary equipment and sometimes capital, and handles marketing efforts for the network.

Within a network structure, partners are linked by supplier–customer relationships that resemble a free market system. That is, goods are bought and sold between network partners just as they would be on the open market. In this way competitive pressures on the supplying partners keep downward pressure on prices. Also, the use of market mechanisms to coordinate activities eliminates much of the need for the vertical hierarchy of traditional organizations and this reduces administrative overhead. These characteristics of network organizations reduce their overall costs and increase efficiency and profitability, which help keep the network competitive. The German TV industry provides an example of a network of temporary project-based organizations.[9] When a broadcaster commissions a TV program, producers bring together mostly independent writers, directors, camera people, actors, and other media specialists to work on the project. The collaboration ends when the program is completed.

There are some advantages associated with networks: they encourage information sharing, liberate decision making and inspire innovation. Also, networks are capable of extremely rapid information exchange because they can process information in multiple directions at the same time. Rapid information exchange enables network partners to exploit opportunities often before non-networked competitors even become aware that they exist. Relative independence of decision making allows experimentation and learning, and new learning can be rapidly diffused throughout the network. By enhancing the spread of information and bringing together different logics and novel combinations of information, networks provide the conditions for innovation. On the other hand, a simple economic relationship between network partners can lead to exploitation by partners who gain control of critical information or resources, such as by key suppliers who are able to create and take advantage of dependencies in the larger system (i.e., charging higher prices once demand for their products is generated by the rest of the network). In these situations, one segment of the network holds the rest hostage for higher profits. This is where networks developed upon more than economic relationships have an advantage. For instance, relationships built on friendship, reputation, or shared ideology may prove more effective due to their greater ability to generate trust and cooperation.

Many of the advantages networks enjoy depend upon members working voluntarily together to innovate, solve problems of mutual concern, and coordinate their activities. This demands a level of organizational teamwork that cannot be taken for granted. Networks create webs of information exchange and mutual obligation that can provide a foundation for deeper relationships, but these relationships are not automatic—they must be managed. Network partners may undermine network effectiveness by pursuing self-interest and middle managers and technical specialists within network organizations may not always be enthusiastic about cooperation. Probably the greatest challenge in managing network relationships is developing and maintaining an organizational identity and sense of purpose in the face of geographic and/or cultural diversity and loosely coupled interests and activities.

Organizational Change

The network approach to organizational design marks a shift from thinking about stable patterns of interaction to recognizing the need for constant change in support of organizational adaptation to environmental complexity and dynamism. This shift of attention from stability to change brings us to our second application of theory to practice—how to bring about organizational change. While many dynamic theories have been presented elsewhere in this book, it is now time to consider some of their prescriptive implications. The theories described below directly address questions concerning how to introduce change in organizations and what happens when change is introduced.

Although by no means exhaustive of the myriad possibilities for applying organization theory to the practical problems involved in organizational change, the two theories presented in this section are perhaps the most recognizable in the field of organizational change management. The first is Kurt Lewin's unfreezing/movement/refreezing model. This is one of the earliest models of planned organizational change and is still in use today by many change agents. Next we will consider Max Weber's equally important theory of the routinization of charisma, which describes organizational responses to leader-induced change. Later in the chapter I will introduce you to more recent contributions to organizational change theory including knowledge management and organizational learning.

Lewin's Model for Change: Unfreezing, Movement, Refreezing

In the 1950s, Kurt Lewin developed a theory of social change that defined social institutions as a balance of forces, some driving change and the others restraining it.[10] In Lewin's theory, stability was not maintained only by the forces opposing change, it was a stalemate between forces for and against change. For Lewin, change was transient instability interrupting an otherwise stable equilibrium and his theory offered prescriptions for managing instability to bring about change. According to his model, change involves three separate activities: unfreezing, movement and refreezing (see Figure 9.6).

Unfreezing unbalances the equilibrium that sustains organizational stability. According to Lewin, destabilizing present behavioral patterns overcomes resistance to

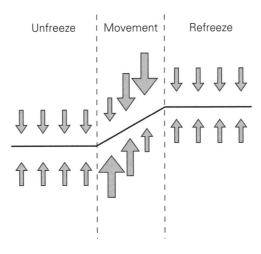

Figure 9.6 Lewin's model of organizational change

Change results from disturbances in the force field sustaining organizational stability. Whenever forces favoring change are greater than forces resisting it, the organization will move from one state to another. In planned change, movement can be induced via unfreezing the old equilibrium and then refreezing around a new one. *Based on*: Lewin (1951, 1958).

change. For example, locating and then taking advantage of existing stress or dissatisfaction is one strategy to bring about unfreezing by increasing the forces for change within a system. However, unfreezing can also be brought about by reducing resistance, for example, through education concerning the need for change. Once unfreezing has occurred, **movement** involves influencing the direction of change in the now destabilized system. Strategies for influencing the direction of change during movement include training new behavioral patterns, altering reporting relationships and reward systems, and introducing different styles of management (e.g., replacing an authoritarian with a participative management style). Movement continues until a new balance between driving and restraining forces is achieved by **refreezing**. Refreezing occurs when new behavioral patterns are institutionalized. An example of a refreezing strategy would be formalizing new recruiting policies to assure that new hires share the organizational culture and work well within the new structure and reward systems and with the new managerial style.

A large proportion of the case studies and theoretical discussions of organizational change that comprise the field of organization development are formulated in the tradition that Lewin's model helped to establish. The field of organization development provides well-documented illustrations of the unfreezing/movement/refreezing processes. To give just one example, American organization development specialists Leonard Goodstein and Warner Burke applied Lewin's model to analyze changes undertaken at British Airways (BA) in the early 1980s.[11]

Goodstein and Burke claimed that changes at BA were made when two environmental influences combined with poor corporate performance. First, Margaret Thatcher, who was then Prime Minister of Britain, opposed public ownership of business, and second, governments around the world deregulated international air traffic with consequent intense air fare competition among airlines. BA's lack of profitability in the prior years was complicated by the challenges of its impending privatization and the fare wars. For instance, in 1982 the airline lost nearly $900 million (USD) requiring large government subsidies, which further encouraged the Thatcher government to privatize BA. As the noose tightened, BA recognized the need for radical change that it then undertook to achieve from 1982 to 1987. Goodstein and Burke reported that during this period, BA went from government ownership and a bureaucratic command and control culture that was facing huge losses and a decreasing market share to a privately owned company having a service-oriented and market-driven culture with profits of over $400 million (USD) and a rising market share.

Goodstein and Burke identified many different elements in BA's change effort. First, BA reduced the size of its workforce from 59,000 to 37,000. Second, it welcomed an industrialist as chairman of its board and named a new CEO with a marketing background. These leaders differed considerably from their predecessors, many of whom had been retired Royal Air Force officers. Goodstein and Burke argued that the effect of these new appointments was to signal an imminent change in BA's values. Third, training programs were initiated to help 'line workers and managers understand the service nature of the airline industry'. The combination of workforce reductions, a new top management and some extensive employee training programs accomplished unfreezing.

Movement was accomplished through management training programs, changes in structure and reward systems, a new, more user-friendly management information system and team-building. Management training programs helped BA move to a participative management style that emphasized employee commitment and involvement. Two elements of the unfreezing stage (cross-functional, cross-level teams planned the change effort plus reductions in middle management) signaled a participative management style that was symbolically reinforced during the movement process by the introduction of a new user-friendly computer system, profit sharing and a bottom-up budgeting process. During movement, the CEO also became a symbol of participation by engaging in question and answer sessions during training programs. Goodstein and Burke claimed that it was in this phase that BA made a critical identity change from a transportation to a service company. The core idea of emotional labor was a key part of the new service identity and involved developing emotional support systems that allowed employees to offset the burnout that service providers often experience.

BA accomplished refreezing via orientation programs for new employees at all levels, establishment of a policy of promoting people who symbolized the new corporate values, and education programs for executives and managers called Top Flight Academies. In addition, performance appraisal and compensation systems were developed around the principle of rewarding customer service and employee development. Meanwhile, new uniforms, refurbished aircraft, and a new logo with the motto 'We fly to serve', communicated BA's new identity. Continued use of teamwork and data feedback to management helped BA maintain its new participative management style. Of course, as Goodstein and Burke pointed out, moving from a known but undesirable state to a desired but unknown future state involved a transition period of disorganization and lowered effectiveness during which, these researchers claimed, courageous and committed leadership offset anger, uncertainty and fear.[12]

Although Lewin's model specifies a path for introducing desired change into a society or organization, it does not tell you much about the ways in which a system responds to the introduction of programmatic change. An early theory proposed by sociologist Max Weber provided insight into this process and thus complements Lewin's theory of planned change.

Weber's Routinization of Charisma

Weber emphasized the dynamics of cultural change in his theory of the **routinization of charisma**.[13] According to Weber, all change in culture originates with the introduction of new ideas by a charismatic leader, but change at the level of everyday life follows the path of the routinization of this charismatic influence. In Weber's words:

> The term 'charisma' will be applied to a certain quality of an individual personality by virtue of which he is considered extraordinary and treated as endowed with supernatural, superhuman, or at least specifically exceptional powers or qualities. These as such are not accessible to the ordinary person, but are regarded as of divine origin or as exemplary, and on the basis of them the individual concerned is treated as a 'leader'.[14]

Weber was particularly concerned with authority and the different forms of domination typical within premodern and modern societies. His focus on charismatic authority represented his explanation of how, under extraordinary circumstances including 'suffering, conflicts or enthusiasm', revolutionary change in worldviews and their consequent influence on social action occurred.[15] Weber explained how charisma works:

> The genuine prophet, like the genuine military leader and every true leader in this sense, preaches, creates, or demands *new* obligations—most typically, by virtue of revelation, oracle, inspiration, or of his own will—which are recognized by the members of the religious, military, or party group because they come from such a source.... The ... revolutionary force of 'reason' works from *without*: by altering the situations of life and hence its problems, finally in this way changing men's attitudes toward them; or it intellectualizes the individual. Charisma, on the other hand, *may* effect a subjective or *internal* reorientation born out of suffering, conflicts, or enthusiasm. It may then result in a radical alteration of the central attitudes and directions of action with a completely new orientation of all attitudes toward the different problems of the 'world'.[16]

He then described what happens after the introduction of the revolutionary influence of a charismatic leader into a culture. However, although charismatic leadership is influential, Weber went on to explain that, because it is routinized, charisma is not as influential as it might at first seem. The processes of systematization and accommodation explain how charisma is routinized to serve the needs and interests of those whose everyday life constructs culture.

By championing the leader's ideas, those whom Weber called disciples of the charismatic leader link and extend charismatic influence to everyday life through the process of **systematization**. In other words, their actions make the leader's ideas systemic. However, some of the revolutionary appeal of the leader's initial influence dissipates through this application to the various mundane aspects of everyday life.[17] **Accommodation** involves negotiation over the interpretations and implementations of new beliefs and obligations suggested or implied by the new ideas. The politics of these negotiations shape and alter the charismatic influence in ways that bring it further into line with the familiar and that cause it to conform, more or less, to existing power relations. It is therefore through routinization, Weber argued, that new ideas introduced by charismatic individuals constitute cultural change but are also transformed (routinized) by that very process (i.e., via systematization and accommodation) because everyday life places demands on followers who not only wish to participate in the worldview of the charismatic leader but also seek to maintain the stability of their social position and their material well-being (e.g., serve their family obligations, and their political and economic interests). Thus Weber claimed charismatic authority as the primary source of cultural change, but allowed that its routinization gave cultural members considerable influence within the change process. In his view, the subjects of charismatic authority alter the ideas leaders introduce to suit their everyday life and its political, religious, intellectual and economic interests.

Although Weber acknowledged that leaders would probably not regard their charisma as dependent on the attitudes of the masses toward them, he claimed that their authority nevertheless rests on how their followers and subordinates regard them: 'In general it should be kept clearly in mind that the basis of every authority, and correspondingly of every kind of willingness to obey, is a *belief*, a belief by virtue of which persons exercising authority are lent prestige.'[18]

In other words, the beliefs of cultural members determine not only how a leader will be regarded, but who will be regarded as a leader. Furthermore, when Weber described the source of the belief that sustains authority as an 'inner logic of world-views', he firmly placed both leadership authority and culture (worldviews) within the realm of subjectivity (*inner* logic), thus anticipating symbolic-interpretive organizational culture theory (see Chapter 6).[19] Weber also anticipated organizational learning theory when he differentiated the forces of reason that work from without to change situations and problems objectively, from the subjective forces of change that work from within to cause a reorientation toward self and the world.

Organizational Learning and Knowledge Management

Both Lewin and Weber described organizational change as a process of incorporating new ideas or practices into everyday organizational life. Contemporary organization theorists continue to study this phenomenon but more often label their theories knowledge management or organizational learning rather than organizational change.

Students of organizational learning and knowledge management often build on cybernetic theory. You should remember from Chapter 8 that the cybernetic theory of feedback control describes organizations as self-correcting systems underpinned by the routinization of organizational activity. Cybernetic learning theory underlies common business practices such as information technology (IT), management information systems (MIS), financial accounting controls (e.g., budgets) and performance evaluations. But organizations today face increasing pressures to innovate and innovation lies in exceptions, not routines. The very foundations of traditional management are shaken by demands to alter the hegemonic forces built into traditional hierarchical structures (as well as into the modernist perspective of organization theory!).

James March proposed that organizations must constantly balance their need for efficiency against their need for flexibility.[20] He emphasized the differences between two modes of **organizational learning**—exploitation and exploration. **Exploitation** refers to the use of existing knowledge and resources to reap value from what is already known, for example, by refining procedures in order to do the same things more efficiently. **Exploration** is akin to rethinking knowledge and redeploying resources in previously unforeseen ways including searching for new options, experimenting and conducting research, all of which represent organizational flexibility and create organizational change. When it focuses on exploration, the notion of organizational learning presents a challenge to traditional organizational change theories and introduces the metaphor of the **learning organization** as a means to change how we think about change and react to or enact it.

Learning Curves, Tacit Knowledge and Knowledge Transfer

In an article she wrote with James March, American organization theorist Barbara Leavitt claimed that experience curves provide evidence that organizations learn.[21] Whether they do or not, the experience curve has become such a powerful symbol for organizational learning that many people now call it the learning curve. **Learning curves** demonstrate and trace the path of the negative relationship between production costs and the quantity of an item manufactured. For example, as more of a particular aircraft are built the cost of producing one of them falls, indicating that something about aircraft production has been learned even though no one may be able to say explicitly *what* was learned. The ambiguity of learning outcomes such as these demonstrates the need to distinguish between tacit and explicit knowledge, a distinction made by Austrian-born British chemist, philosopher and social scientist, Michael Polanyi. According to Polanyi, **explicit knowledge** is that which you can articulate, whereas tacit knowledge cannot be articulated. **Tacit knowledge** comprises all the personal, intuitive and context-dependent knowledge that allows you to perform competently within a given social context.

American philosopher Scott Cook and public administration theorist Dvora Yanow exposed tacit knowledge in an organization when they studied the process by which the finest flutes in the world were manufactured by highly skilled craftspeople.[22] Cook and Yanow observed the flute makers as they produced their flutes and recorded what they talked about as they performed their jobs. The flute makers employed a sequential process in which each person contributed something unique to the evolving instrument—drilled holes, connected springs and keys, glued keypads onto the keys, adjusted keys and keypads, and so on. At any stage of the production process a given worker might return the flute they were working on to someone who preceded them in the process, saying only that 'This flute does not feel right'. As it progressed, a flute of superior quality emerged through a process that was in many respects collaborative and communal. What is more, Cook and Yanow claimed, the organization as a whole continuously employed tacit knowledge—the knowledge of how a flute should feel at various stages of its manufacture—and updated this knowledge through constant learning, making the flute manufacturing company an example of the learning organization.

It is just this sort of organizational learning that American strategy theorist Jay Barney touted as an often overlooked source of competitive advantage. Barney claimed that an organization's tacit knowledge has competitive value because the firm's competitors cannot replicate it and he concluded that the concept of organizational culture accounts for this advantage.[23] An organization whose culture influences organizational decision making and behavior provides evidence of Barney's claim. Johnson & Johnson, the American baby product and pharmaceutical company, has long subscribed to a corporate Credo, created by its founder, but only formalized by his grandson during his tenure as CEO. To this day all J&J employees have the right to question any decision or action taken at any level in the organization on the grounds of its fit to the corporate principles laid out in the Credo, and the culture supports their doing so such that there is continuous monitoring of all behavior in which this company engages. This constant scrutiny creates an environment conducive to ethical behavior and thus gives J & J an important strategic advantage in the

Table 9.1 Nonaka and Takeuchi: Four modes of knowledge transfer

Mode	Process by which transfer occurs	Domain/Method
Tacit → Tacit	Socialization	Culture/Ethnography
Tacit → Explicit	Codification	Academia/Conceptualizing and theorizing
Explicit → Explicit	Combination	Knowledge management/Information systems development and use
Explicit → Tacit	Internalization	Practice (including applications of theory)/Action research

Based on: Nonaka and Takeuchi (1995).

highly competitive pharmaceutical industry. Even though J&J publishes its Credo, no competitor as yet has been able to reproduce its effectiveness thus showing the importance of tacit knowledge concerning how to implement the Credo embedded in J & J culture.[24]

Cook and Yanow's study in combination with Barney's insights about organizational culture as a strategic competence raise questions about how learning and culture are related to Polanyi's knowledge types. Two Japanese knowledge management experts, Ikujiro Nonaka and Hirotaka Takeuchi, provided an answer to this question. Nonaka and Takeuchi described four possible modes of **knowledge transfer** using Polanyi's distinction between explicit and tacit knowledge.[25] According to these researchers, knowledge transfer is conducted in different modes depending on whether the knowledge in question is explicit or tacit, or whether its transfer depends upon shifting it from one of these domains to the other (see Table 9.1). Their framework can be helpful in understanding not only how to transfer knowledge between domains, but what methods are most appropriate for doing so. For example, because tacit knowledge is transferred through direct contact with cultural members via socialization, ethnographic methods (see Chapter 6) yield the most insight for studies of tacit-to-tacit knowledge transfer. Alternatively, action research, in which researchers participate as change agents, is better suited to the domain of practice where explicit-to-tacit knowledge transfer takes place.[26]

Single- and Double-Loop Learning in Organizations

One influential contributor to organizational learning, American philosopher Donald Schön built his theory upon the idea that rapid technological change has already caused organizations to make a radical shift away from operational routines. In 1973 Schön wrote in *Beyond the Stable State* that:

> The loss of the stable state means that our society and all of its institutions are in *continuous* processes of transformation. We cannot expect new stable states that will endure for our own lifetimes.... We must become able not only to transform our institutions, in response to changing situations and requirements; we must invent and develop institutions which are 'learning systems', that is to say, systems capable of bringing about their own continuing transformation. The task which the loss of the stable state makes imperative, for the person, for our institutions, for our society as a whole, is to learn about learning.[27]

Schön's ideas about learning to learn formed the foundation of a theory of double-loop learning that he developed with his colleague Chris Argyris, a professor of organizational behavior.

Single-loop learning involves learning from the consequences of previous actions in order to develop successful patterns of behavior. In Argyris and Schön's theory, this type of learning results from feedback generated by a process of observing the consequences of action and using this knowledge to adjust subsequent action in order to avoid similar mistakes in the future.[28] They exemplified the single-loop learning process with a thermostat that detects when it is too hot or too cold in a room and adjusts by turning the heating or cooling unit on or off. The use of budgets is a good example of single-loop organizational learning (review Figure 8.1). The budget is an ideal or target for capital expenditures to which comparison of actual results can be made. When there is a deviation from the target or ideal, the budget review process will highlight it so that corrective action can be taken. In this way the budgeting process acts as a thermostat controlling unit level spending.

According to Argyris, single-loop learning solves problems as presented but cannot discover why the problems arose in the first place. Although this form of learning can appear intelligent in that single-loop systems can operate on their own (for instance, to keep the temperature of a room or building stable over long periods of time and across extreme variations in external temperatures), the system cannot under any circumstances establish its own standards of appropriate behavior. A system outside the thermostat must determine what temperature it should achieve. If the temperature is not set properly, the thermostat will go merrily on regulating for an undesired result. Similarly, budgeting tends to produce stable spending over long periods of time regardless of variations in the organization's environmental conditions. If the wrong targets are set, the single-loop learning system is helpless to alter them.

In addition to monitoring and correcting behavior to achieve predetermined outcomes, systems embracing **double-loop learning** can determine what is appropriate behavior. Since questioning the appropriateness of behavior involves making a value judgment, double-loop learning lies beyond the domain of the single-loop model. Because it involves subjective judgment, the symbolic-interpretive perspective is implicated, and to the extent that double-loop learning requires that the system questions its own underlying assumptions and values and risk, fundamentally changing the terms of its own organizing, postmodernism can be accommodated. The reflexive property of double-loop learning is also associated with the idea of a self-organizing system first proposed by Chilean systems theorists Humberto Maturana and Francisco Varela.[29]

Self-organizing systems learn to learn and thus become intelligent enough to define their own fundamental operating criteria, behavior and identity. As double-loop learning diffuses throughout an organization, organizational stability disappears and new organizational orders—such as self-organizing systems—emerge from the internal dynamics of the organization rather than at the behest of top management. Of course, self-organizing properties were observed much earlier by socio-technical systems theorists (see Chapter 2) who found that when job specifications are minimized, and appropriate training and development opportunities are offered, employees will reorganize their work to adapt to changing circumstances, thus continually optimizing the fit between the social and technical aspects of the workplace.[30] We will return to the topic of emergence in the context of complex adaptive systems in Chapter 10. For now let us proceed to some recent discussions of organizational learning processes that implicate both planned and emergent organizational change as well as drawing from both modernist and symbolic-interpretive perspectives.

Diversity, CSR and Corporate Branding: Revealing the Dynamics of Organizational Change in Response to Social and Symbolic Issues

Several studies of organizational change initiatives have independently traced similar organizational learning processes. Although the studies focused on business issues ranging from diversity and corporate social responsibility (CSR) to corporate brand management, they seem to converge on a single organizational learning model and thus offer a chance to show you what empirically grounded theorizing about organizational change might look like.

In their longitudinal study of a group of organizations that had created diversity programs, David Thomas and Robin Ely identified three stages of development organizations go through on their way to learning how to make the most of diversity. Thomas and Ely characterized the first stage as organizational concern for **discrimination and fairness**. The focus of executives during this phase was on compliance with Federal regulations governing equal opportunity employment and fair treatment of employees. For instance, firms in this stage typically set up systems of self-assessment using recommended metrics for the recruitment and retention of members of various identity groups (e.g., women, people of color). Although this approach usually resulted in greater diversification of staff, it did not necessarily have any impact on the nature of the work the organization performed and thus the organization gained little if any value from complying with outside pressures to increase employee diversity. Thomas and Ely noted that fear of organizational culture change due to incorporating diversity often created resistance to moving out of this stage and so some companies never moved beyond compliance.

Firms in the second stage, called **access and legitimacy**, sought to exploit the unique attributes of their diversity employees, often doing so in only the most obvious ways such as having employees in race or gender categories serve similarly segmented stakeholder groups. For instance, Latino employees might be assigned the task of selling to the firm's Latino customers or serving the accounts of Latino clients. As a consequence, diversity employees had access to more and better job opportunities within the organization—up to a point. Although employees of firms in the access stage enjoyed more legitimacy and opportunity for advancement within the organization than did those of firms in compliance, organizations in the access and legitimacy stage did not fully understand the differences diversity brought to the organization. To use March's terms, they only exploited these differences, they did not explore them. Thomas and Ely characterized the mindset of a stage two company in this way:

> We are living in an increasingly multicultural country, and new ethnic groups are quickly gaining consumer power. Our company needs a demographically more diverse workforce to help us

gain access to these differentiated segments. We need employees with multilingual skills in order to understand and serve our customers better and to gain legitimacy with them. Diversity isn't just fair, it makes business sense.[31]

Nonetheless, although access and legitimacy typically resulted in promotions for some diversity candidates, their new positions were usually within the areas carved out by the segmentation strategy and employees continued to feel stifled by the glass ceiling they perceived as preventing their promotion to the executive level.

The third stage, not attained by many companies even today, was described by Thomas and Ely as the stage when the organization learns to take full advantage of the benefits diversity brings. The **learning and effectiveness** stage is entered when companies redefine their markets, products, strategies, business practices and organizational cultures in response to their acceptance of the influence diversity brings. In other words, organizations in stage three are transformed by the learning that occurs through internalizing employee differences and adapting to them. Such companies naturally enjoy better recruitment and retention outcomes, but above all they find opportunities they never before imagined such as new product ideas, new customer bases and new business.

In the context of their study of companies that are taking on the challenges of corporate social responsibility (CSR), Philip Mirvis and Bradley Googins developed a model with striking similarities to that of Thomas and Ely. CSR has to do with organizational responses to issues like climate change, poverty, hunger and human rights. While at first companies interpreted these concerns as social issues rather than organizational ones, efforts to broaden corporate responsibility to include not just shareholders, but all stakeholders, have caused some organizations to start down the path of learning to address CSR. The list of changes taking place under the banner of CSR is long, but a few examples should give you a sense of what is being undertaken: protecting human rights in a company's overseas operations, creating eco-friendly technologies, ensuring transparency in financial disclosure, being a family-friendly employer and using nondiscriminatory employment practices.

Although their longitudinal study of organization's engaging in CSR leaves room for divergent learning paths, in general Mirvis and Googins also found that compliance with external pressures (e.g., legal, special interests) marked the first stage in which the companies they studied learned to address CSR. By learning to use the resources allocated to CSR-related activities in obvious ways (e.g., exploitation), the companies moved from compliance to more active engagement, such as strategic philanthropy and public relations campaigns. A period of innovation followed as a third stage during which new products or services were invented or discovered as a byproduct of new activities (e.g., exploration) that typically led to many, often fragmented and uncoordinated efforts that needed to be integrated during the fourth stage. A fifth and final stage occurred as integration efforts established new values within the deep layers of culture and transformed the organization's identity as perceived from both inside and out. This stage was accompanied by market creation and substantial external attention to a firm now regarded as visionary.

An example of a company that has achieved Mirvis and Googin's fifth stage was provided by Ramona Amodeo. Amodeo conducted a retrospective case study of the organizational change by which Interface Flooring Systems became an environmentally sustainable company.[32] A global manufacturer of commercial carpet, this company learned to produce its innovative carpet tiles from recycled materials and then secured an endless supply of recyclable material for its manufacturing process by renting its carpet to other businesses around the world. In this way Interface not only became sustainable itself, but now helps other companies start down their own path to sustainability by using recycled materials in their facilities and by subsequently recycling them. After videotaping and analyzing stories about how the change took place as told by a variety of Interface's members including founder and CEO Ray Anderson, Amodeo described the stages of this company's development as awakening, cocooning, metamorphosis and emergence. During awakening Anderson recognized his responsibility as a leader and member of society to preserve the planet for future generations. As a consequence he set out to influence other members of his organization to help Interface change in the direction of environmental sustainability. An internal dialogue ensued as members of the organization confronted their leader's profound change and considered his challenge to the company to follow suit. Also during this cocooning phase, Anderson introduced persuasive members of the sustainability movement, such as Paul Hawkin, to the organization by creating an advisory board to guide the change process. Transformation to accommodate the value for sustainability occurred next during which time company engineers worked out methods for profitably pursuing the goals suggested by the value for sustainability and marketers developed relationships with interested customers. As more and more members of the organization and its key stakeholders became enthusiastic, deep cultural change at Interface took place. Finally, in emergence, Anderson and others began taking the story of their transformation and the message of sustainability to the world, with Anderson, for example, being invited to tell the company's story in the documentary *The Corporation* and Interface receiving multiple sustainability awards.

Finally, Majken Schultz and I studied an organizational change at LEGO Company, the Danish toymaker, as it implemented its new corporate brand strategy. Not unlike the three studies described above, we discovered four cycles of change that we labeled stating, linking, involving and integrating, noting that the change process was not complete at the time at which we ended our study.[33] During the stating phase the company reviewed the heritage of the LEGO brand and studied its image in the marketplace, on the basis of which top managers introduced a new brand vision and architecture and announced a program of organizational change to support it. The linking phase was devoted to structurally reorganizing the company around corporate branding activities by creating a Brand Council, appointing a senior vice president of global brand communication and forming cross-functional global brand teams. During the involving phase, LEGO Company created a Brand School that allowed its employees to learn about and influence top management decisions about the brand and altered its market segmentation strategy to eradicate age-based categories and open new channels of communication with customers. Integrating involved formalizing guidelines for brand use and expression, designing and building branded retail outlets, conducting a company-wide value chain analysis and developing user communities along with the company's ability to use their input to shape the brand as well as new product development processes.

Although these studies focused on organizational change in response to markedly different business issues, taken together they suggest there is a pattern underlying issue-based organizational change (see Table 9.2). Change begins in one part of the organization, spreads through the dedication of resources and introduction of new activities, practices and structures to other parts of the organization, and as the new becomes integrated with the old, learning occurs through which change finds its way into the core of the organization's culture where values are revised and often revitalized along the lines suggested by Gagliardi's model of incremental culture change (see Chapter 6). In addition, all the models seem to provide evidence that organizations must first see some economic value before they will engage with change on the level of culture, a view that supports Schein's model of cultural change as well as Weber's theory of the routinization of charisma.

Table 9.2 Comparison of four studies of organizational change processes

Model proposed by	Business issue studied	Stages identified in organizational change processes
Thomas and Ely (1996)	Diversity	Discrimination and fairness—compliance with laws and other institutionalized expectations
		Access and legitimacy—to jobs for diversity employees, to market for firms
		Learning and effectiveness—on the part of the total organization
Mirvis and Googins (2005)	Corporate social responsibility (CSR)	Basic—compliance with laws and standards
		Engaged—first awareness that CSR and environmental sustainability involve more than compliance
		Innovative—outreach by functional departments to their social and environmental stakeholders
		Integrated—comprehensive view of CSR and sustainability built into internal organization
		Transformative—business model, products and services express CSR/sustainability values
Amodeo (2005)	Sustainability	Awakening—leader recognizes responsibility and influences others
		Cocooning—internal dialog and confrontation with need for change
		Metamorphosis—company undergoes significant transformation to accommodate value for sustainability (exploration)
		Emergence—letting the outside world hear the company's story about its road to sustainability (exploitation)
Schultz and Hatch (2003)	Corporate branding	Stating—company reconnects with its heritage and its customer base
		Linking—restructuring to emphasize desired change
		Involving—getting internal and external stakeholders on board
		Integrating—creating coherence in practices, policies and communications

Although this abstraction of the stages of change built upon the various models discussed in this section and elsewhere in the book is not formally a part of organization theory, I offer it here as an example of how theorizing develops on the foundation of studies that often come from different parts of the literature and sometimes from different discourses. You should now be ready to go back through Part II of the book and discover many theories to apply to organizational issues to enhance your understanding of organizational learning and change. However, before leaving this topic, I want to offer you a few warnings about organizational learning processes.

Some Caveats about Organizational Learning

Leavitt and March pointed out that there are many difficulties strewn along the learning path among which you need to look out for superstitious learning, the ambiguity of success and competency traps.

Superstitious learning can cause organizations to learn the wrong things. Superstitious learning occurs when the connections between actions and outcomes are incorrectly specified, for example, when promotions are taken to indicate high levels of performance but in fact are given because the promoted individuals duplicate the characteristics of existing leaders (e.g., white, male, domineering). This misattribution leads to superstitious learning when the promoted individuals develop self-confidence in their performance, leading them to overestimate their ability to make sound decisions for the organization. Profitability can also lead to misattribution when an organization or division believes it knows what it is doing just because it is making money. This phenomenon was satirized by Donald McClosky in his 1990 narrative analysis of the discourse of economists entitled *If You're So Smart: The Narrative of Economic Expertise*, which alludes to the query: 'If you're so smart, why aren't you rich?'[34]

Learning failures also occur due to the **ambiguity of success**. It is often difficult to know when organizational success has occurred because the indicators of success are constantly modified (the target keeps moving), and levels of aspiration toward particular indicators also shift over time. It is a common error to assume that organizational success means superior organizational or management practices. Claiming organizational success can be a political act having little to do with the link between organizational behavior and organizational performance. Similarly, negative outcomes create uncertainty about what organizations have actually achieved and this can serve to confuse the causal picture. When success is difficult to pinpoint, it is tough to learn on the basis of what has worked in the past.

Competency traps can lead to improvements in procedures that have limited or no competitive advantage. Such traps occur when the organization makes improvements in one or more of its frequently used procedures such that the procedure results in a series of successful local outcomes, thereby reinforcing its use and reducing motivation to search for better procedures (double-loop sacrificed to single-loop learning). If competitors are meanwhile developing better procedures, the organization can be caught in a competency trap created by its own learning process.

SUMMARY

Organizational design is a fundamental concern for managers because it provides the basis for the coordination of organizational work and activities. Applying the structure metaphor, design is the skeleton of the organization. We have seen that organizational design requires understanding how the various dimensions of organization structure such as differentiation and integration inter-relate to form a particular organizational design. It is also important to understand the advantages and disadvantages of each design. Contingency theorists claim that there is no one design appropriate for every organization. They recommend that managers consider environmental, task/technological, human and other factors, as a basis for determining which organizational design will be most appropriate to their organization's situation. For example, matrix structures are regarded as being more suited to changing environments, complex technologies and customer-driven products or services, whereas functional organizations are effective in more stable environments and where the organization is producing large quantities of fairly standardized products and services—hence government bureaucracy.

However, because organizations and their environments are rarely static, it is important to continually monitor and evaluate organizational design to ensure it enhances rather than impedes goal achievement. The example of structural and cultural change at British Airways reinforced this point, along with the importance of understanding change and learning processes. Change is an inevitable part of organizational life and does not just occur through intervention by top management. Successful change often depends on organizational members recognizing the need for change and participating in its implementation. Implemented changes need to be institutionalized (refrozen or routinized) in organizational practice—while also maintaining a degree of flexibility and openness to further change.

Finally, learning is key if organizations are to survive, compete, and manage their surroundings. The current interest in organizational learning and knowledge management emphasizes the role tacit learning plays in organizational effectiveness and explores ways of making such learning more explicit and more easily shared. In particular, double-loop learning—questioning assumptions, current mindsets, organizational designs, processes and practices—is essential to effective change.

KEY TERMS

organizational design
  simple design
  functional design
  multidivisional form (M-form)
  matrix design
  hybrid design
  strategic alliance
  joint venture
  multinational organization
  global organization
  network organization
  virtual organization
organizational change
  unfreezing/movement/refreezing
  routinization of charisma
  systematization

accommodation
organizational learning
  learning organization
  learning curves
  explicit and tacit knowledge
  knowledge transfer
  single and double-loop
    learning
  self-organizing systems
management issues
  diversity
  CSR
  corporate branding
superstitious learning
ambiguity of success
competency traps

ENDNOTES

1. www.co.honolulu.hi.us/budget/cityorganization/
2. www.grc.nasa.gov/WWW/RT2002/intro/b-divchart.html
3. www.btplc.com/Corporateinformation/Principalactivities/BTstructure.html
4. www.usgs.gov/bio/USGS/orgcharts.html
5. Tosi (1974).
6. Rumelt (1986).
7. www.airbus.com
8. www.wikipedia.org
9. Windeler and Sydow (2001).
10. Lewin (1951, 1958).
11. Goodstein and Burke (1991).
12. To read about subsequent changes at BA over the last decade, see Hatch and Schultz (2003).
13. Weber (1968/78); see also Schroeder (1992).
14. Weber (1968/78: 241).
15. Weber (1968/78: 241–49).
16. Weber (1968/78: 243–45, emphasis in the original).
17. Schroeder (1992: 10).
18. Weber (1968/78: 263, emphasis in the original).
19. Weber (1948: 328, cited by Schroeder 1992: 11).
20. March (1991); see also Levinthal and March (1993).
21. Leavitt and March (1988).
22. Cook and Yanow (1993); see also Yanow (2000).
23. Barney (1986).
24. www.jnj.com/our_company/our_credo/
25. Nonaka and Takeuchi (1995).
26. See Reason and Rowan (1981) for an introduction to action research.
27. Schön (1973: 28–29).
28. Argyris and Schön (1978).
29. Maturana and Varela (1980).
30. Emery (1969); see also Emergy and Trist (1973) and Weick (1977).
31. Thomas and Ely (1996: 83).
32. Amodeo (2005).
33. Schultz and Hatch (2003, 2005) and Schultz, Hatch and Ciccolella (2005).
34. McClosky (1990).

REFERENCES

Amodeo, Ramona (2005). 'Becoming sustainable': Identity dynamics within transformational culture change at interface. Ph.D. Dissertation, Benedictine University.

Argyris, Chris, and Schön, Donald A. (1978). *Organizational learning: A theory of action perspective*. Reading, Mass.: Addison-Wesley.

Barney, Jay B. (1986). Organizational culture: Can it be a source of sustained competitive advantage? *Academy of Management Review*, 11: 656–65.

Cook, Scott, and Yanow, Dvora (1993). Culture and organizational learning. *Journal of Management Inquiry*, 7: 373–90.

Emery, Fred E. (1969). *Systems thinking*. Harmondsworth, England: Penguin.

—— and Trist, Eric L. (1973). *Toward a social ecology*. London: Tavistock.

Goodstein, Leonard D., and Burke, W. Warner (1991). Creating successful organization change. *Organizational Dynamics*, Spring: 5–17.

Hatch, M. J., and Schultz, M. S. (2003). Bringing the corporation into corporate branding. *European Journal of Marketing*, 37: 1041–64.

Leavitt, Barbara, and March, James G. (1988). Organizational learning. *Annual Review of Sociology*, 14: 319–40.

Levinthal, Daniel A., and March, James G. (1993). The myopia of learning. *Strategic Management Journal*, 14: 95–112.

Lewin, Kurt (1951). *Field theory in social science*. New York: Harper & Row.

—— (1958). Group decisions and social change. In E. E. Maccobby, T. M. Newcomb and E. L. Hartley (eds.), *Readings in social psychology*. New York: Holt, Rinehart & Winston, 459–73.

March, James G. (1991). Exploration and exploitation in organized learning. *Organization Science*, 2: 71–87.

Maturana, Humberto, and Varela, Francisco (1980). *Autopoiesis and cognition: The realization of the living*. London: Reidl.

McCloskey, Donald N. (1990). *If you're so smart: The narrative of economic expertise*. Chicago: University of Chicago Press.

Mirvis, Philip H., and Googins, Bradley (2005). *Stages of corporate citizenship: A developmental framework*. Boston: Center for Corporate Citizenship, Boston College.

Nonaka, Ikujiro, and Takeuchi, Hirotaka (1995). *The knowledge-creating company: How Japanese companies create the dynamics of innovation*. Oxford: Oxford University Press.

Reason, Peter, and Rowan, John (1981) (eds.). *Human inquiry: A sourcebook of new paradigm research*. Chichester: John Wiley and Sons.

Rumelt, Richard (1986). *Strategy, structure and economic performance*. Boston: Harvard Business School Press (first edition 1974).

Schön, Donald (1973). *Beyond the stable state*. Harmondsworth: Penguin.

Schroeder, Richard (1992). *Max Weber and the sociology of culture*. London: Sage.

Schultz, Majken S., and Hatch, Mary Jo (2003). The cycles of corporate branding: The case of LEGO Company. *California Management Review*, 46/1: 6–26.

—— —— (2005). A cultural perspective on corporate branding: The case of the LEGO Group. In J. Schroeder and M. Salzer (eds.) (in press), *Brand Culture*. London: Routledge.

—— —— and Ciccolella, F. (2005). Expressing the corporate brand through symbols and artifacts. In A. Rafaeli and M. Pratt (eds.), *Artifacts in organizations: Beyond mere symbolism*. New York: Lawrence Erlbaum & Associates, 141–60.

Thomas, David A., and Ely, Robin J. (1996). Making differences matter: A new paradigm for managing diversity. *Harvard Business Review*, Sept.–Oct.: 80–90.

Tosi, Henry L. (1974). The human effects of budgeting systems on management. *MSU Business Topics*, Autumn: 53–63.

Weber, Max (1968/78). *Economy and society* (eds. G. Roth and C. Wittich). Berkeley: University of California Press.

Weick, Karl (1977). Organization design: Organizations as self-designing systems. *Organizational Dynamics*, Autumn: 38–49.

Windeler, Arnold, and Sydow, Jörg (2001). Project networks and changing industry practices: Collaborative content production in the German TV industry. *Organization Studies*, 22: 1035–60.

Yanow, Dvora (2000). Seeing organizational learning: A 'cultural' view. *Organization*, 7: 247–68.

FURTHER READING

Argyris, Chris (1982). *Reasoning, learning and action*. San Francisco: Jossey-Bass.

—— (1990). *Overcoming organizational defenses: Facilitating organizational learning*. Boston: Allyn and Bacon.

Barney, Jay (2001). *Gaining and sustaining competitive advantage*. Reading, Mass.: Prentice-Hall.

Bate, Paul (1995). *Strategies for cultural change*. Oxford: Butterworth-Heinemann.

Cohen, Michael D., and Sproull, Lee (1995) (eds.). *Organizational learning*. Newbury Park, Calif.: Sage.

Galbraith, Jay (1977). *Organization design*. Reading, Mass.: Addison-Wesley.

Kanter, Rosabeth Moss, Stein, Barry A., and Jick, Todd D. (1992). *The challenge of organizational change: How companies experience it and leaders guide it*. New York: Free Press.

Senge, Peter M. (1990). *The fifth discipline: The art and practice of the learning organization*. London: Century.

Watson, Tony J. (2001). *In Search of Management* (reissued edn.). London: Thomson Learning.

10

New Directions in Organization Theory

This final chapter presents recent developments in organization theory and I invite you to ponder with me what they mean for the future of the field. Together we will consider critical realism, complexity theory, network theories, organizational identity and organizational aesthetics. While space makes it impossible to cover all the topics that might be considered under this heading, my ambition is to give you some sense of the range of ideas organization theorists are getting involved in these days and an appreciation for how this field is developing.

Be sure to notice that most of the ideas presented in this chapter do not fit neatly into the modern, symbolic or postmodern perspective. This ambiguity is part of the messy business of theorizing. Many new theories are developed when someone fits seemingly incompatible ideas together in a way that reveals a new phenomenon or defines a perspective that no one has tried before. In organization theory it is not uncommon for this to involve borrowing an idea from another discipline (as Figure 1.1 showed). But increasingly, once a topic has been proposed, it attracts theorists from different perspectives who bring their assumptions with them as they collectively develop a new branch of organization theory. This makes describing new directions in the field particularly challenging.

To provide historical context for our discussion, I want to revisit the topic of multiple perspectives and tell you some of the story behind how organization theory came to terms with its multidisciplinarity. This history will help you to understand what theorizing demands and how theorists go about their work in the context of their own discourses and subcultures. It begins with war.

The Paradigm Wars, Revisited

The paradigm wars got underway in 1979 following the publication of Gibson Burrell and Gareth Morgan's book *Sociological Paradigms and Organizational Analysis*. This book overturned an assumption that lay at the very core of the discipline—that organization theorists were all doing similar work in more or less compatible ways. In hindsight, the 1960s and early 1970s were the golden age of modernism, a period when organization theory was dominated by the structural analysis of large bureaucratic organizations, and systems and contingency theories prevailed. Into this relative bliss, Burrell and Morgan introduced a way of mapping the field that suggested organization theory was composed of competing approaches, rather than being defined by one integrated view. This upsetting idea provoked many battles, some fought over the legitimacy of the various perspectives in use, and others over whether organization theory was better served by its former (if illusionary) unity or by the pluralism of many voices.

All the commotion came to be called the paradigm wars in honor of Thomas Kuhn, a philosopher of science, who argued that scientists hold shared assumptions that define acceptable scientific knowledge and dictate how it should be produced. Those scientists who share assumptions create and occupy a **paradigm**, which in turn both defines a discourse and constitutes a subculture of the scientific community.[1] Kuhn called the dominant paradigm within a given scientific discipline **normal science**. He claimed that normal science exists in a state that is perpetually open to challenge by revolutionary paradigms comprised of scientists with new knowledge and/or new ways of knowing. As a revolutionary paradigm becomes accepted, normal science shifts to accommodate it and then carries on until another revolutionary paradigm emerges, and so on.

In 1979, brandishing Kuhn's highly acclaimed insights about the development of scientific revolutions, Burrell and Morgan argued that, not one, but three revolutionary paradigms were competing to replace the normal science of modernist organization theory. They defined all four paradigms using two dimensions (see if you can draw their 2 x 2). One dimension concerned assumptions about the nature of science and was bifurcated into our old friends: objectivism and subjectivism. The other involved different assumptions about the nature of society (remember, Burrell and Morgan are sociologists): either society was assumed to be consensual as a result of being integrated by shared values or it was assumed to be fundamentally conflicted along the lines first theorized by Marx.

Burrell and Morgan located the functionalist paradigm at the intersection of positivist/consensual assumptions and is what, roughly speaking, you have learned to call the modernist perspective. Burrell and Morgan called the paradigm conjoining subjectivist and consensual assumptions interpretivist; however, given developments since 1979, the consensual assumption only fits some symbolic-interpretivists. The remaining two paradigms—radical humanist and radical structuralist—are versions of critical theory. The radical humanists in Burrell and Morgan's framework were interested in human consciousness as it relates to alienation, motivation and emancipation, while the radical structuralists studied conflict and how structures, and the managerial ideology they carry, oppress workers. The main difference between the conflict-oriented paradigms is their level of analysis. In their explanations of organizations and organizing, radical humanists privilege agency, while radical structuralists privilege, you guessed it, structure. Burrell and Morgan did not include postmodernism in their scheme, probably because this perspective had yet to influence much sociology or organization theory by the time of their writing.

One of the most contentious claims Burrell and Morgan made was that paradigms are mutually exclusive or incommensurable. **Paradigm incommensurability** means that the assumptions, interests and methods of one paradigm contradict those of any other paradigm and therefore translations between them are impossible. These theorists also maintained that, because the assumptions underlying each paradigm are so completely different, no one can operate from more than one paradigm at a time, and that changing paradigms is rare: something akin to religious conversion.

While Burrell and Morgan's book was extraordinarily influential within organization theory, there was considerable resistance to its key ideas including that: (1) organization theorists can be boxed into paradigms; (2) paradigms are incommensurable; and (3) because of the impossibility of comparison, there is no way to assess the relative merits of different paradigms.[2] A number of mostly modernist organization theorists argued that accepting the idea of incommensurable paradigms would lead to proliferation and polarization of perspectives and this would surely undermine whatever legitimacy organization theory could claim. A major proponent of this view, Jeffrey Pfeffer, argued that paradigm proliferation would result in anarchy and that organization studies could be saved from this fate only if the field rallied behind a single paradigm, an act that would, by the way, enhance the field's prestige, influence and grant-getting ability (do you recognize this argument as an application of Pfeffer and Salancik's resource dependence theory?).

Pfeffer's position was shared by Lex Donaldson, an Australian organization theorist. Donaldson claimed that the modernist/functionalist paradigm was able to incorporate all the intellectual and practical demands raised by the warring paradigms. He wanted to make contingency theory the poster child for modernism, awarding it the coveted title of normal science.[3] You can imagine the glee with which postmodern and critical theorists attacked Donaldson's and Pfeffer's positions! For instance, a group of postmodern scholars led by Burrell suggested that calls for paradigm unification fed modernist needs for control and their desires to establish modernism as the dominant ideology of organization theory. Burrell sided with the pluralists reasoning that the alternative forms of knowledge legitimated by different paradigms leads to richer intellectual debate and thus to improvements to theorizing in all paradigms. Meanwhile John van Maanen, who also stood with the pluralists, publicly referred to the idea of unifying organization theory as a Pfefferdigm.[4]

Conflict over whose paradigm had the most explanatory power was not just an occasion for ideological rhetoric. Because academic survival (via publication and tenure) depended upon each paradigm's influence within the field, dividing lines became entrenched, both intellectually and geographically, and sometime institutionally as particular schools aligned with one paradigm while others became known as tolerant of multiple perspectives. Geographically, regional differences appeared. For example, a number of European academics aligned with radicals like Michel Foucault and Jacques Derrida arguing for a philosophically informed organization theory, while the majority of American academics insisted on being pragmatic, which they interpreted as sticking to modernism. Can you imagine what happened to the concept of truth amid this upheaval? Does the postmodern query—*whose* truth?—take on greater importance in the context of a history like this one?

One group of mostly younger scholars tried to avoid the paradigm wars waged by their elders by denying the ground of paradigm incommensurability on which the war was fought. They insisted on either crossing paradigms or maintaining open dialogue between them.[5] John Hassard, for example, was one of the first to engage in multi-paradigm research when he analyzed a department of the British Fire Service four times over, each time using a different paradigm.[6] Based on this experience, Hassard suggested that the assumptions and research methods of multiple paradigms reveal different aspects of organizations and can be handled in ways that do not privilege any one of them and without blurring their distinctions. Thus was the multiple perspectives approach introduced into organization theory as a peaceable alternative to continuing the paradigm wars.

While defining and defending paradigms may seem a purely philosophical exercise, consider how the implications of this debate echo still across Business Schools and academic conferences, particularly in the United States, where the modernist perspective overshadows all others and where careers are defined by conformity or nonconformity to mainstream academic interests. It was only around the time of the first edition of this book in 1997 that symbolic-interpretivism and postmodernism were accepted as part of mainstream organization theory, and more recently still that the possibility of including other perspectives has been entertained. Perhaps as you were reading through this book you caught yourself using the modernist perspective to think about these matters. For example, did you ever ask yourself: why not just study organization from one perspective, or, isn't one perspective better than the others? These were the questions that fueled the paradigm wars in the 1980s and that lie behind many persistent quarrels about how to do organization theory.

In the remainder of this chapter we will explore theories and perspectives that are not (yet anyway) clear articulations of any of the recognized perspectives or paradigms of organization theory. Some of these, like critical realism, are attempting to lay claim to unique philosophical positions. Others are as yet unclear about how to position themselves. Some are even experiencing their own paradigm wars! In spite of the confusion, the excitement of new ideas compensates for the difficulties and, in any case, organization theory depends upon those who dare to accept the challenge of exploring new directions.

Critical Realism

Critical realism provides an example of crossing paradigms. Its proponents claim to be developing a new position that lies somewhere between the modern and symbolic-interpretive perspectives.[7] Recall that modernists believe reality has a structure existing independently of the individuals who experience it—in other words, reality is real and can be observed and studied like any other object. Rom Harré recognized that this modernist ontological assumption is the mainstay of **philosophical realism**, which offers three epistemological imperatives: (1) empirical adequacy—theories and laws must offer causal explanations and allow predictions about future behavior; (2) theories are acceptable only when they represent reality accurately and are truthful; and (3) researchers must be able to verify the accuracy of a theory and replicate its results through experimentation that provides inductive evidence.[8]

Social constructionist ontology and epistemology deny the imperatives of realism by assuming that reality is constructed with others in the course of everyday interaction. Consequently we cannot separate reality (ontology) from our knowledge of reality (epistemology)—they are hopelessly entwined. Knowledge is therefore dependent upon the context and moment in which meaning is created and no one can be neutral or disinterested. From a realist philosophical position, social constructionism amounts to relativism—it promotes the belief that truth, meaning and knowledge are not universals but are relative to the context in which they are produced. Meanwhile, from a social constructionist position, realism amounts to determinism—it leaves little room for choice because human nature and action are causally determined.

Several philosophers and social theorists became dissatisfied with both what they considered to be the over-determinism of positivism and the total relativism of constructionism. In response they proposed a postpositivist philosophy of science called critical realism. Although the roots of critical realism trace indirectly to an early twentieth-century movement called American critical realism, and to two essays written by Maurice Mandelbaum in the 1950s (*Societal Facts* and *Societal Laws*),[9] it is more common for organization theorists who use critical realism to look to British philosopher Roy Bhaskar for inspiration.

Bhaskar was concerned with questions of ontology, particularly how unspoken assumptions about the nature of reality influenced positivist approaches to science and the impact this had on our world and on human freedom. In his 1975 book, *A Realist Theory of Science*, he reworked Harré's realist notions of reality (ontology) and explored their impact on how we generate knowledge (epistemology). The main contentions of Bhaskar's critical realism are:

- Society is an ensemble of real structures comprised of practices and conventions that are reproduced and transformed by individuals. While society pre-exists its members, it is not independent of human activity because, not only do we take these structures into account as we get on with our lives, but elements of social life that emerge in our interactions become objectified (i.e., socially real) once human activity comes to depend on them. The hierarchy of an organization, for example, emerges from the ways employees interact with their supervisors and managers, and how they show deference to authority.

- Reality is stratified, consisting of underlying structures and mechanisms that shape surface events. So, while individuals may change, institutions with their practices and roles persist, governed by causal laws or generative mechanisms. Critical realists seek to identify these **generative mechanisms** and the deep structures they imply as a means of explaining the surface events and outcomes we experience as social life.

- Knowledge is socially produced, but not to the extent that it can be reduced purely to discursive and textual practices as claimed by postmodernists. Rather, it is produced through a continual dialectic of constructing and testing explanations and models. The aim is to understand, rather than predict, phenomena including social behavior.

Bhaskar's position combines ontological realism (real structures) and epistemological relativism (knowledge is socially produced). His approach is critical because of its emphasis on the political and ethical implications of scientific knowledge for human freedom and for defining possibilities for social transformation. In a way, critical realism selectively combines assumptions from the modernist, symbolic-interpretive and critical theory perspectives. Is this a new perspective, as critical realists claim, or another product of modernist grand narrative?

A number of organization theorists have taken up critical realism, suggesting that it offers a way of explaining how organizational forms emerge from the interaction of complex and often competing forces. Their work addresses the structures and mechanisms underlying institutional forms and practices; how these emerge over time; how they might constrain and empower social actors; and how such forms might be critiqued and changed. Critical realist organization theorists conceptualize organizations as socially structured forms in which collective action emerges and transforms itself through dynamic power struggles.[10]

To give you an example, British organizational theorist Michael Reed studied different types of organizations that had shifted to low trust/high control structures. In cases involving the restructuring of British health care organizations, for example, he found that conflicting interests in matters such as market price, bureaucratic regulation and professional expertise led to the adoption of a new institutional form—hospital trusts. Reed explained that hospital trusts emerged as a result of the new generative mechanism of delegated control—a paradoxical mix of centralized control of strategic policy and local autonomy. Hospital trusts were to be freestanding organizations with control over their own capital spending and employment issues, but accountable to the Secretary of State for implementing government health policy. Reed suggested that delegated control, and the resulting power struggles between stakeholders trying to influence trust managers, led to low trust cultures yet also provided the mechanism by which new forms of public sector governance emerged.

Reed's study showed how critical realists explain the creation of social institutions, like hospital trusts, by identifying their generative mechanisms and the social, economic, political, and historical forces that shape them. Because they talk about the interaction between structure and agency, critical realists face the challenge of distinguishing their perspective from structuration theory. Can you tell the difference? One of the ways that new perspectives make their mark on organization theory is by successfully differentiating themselves from previously established theories.

Complexity Theory

When we talk about organizations, environments, systems or technology being complex, as we often have in previous chapters, we usually mean that they are complicated. **Complexity theory** is about a different type of complexity and carries specific assumptions about the nature of complex systems, mainly that they are emergent phenomena characterized by nonlinearity and feedback loops. So, within the field of organization theory, we might talk about organizations being complicated by the many different characteristics and factors influencing their operation, but unless they operate in nonlinear ways, generate variation (rather than uniformity) and are adaptive, they are not complex in the sense meant by complexity theorists. Let me begin by presenting a little history and the main principles of complexity theory.

Complexity theory first emerged in the sciences, mainly in the field of physics, which seeks laws to explain nature's complexity. Linear models had proven ineffective for explaining complex physical phenomena like jet contrails, and new methods sensitive to the many variables and to the emergent nature of these systems were needed. Complexity theory provided the promise of an answer. In the 1980s a number of interdisciplinary research institutes developed around applications of complexity theory to scientific and social problems, two of the most famous being the Santa Fe Institute in the United States (a research center studying complex adaptive systems such as epidemics, city development and decay, and stock market behavior) and, in Germany, the Max-Planck Institute for Physics of Complex Systems. Computer scientists and a few organization theorists also began using complexity theory around this time.

Complexity theory involves studying how patterns emerge from randomness to form complex dynamic systems. Such systems have a number of characteristics:

- Each complex system is unique because it consists of many different elements with multiple interactions and feedback loops between elements. Complex systems are dynamic because they exist in changing environments and so need to be adaptable.

- Each element of a complex system responds only to local information not to broader system information.

- Interactions within complex systems are nonlinear, which means that they contain multiple components and interactions that are rarely explained by simple cause-effect relationships. As the result of nonlinearity, small changes in one part of a complex system can have major effects in other parts. Take the example of Edward Lorenz's 'Butterfly Effect': the flap of a butterfly's wings in Africa can cause a tornado in the Caribbean when minor factors become magnified as they move through time and space. Nonlinearity means that, although we might be able to model how they unfold, we are unable to make precise predictions about the behavior of complex systems. For example, we cannot predict the weather precisely, nor can anyone say when or where the next earthquakes will occur.

- Complex systems constantly change and evolve over time in unpredictable ways as a result of their nonlinearity. They also contain attractors or magnets for chaos, so just as rocks in a stream attract turbulent water, a problematic part of a work process can lead to a flurry of activity surrounding it. Such systems also become more complex as they evolve; complexity theorists therefore study how systems emerge—a property known as emergence—as a means of understanding them.

- Complexity theorists also study how order can emerge from chaos in the form of **self-organization**. For example, if you pour sand in a heap it will maintain a particular shape, if you study drivers' responses to an accident or to road work you will be able to identify emergent traffic patterns, and autonomous teams find ways to organize their own activities.

Organization theorists who use complexity theory suggest that organizations are **complex adaptive systems** existing on the edge of chaos. Ralph Stacey, Director of the Complexity and Management Centre in the United Kingdom, has written extensively about organizational complexity and chaos.[11] He asserts that, because today's business environment is complex and ever-changing, organizations must be complex adaptive systems comprising large numbers of interacting agents behaving in nonlinear ways, and that managers need to use complexity theory as a frame of reference for managing them. In particular, Stacey promotes using complexity theory as a springboard for greater creativity in the areas of business development, business strategy and new product development.

Similar ideas were expressed in *Harnessing Complexity*, a book written by Robert Axelrod and Michael Cohen, two professors of public policy and contributors to the Santa Fe Institute. They suggested that organizations can harness complexity to produce new structures and strategies appropriate for complex environments. These researchers prescribed three qualities of complex adaptive systems that managers should cultivate in their organization: variation, interaction and selection. *Variation* means encouraging a variety of practices and solutions (as opposed to one fixed answer) and is associated with decentralized problem solving. Managers need to encourage *interaction* between all organizational elements by establishing and supporting networks and their linkages. *Selection* means creating appropriate standards and measures to guide choices among new strategies.

Organization theorists have also analyzed organizations through the lens of complexity theory.[12] For example, Alexander Styhre studied change in a Swedish telecommunications company arguing that, while many models of organization are based on the notion of change as incremental, linear and planned, in reality change is nonlinear.[13] In the organization he studied, planned change centered on the introduction of a new manufacturing unit with an egalitarian style of management. However, the change process was characterized by nonlinearity caused by unanticipated events and periods of major change, stability and decline. For example, new employees were hired and then fired after an unanticipated market demand fluctuation, the attack on the World Trade Center led to an unpredictable recession in the world market, and the company experienced problems in determining the technical specifications for new products when engineers and customers unexpectedly required changes. The lack of success of the planned change was pinned on the dynamics of complexity, but the linear thinking of managers could also be to blame.

Many modernists believe that complexity theory can provide insight into ways of designing and managing organizations in today's dynamic environments. By framing organizations as complex adaptive systems operating in nonlinear ways, managers can design more fluid and adaptive organizational forms and practices. Symbolic-interpretivists and postmodernists, however, are more inclined to view the phenomenon of complexity as providing empirical evidence that contravenes modernist methods, and possibly the modernist perspective itself. For example, Greek organization theorist Haridimos Tsoukas and I proposed using the narrative approach as an alternative means to address the phenomena described by complexity theory.[14]

Network Theories of Organizing

Many organization theorists believe that complexity is best addressed using one or another version of network theory. We have already discussed several network phenomena: interorganizational networks, network organizations and organizations as social networks or communities. **Social network theory** attempts to explain, in a modernist way, all of these phenomena by describing the structure of relationships between actors (individuals, groups, organizations).[15] It emphasizes methods for describing networks by identifying their nodes (network members) and then focusing on the relationships between them.

Applications of social network analysis to organizations reveal how the ties that organizations maintain in their interorganizational networks provide them with information and ways to deter competitors. For example, one interesting property that economist Mark Granovetter derived from interorganizational network analysis is **the power of weak ties**. Granovetter's studies showed that networks (e.g., organizations) acquire some of their most critical information from actors who operate on the fringe of two or more networks, even though such actors typically are not strongly linked into any network.[16]

Social capital is another concept that has been abstracted from studies involving social network theory. Londoners Janine Nahapiet and Sumatra Ghoshal, two strategy theorists, identified three dimensions of social capital: structural, relational and cognitive.[17] Their structural dimension maps an actor's ability to make connections to others within a community through information exchange. An advantage of this dimension is that it reduces the amount of time and investment required of an individual to gather information. The significance of the relational dimension of social capital is that it facilitates development of trust, shared norms, mutual obligations and identification, as well as the ability to exploit weak ties between networks. The cognitive dimension suggests that social capital could facilitate the development of intellectual capital among people by exchanging information and sharing knowledge. Differences in language and codes keep people apart, while shared narratives bring them together.

In almost every discussion of social capital, trust is given a central role. For example, Robert Putnam argued that trust and social capital go hand in hand due to reciprocity—trust breeds trust and this builds social capital into organizations and societies.[18] Putnam based this theory on studies of Italian villagers whose increased trust, following WWII, aided the spread of democracy and economic development in their region. He followed this uplifting work with an alarming study of the recent loss of trust and plummeting social capital in the United States. His theory is that increases in social isolation, a phenomenon that he described metaphorically with the image of bowling alone, were producing these negative consequences within U.S. culture. The implications of bowling alone for the role organizations play in society are enormous—organizations are increasingly becoming default sources of community support for those whose other communities have all but disappeared.

The implications of social capital, however, bring us closer to the perspective offered by actor network theory, which is more compatible with interpretive epistemology than is social network theory. **Actor network theory** or ANT crosses paradigm boundaries to explore relationships between human and nonhuman network elements. Like critical realism, actor network theory is not just a theory about what organization is (ontologically what exists is the network), but is concerned with how knowledge is created (epistemologically we know reality through our positions in our networks).

Actor network theory emerged from the initially controversial work of Bruno Latour who studied philosophy and theology in his native France but became interested in anthropology while engaged in military service on Africa's Ivory Coast. Following these formative experiences, he decided to spend two years doing an ethnographic study of research at the Salk Institute for Biological Studies in California:

> 'Because I wanted to go to the States to see the opposite part of the world, I decided to do an anthropology of science. From the beginning I felt my interest in philosophy, theology, and anthropology was the same thing—that is, I was trying to account for the various ways in which truth is built.'[19]

In 1979 Latour presented his findings in *Laboratory Life: The Social Construction of Scientific Facts*, a book he wrote with British sociologist Steve Woolgar. The two argued that knowledge is a social product, created in a network that orders and translates various interacting materials (machines, people, buildings, concepts, written documents). Any observed order is fleeting because such networks fragment and shift as materials change and mingle to form different effects.

Laboratory Life generated considerable controversy for two reasons. First, Latour's ethnographic method surprised practitioners of normal science who, in those days, expected any study of science to be conducted using accepted scientific methods. Second, Latour and Woolgar claimed that the scientific work they observed was socially constructed from a 'seething mass of alternative interpretations' and from 'the confrontation and negotiation of utter confusion'. Rather than being based on organized and coherent scientific rationality, science was political.[20] ANT was born from the controversy and attention that these ideas generated.

Like critical realism, ANT draws from multiple perspectives; in ANT's case these are: modernism's focus on the object, symbolic-interactionism's idea that agency is constituted as an effect of the interaction of many different materials, and postmodernism's decentering of the subject. Actor-network theorists see society, organizations and identities as effects created in networks of heterogeneous materials. As Latour stated, 'ANT is not a theory of the social, it is a theory of a space in which the social has become a certain type of circulation.'[21] ANT depends upon two main assumptions. First, the social world is **materially heterogeneous**, in other words, buildings, machines, actors, bodies, physical material and talk are all involved in the process of socio-technical ordering, which includes making sense of, constructing and maintaining a network. Second, the elements of a network only achieve significance in relation to other elements, they do not have a fixed independent significance—this is known as the principle of **relationality**.

Based on these assumptions, organization theorists using ANT study organizational structures as networks consisting of both human and nonhuman materials (technical, physical, natural, body, thought, text, etc.). The human actor is no more or less important than any other material, but acts as a translator who builds coherence and organization from all the bits and pieces. Network objects are fluid and many of the ways that network materials adapt to particular circumstances are invisible.[22] Let's take an example of a company manufacturing the high pressure mercury lamps used in street lighting. Decreased demand for mercury lamps and a growing demand for the higher quality, more efficient natural light provided by metal halide lamps, convince production and design engineers to modify the company's existing machine so that it will produce the new type of lamp. The physical shape and design of the machine, its components, raw material inputs, operating procedures, operator behavior, problem-solving activities and interactions, quality standards and so on will change as all these elements of the network interact and try to organize and adapt themselves to the demands of manufacturing the new product.

You would be right in assuming that technology is an integral part of the network in Actor Network Theory, which means ANT theorists need to differentiate their position from that taken by social construction of technology (SCOT) theorists. You may recall from Chapter 5 that SCOT theorists see technology and people as interacting but separate entities, whereas from an ANT perspective, as Latour stated: 'It is as if we might call technology the moment when social assemblages gain stability by aligning actors and observers. Society and technology are not two ontologically distinct entities but more like phases of the same essential action.'[23] Technology achieves meaning and thereby exists because of relationality (between people, work, artifacts, and so on) and therefore must be studied and managed within the context of the network. Similar to social network theory, ANT focuses on the relationships between elements in the network rather than on the elements themselves, but unlike social network theory, ANT theorists adopt the assumptions of interpretive epistemology presumed by their ethnographic methods. In addition, downplaying the importance of human actors introduces a hint of postmodernism.

Organizational Identity

The concept of **organizational identity** was introduced to organization theory in 1985 by American organization theorists Stuart Albert and David Whetten.[24] According to Albert and Whetten you can observe the phenomenon of organizational identity whenever members of an organization address questions like: 'Who are we?', 'What business are we in?' or 'What do we want to be?' Using observations of their university's struggle to answer these questions, these authors proposed a modernist definition of organizational identity as that which is central, distinctive and enduring about an organization.

Albert and Whetten were by no means the only organization theorists to tackle the subject of identity. Theorists steeped in other perspectives have also tried their hand at specifying what this concept might offer to organization theory. One of these was Howard Schwartz who contributed a psychoanalytic theory of the risks of organizational identity. Schwartz explained how the **organization ideal** could potentially substitute for the ego ideal that Sigmund Freud claimed individuals aspire to in their search for a return to the infantile narcissistic state of total love and protection. Thus, at least for some organizational participants, the organization ideal makes the identity of the organization into a source of security and possibly even a love object. Schwartz used his theory of the organization ideal to explain why some individuals perform unethical or illegal acts to protect their company, as did the individuals responsible for covering up negligent safety practices in the early 1970s at their plutonium fuel production plant in Oklahoma. The fight of employee Karen Silkwood to expose her company's illegal and life-threatening activities is documented in the film *Silkwood*.[25]

Swedish organization theorist Mats Alvesson proposed another theory of organizational identity to explain how a company's overemphasis on its image can lead to the loss of its culture. He defined corporate image as: 'a holistic and vivid impression held by a particular group towards a corporation, partly as a result of information processing (sense-making) carried out by the group's members . . . and partly by the aggregated communication of the corporation in question concerning its nature, i.e., the fabricated and projected picture of itself'. Drawing on postmodernism, Alvesson added this important caveat to his definition: 'An image is something we get primarily through coincidental, infrequent, superficial and/or mediated information, through mass media, public appearances, from second-hand sources etc., not through our own direct, lasting experiences and perceptions of the "core" of the object.'[26] Thus conceptualizing image and identity separately, Alvesson posited his theory of the relationship between them as one of substitutability. His theory is that, in the face of ambiguity or psychological distance from the corporation (conditions he equates with postmodern times), management-instilled images replace personal experiences of the corporation in the mental representations of its participants. In short, image replaces substance and organizational culture suffers or dies as a result.

Barbara Czarniawska's narrative theory of organizational identity draws on symbolic-interpretive ideas. Her studies of several Swedish public sector organizations showed that identity is a 'continuous process of narration where both the narrator and audience formulate, edit, applaud and refuse various elements of the ever-produced narrative'.[27] Czarniawska compared the narratives of organizational identity she heard in the organizations she studied to serial novels and television soap operas (see Chapter 6).

The idea that organizational identities change over time was taken up by a theory of the dynamics of organizational identity I developed with Majken Schultz.[28] We built our model on George Herbert Mead's theory that individual identities are constituted as a sense of self produced by interactions with others and experiences in the world. Mead believed that individual identity arises as the human psyche grapples with the separate existence of others, reasoning that, if others exist, then who am I? In learning to conceptualize others, the infant comes to a preliminary notion of its self and thus begins a process of development that produces a lifelong conversation between the 'I' (the individual's self-definition) and the 'me' (how others define the individual in ways that the individual accepts into his or her concept of self). We proposed that a similar conversation occurs at the organizational level as an extrapolation of Mead's **identity dynamics**. Using this logic, we defined organizational identity as the meaning-making an organization does in respect of itself, and claimed that such meaning is embedded in organizational culture (which produces the organizational 'I') but is also tempered by the many encounters organizational members have with the organization's stakeholders (thus producing the organizational 'me'). The set of identity-producing interactions are like a conversation between the organizational 'I' and 'me' that moves in and out of the contexts created by the organization's culture and the cultural sector of its broader environment. Our theory specified four interwoven processes that enable and constrain the organizational identity conversation and explain how image and culture influence each other by intentionally or unconsciously: (1) *expressing* organizational beliefs and values, (2) *impressing* others with organizational identity claims, (3) *mirroring* feedback from stakeholders, and (4) *reflecting* upon outsiders' images of the organization in relation to what insiders believe its identity is or should be.

From the perspective of critical theory, Alvesson and Hugh Willmott described how managers of organizations use culture to form and transform identity through acts of identity regulation, that is, by defining the person, their morals and values, knowledge and skills via the use of group categorizations, rule enforcement and the social construction of the organizational context/culture.[29] These authors concluded that managerial attempts to regulate identity are accomplished through sophisticated discursive practices that influence the identity work in which employees engage when they use organizationally influenced narratives to form, repair, maintain, strengthen or revise their sense of self. However, although Alvesson and Willmott's primary purpose was to show how identity regulation serves oppressive ends, they also considered how it might be used to liberate individuals. They claimed that those who work in new flexible and decentralized organizations confront the opportunity for micro-emancipation because the properties of these organizational forms free them to redefine their work, skills and organizational values, and thus their organization's identity, for their own purposes.

The organizational identity theories described above offer a microcosm of organization theory in that, collectively, they draw on all the perspectives organization theory currently offers. Like organization theory in general, this range of perspectives defies integration.[30] However, this does not relieve organization theorists of the task of refining their theories by exposing them to empirical evidence and practical application. This empirical work began with a study of the New York and New Jersey Port Authority conducted by American organizational researchers Jane Dutton and Janet Dukerich.[31] These researchers observed that this organization's identity had been threatened by negative public opinion created by numerous encounters with the homeless people who loitered in the Port Authority's bus and train stations. Public images associating homelessness with the Port Authority led organization members to take responsibility for setting up homeless shelters, a move that renewed the organization's reputation among an appreciative public, but also changed the organization's identity.

Empirical study of organizational identity will no doubt continue for a long time to come. Two recent examples of empirical studies of organizational identity are offered below to give you insight into how theories as complex as those relating to organizational identity are refined through empirical study.

Kimberly Elsbach and Roderick Kramer studied the ways in which organizational identities were shaped in a set of U.S. business schools that had recently been ranked in a national poll that had received high levels of media coverage.[32] These researchers found that all the schools they sampled, including those highly ranked, perceived the rankings as threatening and defined two sources of perceived threat. The first was the threat to members' abilities to define their organization's core, distinctive and enduring qualities for themselves. *Business Week*'s reliance on student and recruiter opinions challenged traditional definitions of identity rooted in the schools' research reputations. The second was the threat posed by pinpointing a particular school's position in a presumed status hierarchy. *Business Week* gave each school an explicit positional ranking vis-à-vis other top 20 schools. School members tended to respond to these perceived threats either by emphasizing aspects of their organizational identity that were not measured by *Business Week* magazine's ranking system (e.g., research excellence, diverse student body) or by selective categorization within the *Business Week* system (e.g., we did well for a public school amidst so many better-funded private schools); thus Elsbach and Kramer showed the power of images produced by the ranking system to affect internal identity-producing processes, thereby supporting theories that connect image and identity.

Italian organization theorist Davide Ravasi along with Majken Schultz conducted a longitudinal study of Bang & Olufsen that supported theories that connect identity with culture.[33] Conducting participant observation and examining historical records over a period of twenty-five years, these researchers found clear indications that organizational members repeatedly used the meanings and artifacts of their organizational culture to help them make sense of environmental demands for change and forge responses to them, including reaffirming and reinterpreting their sense of organizational identity. Many more studies like these have been conducted, with more on the way, from which you can expect further developments in organizational identity theory.[34]

The Aesthetics of Organizations and Organizing

Can you think of any moment in your life that, when you recall it, gives you an overpowering sense of joy or fear or anger? Have you ever had a memory triggered by a sight or smell? Is there a piece of music or art that evokes very strong emotions for you? Your senses can lead to a very different appreciation of experience than that which comes from your intellect and these appreciations form the departure point for **organizational aesthetics**.

For example, a few years ago Ann, who helped me write this book, arranged interviews with the president and senior managers of a small textile company as part of a research project. As she walked through the door, the smell of damp material immediately took her back to childhood visits to her grandmother who worked in a textile mill in Lancashire, England. She reports: 'I almost felt I was back there, holding my grandmother's hand as I walked past lines of noisy machines weaving tapestries of richly colored cloth.' Ann's revery makes the point that aesthetic experiences pervade our work just as they do the rest of our lives, giving color, texture and form to our existence.

Memories and experiences like Ann's are the focus of those who study organizational aesthetics. This perspective assumes that human senses and perceptions play a major role in constructing and appreciating organizations and that 'experience of the real is first and foremost sensory experience of a physical reality'.[35] Aesthetic knowledge comes through sensory experience as opposed to intellectual effort, and the methods of studying, creating and managing organizations aesthetically extend to the poetic/artistic. Somewhat aligned with the philosophical positions of both symbolic-interpretivism and the creative and optimistic aspects of postmodernism, those interested in organizational aesthetics place their attention on the **felt experiences** of organizational members and those who study them (or with them as is more usually the case). Aesthetic inquiry explores how organizations can be experienced as beautiful, sublime, comic and gracious (i.e., aesthetically pleasing); or as ugly, grotesque, painful and repugnant. It can reveal the beauty and joy experienced in the rhythm and flow of work; or the comedy and irony of everyday interactions expressed in jokes and stories told by colleagues.

Italian organizational sociologist Antonio Strati, originally a student of organizational culture and an art photographer, recognized the importance of organizational aesthetics to organization theory early on. Strati articulated several different ways to approach the study of organizations aesthetically by studying: (a) images relating to organizational identity, (b) the physical space of organizations, (c) physical artifacts, (d) aesthetic understandings such as the manager as artist, or the beauty, comedy, etc., of social organization, and (e) how management can learn from artistic form and content by using, for example, music, dance, storytelling, drawing, painting or sculpture.[36]

Italian organization theorist Pasquale Gagliardi was another early contributor to the study of organizational aesthetics. Gagliardi claimed that organizational cultures are sensory maps built from aesthetic responses employees have to their physical-cultural setting, and that cultures should be studied, not only in relation to their values and assumptions (an organization's essence or raison d'être) and ethos (rules, morals and ethical codes), but also in relation to their **pathos**—how organizational life is felt and experienced.[37] Because pathos (an ancient Greek concept originally defined in opposition to the concepts of logos and ethos) is intuitive and instinctive, Gagliardi concluded that aesthetics is basic to all other forms of knowing (including logos and ethos) and therefore should be incorporated into the study of organizations.

Other field studies have focused on aesthetic labor, how workplace performances are not just acts or acting (as Goffman suggested) but embodied feelings. One study of workplace performance focused on the embodied nature of service work.[38] The authors found that a particular hotel chain created an aesthetic experience for guests, not just through physical artifacts but also through the labor of aesthetic organizing. The company hired people with the right image (based on personality, passion and style) and transformed them and their activities into aesthetic labor by training them in grooming and deportment. However, while some employees embraced the aesthetic performance, others felt the costs. These results complement those of Heather Höpfl's study of airline employees who lost part of themselves and experienced emotional stress as the result of the demands for workplace performance placed on them by their managers (see Chapter 6).

Patricia Martin explored the emotional and sensory experience (sight, smell, sound) of organizations in her study of old people's homes in the United Kingdom. She suggested these homes provoke profound aesthetic experiences because of their association with physical and mental decline, and the way that residents' bodies are defined and dealt with. For example, bodies are managed (cleaned, dressed, given medication), controlled (when and where to walk), and placed in locations (bedrooms, dining table assignments) depending on how residents are categorized. By talking to residents and employees, and through her sensory experiences, Martin discovered that some places have a homey while others have an institutional feel. She suggested that by taking an aesthetic approach she was able to help others appreciate what it feels like to live and work in these organizations and to show how aesthetic experience and power are interrelated, creating either a healthy environment or one conducive to ill-health.[39]

A less analytical approach to organizational aesthetics is practiced by members of AACORN (Arts, Aesthetics, Creativity and Organizations Research Network).[40] Many AACORNers devote their research energies to performance art in organizational settings or use organizations as subjects and/or media for artistic expression. For example Steven Taylor, an organization theorist and playwright, wrote and directed multiple plays about the life of young academics that express and provoke aesthetic responses to the conditions of work they experience. His casts were drawn from members of the profession and performed for audiences comprised of their colleagues. Immediately following each performance, Taylor invited cast and audience members to reflect on their aesthetic experiences of the play and their lives through dialog, and some of these responses, along with two plays, have been published in academic journals.[41] Thus, through drama, Taylor and his company reflexively (re)cast and dramatize their own academic practices while invading the discourse of mainstream organization theory.

Other ACORN members seek to produce aesthetic experiences in business organizations. For example, Philip Mirvis uses drama and other art forms (including mask making and movement) to create aesthetic contexts for transformational change in large organizations. The Dutch foods division of Unilever used this approach to take organizational members on a journey through the Scottish highlands, and later on a trek through the Jordan desert where the leadership of the foods group was passed to a new manager.[42] These events dramatized and thereby signified the importance of change within this organization. But the events also provided the context for doing the work of change in a more inspired way. Over 200 managers formed teams and planned how they would transform their organizations as they journeyed across ancient lands. The historically rich travels of these managers also provided them with time and space in which to build community through the sharing of personal and work stories told around numerous campfires.

Efforts like those of the Unilever managers to give aesthetic experience a place in their organizations are critiqued by other organizational theorists for appropriating aesthetics for the purpose of domination. For example, British organization theorists Catrina Alferoff and David Knights concluded on the basis of their study of three UK call centers that the aesthetics of a workplace can be used as a form of control via the seductions of organizational commitment.[43] They explored how physical layout and artifacts such as posters, signs, decorations, dress, competitions and theme days (e.g., World Cup Soccer Day where employees dress up in the costumes of national teams and managers use images of soccer goals superimposed on performance targets) presented work as fun, claiming the managers were subtly trying to intensify and control work activity. Alferoff and Knights found that some employees perceived these activities as threats to their identity and resisted these attempts at control by refusing to wear team jerseys. Their study shows that, while managerial control can be literally dressed up as a fun aesthetic activity designed to playfully express and engage the instrumental ambitions of the organization, pathos may intervene and cause the effort to be experienced differently and to redirect energies toward unintended outcomes.

Like the other new directions we have examined, organizational aesthetics has only recently emerged in organization theory and is attracting the attentions of researchers who bring a variety of perspectives. Just where this or any other new direction presented to the field will lead is anyone's guess.

SUMMARY

This book has told a story of how the normal science of modernist organization theory was revolutionized by the proponents of symbolic-interpretivism and postmodernism and this chapter has claimed that this story is not finished. Organization theory will continue to confront questions about the value of pluralism offered by its multiple perspectives and will no doubt undergo many revisions as new developments like those described in this chapter lead to interesting new ways of studying and managing organizations.

There is no one answer to questions concerning how to define this field of study. Like the organizational theorists caught up in the paradigm wars, everyone will have their own view. My position as you well know by now is that, by reflecting on different perspectives and opening up your assumptions and practices to reflexive critique, you will learn to appreciate beliefs that differ from your own and thereby gain the option of exposing and exploring your taken-for-granted assumptions and behaviors and their often hidden and unintended consequences. I hope that my emphasis on multiple perspectives in this book will help you to develop more responsive, creative and ethical ways of managing organizations.[44] On the question of mixing perspectives or waging paradigm war, I hope that you will consider the possible value of any distinction you meet before you disagree with or abandon it. Beware of thinking that you are crossing a boundary or combining two positions when you are merely permitting one to dominate the other, thereby denying or destroying value. If you take one thing away from this book, may it be this one: appreciate how others know their world even as you construct your own.

KEY TERMS

paradigm
normal science
paradigm incommensurability
critical realism
  philosophical realism
  generative mechanisms
complexity theory
  emergence
  self-organization
  complex adaptive systems
network theory
  social network theory

power of weak ties
social capital
actor network theory (ANT)
materially heterogeneous
relationality
organizational identity and image
  organization ideal (psychoanalytic)
  identity dynamics
organizational aesthetics
  felt experience
  pathos

ENDNOTES

1. Kuhn (1970).

2. Burrell and Morgan (1979).

3. Pfeffer (1993), Donaldson (1985).

4. Van Maanen (1995).

5. See Gioia and Pitre (1990), Willmott (1990, 1993), Weaver and Gioia (1994), Schultz and Hatch (1996).

6. Hassard (1991).

7. Bhaskar (1989), Lawson (2005).

8. Harré (1993).

9. Mandelbaum (1955, 1957).

10. Archer (2000).

11. Stacey (1996).

12. See, for example, the special issue of the academic journal *Organization Science*, devoted to organizational applications of complexity theory (1999).

13. Styhre (2002).

14. Tsoukas and Hatch (2001).

15. Ronald Burt is often given credit for establishing social network theory and its methods of study. A sociologist, Burt's many books and papers have been highly influential within organization theory. See, for example: Burt (1982, 1992).

16. Granovetter (1985).

17. Nahapiet and Ghoshal (1998).

18. Putnam (1993a, 1993b, 2000).

19. From Crawford (1993).

20. Latour and Woolgar (1979: 36).

21. Latour (1998).

22. deLaet and Mol (2000), Law and Singleton (2003).

23. Latour (1991: 129).

24. Albert and Whetten (1985).

25. Schwartz (1987).

26. Alvesson (1990: 376).

27. Czarniawska (1997).

28. Hatch and Schultz (2002).

29. Alvesson and Willmott (2002).

30. Corley et al. (in press) recently attempted a comprehensive description of organizational identity research and theory.

31. Dutton and Dukerich (1991).

32. Elsbach and Kramer (1996).

33. Ravasi and Schultz (forthcoming).

34. See, for example, Gioia and Thomas (1996), Gioia, Schultz and Corley (2000), Glynn (2000), Corley and Gioia (2004).

35. Gagliardi, in Clegg and Hardy (1999: 311).

36. Strati (1999, 2000). See also Barry (1996), Ottensmeyer (1996), Barrett (2000), Guillet de Monthoux (2004), Nissley, Taylor and Butler (2002), Taylor and Hansen (in press).

37. Gagliardi (1990); see also (1996).

38. Witz, Warhurst and Nickson (2003).

39. Martin (2002).

40. http://aacorn.net/index.htm

41. Taylor (2000, 2003), Rosile (2003).

42. Mirvis, Ayas and Roth (2003).

43. Alferoff and Knights (2003).

44. See also Cunliffe and Jun (2005).

REFERENCES

Albert, Stuart, and Whetten, David A. (1985). Organizational identity. In L. L. Cummings and M. M. Staw (eds.), *Research in Organizational Behavior*. Greenwich, Conn.: JAI Press, 7: 263–95.

Alferoff, C., and Knights, David (2003). We're all partying here: Targets and games, or targets as games in call centre management. In A. Carr and P. Hancock, *Art and aesthetics at work*. London: Palgrave, 70–92.

Alvesson, Mats (1990). Organization: From substance to image? *Organization Studies*, 11: 373–94.

—— and Willmott, Hugh (2002). Organizational control producing the 'appropriate individual'. *Journal of Management Studies*, 39: 619–44.

Archer, M. (2000). *Being Human: The Problem of Agency*. Cambridge: Cambridge University Press.

Barrett, Frank J. (2000). Cultivating an aesthetic of unfolding: Jazz improvisation as a self-organizing system. In S. Linstead and H. Höpfl (eds.), *The Aesthetics of Organization*. London: Sage, 228–45.

Barry, David (1996). Artful inquiry: A symbolic constructivist approach to social science research. *Qualitative Inquiry*, 2: 411–38.

Bhaskar, Roy (1975). *A Realist Theory of Science*. Leeds, UK: Leeds Books Ltd.

—— (1989). *Reclaiming Reality: A Critical Introduction to Contemporary Philosophy*. London: Verso.

Burrell, Gibson, and Morgan, Gareth (1979). *Sociological paradigms and organizational analysis*. London: Heineman.

Burt, Ronald S. (1982). *Toward a structural theory of action*. New York: Academic Press.

—— (1992). *Structural holes*. Cambridge, Mass.: Harvard University Press.

Corley, Kevin, and Gioia, Dennis (2004). Identity ambiguity and change in the wake of a corporate spin-off. *Administrative Science Quarterly*, 49: 173–208.

—— Harquail, C. V., Pratt, Michael, Glynn, Maryann, Fiol, Marlene, and Hatch, Mary Jo (in press). Guiding organizational identity through aged adolescence. *Journal of Management Inquiry*.

Crawford, T. H. (1993). An interview with Bruno Latour. *Configurations*, 1: 247–68. Interview conducted October 1990. http://prelectur.stanford.edu/lecturers/latour/latouron.html (accessed 7/8/2005).

Cunliffe, Ann L., and Jun, J. (2005). The need for reflexivity in public administration. *Administration and Society*, 37: 225–42.

Czarniawska, Barbara (1997). Narratives of individual and organizational identities. *Communication Yearbook*, 17: 193–221.

de Laet, M., and Mol, A. (2000). The Zimbabwe bush pump: Mechanics of a fluid technology. *Social Studies of Science*, 30: 225–63.

Donaldson, Lex (1985). *In defense of organization theory*. Cambridge: Cambridge University Press.

Dutton, J., and Dukerich, J. (1991). Keeping an eye on the mirror: Image and identity in organizational adaptation. *Academy of Management Journal*, 34: 517–54.

Elsbach, Kimberly D., and Kramer, Roderick, M. (1996). Members' responses to organizational identity threats: Encountering and countering the *Business Week* rankings. *Administrative Science Quarterly*, 41: 442–76.

Gagliardi, Pasquali (1990) (ed.). *Symbols and artifacts: Views of the corporate landscape*. Berlin and New York: de Gruyter.

—— (1996). Exploring the aesthetic side of organizational life. In S. R. Clegg and C. Hardy (eds.), *Studying Organization: Theory & Method*. London: Sage, 311–26.

Gioia, Dennis A., and Pitre, Evelyn (1990). Multiparadigm perspectives on theory building. *Academy of Management Review*, 15: 584–602.

—— Schultz, Majken, and Corley, Kevin (2000). Organizational identity, image and adaptive instability. *Academy of Management Review*, 25: 63–82.

—— and Thomas, J. B. (1996). Identity, image, and issue interpretation: Sensemaking during strategic change in academia. *Administrative Science Quarterly*, 41/3: 370–403.

Glynn, Mary Ann (2000). When cymbals become symbols: Conflict over organizational identity within a symphony orchestra. *Organization Science*, 11/3: 285–98.

Granovetter, Mark (1985). Economic action and social structure: The problem of embeddedness. *American Journal of Sociology*, 91: 481–510.

Guillet de Monthoux, Pierre (2004). *The art firm: Aesthetic management and metaphysical marketing*. Palo Alto, Calif.: Stanford University Press.

Harré, Rom (1993). *Realism: An Inductive Defense*. Paper presented at the University of New Hampshire, USA (September).

Hassard, John (1991). Multiple paradigms and organizational analysis: A case study. *Organization Studies*, 12: 275–99.

Hatch, Mary Jo, and Schultz, Majken (2002). The dynamics of organizational identity. *Human Relations*, 55: 989–1019.

Kuhn, Thomas S. (1970). *The Structure of Scientific Revolutions*. Chicago: University of Chicago Press.

Latour, Bruno (1991). Technology is society made durable. In John Law (ed.), *A sociology of monsters: Essays on power, technology and domination*. London: Routledge, 103–31.

—— (1998). *Keynote Speech: On Recalling ANT*. Department of Sociology, Lancaster University, UK. http://www.comp.lancs.ac.uk/sociology/papers/Latour-Recalling-ANT.pdf (accessed 4/19/2005).

—— and Woolgar, Steven (1979). *Laboratory life: The social construction of scientific facts*. Beverley Hills, Calif.: Sage.

Law, John, and Singleton, Vicky (2003). Object lessons. Centre for Science Studies, Lancaster University. http://www.lancs.ac.uk/fss/sociology/papers/law-singleton-object-lessons.pdf (accessed 7/12/2005).

Lawson, T. (2005). *A Conception of Ontology: Some Critical Realist Reflections*. Keynote speech at the Fourth International Critical Management Studies Conference, Cambridge University, July.

Mandelbaum, Maurice (1955). Societal facts. *British Journal of Sociology*, 6: 305–17.

—— (1957). Societal laws. *British Journal for the Philosophy of Sciences*, 8: 211–24.

Martin, Patricia (2002). Sensations, bodies, and the 'spirit of a place': Aesthetics in residential organizations for the elderly. *Human Relations*, 55: 861–85.

Mirvis, Philip, Ayas, Karen, and Roth, George (2003). *To the desert and back*. San Francisco: Jossey-Bass.

Nahapiet, J., and Ghoshal, S. (1998). Social capital, intellectual capital and the organizational advantage. *Academy of Management Review*, 23/2: 242–66.

Nissley, Nick, Taylor, S., and Butler, O. (2002). The power of organizational song: An organizational discourse and aesthetic expression of organizational culture. *Tamara: Journal of Critical Postmodern Organizational Science*, 2: 47–62.

Organization Science (1999). Special Issue on Applications of Complexity Theory to Organization Science, 10.

Ottensmeyer, Edward (1996). Too strong to stop; too sweet to lose: Aesthetics as a way to know organizations. *Organization*, 3: 189–94.

Pfeffer, Jeffrey (1993). Barriers to the advance of organizational science: Paradigm development as a dependent variable. *Academy of Management Review*, 18: 599–620.

Putnam, Robert D. (1993a). *Making democracy work: Civic traditions in modern Italy*. Princeton, NJ: Princeton University Press.

—— (1993b). The prosperous community: Social capital and public life. *American Prospect*, 13: 35–42.

—— (2000). *Bowling alone: The collapse and revival of American community*. New York: Simon Schuster.

Ravasi, Davide, and Schultz, Majken (forthcoming). Responding to organizational identity threats: Exploring the role of organizational culture. *Academy of Management Journal*.

Rosile, Grace Ann (2003). Critical dramaturgy and artful ambiguity: Audience reflections on 'Ties that Bind'. *Management Communication Quarterly*, 17: 308–14.

Schultz, Majken, and Hatch, Mary Jo (1996). Living with multiple paradigms: The case of paradigm interplay in organizational culture studies. *Academy of Management Review*, 21: 529–57.

Schwartz, Howard S. (1987). Anti-social actions of committed organizational participants: An

existential psychoanalytic perspective. *Organization Studies*, 87: 327–40.

Stacey, R. D. (1996). *Complexity and creativity in organizations*. San Francisco: Berrett-Koehler.

Strati, Antonio (1999). *Organization and aesthetics*. London: Sage.

—— (2000). The aesthetic approach in organization studies. In S. Linstead and H. Höpfl (eds.), *The aesthetics of organization*. London: Sage.

Styhre, A. (2002). Non-linear change in organizations: Organizational change management informed by complexity theory. *Leadership and Organizational Development Change Journal*, 23: 343–52.

Taylor, Steven S. (2000). Aesthetic knowledge in academia: Capitalist Pigs at the Academy of Management. *Journal of Management Inquiry* 9: 304–28.

—— (2003). Ties that bind. *Management Communication Quarterly*, 17: 280–300.

—— and Hansen, Hans (in press). Finding form: Looking at the field of organizational aesthetics. *Journal of Management Studies*, 42/6.

Tsoukas, Haridimos, and Hatch, Mary Jo (2001). Complex thinking, complex practice: The case for a narrative approach to organizational complexity. *Human Relations*, 54: 979–1013.

Van Maanen, John (1995). Style as theory. *Organization Science*, 6: 133–43.

Weaver, Gary, and Gioia, Dennis (1994). Paradigms lost: Incommensurability, structuration and the restructuring of organizational inquiry. *Organization Studies*, 15: 565–90.

Willmott, Hugh (1990). Beyond paradigmatic closure in organisational enquiry. In J. Hassard and D. Pym (eds.), *The theory and philosophy of organization*. London: Routledge, 44–62.

—— (1993). Breaking the paradigm mentality. *Organization Studies*, 14: 681–720.

Witz, A., Warhurst, C., and Nickson, D. (2003). The labour of aesthetics and the aesthetics of organization. *Organization*, 10: 33–55.

FURTHER READING

Actor Network Resource, Department of Sociology and Centre for Science Studies, Lancaster University, UK. http://www.lancs.ac.uk/fss/sociology/css/antres/antres.htm

Archer, M., Bhaskar, R., Collier, A., Lawson, T., and Norrie, A. (eds.), *Critical Realism: Essential Readings*. London: Routledge.

Bhaskar, R. (1978). On the possibility of social scientific knowledge and the limits of naturalism. *Journal for the Theory of Social Behavior*, 8: 1–28.

Bouchiki, Hamid, and Kimberly, J. R. (2003). Escaping the identity trap. *Sloan Management Review*, 44/3: 20–26.

Deetz, Stanley (1996). Describing differences in approaches to organization science: Rethinking Burrell and Morgan and their legacy. *Organization Science*, 7: 1991–2007.

Fiol, Marlene C. (2002). Capitalizing on paradox: The role of language in transforming organizational identities. *Organization Science*, 13: 653–66.

Fleetwood, S. (2005). Ontology in organization and management studies: A critical realist perspective. *Organization*, 12: 197–222.

Harré, Rom (1986). *Varieties of Realism: A Rationale for the Natural Sciences*. Oxford: Blackwell.

Hatch, Mary Jo, and Schultz, Majken (eds.) (2004). *Organizational identity: A reader*. Oxford: Oxford University Press.

Jackson, Norman, and Carter, Pippa (1991). In defense of paradigm incommensurability. *Organization Studies*, 12/1: 109–28.

Law, John (1994). *Organizing modernity*. Oxford: Blackwell.

Linstead, Stephen, and Hopfl, Heather (eds.) (2000). *The aesthetics of organization*. London: Sage.

Moldoveanu, M. C., and Bauer, R. M. (2004). On the relationship between organizational complexity and organizational structuration. *Organization Science*, 15: 98–119.

Nissley, Nick, Taylor, S., and Butler, O. (2002). The power of organizational song: An organizational discourse and aesthetic expression of organizational culture. *Tamara: Journal of Critical Postmodern Organizational Science*, 2: 47–62.

Pelzer, P. (2002). Disgust and organization. *Human Relations*, 55: 841–59.

Pratt, M. G., and Rafaeli, A. (1997). Organizational dress as a symbol of multilayered social identities. *Academy of Management Journal*, 40: 862–98.

Schultz, M., Hatch, M. J., and Larsen, M. H. (2000) (eds.). *The expressive organization: Linking identity, reputation, and the corporate brand*. Oxford: Oxford University Press, 13–35.

Stacey, R. D. (1991). *The chaos frontier: Creative strategic control for business*. Oxford: Butterworth Heinemann.

Suchman, L., Blomberg, J., Orr, J. E., and Trigg, R. (1999). Reconstructing technologies as social practice. *American Behavioral Scientist*, 43: 392–411.

Tsoukas, Haridimos (2004). *Complex knowledge: Studies in organizational epistemology*. Oxford: Oxford University Press.

■ INDEX